W9-BID-288

Frommer's

2nd Edition

Maryland
&
Delaware

by Patricia Tunison Preston
and John J. Preston

Macmillan • USA

MACMILLAN TRAVEL

A Simon & Schuster Macmillan Company
1633 Broadway
New York, NY 10019
Find us online at **http://www.mcp.com/mgr/travel** or
on America Online at Keyword: **SuperLibrary.**

ISBN 0-02-860872-0
ISSN 1072-8015

Editor: Jim Moore
Design by Michele Laseau
Digital Cartography by Jim Moore and Ortelius Design

SPECIAL SALES

Bulk purchases (10+ copies) of Frommer's travel guides are available to corporations
at special discounts. The Special Sales Department can produce custom editions to
be used as premiums and/or for sales promotion to suit individual needs. Existing
editions can be produced with custom cover imprints such as corporate logos.
For more information write to: Special Sales, Simon & Schuster, 8th floor,
1633 Broadway, New York, NY 10019.

Manufactured in the United States of America

Contents

List of Maps

AN INVITATION TO THE READER

In researching this book, we discovered many wonderful places—hotels, restaurants, shops, and more. We're sure you'll find others. Please tell us about them, so we can share the information with your fellow travelers in upcoming editions. If you were disappointed with a recommendation, we'd love to know that, too. Please write to:

Frommer's Maryland & Delaware, 2nd Edition
Macmillan Travel
1633 Broadway
New York, NY 10019

AN ADDITIONAL NOTE

Please be advised that travel information is subject to change at any time—and this is especially true of prices. We therefore suggest that you write or call ahead for confirmation when making your travel plans. The authors, editors, and publisher cannot be held responsible for the experiences of readers while traveling. Your safety is important to us, however, so we encourage you to stay alert and be aware of your surroundings. Keep a close eye on cameras, purses, and wallets, all favorite targets of thieves and pickpockets.

WHAT THE SYMBOLS MEAN

✪ Frommer's Favorites

Hotels, restaurants, attractions, and entertainment you should not miss.

⑤ Super-Special Values

Hotels and restaurants that offer great value for your money.

The following abbreviations are used for credit cards:

AE	American Express	EU	Eurocard
CB	Carte Blanche	JCB	Japan Credit Bank
DC	Diners Club	MC	MasterCard
DISC	Discover	V	Visa
ER	enRoute		

Dedicated to Gigi, Larry, Tara, and Michael Windley

ACKNOWLEDGMENTS

With special thanks to the Preston, Tunison, and Sabalis families and to our many friends, especially Fr. Charlie Coen and Fr. John Fagan, for their constant encouragement to us. We would also like to acknowledge the tremendous help, guidance, and enthusiasm of many people in Delaware and Maryland.

In particular, we extend a big "thank you" to the following:

In Delaware   Gigi Dux Windley and Carol Myers of the Delaware Tourism Office; Ralph Williams and Carol Kraft of Wilmington Convention and Visitors Bureau; Mary Skelton of Kent County Tourism Corporation; JoAnne LaMere of the Lewes Chamber of Commerce; Kay Anderson of the Bethany Beach-Fenwick Island Area Chamber of Commerce.

In Maryland   Anne Mannix, Maryland Office of Tourism Development; Gil Stotler of Baltimore Area Convention & Visitors Association; Kristin Witzenburg of Annapolis & Anne Arundel Conference & Visitors Bureau; Shirley Wisenburg and Natalie Chabot of Allegany County Visitors Bureau; Lynn Morrison of the Ocean City Convention & Visitors Bureau; Diane Wolfe of Deep Creek Lake and Garrett County Promotion Council; Stephanie Price of the Talbot County Chamber of Commerce; Jeanne Vasold of the Tourism Council of Frederick County; Patricia Piposzar of Kent County Chamber of Commerce; Natalie Scheeler Ricci of Cecil County Economic Development Office; and Lewis Carman of the Wicomico County Convention & Visitors Bureau.

At Amtrak   Patricia Kelly.

Introducing Maryland

"**A**merica in miniature" is the way Maryland is often described. From its snowcapped Allegheny Mountains and the sandy Ocean City beaches to the metropolis of Baltimore and the fertile horse farms of Frederick, Maryland is a state of many sights and experiences. "Truly a delightsome land," remarked Capt. John Smith in 1608 as he sailed up the Chesapeake Bay into the Potomac.

In the heart of the mid-Atlantic region, Maryland extends from the Atlantic Ocean and the Chesapeake Bay on the east to the Allegheny Mountains on the west, offering easy access from many Eastern seaboard cities. Bordered by Virginia and West Virginia to the south and west, and by Pennsylvania and Delaware to the north and east, Maryland shares common bonds with states on both sides of the Mason-Dixon line.

With an ever-changing kaleidoscope of farmlands and natural vistas, Maryland offers many opportunities for outdoor recreation and sport. The western part of the state around Deep Creek Lake is etched with mountains and hillsides suitable for skiing; the Atlantic coastal resort of Ocean City offers miles of sandy beaches and oceanfront activities; and the Chesapeake Bay shoreline is a haven for boaters and water-sports enthusiasts.

In all, Maryland enjoys 3,190 miles of tidal shoreline and a coast that touches the Atlantic, Chesapeake, and Potomac, plus more than 4,000 lakes. It is also the home of more than 50 state parks and forests and is a prime area on the Atlantic flyway for wintering waterfowl.

The state has a total area of about 10,000 square miles and a population of more than four million. It's just big enough (more than 200 miles at its widest) to offer a great variety of attractions, and small enough (two miles at its narrowest point) to get to know easily. The terrain ranges from sandy seashore beaches to mountain ski slopes reaching to 3,300 feet above sea level.

1 Maryland Today

Maryland preserves its past and melds it into the 20th century. From Annapolis to Princess Anne, from Chestertown to Cumberland, and from Salisbury to Sharpsburg, you'll find gracious southern

> ## ❓ Did You Know?
>
> - Lacrosse, the oldest sport in North America, was popularized as a collegiate game by colleges and universities in Maryland.
> - Maryland's most prominent feature, the Chesapeake Bay, gives the state a coastline of more than 3,000 miles.
> - Maryland's Pimlico racetrack is the home of the Preakness Stakes, second jewel of the Triple Crown races. First run in 1873, the Preakness was named after a popular horse of the late 19th century.
> - The Maryland Department of Natural Resources estimates that there are about 500 bald eagles living in Maryland, including more than 150 nesting pairs.
> - Maryland is known as the "Old Line State"; the nickname can be traced to Colonial times, when Marylanders led the way in many Revolutionary War encounters.
> - America's national anthem, "The Star-Spangled Banner," was composed in Maryland by Marylander Francis Scott Key during the War of 1812.
> - In southern Maryland, tobacco was once so prized that it served as legal tender.
> - Centrally located among the original 13 colonies, Maryland donated the land on which the nation's capital, Washington, D.C., was built.
> - Maryland is the only state with an official sport, jousting, still practiced at tournaments.
> - Maryland's state tree, the 450-year-old Wye Oak in Talbot County, has a circumference of more than 31 feet and a crown spread of 102 feet, making it the nation's largest white oak.

mansions and restored Federal-style townhouses doing double duty as restaurants, bed-and-breakfast inns, and sightseeing attractions. You'll also come across high-tech industry and manufacturing plants, side by side with sprawling tobacco farms, meandering apple orchards, and mammoth poultry farms.

As a vital part of the Chesapeake Bay area, Maryland is also watermen's territory—and a seafood-lover's paradise. The waters surrounding the state's Eastern Shore yield some 30 million pounds of hard-shell crabs a year, not to mention about two million pounds of soft-shell crabs, two million bushels of oysters, and 500,000 bushels of clams.

Everywhere you go in this state, you'll find fresh seafood on the menu. The king of Maryland cuisine, however, is crab (in season from April through December). Crab is to Maryland what the peanut is to Georgia and the pineapple is to Hawaii. To get the most out of crab cuisine, you may consider a few tasty tips:

First, crab is at its best served au naturel—fresh from the bay, steamed, and lightly spiced in the shell. Many restaurants feature crab this way, but be prepared to work at your dinner, cracking and breaking open the shells to obtain the tasty morsels (mallets and other helpful utensils are always supplied).

Soft-shell crabs are also plentiful and served in many ways, from a simple sauté to amandine or stuffed with succulent lump crabmeat. In Maryland, soft-shell crabs are simply known as "soft" crabs.

Why will you ask for other glories when you have soft crabs?
—Oliver Wendell Holmes, *The Professor at the Breakfast Table,* 1859

For those who don't want to crack shells and work for their dinner, then the dish to choose is crab imperial. This is usually in casserole form with lots of lump or backfin crabmeat topped with a creamy white sauce, often with a touch of sherry or other "secret recipe" ingredients. Last but not least, there are crab cakes. Although they vary from restaurant to restaurant, a classic crab cake is basically a scoop of crab (either lump or backfin) formed into the size of a hamburger. The crab is usually mixed with breadcrumbs, a bit of ham, green and red peppers, or other compatible ingredients, and then deep-fried or broiled. The secret of a good crab cake is lots of crab and very little filler. Some of the best crab cakes are dished up at Crisfield on Maryland's Eastern Shore, otherwise known as the "Seafood Capital of the World."

Maryland is also a big chicken-producing state; Salisbury, headquarters of the Perdue enterprises, is considered "the poultry capital of the world." Chicken is served many ways throughout the state, but "southern fried" is the most prevalent. Maryland's rich soil also produces sweet corn, tomatoes, soybeans, melons, strawberries, and peaches; many roadside stands offer fresh produce, available packed to order or on a pick-your-own basis. Vineyards and wineries are also prevalent throughout the central part of the state, with tours and tastings always on tap for visitors.

2   A Look at the Past

EARLY EXPLORATIONS & SETTLEMENT

The area that is present-day Maryland was initially settled, long before the coming of Columbus, by various Native American tribes including the Algonquin, Lenni Lenape, and Nanticoke. The first European to catch sight of the coast of Maryland was probably the Dutchman Henry Hudson as he sailed in from the Atlantic and along the body of water now known as Delaware Bay.

After Hudson, the Dutch made their mark several more times in the New World and as early as 1629 were attempting to establish a whaling colony in Delaware. While the Dutch were busy in Delaware, the English set their sights on neighboring territory, on the southern rim of what is now Maryland. In 1634 more than 140 English colonists arrived at the mouth of the Potomac River on two ships, *The Ark* and *The Dove.* These stalwart settlers set up a community that served as the state's first capital until 1694. It was Lord Baltimore's brother, Leonard Calvert, who christened the land in honor of Henrietta Maria, wife

Dateline

- **1634** English colonists sail into the Potomac and found St. Mary's City, Maryland's first capital.
- **1649** Puritans find a home in Annapolis.
- **1729** Baltimore founded.
- **1776** Declaration of Independence adopted.
- **1783–84** Annapolis becomes capital of colonies for nine months; Treaty of Paris signed at Annapolis in 1784.
- **1788** Maryland ratifies constitution and becomes seventh state.
- **1814** "Star-Spangled Banner" written at Baltimore.
- **1829** Chesapeake and Delaware Canal completed.

continues

- 1845 U.S. Naval Academy founded at Annapolis.
- 1850 Chesapeake and Ohio Canal reaches terminus at Cumberland.
- 1861 Abraham Lincoln passes through Baltimore's President Street Station on way to his inauguration. "First Blood of the Civil War" shed at Baltimore.
- 1862 Battle of Antietam.
- 1875 Ocean City, Maryland, opened as beach resort.
- 1925 Deep Creek Lake created.
- 1952 William Preston Lane Jr. Bridge opens up the Eastern Shore.
- 1981 Harborplace debuts in Baltimore.
- 1992 Oriole Park at Camden Yards opens in Baltimore.
- 1997 Baltimore celebrates its 200th anniversary with opening of new $150 million Convention Center at the Inner Harbor.

of King Charles I, calling it "St. Marie's Citty" (or St. Mary's City). Among the achievements of this early city was the enactment of the first laws recognizing religious tolerance.

THE PURITANS ESTABLISH A BASE   In 1649 another group from England, the Puritans, came on the scene. They landed first in Virginia but, encountering religious intolerance there, moved northward to what is now Annapolis and settled at the mouth of the Severn River, near Chesapeake Bay. These early inhabitants called their new settlement Anne Arundel Town, after the wife of the second Lord Baltimore, proprietor of the colony of Maryland. In 1695 the town was renamed Annapolis in honor of Princess Anne of England, and the colonial government of Maryland was moved here from St. Mary's City; it has been Maryland's capital ever since. Shortly afterward, another city began to take shape on the Patapsco River—Baltimore, named after Lord Baltimore of England and founded in 1729.

As events propelled the American colonies toward the quest for independence from England, Maryland was in the forefront of the struggle.

THE STRUGGLE FOR INDEPENDENCE Although Philadelphia was the capital of the colonies for most of the period from 1774 to 1800, during the First and Second Continental Congresses and the major part of the Revolutionary War, Maryland's colonial hub also took a turn as capital. As the hostilities of the war drew to a close, Philadelphia relinquished its preeminence and Annapolis reigned as the first peacetime capital of the United States (from November 26, 1783, until August 13, 1784) and served as the site for the ratification of the Treaty of Paris, the document in which Great Britain formally recognized the independence of the United States.

After almost nine months in Annapolis, the capital was once again firmly back in Philadelphia, and in 1787 a Federal Convention of 55 delegates gathered at Independence Hall. For four months, they met, debated, and revised the Articles of Confederation and ultimately developed the Constitution of the United States.

STATEHOOD, EARLY GROWTH & A NATIONAL ANTHEM   Maryland ratified the Constitution on April 28, 1788, becoming the seventh of the original 13 colonies to do so. The post–Revolutionary War era was one of growth and expansion for the new states, and farming was pivotal to the development of all the states, including Maryland.

Transportation avenues blossomed—the 19th century soon became the age of the railroad, the steamboat, and the canal, and rivers were harnessed for milling and industrial use. National roads were built and western Maryland via Cumberland became a gateway to the West. In 1829, the completion of the Chesapeake and Delaware Canal provided a shortcut from Chesapeake Bay to the

Atlantic. The Chesapeake and Ohio Canal, stretching westward across Maryland from Georgetown, reached Cumberland in 1850.

This was a relatively peaceful era for the region, with the exception of the War of 1812, which began with a British blockade of the Chesapeake and Delaware bays. By 1813 much of the action had shifted westward toward the Great Lakes, but one of the war's most notable events occurred in Baltimore in 1814 as the Americans were holding off a siege of Fort McHenry by the British. Francis Scott Key, a native Marylander, was inspired to write the words of "The Star-Spangled Banner," the song that would become the country's national anthem.

CIVIL WAR YEARS   The Civil War (1861–65) was to have a big effect on the entire mid-Atlantic area including Maryland. On February 23, 1861, Abraham Lincoln passed through Baltimore's President Street Railroad Station on the way to his first inauguration. A few months later, the Sixth Massachusetts Union Army Troops and the Pennsylvania Volunteer Washington Brigade passed through the same station on April 19, 1861, on their way to the nation's capital. While the troops attempted to march to nearby Camden Station, a mob quickly gathered and blocked their passage. The skirmish resulted in the deaths of four soldiers and 12 civilians, and the incident became known as the "First Blood of the Civil War." More than a year later one of the most significant battles also took place in the state. On September 17, 1862, the Battle of Antietam at Sharpsburg, Maryland, became the bloodiest single-day battle of the war, with the dead and wounded on both sides exceeding 23,000.

MODERN MILESTONES   In the 35 years from the Civil War's end to the dawn of the 20th century, the United States moved quickly from a war-torn nation to a leading industrial power. Tourism-related developments were also coming to pass that would have local impact in the state of Maryland, such as the official opening on July 4, 1875, of Ocean City as a beach resort.

Events of particular significance to Maryland during the 20th century include the construction in 1925 of the 12-mile-long Deep Creek Lake as a year-round water- and winter-sports playground in western Maryland. In 1952 the William Preston Lane Jr. Bridge was built, stretching from Annapolis to Kent Island, making the Eastern Shore truly accessible to the rest of the state. And in 1980 the cornerstone of waterfront urban development in Baltimore, Harborplace, was opened. This spurred further expansions of the waterfront area, encouraging investment in many new restaurants, hotels, and attractions including the National Aquarium in 1981, the Pier Six Concert Pavilion in 1991, Oriole Park at Camden Yards in 1992, and a $150 million Convention Center, slated for completion on April 1, 1997.

3 Visitor Information & Money

VISITOR INFORMATION   For brochures and printed information about Maryland, contact the **Maryland Office of Tourism Development,** 9th floor, 217 E. Redwood St., Baltimore, MD 21202 (☎ 410/333-6611 or 800/MD-IS-FUN, ext. 123).

PRICE GUIDELINES   In general, the lowest prices for hotel rooms in cities, such as Baltimore and Annapolis, are available on weekends and in the peak summer months, when business traffic is slow. In contrast, the best deals prevail

What Things Cost in Maryland

Deluxe hotel room overlooking Baltimore's Inner Harbor (Hyatt Regency)	$190.00–250.00
Moderate/budget hotel room in downtown Baltimore (Mount Vernon Hotel)	$69.00–125.00
Room/suite at a 19th-century inn in Baltimore's Fells Point (Admiral Fell Inn)	$120.00–195.00
Lunch for one at a downtown Baltimore budget restaurant (Women's Industrial Exchange)	$4.00
Expensive dinner for two in Baltimore's Little Italy (Da Mimmo)	from $80.00
All-you-can-eat crab dinner for two in Baltimore's Fells Point (Obrycki's)	from $70.00
Ride on Baltimore's Light Rail system between the Inner Harbor and Mount Vernon Place	$1.25
Admission to the National Aquarium in Baltimore	$11.50
All-day pass on Baltimore's water taxi	$3.25
Two-hour narrated lunch cruise with entertainment from Baltimore Harbor (Bay Lady)	$21.95
Admission to an Oriole's baseball game at Oriole Park at Camden Yards	$5.00–28.00
Concert at Baltimore's Peabody Conservatory of Music	$10.00
Room at one of the Historic Inns of Annapolis	$105.00–195.00
Room at budget motel outside of Annapolis (Courtyard by Marriott)	$69.00–99.00
Dinner for two at a historic downtown Annapolis inn (Reynolds Tavern)	from $60.00
Budget lunch at a local Annapolis deli (Chick and Ruth's)	$3.00–5.00
Guided tour of the U.S. Naval Academy at Annapolis	$5.00
Two-hour sailing trip in Annapolis harbor	$22.00–25.00
Room at a deluxe inn on the Eastern Shore (Robert Morris Inn, Oxford)	$70.00–220.00
"Down-home" seafood dinner for two on the Eastern Shore (Harrison's Chesapeake House, Tilghman)	$50.00

at the Eastern Shore bay and beach resorts during weekdays, and especially in the off-season (October or November through April). Always inquire about package deals. Both city and country destinations frequently offer weekend or mid-week packages that include accommodations, some meals, and many extras. These packages not only save money and time, but usually include some local highlights that you might otherwise miss.

All-you-can-eat crab dinner for two at budget restaurant on the Eastern Shore (Crab Claw, St. Michaels)	$40.00
Deluxe oceanfront hotel room with balcony at Ocean City (Dunes Manor)	$145.00–210.00
Budget bay-side motel room at Ocean City (Talbot Inn)	$30.00–85.00
Expensive dinner for two at Ocean City (Reflections)	from $80.00
Crab seafood dinner at moderate restaurant in Ocean City (Phillips' Crab House)	from $60.00
Smorgasbord dinner for one at Ocean City (Paul Revere's)	$7.99
Half-day headboat fishing-boat trip from Ocean City	$16.00–20.00
Deluxe room with breakfast and dinner for two at country inn near Frederick (Inn at Buckeystown)	$225.00
Bed-and-breakfast room at New Market (National Pike Inn)	$75.00–125.00
Admission to Antietam Battlefield	$2.00
A day's guided biking with lunch beside the C&O Canal at Cumberland	$25.00–40.00
32-mile round-trip steam train ride on the Western Maryland Scenic Railroad	$13.75–15.75
Room at a downtown bed-and-breakfast inn in Cumberland (Inn at Walnut Bottom)	$65.00–90.00
Dinner for two at a moderate restaurant in Cumberland (Oxford Inn)	$50.00
A day's skiing at Wisp Resort, Deep Creek Lake	$30.00–37.00
Moderate/budget room at a lakeside motel at Deep Creek Lake (Point View Inn)	$50.00–75.00

Accommodations—The Average Cost of a Double Room, Excluding Tax:
Very Expensive, $200 and up; Expensive, $125 to $200; Moderate, $75 to
$125; Inexpensive, Under $75.

Dining—The Prices of Most Main Courses on the Menu: Very Expensive,
Over $25; Expensive, $17 to $25; Moderate, $10 to $17; Inexpensive,
Under $10.

In calculating the price categories within this book, the following guidelines have
been used:

AREA CODE   The state of Maryland has two area codes: 410 for most numbers
in the eastern half of the state, and 301 for numbers in the western half of the state.

SALES TAX   The sales tax in Maryland is 5%. Some counties also levy a lodging tax of an additional 3% to 8%.

4 When to Go

CLIMATE   With an elevation that ranges from sea level along the seashore to 3,360 feet in the mountains, Maryland has an equally diverse climate.

	Baltimore Area	Central Area	Western Area	Eastern Shore
Avg. Summer Temp. (°F)	77	72–74	65–72	75
Avg. Winter Temp. (°F)	37	32–36	28–32	38
Rainfall (in.)	41	40–46	36–47	46
Snowfall (in.)	23	22–36	35–82	14.7
Frost-free days	232	194	122–168	201

MARYLAND CALENDAR OF EVENTS

January

- **Annapolis Heritage Antiques Show,** Annapolis. Quality antiques, spanning centuries, shown at the National Guard Armory. Last weekend of January.
- ✪ **Baltimore Bicentennial, 1797–1997.** Throughout 1997, the city of Baltimore will be celebrating the 200th anniversary of its incorporation as a city. A full program of festive events, not final at press time, will be taking place.

   Where: Throughout City of Baltimore. **When:** Jan–Dec 1997. **How:** For a program of events and complete details, contact the Baltimore Area Convention and Visitors Association, 100 Light St., 12th floor, Baltimore, MD 21202 (☎ 410/659-7300 or 800/343-3468).

February

- **Babe Ruth Birthday Party,** Baltimore. An annual celebration in honor of the city's all-time baseball hero (born in 1895 in Baltimore). February 6.
- **Winterfest at Wisp, Deep Creek Lake.** A weekend celebration of winter, with ski races, snowboarding, torchlight parades, fireworks, entertainment, and more. Late February or early March.

March

- **Maryland Days,** St. Mary's City. This annual celebration commemorates the founding of Maryland, with addresses by state and city officials, and entertainment. March 25–26.

April

- ✪ **Annapolis Spring Boat Show.** Staged along the waterfront, this is the region's largest spring boat show, featuring new and used powerboats and sailboats plus boating, fishing, and water-sports equipment.

   Where: Annapolis City Dock. **When:** Third weekend of April. **How:** Tickets are $6 for adults, $3 for children aged 12 and under. Contact the Annapolis and Anne Arundel Conference and Visitors Bureau, 26 West St., Annapolis, MD 21401 (☎ 410/280-0445 or 410/268-TOUR).
- ✪ **Mid-Atlantic Maritime Festival.** A three-day nautical celebration featuring exhibits and demonstrations of ship models, paintings, photographs, nautical crafts, collectibles, plus music, seafoods, a parade of tall ships, and more.

Where: Easton downtown. **When:** Third weekend in April. **How:** Three-day pass is $10 for adults, $5 for children aged 6 to 12; one-day ticket is $5 adults, $2 children aged 6 to 12. Contact Mid-Atlantic Maritime Festival, P.O. Box 2409, 11 Federal St., Easton, MD 21601 (☎ 410/822-4606).

○ **Annapolis Waterfront Festival.** More than 100 artisans and craftspeople display their work along the waterfront, in an atmosphere of celebration, with a flotilla of historic boats and tall ships, boat races, sailboat minilessons, and performances by barbershop quartets, chorale societies, and folk, gospel, and rock groups.

Where: Annapolis City Dock. **When:** Last weekend of April. **How:** Admission is $4 for adults and $1 for children under 12. Contact Annapolis and Anne Arundel Conference and Visitors Bureau, 26 West St., Annapolis, MD 21401 (☎ 410/280-0445 or 410/268-TOUR).

May

• **Chesapeake Bay Bridge Walk,** Annapolis. Marylanders and visitors enjoy a leisurely 4.3-mile stroll across the east-bound span of the Bay Bridge. First Sunday in May.

○ **Preakness Celebration.** The best known of Maryland's annual festivals, this citywide event revolves around the Preakness Stakes race at the Pimlico Race Course. The middle jewel in horse racing's Triple Crown, the Preakness is regarded as one of the prime sporting events in the world. The week-long hoopla includes a 5-K run, music festival, hot-air balloon races, a polo match, golf tournament, frog hop, boating, food-eating contests, and waterside activities at the Inner Harbor. On the eve of the big race, there is also a parade with floats, drill teams, and marching bands.

Where: Baltimore. **When:** Mid-May. **How:** Many events are free; all seats at the Preakness race must be reserved in advance. For details of price and availability, contact the Pimlico Race Course, Park Heights and Belvedere avenues (☎ 301/542-9400 or 800/638-3811).

○ **Frederick Craft Fair.** One of the largest arts and crafts fairs in western Maryland, this juried show features "made in America" goods, produced by more than 300 of the top U.S. craft designers, as well as nationally known musical entertainment, craft demonstrations, and all kinds of food.

Where: Frederick Fairgrounds, Frederick. **When:** Third weekend of May. **How:** Tickets are $5 for all persons over 12 years of age. Contact the Tourism Council of Frederick County, 19 E. Church St., Frederick, MD 21701 (☎ 410/663-8687).

• **Chestertown Tea Party Festival,** Chestertown. This is an annual reenactment of a 1774 event, with crafts, parade, art show, and entertainment. Fourth Sunday of May.

June

• **Queen Anne's County Waterman's Festival,** Grasonville. This event pays tribute to the Maryland watermen and the seafood industry, with music, arts, crafts, food, and a docking-and-anchor-throwing contest. First Sunday of June.

• **Canal Day,** Chesapeake City. On this one-day celebration, the banks of the C&D Canal are lined with more than 100 artisans, food vendors, and entertainers. Last Saturday in June.

July

✪ **C&O Canal Boat Festival.** Focusing on western Maryland of the 1800s, this two-day event features reenactments of Civil War days and frontier life. Activities include crafts demonstrations, country music sessions, and walking tours of the 93-foot canal boat replica, as well as stagecoach, carriage and pony rides.

Where: North Branch of the C&O Canal Park, PPG Rd., 5 miles south of Cumberland off Route 51. **When:** Third weekend of July. **How:** No admission charge, but $1 donation per person is expected. Contact Allegany County Visitors Bureau, Western Maryland Station Center, Mechanic and Harrison streets, Cumberland, MD 21502 (☎ 301/777-5905).

• **Artscape,** Baltimore. This is Baltimore's annual Festival of the Arts, staged in the Mount Royal cultural district, with a panorama of literary, performing, and visual arts. Third weekend of July.

• **Celebrate Annapolis: Wine, Food, and Music Festival,** Annapolis. Staged beside the Navy/Marine Stadium, this weekend focuses on Maryland's wines, micro-brewed beers, regional foods, crafts, and acoustic rock music. Third or fourth weekend of July.

August

• **St. Mary's Governor's Cup Yacht Race,** St. Mary's City. This is one of the largest overnight sailboat races on the East Coast. First weekend of August.

✪ **Rocky Gap Country/Bluegrass Music Festival.** This annual jamboree features nationally known music stars—such as Willie Nelson, Hank Williams Jr., and Dolly Parton—local music acts, musical workshops, arts and crafts, and sports activities.

Where: Rocky Gap State Park, near Cumberland. **When:** First weekend of August. **How:** Tickets are $66 and up for a three-day pass or from $20–$30 per day for adults, $2 per day for children eight years and under. Contact Rocky Gap Country Bluegrass Festival, P.O. Box 1996, Cumberland, MD 21502 (☎ 301/724-2511 or 800/424-2511).

• **White Marlin Open and White Marlin Tournament,** Ocean City. These two competitions draw fishermen from far and wide to the "white marlin capital of the world." Early to mid-August; and the last weekend of August or first weekend of September.

✪ **Maryland Renaissance Festival.** Maryland's state sport of jousting is featured at this annual eight-weekend event, along with all types of entertainment, from musicians and singers to mimes, jugglers, magicians, fire-eaters, stilt-walkers, and actors dressed in medieval costume.

Where: Crownsville, 8 miles NW of Annapolis. **When:** Late August through early October. **How:** Admission $11.95 adults, $9.25 seniors, $4.95 children aged 7 to 15. For details, contact Maryland Renaissance Festival, P.O. Box 315, Crownsville, MD 21032 (☎ 410/266-7304 or 800/296-7304).

September

✪ **National Hard Crab Derby and Fair.** Since 1947, this has been a major fixture on the late summer calendar. The focal point is a crab race in which crustaceans from states as far away as Hawaii try to match the speed of the Eastern Shore crabs. Other highlights include crab-picking and crab-cooking competitions, tennis and fishing tournaments, a beauty contest, fireworks, and a parade.

Where: Crisfield. **When:** Labor Day weekend. **How:** Admission is $3 for adults, $1 for children under 12. Contact the Crisfield Chamber of Commerce, P.O. Box 215, Crisfield, MD 21817 (☎ 301/968-2682 or 800/782-3913).

- **Maryland Seafood Festival,** Annapolis. Staged at the Sandy Point State Park, this three-day event focuses on sampling the various seafood delicacies of the Chesapeake Bay area, plus beach activities, entertainment, arts, and crafts. Second weekend of September.
- **New Market Days,** New Market. The "antiques capital of Maryland" hosts a three-day celebration of crafts, music, and food, with Civil War reenactments and other pageantry. Fourth weekend of September.
- **Kunta Kinte Heritage Festival,** Annapolis. African American connections and achievements in Maryland are the focus of this two-day festival of arts and crafts, cuisine, and music. Last weekend of September.
- **Sunfest,** Ocean City. A four-day beachside gathering for arts and crafts, music, and other entertainment. Last weekend of September.

October
- **Maryland Railfest,** Cumberland. This is a nine-day celebration of the state's railroading heritage, with daily excursions on a 1916 steam locomotive, displays of train memorabilia, and craft and music shows. First week of October.
- **U.S. Sailboat Show,** Annapolis. Staged at the City Dock, this event is a showcase for new sailboats and products from the world's leading manufacturers. First weekend of October.
- ✪ **Old Princess Anne Days.** More than 20 historic 18th- and 19th-century houses, mansions, and cottages—from Federal and Victorian to Italianate and Georgian—open their doors once a year for this open-air walking tour celebration, with narration by costumed guides.

  Where: Princess Anne. **When:** First weekend of October. **How:** Tickets are $10 per person. Contact Somerset County Tourism Office, P.O. Box 243, Rte. 13, Princess Anne, MD 21853 (☎ 410/651-2968 or 800/521-9189).
- **Autumn Glory Festival,** Deep Creek Lake. The peak of fall foliage is celebrated at this three-day event, with banjo and fiddle championships, a tournament of bands, parades, Oktoberfest, arts, crafts, antique sales, and concerts. Second weekend of October.
- **U.S. Power Boat Show,** Annapolis. Held at the City Dock, this show presents new powerboats and products from the world's leading boat-product manufacturers. Second weekend of October.
- **St. Mary's County Oyster Festival,** Leonardtown. This annual event draws people from many lands for the World Oyster-Shucking Competition, as well as oyster sampling, cooking contests, music, and crafts. Third weekend of October.

November
- ✪ **Waterfowl Festival.** A major Eastern Shore fixture since 1971, this three-day event is attended by waterfowl artists, carvers, sculptors, photographers, collectors, and anyone interested in waterfowl. Activities include duck- and goose-calling contests, workshops, auctions of antique decoys, dog trials, and exhibits of waterfowl paintings, artifacts, books, carvings, duck stamps, and memorabilia.

Where: Easton. **When:** Second weekend of November. **How:** $15 for three-day pass; children under 14 with an adult are admitted free. Contact the Waterfowl Festival, 40 S. Harrison St., P.O. Box 929, Easton, MD 21601 (☎ 410/822-4567).

December

- **Victorian Christmas,** Berlin. Celebrate the holidays in a Victorian town, with Christmas recitals, brass quintets, concerts, horse and carriage rides, and an annual parade. Throughout December.
- **Victorian Christmas at History House,** Cumberland. Holiday candlelight tours of an 18-room Victorian town house decorated with candles, live greens, and handmade ornaments. Second and third weeks of December.
- **Historic Annapolis Christmas Celebration,** Annapolis. A Yuletide event in an 18th-century setting with music, refreshments, and decorations. Second weekend of December.
- **Christmas in Historic Chestertown and Kent County,** Chestertown. Walking tours of historic homes decorated for the holiday season. Third weekend of December.

5 Getting There

BY PLANE   The gateway to Maryland is **Baltimore-Washington International Airport,** situated 10 miles south of Baltimore and 20 miles north of the state capital at Annapolis. Hundreds of domestic and international flights a day land and depart from this gateway. Most Maryland cities and towns are also convenient to Dulles International Airport and Washington National Airport.

In addition, commuter flights operate into **Easton Airport, Salisbury Airport,** and **Ocean City Airport** on Maryland's Eastern Shore, and into **Cumberland Regional Airport** in the western part of the state.

BY TRAIN   **Amtrak** offers convenient daily service into Baltimore, arriving at the beautifully restored Beaux Arts–style station in downtown. In addition, there is more limited service into Cumberland in western Maryland.

BY BUS   **Greyhound/Trailways** serve major points in Maryland such as Baltimore, Ocean City, Salisbury, Easton, Frederick, and Cumberland.

BY CAR   **I-95,** the eastern seaboard's major north-south link from Maine to Florida, passes through the state via Baltimore and central Maryland. Other interstate highways that traverse Maryland are **I-83, I-81, I-70,** and **I-68.** U.S. **Route 40,** part of the original National Pike, runs from Baltimore westward via Frederick and Cumberland. U.S. routes **50 and 301** connect Maryland's eastern and western shores via the William Preston Lane Jr. Memorial Bridge over the Chesapeake Bay. The Eastern Shore is also served by U.S. **Route 13.**

6 Getting Around

BY PLANE   Commuter flights within the state are operated from Baltimore-Washington International Airport to several smaller airports, such as Salisbury, Ocean City, and Cumberland.

BY CAR   In addition to the major interstate highways and routes, Maryland is well served with local roads, such as Route 413, which will take you to Crisfield, and Route 219, which leads to Deep Creek Lake. Driving in Maryland is a pleasant experience with fertile farmland scenes on the western shore and dozens of seaport towns on the eastern side of the Chesapeake. As Route 40 and Route Alternate 40 lead west toward Cumberland, they provide a gateway to panoramic mountain vistas.

2 Baltimore

Baltimore, situated on the Atlantic coast, has been a key seaport since the American Revolution. Named after the British colonizer of what is now Maryland (George Calvert, later Lord Baltimore, around 1580–1632), the city was founded in 1729 and incorporated in 1797. It has many claims to fame.

Birthplace of "The Star-Spangled Banner" and the famous Baltimore clipper ships, Baltimore was briefly the nation's capital; it was also the starting point for the first U.S. railroad and the site of the first railroad passenger and freight station. The first telegraph communication ("What hath God wrought") was sent to Baltimore in 1844, and the nation's oldest cathedral is also here. Over the years, Baltimore has been home to a parade of personalities, among them Edgar Allan Poe, H. L. Mencken, Babe Ruth, and Wallis Warfield, better known as the duchess of Windsor.

In the last two decades, Baltimore has been particularly hard hit by a skyrocketing crime rate, racial tensions, and a decaying urban infrastructure. It's not a sleek, perfectly manicured city by any stretch of the imagination—there are some bad neighborhoods you'll want to avoid. And local fans were crushed when Baltimore's NFL franchise departed for St. Louis, a move that seemed symbolic of the city's decline.

But there have been bright spots in the last few years. With the Browns' move from Cleveland to Baltimore for the 1996 season, football fans will once again have a hometown team to root for. Harborplace was meant to be a major urban development of the waterfront area, and it's been successful to a degree, though, like South Street Seaport in New York, it's nothing more than a glorified shopping mall, full of tourists frequenting shops you could find in Anytown, U.S.A. But despite the bland gentrification of its downtown, which is full of those anonymous glass skyscrapers that so afflict most American cities, there's still an authentic, old-fashioned charm in certain neighborhoods. It's a city of row houses—some blocks are lined with lovely Federal-style town houses. And the most encouraging development in recent years was the construction of a real old-fashioned ballpark: Camden Yards, the new home of the Baltimore Orioles. This project maintained the integrity of the historic buildings around it, and it's been a wild success. Baseball fans have been flocking to the stadium in droves.

Baltimore has also made an appearance on the large and small screens in the last decade. Hometown boy Barry Levinson has often used the city as the setting for his work, including the films *Avalon* and *Diner*. He's currently the executive producer of *Homicide: Life on the Street,* a highly acclaimed crime drama that uses a gritty backdrop to great effect. Baltimore is also the setting favored by another homegrown talent, John Waters, the director of such notoriously sick, hilarious, and quirky epics as *Polyester,* starring the late Divine, and the more mainstream comedy *Serial Mom.*

It's an offbeat city, where the visitor can enjoy a couple of traditional "attractions," including the really fascinating National Aquarium, or venture a little farther off the beaten track in search of a more scruffy sort of charm—say, scouring Fells Point for funky retro-style antiques or downing a dozen oysters on the half shell at a fish market. It's a city that exists on a small scale and you can get to know it intimately.

On the Patapsco River off Chesapeake Bay, Baltimore is a major seaport with 45 miles of waterfront, the third-largest in the United States, located 37 miles north of Washington and 96 miles south of Philadelphia. With a 79-mile square area, it is also Maryland's major urban center and a prime economic and manufacturing center, with a city population of 736,000 and a metropolitan area population of 2,357,700.

1   Orientation

ARRIVING

BY PLANE   The **Baltimore-Washington International Airport,** Route 46 (☎ 410/859-7111), is 10 miles south of downtown Baltimore. To drive to downtown Baltimore from the airport, take I-195 west to I-295 north, which will take you into downtown. Also, **SuperShuttle** (☎ 800/809-7080) operates vans between the airport and all the major downtown hotels. Departures are scheduled every 30 minutes between 6am and 12:30am, and the cost is $10 per person one way or $15 round-trip.

Each day, hundreds of flights from both domestic and international points land at this airport. Some useful airline telephone numbers are **American** (☎ 800/433-7300); **Delta** (☎ 800/221-1212); **Continental** (☎ 800/525-0280); **Northwest** (☎ 800/225-2525); **Southwest** (☎ 800/435-9792); **TWA** (☎ 800/221-2000); **United** (☎ 800/241-2000); and **USAir** (☎ 800/428-4322).

BY CAR   From the northeast and south, **I-95** has access to downtown areas via **I-695** and the Baltimore-Washington Parkway (**I-295**). From the north, Exit 53 off I-95 south will lead straight into the center of town. Traffic from the west approaches downtown from **I-70**, I-695, and **Route 40.** Southbound access is via **I-83.** The **Fort McHenry Tunnel** (I-895) is the final connection of I-95 through Baltimore, running under the Patapsco River and providing easy access from the north to downtown Baltimore. This eight-lane structure is the widest tunnel in the world and one of the largest public works developments in history; the toll per car is $1.

Impressions

I could not love New York so much loved I not Baltimore.

—Ogden Nash

What's Special About Baltimore

Sightseeing
- National Aquarium, a must-see complex of sea creatures.
- Fort McHenry National Monument and Historic Shrine, birthplace of the "Star-Spangled Banner" and now a national park.
- Harborplace, the focal point of the Inner Harbor, with shops, boutiques, food markets, restaurants, music, and more.

Activities
- Sightseeing cruises around the waters of the Inner Harbor.
- Sailing on board *Clipper City*, the tallest ship licensed to carry passengers in the United States.
- All-day trolley-style tours of the city.

Events & Festivals
- Harbor Lights Music Festival, featuring top-name stars in concert beside the Inner Harbor.
- Preakness Celebration, the second jewel in Thoroughbred racing's Triple Crown.

Museums & Galleries
- Maryland Science Center, with a hands-on exhibit of Baltimore and the Chesapeake Bay, plus a planetarium and IMAX theater.
- Walters Art Gallery, world-class repository of art spanning 5,000 years.
- Star-Spangled Banner Flag House and 1812 Museum.
- Babe Ruth Birthplace and Museum, also housing Maryland's Baseball Hall of Fame.

Shopping
- Harborplace, with more than 135 shops.
- "Antique Row," where you can comb through 40 shops looking for treasures.
- Lexington Market, the oldest continuously operating market in the United States.
- Fells Point arts and crafts shops, including some great places for funky retrostyle antiques.

Once you arrive, you'll find that many hotels provide indoor parking; otherwise, public metered lots and street parking are available throughout the city. Rates at the numerous commercial lots and garages average about $2 an hour or $8 to $12 a day. Most maps produced by the tourism office indicate public parking places.

BY TRAIN   Baltimore is a stop on the main East Coast corridor of **Amtrak,** between Wilmington and Washington, D.C. All trains arrive at and depart from Baltimore's busy Pennsylvania Station, 1500 N. Charles St. (☎ 410/291-4260 or 800/872-7245), on the north side of the city. Recently restored to the tune of $3.5 million, this building is a Beaux Arts gem. In addition, the local Penn Line of **MARC,** a division of Amtrak operated in conjunction with the Maryland Department of Transportation, provides rail service between downtown Baltimore (Amtrak Station) and Baltimore International Airport. Service is daily from approximately 6am to 10pm and the fare is $3 one way. For more information, call 800/325-RAIL.

BY BUS   Regular bus service is provided to and from Baltimore via **Greyhound/ Trailways**, 210 W. Fayette St. (☎ 410/744-9311).

VISITOR INFORMATION

For advance information to help plan a visit, contact the **Baltimore Area Convention and Visitors Association** (BACVA), 100 Light St., 12th floor, Baltimore, MD 21202 (☎ 410/659-7300 or 800/343-3468). Once you are in town, there are several **BACVA visitor centers** open daily for on-the-spot inquiries. These locations include a ground-floor walk-in office at Constellation Pier, 301 E. Pratt St. (☎ 410/837-4636 or 800/282-6632); a kiosk in the main lobby of the Pennsylvania Railroad Station, 1525 N. Charles St.; and booths at the Baltimore-Washington International Airport at Pier C (main entrance) and Pier D (international terminal). In addition to general sightseeing brochures, all offices distribute copies of the *Quick Guide*, a comprehensive, magazine-style guide to what's happening in and around the city.

CITY LAYOUT

Sooner or later, you'll wind up at the Inner Harbor at the city's southern edge. With its pavilions of boutiques, markets, and restaurants, and its modern museums, open-air concert decks, state-of-the-art convention center, and boats of all sizes, the Inner Harbor is a showplace of Baltimore at its best. Once a row of abandoned warehouses and factories, this waterfront area is a successful if bland urban restoration.

MAIN ARTERIES & STREETS   The main downtown area radiates around the Charles Center, a 33-acre complex incorporating apartments, office buildings, hotels, shops, landscaped plazas, and a theater, all connected by an overhead walkway. It is bounded by Liberty, Saratoga, Lombard, and Charles streets, the last of which divides Baltimore from east to west.

Also within this perimeter is Baltimore Street, which divides the city from north to south. Almost all downtown streets run only one way, although the important exceptions are Howard and Eutaw streets. All of Baltimore's numbered streets run east and west.

NEIGHBORHOODS IN BRIEF   Toward the northern end of Charles Street is an area known as **Mount Vernon,** dominated by a 178-foot monument dedicated to George Washington. Laid out in 1827, Mount Vernon was once the city's most fashionable residential district, and it is still a delight, with its elegant town houses and four parklike squares. This is also the location of many of the city's oldest churches and cultural institutions, including the Peabody Conservatory of Music, one of the leading music schools in the world, and the Walters Art Gallery.

To the east of the Inner Harbor is **Little Italy,** one of Baltimore's most colorful and self-contained ethnic neighborhoods and the location of about two dozen fine Italian restaurants. Here you will also see some fine examples of neighborhood row houses, with their gleaming white marble front stoops, which the residents still scrub daily. In this section, as in many of the Baltimore ethnic neighborhoods, the practice of window-screen painting is still carried on by craftspeople. Passersby can't see in, but window sitters can see out.

Moving still more to the east is the **Fells Point** section, the old seaport where Baltimore originally started. Fells Point today is an old-world area with brick-lined streets and more than 350 original residential structures reflecting the architecture of the American Federal period.

MAPS   For maps, brochures, and useful pamphlets to help you plan and enjoy your trip, contact the Baltimore Area Visitors Center, Constellation Pier, 301 E. Pratt St., Baltimore, MD 21201 (☎ 410/837-4636 or 800/282-6632).

2 Getting Around

BY PUBLIC TRANSPORTATION

BY RAIL   Baltimore's Mass Transit Administration (MTA), operates **Light Rail,** a 27-mile system of above-ground rail lines reminiscent of the city's old trolleys. It travels in a north-south direction from the suburb of Timonium to the north and Glen Burnie to the south. Seven of the 24 stops are located on Howard Street in the downtown area. The key stop within the city is Camden Station, next to the Orioles' ballpark. It's the ideal way to get to a game or to travel within the downtown area between Camden Yards and the Inner Harbor, to Lexington Market, and the cultural center or antique area around Mount Vernon Place.

Tickets are dispensed at machines at each stop; exact change is required, but change-making machines are also on site. Light Rail runs weekdays every 15 minutes between 6am and 11pm; Saturday, every 15 minutes between 8am and 11pm; and Sunday, every 15 minutes between 11am and 7pm. Minimum fare is $1.25. For information, call 410/539-5000 or 800/543-9809.

BY SUBWAY   For those interested in reaching the area north of the city, Baltimore's MTA operates **Metro,** a subway system that connects the downtown area with northwest suburbs. Service runs from Monday through Saturday, with varying hours. The minimum subway fare is $1.25; for more information, call 410/539-5000 or 800/543-9809.

BY BUS   The MTA also operates a network of buses that connect all sections of the city. Service is daily, but hours vary. The base fare is $1.25 and exact change is necessary. For information and schedules, call 410/539-5000 or 800/543-9809.

BY TROLLEY   One of the best ways to tour Baltimore is via the **Baltimore Trolley,** a motorized trolley-style bus that is a replica of Baltimore's original cabled vehicles. The trolley ride, which is fully narrated, operates continuously, stopping at all major hotels and attractions. You can board at any point along the route, ride the complete circuit, board and reboard as many times as you wish for an inclusive one-day price. The cost is $12 for adults and $4.50 for children 5 to 12; children under 5 ride free. These colorful trolleys operate daily, year-round, from 10am to 4pm, with a slightly reduced schedule from October to April. For full information, call 410/752-2015.

BY CAR

There are many car-rental firms with offices in downtown Baltimore and at Baltimore-Washington International Airport, including: **Avis,** 315 W. Baltimore St. (☎ 800/331-1212) and at the airport (☎ 800/331-1212); **Budget,** 401 W. Pratt St. (☎ 410/685-8743); and at the airport (☎ 410/859-8050); **Enterprise,** at the airport (☎ 410/787-9210); **Hertz,** at the airport (☎ 410/850-7400); and **National,** at the airport (☎ 410/859-8860).

BY TAXI

All taxis in the city are metered; the three largest fleets are **Yellow Cab** (☎ 410/685-1212); **Sun Cab** (☎ 410/235-0300); and **Diamond Cab** (☎ 410/947-3333). For airport trips, call **BWI Shuttle Express** (☎ 410/859-0800).

BY WATER SHUTTLE

Water shuttle is a convenient and very pleasant way to hop between Baltimore's major waterside attractions and neighborhoods. The **Fort McHenry Shuttle** (410/685-4288) is a narrated shuttle service connecting Fort McHenry and Fells Point to the Inner Harbor. An all-stop ticket costs $5 for adults, $3.75 for children under 12; a one-way ticket is $2.50 for adults, $2 for children under 12. The shuttle runs from May to Sept, between 11am and 6pm daily. The **Harbor Shuttle Co.** (410/675-2900) operates to 10 major points along the Inner Harbor corridor. Weekdays, service to all ports costs $2 per person. On weekends, service to six ports costs $3, 10 ports costs $4. The shuttle runs from April through September, weekdays between 11am and 11pm, weekends between 10am and midnight. From October to March service is reduced according to demand.

Water Taxi (410/563-3901) runs a continual service, like a water bus, between Pier 1 and a dozen other Inner Harbor locations including Harborplace, Fells Point, and Little Italy. To hail a water taxi, just stand next to the (water taxi) sign at a designated stop or on the adjacent floating dock. Each ticket entitles the passenger to unlimited use of the water taxi for a full day. The cost is $3.25 for adults and $2.25 for children under 10. Service operates from May through September, Monday through Thursday between 11am and 11pm, Friday between 11am and midnight, Saturday from 10am to midnight, and Sunday from 10am to 11pm; October and April, Monday through Thursday and Sunday from 11am to 9pm, Saturday between 10am and midnight; November, February, and March, Wednesday through Sunday from 11am to 6pm.

ON FOOT

Although Baltimore is an easy city to walk, the trek from downtown Charles Center to the Inner Harbor is made even easier by an elevated pedestrian walkway called **Skywalk**. Following an indoor-outdoor path, the well-posted route begins at Charles and Saratoga streets and ends at Harborplace, connecting commercial buildings, shops, theaters, pedestrian plazas, the Baltimore Convention Center, restaurants, and hotels along its safe and traffic-free route.

FAST FACTS: Baltimore

Area Code   Baltimore's area code is 410.

Car Rentals   See "Getting Around" earlier in this chapter.

Climate   See "When to Go" in Chapter 1.

Drugstores   Downtown branches of major chains include **Rite Aid** at 200 E. Baltimore St. (☎ 410/727-4494) and 201 N. Charles St. (☎ 410/539-1541), and **Valu-Rite**, 900 N. Charles St. (☎ 410/539-5555).

Emergencies   Dial 911 for fire, police, or ambulance.

Eyeglasses   Many national optical chains operate in the Baltimore area, including **Lens Crafters** and **Pearle Vision Center.** For exact locations, consult the yellow pages.

Film   See "Photographic Needs" below.

Hospitals   The **Johns Hopkins Hospital,** 600 N. Wolfe St. (☎ 410/955-5000); **University of Maryland Medical Center,** 22 S. Greene St. (☎ 410/328-6040); and **Mercy Medical Center,** 301 St. Paul Place (☎ 410/332-9000).

Information   See "Visitor Information" earlier in this chapter.

Libraries   **Enoch Pratt Free Library** is at 400 Cathedral St. (☎ 410/396-5500). There are more than 30 branches throughout the city.

Liquor Laws   Restaurants, bars, hotels, and other places serving alcoholic beverages may be open from 6am to 2am except on Sunday and election days, when some opt to close. The minimum age for buying or consuming alcohol is 21.

Newspapers and Magazines   The major daily newspaper is the *Baltimore Sun;* the *Washington Post* is also widely read. The leading monthly local magazine is *Baltimore.*

Pharmacies   See "Drugstores" above.

Photographic Needs   Reliable downtown shops include **The Camera Doctor,** 133 S. Broadway (☎ 410/732-1717) for repairs; and the **Ritz Camera Center,** 37 S. Charles St. (☎ 410/727-0220) and 200 E. Pratt (☎ 410/685-0077), and **The Dark Room,** 308 N. Charles St. (☎ 410/539-5639), for one-hour processing.

Police   Dial 911.

Post Office   The **main post office** is at 900 E. Fayette St. (☎ 410/347-4425). Hours are 8:30am to 5pm.

Safety   Frequent patrols through the Inner Harbor and the other main tourist areas by both police and the Clean and Safe Team have cut down on the number of muggings, pickpocketings, or purse snatchings in these areas. But use common sense, as you would anywhere else: walk only in well-lit, well-populated streets. It's not a good idea to walk down Lombard Street east of Cornbeef Row after dark.

Taxes   The state sales tax is 5%. The local hotel tax is an additional 7%.

Taxis   See "Getting Around" earlier in this chapter.

Telegrams and Telex   **Western Union,** 17 Commerce St. (☎ 410/685-6020 or 800/227-5899).

Transit Information   Call Baltimore's **Mass Transit Administration** (MTA) at 410/539-5000.

3 Accommodations

In recent years, new properties have sprung up, especially around the Inner Harbor, and the grand older properties have been restored and renovated. There are now more than 5,600 hotel rooms, most of them first class and deluxe. This means that it can be hard to find a double for under $100 during the week; happily, most hotels offer special weekend rates and inclusive weekend packages that represent savings of 35% to 50% off normal Sunday through Thursday tariffs. So don't be scared off by your first look at the room prices—try to time your visit for a weekend.

INNER HARBOR AREA
Very Expensive

✪ Harbor Court Hotel

550 Light St., Baltimore, MD 21202. ☎ **410/234-0550** or 800/824-0076. Fax 410/659-5925. 203 rms. 25 suites. A/C MINIBAR TV TEL. $210–$250 double; $375–$2,000 suite. AE, CB, DC, MC, V. Self-parking $9.50; valet parking $12.

For the best location overlooking the water, treat yourself to a stay at this lovely, intimate property with old-world charm. With a distinctive brick facade, it offers marble floors, crystal chandeliers, paneled walls, masterful artworks, and fine reproduction furniture. Over half the spacious guest rooms face the harbor and each is outfitted with period-style furnishings and designer fabrics.

Dining/Entertainment: The choices include the informal cafe Brightons; Hampton's, for American cuisine; and Explorer's Lounge, a cozy enclave with piano music nightly.

Services: 24-hour room service, full-time concierge, valet parking.

Facilities: Health club, swimming pool, whirlpool, saunas, exercise room, racquetball, squash, tennis, and croquet.

✪ Hyatt Regency Baltimore

300 Light St., Baltimore, MD 21202. ☎ **410/528-1234** or 800/233-1234. Fax 410/685-3362. 490 rms. A/C MINIBAR TV TEL. $190–$250 double; weekend packages available. AE, CB, DC, MC, V. Self-parking $9; valet parking $12.

Located opposite the Light Street Pavilion of Harborplace, this ultramodern hotel is right on the Inner Harbor, adjacent to the convention center. The mirrored glass exterior reflects the passing boats and Harborplace. A bank of rounded glass elevators, rising from the customary Hyatt atrium, whisks guests to bedrooms that are contemporary, with light woods, brass fixtures, modern art, live plants, mirrored closets, and marble bathrooms, and with emphasis on wide windows and dramatic views of the water or the city. Guests have direct access to the convention center.

Dining/Entertainment: Choices include a rooftop (15th-floor) restaurant/lounge, Berry and Elliott's (see "Dining" later in this chapter), spacious lobby level bar, and informal bistro.

Facilities: Outdoor pool, tennis courts, jogging track, health club, gift shop, and business center.

Stouffer Renaissance Harborplace Hotel

202 E. Pratt St., Baltimore, MD 21202. ☎ **410/547-1200** or 800/468-3571. Fax 410/783-9676. 622 rms. A/C MINIBAR TV TEL. $175–$235 double; weekend packages available. AE, CB, DC, MC, V. Self-parking $8; valet parking $11.

With Harborplace at its doorstep, fine views are a draw at this hotel, one of the largest in the waterfront area. It's part of the Gallery at Harborplace, a complex that includes an office tower, underground parking garage, and a glass-enclosed atrium of 75 shops and restaurants. Each guest room has a contemporary decor and sweeping views of the harbor or cityscape.

Dining/Entertainment: Windows, an all-day restaurant/lounge, offers expansive views of the Inner Harbor (see "Dining"); there is also a lobby bar for cocktails.

Services: Concierge desk, valet service, complimentary coffee and newspaper, 24-hour room service, evening turndown service.

Facilities: Indoor pool, health club, sauna, and whirlpool.

EXPENSIVE

Baltimore Marriott Inner Harbor

110 S. Eutaw St., Baltimore, MD 21201. ☎ **410/962-0202** or 800/228-9290. Fax 410/ 962-8585. 525 rms, 12 suites. A/C MINIBAR TV TEL. $129–$195 double; $230–$650 suite, weekend packages available. AE, CB, DC, MC, V. Parking $8.

With a dramatic 10-story, crescent-shaped facade, this hotel has a great location— a couple of blocks from the Charles Center, Harborplace, and the convention center, and across the street from Camden Yards. The busy lobby centers around a cascading waterfall, while the bedrooms are designed in contemporary style. Other facilities include a garden-themed restaurant and cocktail dance bar; game room; indoor swimming pool and fitness center with sauna and whirlpool. There is also a video checkout and message system.

✪ Clarion Inn Pier 5

Pier 5, 711 Eastern Ave., Baltimore, MD 21202. ☎ **410/783-5553** or 800/CLARION. Fax 410/783-1787. 66 rms, 5 suites. A/C MINIBAR TV TEL. $119–$179 double; $175–$325 suite. AE, CB, DC, DISC, MC, V. Parking $7.

The Clarion's facade reflects the charm of a Chesapeake Bay lighthouse; it's a three-story property right on the water of the Inner Harbor. A nautical decor prevails inside also, with a 40-foot skipjack sailing ship in the center of the atrium-style lobby, and guest rooms named after historic Chesapeake Bay sailing vessels.

Each room has traditional Georgian mahogany furniture, designer fabrics, framed seafaring and wildfowl prints, and a spacious well-lit bathroom with phone and hair dryer. Some rooms have balconies and others have cathedral ceilings; suites have a Jacuzzi bath. Facilities include a restaurant overlooking the harbor, lounge bar, a patio deck, ice-cream parlor, shops, and room service. (*Note:* This hotel, owned by the city of Baltimore, was for sale at press time.)

Sheraton Inner Harbor

300 S. Charles St., Baltimore, MD 21201. ☎ **410/962-8300** or 800/325-3535. Fax 410/ 962-8211. 339 rms. A/C MINIBAR TV TEL. $145–$200 double. AE, CB, DC, MC, V. Parking $10.

The Sheraton is conveniently near Harborplace, the convention center, Camden Yards, and the Skywalk route; harbor views are a plus. The hotel's decor is accented with American art, with emphasis on works by Maryland artists. The modern rooms offer a choice of styles, with computer card access, light wood furnishings, and mirrored closets; the cheaper rooms have city or stadium views. Facilities include a restaurant, lobby-level piano bar, baseball-themed bar, indoor swimming pool, health club, and sauna.

MODERATE/INEXPENSIVE

Days Inn Inner Harbor

100 Hopkins Pl. (between Lombard and Pratt sts.), Baltimore, MD 21202. ☎ **410/576-1000** or 800/325-2525. Fax 410/576-9437. 251 rms. A/C TV TEL. $59–$130 double. AE, CB, DC, MC, V. Parking $7.

This modern nine-story hotel is one of the Inner Harbor area's best bargains. It is conveniently situated between the arena and convention center. Guest rooms offer standard chain motel furnishings, and amenities include an outdoor heated pool, a patio courtyard, and a full-service restaurant.

Baltimore Accommodations & Dining

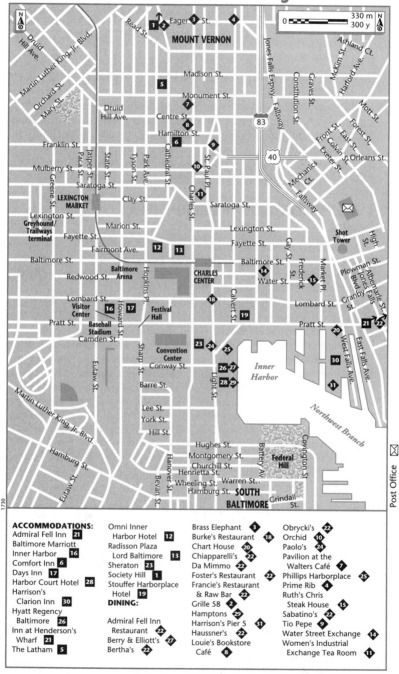

N

330 m
300 y

MOUNT VERNON

Read St.
Eager St.
Madison St.
Monument St.
Druid Hill Ave.
Centre St.
Hamilton St.
Franklin St.
Mulberry St.
Saratoga St.
Clay St.
Marion St.
Fayette St.
Fairmont Ave.
Baltimore St.
Redwood St.
Lombard St.
Pratt St.
Camden St.
Conway St.
Barre St.
Lee St.
York St.
Hill St.
Hughes St.
Montgomery St.
Churchill St.
Henrietta St.
Wheeling St.
Hamburg St.

Druid Hill Ave.
Martin Luther King Jr. Blvd.
Orchard St.
Mary St.
Jasper St.
Paca St.
State St.
Tyson St.
Park Ave.
Cathedral St.
St. Paul Pl.
Charles St.
Greene St.

Jones Falls Expwy. Fallsway
Constitution St.
Graves St.

Ashland Ct.
McKim St.
Harford Ave.
Mott St.
Front St.
Forest St.
Colvin St.
East St.
Exeter St.
Orleans St.
Mechanics Ct.
Fallsway

Shot Tower
High St.
Gay St.
Frederick St.
Market Pl.
Plowman St.
Jones Falls
Granby St.
Albemarle St.
East Falls Ave.
West Falls Ave.

LEXINGTON MARKET

Lexington St.
Greyhound/Trailways terminal

CHARLES CENTER

Baltimore Arena

Hopkins Pl.
Howard St.
Sharp St.

Visitor Center
Baseball Stadium

Festival Hall

Convention Center

Eutaw St.
Light St.
Calvert St.

Inner Harbor

Martin Luther King, Jr. Blvd.
Hamburg St.

Hanover St.
Bevan St.

Battery Ave.

Federal Hill

Covington St.

Northwest Branch

SOUTH BALTIMORE
Warren St.
Grindall St.

Post Office

1730

ACCOMMODATIONS:
Admiral Fell Inn **21**
Baltimore Marriott Inner Harbor **16**
Comfort Inn **6**
Days Inn **17**
Harbor Court Hotel **28**
Harrison's Clarion Inn **30**
Hyatt Regency Baltimore **26**
Inn at Henderson's Wharf **21**
The Latham **5**

Omni Inner Harbor Hotel **12**
Radisson Plaza Lord Baltimore **13**
Sheraton **23**
Society Hill **1**
Stouffer Harborplace Hotel **19**

DINING:

Admiral Fell Inn Restaurant **22**
Berry & Elliott's **27**
Bertha's **22**

Brass Elephant **3**
Burke's Restaurant **18**
Chart House **20**
Chiapparelli's **22**
Da Mimmo **22**
Foster's Restaurant **22**
Francie's Restaurant & Raw Bar **22**
Grille 58 **2**
Hamptons **29**
Harrison's Pier 5 **31**
Haussner's **22**
Louie's Bookstore Café **8**

Obrycki's **22**
Orchid **10**
Paolo's **24**
Pavilion at the Walters Café **7**
Phillips Harborplace **25**
Prime Rib **4**
Ruth's Chris Steak House **15**
Sabatino's **22**
Tio Pepe **9**
Water Street Exchange **14**
Women's Industrial Exchange Tea Room **11**

Holiday Inn Inner Harbor

301 W. Lombard St., Baltimore, MD 21201. ☎ **410/685-3500** or 800/HOLIDAY. Fax 410/727-6169. 374 rms, 3 suites. A/C TV TEL. $99–$119 double, $150–$250 suites. AE, DC, DISC, MC, V. Parking $5.

You know what you get from a Holiday Inn, and for good value and location, it's hard to beat this old-timer. It was the first major chain property in Baltimore. It has since added an executive tower with 175 rooms geared to business travelers, and has been updated and renovated regularly. Guest rooms are decorated with traditional dark wood furniture including a desk and reclining chair, brass fixtures, watercolor art, and wide windows providing views of the city skyline. It is located between the Baltimore Arena and the convention center, a block away from Oriole Park and three blocks from Harborplace. Facilities include a restaurant, lounge, and a health center with glass-enclosed 50-foot indoor swimming pool, sauna, and exercise center.

CHARLES STREET/MOUNT VERNON AREA
EXPENSIVE

Doubletree Inn at the Colonnade

4 West University Pkwy., Baltimore, MD 21218. ☎ **410/235-5400** or 800/222-TREE. Fax 410/235-5572. 125 rms, 33 suites. $89–$159 double, $135–$250 suites; weekend packages available. AE, DC, DISC, MC, V. Self-parking $6; valet parking $8.

Situated 4 miles from the central business district and Inner Harbor, this hotel is a little off the beaten track, but it's a good option if you want to be close to Johns Hopkins University (across the street) and other northside attractions such as the Baltimore Museum of Art. Although the multicolumned entrance is unusually grandiose and the lobby is a bit overwhelming with its collection of original 18th-century European master paintings, a friendly atmosphere comes to the fore from the moment of check-in—guests receive complimentary chocolate chip cookies as a welcome. The rooms are very comfortable with Biedermeier-inspired furnishings and nightly turndown is provided. Facilities include a popular restaurant, the Polo Club (see "Dining"), an indoor glass-domed pool surrounded by Italian marble and Tivoli lights, two Jacuzzis, whirlpool, exercise room, sundeck, and access to the university jogging track and tennis courts. There is also complimentary transportation to the Inner Harbor.

✪ The Latham

612 Cathedral St., Baltimore, MD 21201. ☎ **410/727-7101** or 800/LATHAM-1. Fax 410/789-3312. 104 rms. A/C MINIBAR TV TEL. $150–$170 double. Weekend discounts available. AE, CB, DC, MC, V. Parking $10.

This Mount Vernon–area hotel first opened in 1930; it was later converted into an apartment building, and reemerged in 1985 as the Peabody Court hotel; it became the Latham in 1992. The building has undergone a total renovation and rejuvenation, giving it a European-style ambience and luxury. As you step inside the lobby, dominated by a 6-foot, 500-pound Baccarat crystal chandelier, a sense of grandeur greets you. The public rooms feature period furniture, hand-loomed carpeting, and original art. Each of the guest rooms has period furniture, imported lamps, and a marble bathroom.

Dining/Entertainment: The include the glass-enclosed rooftop Citronelle restaurant for gourmet French cuisine (see "Dining"), and a mezzanine level grill room and cafe.

Facilities/Services: Concierge, nightly turndown and shoeshine services, business center, and use of a local health club.

Omni Inner Harbor Hotel

101 W. Fayette St., Baltimore, MD 21201. ☎ **410/752-1100** or 800/THE-OMNI. Fax 410/752-6832. 702 rms. A/C MINIBAR TV TEL. $125–$175 double. AE, CB, DC, MC, V. Self-parking $9; valet parking $14.

Comprised of two beige towers—27 and 23 floors in height—this property is the largest hotel in Maryland, popular with conventions and groups. In spite of its name, it is not on the Inner Harbor—it is situated in the heart of downtown opposite the Charles Center and the Baltimore Arena. Most bedrooms are L-shaped, with mirrored closets, traditional dark-wood furnishings, and designer fabrics. Facilities include a grill room, cafe, bar, outdoor swimming pool, fitness center, and gift shop.

MODERATE

Radisson Plaza Lord Baltimore

20 W. Baltimore St., Baltimore, MD 21201. ☎ **410/539-8400** or 800/333-3333. Fax 410/625-1060. 440 rms. A/C TV TEL. $109–$159 double. AE, CB, DC, DISC, MC, V. Parking $12.

Dating from 1928, this 19-story French Renaissance–style hotel is located in the heart of the city's theater and financial district, between Charles and Howard streets. In recent years, it has changed hands and been renovated again and again, but it has managed to retain much of its original charm. The entrance is particularly impressive with marble columns; hand-carved artwork; brass fixtures; and a massive central chandelier. Guest rooms, accessible by computer card keys, are tastefully furnished with dark woods, mirrored closets, and floral fabrics. There are concierge and valet laundry services. Facilities include a cafe, bar, fitness center, whirlpool, and sauna.

MODERATE/INEXPENSIVE

Mount Vernon Hotel

24 W. Franklin St., Baltimore, MD 21201. ☎ **410/727-2000** or 800/245-5256. Fax 410/576-9300. 189 rms. A/C TV TEL. $69–$125 double. AE, CB, DC, MC, V. Parking $6.

Situated at the corner of Cathedral Street opposite the basilica and at one time a YMCA, this seven-story historic landmark dates from 1907. Fully renovated and taken over by the Baltimore International Culinary College in 1994, it has rooms of varying sizes furnished in contemporary style; about half are used for students of the college and the remaining rooms are offered for overnight guests. Six of the units have unique loft layouts and a Jacuzzi bath. Other amenities include a guest launderette, valet service, complimentary shuttle service to Inner Harbor, and an in-house restaurant, Washington Cafe (see "Dining"), staffed by eager BICC students and chefs-in-training.

FELLS POINT/LITTLE ITALY
MODERATE

✪ Admiral Fell Inn

888 S. Broadway, Baltimore, MD 21231. ☎ **410/522-7377** or 800/292-4667. Fax 410/522-0707. 80 rms. A/C TV TEL. $120–$195 double. AE, DISC, MC, V. Free parking.

Updated and expanded over the years, this charming inn sits just a block from the harbor in the heart of Fells Point. It is composed of seven buildings, built between 1790 and 1920 and blending Victorian and Federal-style architectures. Originally a boardinghouse for sailors, later a YMCA, and then a vinegar bottling plant, the inn was completely renovated in 1985 and again in 1995, and now includes an antique-filled lobby and library, a restaurant, and an English-style pub. The guest rooms are individually decorated, with modern bathrooms; many have canopied four-poster beds and are named after historical characters (for example, Carroll Room and Calvert Room). Some rooms are "attic" rooms and can be quite small, others are larger and equipped with Jacuzzis. The inn also offers little extras—complimentary van transport to the downtown area and daily newspapers.

Inn at Henderson's Wharf
1000 Fell St., Baltimore, MD 21231. ☎ **410/522-7777** or 800/522-2088. Fax 410/522-7087. 38 rms. A/C TV TEL. $120–$145 double. (Rates include continental breakfast.) AE, CB, DC, MC, V. Free parking.

Located on the waterfront at Fells Point, this inn occupies the ground floor of a former B&O railroad warehouse dating from the 1800s and restored in 1991; the rest of the structure has been converted into a condominium development. The guest rooms, which face the water or the central courtyard with English-style gardens, are decorated with period reproduction furniture, paneled or brick walls, floral quilted fabrics, nautical art, and brass fixtures. There is room service and valet laundry services. Facilities include an exercise studio and a 170-slip marina, for those who prefer to arrive by boat.

4 Dining

"Crabtown" has always been well known for its excellent seafood restaurants, and the recent development of the Inner Harbor has provided an impetus and an ideal setting for even more eateries emphasizing the sea's bounty.

Baltimore is also home to a wide array of restaurants featuring regional and ethnic cuisines, and traditional steak houses. In addition to the waterfront, you'll find clusters of restaurants downtown along Charles Street (known locally as "restaurant row") and in the older neighborhoods such as Little Italy and Fells Point.

INNER HARBOR AREA
VERY EXPENSIVE/EXPENSIVE

✪ Hamptons
550 Light St. ☎ **410/234-0550**. Reservations required. Main courses $22–$32; brunch $19.95–$27.95. AE, CB, DC, MC, V. Dinner Tues–Sat 5:30–11pm, Sun 5:30–10pm; brunch Sun 10:30am–3pm. AMERICAN/FRENCH.

Overlooking the Inner Harbor and the National Aquarium, this highly touted restaurant is the main dining room of the posh Harbor Court Hotel, and well worth a splurge for a special night out or sumptuous brunch. Specialties include pan-roasted lobster with herbs and garlic and crabmeat risotto; boneless breast of duck stuffed with a game bird and herb mousse and served with a confit of duck and an orange glaze with dried cranberries; grilled veal chop with garlic and spicy apple chutney; blackened and Cajun-spiced buffalo with mushroom and shallot marmalade; rack of lamb baked with rosemary and mustard with fresh mint sauce; smoked squab with andouille sausage stuffing and Creole sauce.

EXPENSIVE

✪ Berry & Elliott's

In the Hyatt Regency Hotel, 300 Light St., 15th floor. ☎ **410/528-1234.** Reservations required for dinner. Main courses $17.95–$24.95; lunch $7.95–$13.95. AE, CB, DC, DISC, MC, V. Daily 11:30am–1am. INTERNATIONAL.

Overlooking the Inner Harbor, Camden Yards, and the downtown skyline, this two-tiered rooftop restaurant was voted "Baltimore's best view" by the readers of *Baltimore* magazine. The restaurant is named for a pair of early Baltimore vegetable vendors who used to sell their wares on the spot where the hotel now stands. Menu specialties include Maryland crab cakes; salmon in pastry with spinach and Boursin cheese; roasted red snapper with sesame-soy marinade, plum tomatoes, pancetta, and basil; grilled medaillons of veal with a trio of mushrooms and rich cognac demiglaze; lamb chops served atop a pink peppercorn sauce flavored with rosemary confetti; grilled petit filet mignon with rock lobster tail; and ribbon pasta tossed with roast chicken, asparagus, grilled peppers, tomatoes, and cream.

Chart House

601 E. Pratt St. ☎ **410/539-6616.** Reservations recommended for dinner. Main courses $15.95–$29.95; lunch $6.95–$12.95. AE, CB, DC, DISC, MC, V. Lunch Mon–Sat 11:30am–2:30pm; dinner Mon–Thurs 5–10:30pm, Fri 5pm–11:30pm, Sat 4–11:30pm, Sun 1–10pm. INTERNATIONAL/SEAFOOD.

Just east of Harborplace, this restaurant sits right on the water's edge next to the National Aquarium. Originally a warehouse for the nearby power plant, this building has been tastefully converted into a bilevel restaurant with an outside deck. The decor is appropriately nautical, with ship replicas and carvings, and photos of the sea and the old Baltimore waterfront. Lunch features super deli sandwiches (from crab salad to smoked turkey) and raw-bar selections. Dinner entrées include exotic fish such as mahimahi, mako, and yellowfin tuna, as well as baked stuffed flounder, crab imperial, crab cakes, and lobster tails; steaks and prime rib are also specialties. For dessert, don't miss the mud pie.

Ruth's Chris Steak House

600 Water St. ☎ **410/783-0033.** Reservations required. Main courses $14.95–$30.95. AE, CB, DC, MC, V. Mon–Sat 5–10, Sun 4–9pm. AMERICAN.

Located between South Frederick and Market streets on the first floor of the Brokerage, this restaurant is a favorite with the suit-and-tie crowd. Its clubby atmosphere is created by dark-wood furnishings, tiled floor, globe lanterns, and tree-size leafy plants. It's a place to come for beef—there are six choices of steak on the menu, all butter-bathed and prepared to order, plus prime rib and filet mignon. Alternatively, there is lobster, salmon, swordfish, and blackened tuna, as well as lamb chops and chicken.

EXPENSIVE/MODERATE

✪ Phillips Harborplace

Level 1, Light Street Pavilion, Harborplace. ☎ **410/685-6600.** Reservations not accepted. Main courses $11.95–$22.95; lunch $6.95–$10.95. AE, DISC, MC, V. Daily 11am–11pm. SEAFOOD.

Of the more than a dozen restaurants and sidewalk cafes in the festive Harborplace development, this is a standout. It's a branch of the very successful establishment of the same name that has been an Ocean City, Maryland, landmark since 1956. Dinner is a feast of fresh seafood, featuring crab in many forms—soft-shell crabs, crab and lobster sauté, crab cakes, crab imperial, and all-you-can-eat portions of steamed crab. Other seafoods offered include salmon, swordfish, lobster, oysters, and mahimahi. Steaks and other meats are also available.

This is a fun restaurant with a lively sing-along piano bar and entertainment at night. Even though reservations are not taken, there rarely is too long a wait, except at peak times. Once you are seated, however, service is swift and attentive and the food is great.

Windows

202 E. Pratt St. ☎ **410/547-1200.** Reservations required. Dinner main courses $8.95–$22.95, lunch $6.95–$15.95. AE, DC, DISC, MC, V. Daily 6:30am–11pm. AMERICAN.

Situated on the fifth floor of the Stouffer Renaissance Harborplace Hotel, this restaurant not only offers sweeping views of the Inner Harbor, but it has also earned revered culinary recognition for producing "nonhotel-style" food, by using fresh seasonal Maryland products and ingredients, many of which are grown right in the hotel's own in-house roof garden or come from individual specialist suppliers. Entrées at dinner range from Indian-spiced roast chicken with stewed vegetables, to grilled duck breast with Michigan sun-dried cherries and woodland mushrooms; seared scallops in a smoked salmon and tomato vodka cream sauce; and a variety of fresh-from-the-boat Maryland crab selections. Lunch offers salads, sandwiches, pastas, and light entrées. The hands-on Executive Chef Guy Reinbold is a personality in his own right, often quoted in *Bon Appetit* or *Gourmet*, and usually roaming the dining room to check on customer satisfaction firsthand.

MODERATE/INEXPENSIVE

⑤ Burke's Restaurant

36 Light St. (at Lombard St.). ☎ **410/752-4189.** Reservations recommended for dinner. Main courses $6.95–$18.95; lunch $3–$10. MC, V. Daily 11:30am–1:30am. INTERNATIONAL.

Located opposite Harborplace, this tavern-style restaurant has been a downtown fixture for more than 50 years. There are two rooms—one that features a long dark-wood bar, ceiling fans, aged barrels, pewter tankards, and booth or stool seating, while the other room has a high Tudor-style ceiling, wrought-iron chandeliers, framed prints depicting "Old Maryland" scenes, and traditional table seating. The food is particularly good here; the menu is surprisingly extensive, and the crab cakes are a perennial standout. Dinner entreées include steaks, beef ribs, barbecued chicken, and seafood combination platters. The deep-fried onion rings are a house specialty.

⑤ Paolo's

301 Light St., Harborplace. ☎ **410/539-7060.** Reservations not accepted. Main courses $7.95–$17.95; lunch $4.95–$8.95. AE, CB, DC, MC, V. Weekdays lunch and dinner 11am–midnight; Sat–Sun brunch 10:30am–3pm, dinner 3pm–midnight. ITALIAN/AMERICAN.

Situated on Level 1 of the Light Street Pavilion, this informal, wide-windowed restaurant offers indoor and outdoor seating overlooking the harbor. Working out of an open kitchen, chefs prepare creative food at reasonable prices. Entrées include veal with saffron risotto, grilled rib-eye steak, clay pot-roasted chicken, osso bucco, quail charbroiled with spinach and egg fettuccine, and mixed grills. Also served are a variety of pastas, as well as pizzas made in a wood-burning oven with a variety of traditional and exotic toppings. Same menu all day.

Water Street Exchange
110 Water St. ☎ **410/332-4060.** Reservations recommended. Main courses $5.95–$15.95. AE, CB, DC, MC, V. Mon–Sat 11:30am–9pm. AMERICAN.

Resting on the site of an old wharf just a block north of Pratt Street and Harborplace, this multilevel Victorian-style restaurant has been beautifully restored with original brick walls, local artwork, brass fixtures, and a huge mahogany bar. The menu, which is the same all day, features light fare such as sandwiches, salads, omelets, and burgers, as well as dishes with an international flair, such as Cajun chicken Alfredo, jambalaya pasta, stir-fry Oriental, Monterey chicken melt, and traditional Maryland crab cakes. From March through October, there is also outdoor cafe seating on a brick-lined front courtyard.

CHARLES STREET/MOUNT VERNON
VERY EXPENSIVE

Citronelle
612 Cathedral St. ☎ **410/727-7101.** Reservations required. Main courses $15–$29. AE, CB, DC, DISC, MC, V. Mon–Thurs 6–10pm, Fri–Sat 5:30–10pm, Sun 5–9pm. FRENCH/AMERICAN.

As hotel restaurants go, this glass-enclosed rooftop enclave draws a faithful following unto itself. Situated atop the Latham Hotel overlooking Mount Vernon, it has been highly praised by *Bon Appetit* and other national food magazines. Chef Michel Richard, who also runs restaurants in Santa Barbara and Washington, D.C., is known for innovative dishes such as baby Coho salmon napoleon, crispy crab cakes, lamb rack with minigoat cheese ravioli, venison chop with potato ragout, and peppered capon steak with hay potatoes.

Polo Grill
4 West University Pkwy. ☎ **410/235-8200.** Reservations required. Main courses $16.95–$35.95. AE, DC, DISC, MC, V. Mon–Thurs 6:30am–11pm, Fri 6:30am–midnight, Sat 7am–midnight, Sun 7am–10pm. AMERICAN.

It doesn't matter that this restaurant is 4 miles north of downtown, the movers and shakers of Baltimore gather here each evening from all directions. Often compared to New York's 21 Club or Washington's Jockey Club for atmosphere, this clubby restaurant is handsomely ensconced as the main dining room of at the Doubletree Inn at the Colonnade, opposite the Johns Hopkins University. The menu changes every day, but don't be surprised to find farm-raised emu or roast loin of elk featured, as well as signature dishes such as Panos and Pauls' famous fried lobster tail with drawn butter and honey mustard sauce; penne pasta with blackened chicken; and Oriental-style barbecued salmon with soya butter on warm sesame spinach leaves. Fresh lobster by the pound and prime cut-to-order steaks are also popular.

✪ Prime Rib
1101 N. Calvert St. ☎ **410/539-1804.** Reservations required. Main courses $11.95–$35. AE, CB, DC, MC, V. Dinner Mon–Sat 5pm–midnight. Sun 5–11pm. AMERICAN.

In the heart of the Mount Vernon district, between Biddle and Chase streets, this restaurant has been a standout for fine beef since 1965, often called "the shrine to prime" by locals. In addition to aged midwestern beef, fresh Chesapeake Bay seafood is a specialty of the chef, who has won accolades from the prestigious Chaîne des Rôtisseurs. Most people start with the house trademark, Greenberg potato skins, named after a regular customer. Entrées include prime rib, steaks, rack of lamb, veal chops, and such seafood dishes as blackened swordfish, crab cakes, and lobster tails. It's a favorite with the corporate crowd and those who like to be pampered—in a setting of self-fringed table lamps, leopard-spotted carpeting, and a pianist tinkling softly on the baby grand.

EXPENSIVE

Brass Elephant
924 N. Charles St. ☎ **410/547-8480.** Reservations required. Main courses $13–$23; lunch $5.95–$10.95. AE, DC, MC, V. Lunch Mon–Fri 11:30am–2pm; dinner Mon–Thurs 5:30–9:30pm, Fri–Sat 5:30–10:30pm, Sun 5–9pm. NORTHERN ITALIAN/MEDITERRANEAN.

This trendy restaurant, nestled in the Mount Vernon district between Reade and Eager streets, is housed in a restored 1861 town house, originally the home of businessman Charles Stuart. The decor carries on the 19th-century tradition with an open fireplace, gold-leaf trim, chandeliers, and, as its name implies, lots of brass fixtures. Gentle shades of blue and classical background music add to the serene atmosphere. Lunch ranges from open-faced sandwiches and omelets to pastas and light entrées. Dinner choices include grilled salmon al pesto, yellowfin, seafood cioppino, veal portofino with roasted shallots and shiitake mushrooms, shrimp and scallops cioppino, medaillons of beef Marsala, and rack of lamb.

Orchid
419 N. Charles St. ☎ **410/837-0080.** Reservations recommended for dinner. Main courses $17.95–$27.95; lunch $8.95–$13.95. AE, MC, V. Tues–Thurs 11:30am–2:30pm and 5–10:30pm, Fri–Sat 11:30am–2:30pm and 5–11:30pm, Sun 4pm–9:30pm. INTERNATIONAL.

This restaurant, in a converted row house near Franklin Street, prepares classic French dishes with creative Asian accents. The decor is lovely, with a fireplace, crisp linens, brass chandeliers, and, of course, orchids on each table. The menu is eclectic, with house favorites such as spicy tuna with fresh mango in a warm sesame sauce; mixed grill Escoffier, a combination of veal and beef tenderloins with lamb chops and three different sauces, and filet of flounder "Orchid," with crispy almonds, ginger, pineapple, and lemon butter sauce.

The Owl Bar
1 E. Chase St. ☎ **410/347-0888.** Reservations recommended for dinner. Main courses $16–$28, lunch $5–$10. AE, DC, DISC, MC, V. Mon–Sat 11:30am–11pm or later, Sun 11am–2:30pm. ITALIAN/AMERICAN.

Housed in the once-revered Belvedere Hotel (now condominiums and offices) in the classy Mount Vernon district, this restaurant seeks to restore some of the luster and panache of turn-of-the-century Baltimore. The entrance is lined with photos that tell the story of Baltimore's great citizens and notable visitors, and the interior has all the trappings of yesteryear—brass rail bar, paneled walls, leather furnishings, and the famous blinking owls that gave the bar its name. Only the menu bows to contemporary tastes, with a brick oven that turns out trendy pizzas such as white pizza (made with all white cheeses); Peking pizza (made with Peking duck and hoisin sauce; and hickory-smoked vegetarian pizza, topped with hummus and fontina cheese. Specialty pastas are equally appealing, from penne Granchio, jumbo lump crabmeat sautéed with artichoke hearts, plum tomatoes and penne in a Pinot Grigio butter sauce; to farfalle, butterfly pasta in vodka tomato cream sauce and julienne of proscuitto. Other choices include osso bucco, Black Angus steaks, and free-range chicken stuffed with veal and fresh herbs. The same management is also attempting to breathe life back into two other sections of the former hotel—the adjacent room known as Champagne Tony's, also for contemporary

Italian cuisine, and the 13th-floor rooftop room, Champagne and Truffles, for desserts and cappuccino with piano music and panoramic views of the city.

Tío Pepe

10 E. Franklin St. ☎ **410/539-4675.** Reservations required. Main courses $13.75–$22.75; lunch $7.50–$16.75. AE, DC, DISC, MC, V. Mon–Thurs 11:30am–2:30pm and 5–10:30pm, Fri 11:30am–2:30pm and 5–11pm, Sat 5–11:30pm, Sun 4–10:30pm. SPANISH.

Located just off Charles Street, this highly praised restaurant exudes a Spanish wine cellar atmosphere, with arched cavern-style entranceways, wrought-iron railings, and white stucco walls decorated with colorful ceramic plates. The menu empha-sizes the Catalan region of Spain, offering dishes such as paella; rack of lamb; tournedos Tío Pepe (beef with sherry-wine sauce and mushrooms); chicken with tomatoes, green and red pimentos, and mushrooms; red snapper à la vasca (with green sauce, clams, mussels, asparagus, and boiled egg); filet of sole with bananas and hollandaise sauce; and Spanish prawns flavored with brandy.

MODERATE/INEXPENSIVE

Pavilion at the Walters Cafe

600 N. Charles St. ☎ **410/727-2233.** Reservations required. Main courses $5.95–$11.95. AE, CB, DC, DISC, MC, V. Tues–Fri 11:30am–3:30pm, Sat–Sun 11:30am–4pm. AMERICAN.

Nestled on the lower level of the Walters Art Gallery, this restaurant is surrounded by corridors of great art, and a favorite with Baltimoreans for lunch or brunch. With such a creative atmosphere, it's no wonder that the constantly changing menu is very imaginative. Entrées range from salads and sandwiches to exotic quiches, pizza, and pastas, as well as traditional crab cakes, shaved honey-baked ham, and house specials of barbecued North Atlantic salmon and Moss's white meat loaf (made with herbed turkey).

Washington Cafe

24 W. Franklin St. ☎ **410/727-3000.** Reservations recommended for dinner. Main courses $5.95–$16.95. AE, CB, DC, MC, V. Daily 11am–2pm and 5–10pm. ITALIAN/SEAFOOD.

Housed in the Mount Vernon Hotel and operated by the staff and students of the Baltimore International Culinary College, this restaurant provides a rare oppor-tunity to sample and experiment with the latest in culinary treats at relatively low prices. The decor is an eclectic reflection of Old Baltimore—a ceiling painted with blue sky and clouds and brick walls lined with mounted elk heads, trophy fish, statuary, old kitchen implements, paintings, and the coat of arms of the nearby cathedral. The menu emphasizes multi-ingredient salads, create-your-own pizzas, and pastas, all made fresh daily on the premises. There are also burgers and sand-wiches as well as a variety of daily specials that really show off the talents of the chefs and chefs-in-training, such as chicken breast baked with brie and wrapped in puff pastry topped with orange sauce or deep-fried manicotti shells stuffed with cream cheese and salmon. There is also a very appealing and healthful menu for children aged 12 and under.

INEXPENSIVE

⑤ Louie's Bookstore Cafe

518 N. Charles St. ☎ **410/962-1224.** Reservations not accepted. Main courses $7.95–$13.95; lunch $3.95–$7.95. MC, V. Mon 10am–midnight, Tues–Thurs 10am–12:30am, Fri 10am–1:30am, Sat 11:30am–1:30am, Sun 10:30am–midnight. INTERNATIONAL.

Readers Recommend

CoChin, 800 N. Charles St. ☎ 410/332-0332. *On a recent trip to Baltimore, some old friends took me to CoChin, a local Vietnamese/Japanese restaurant. . . . The food put some of my favorite New York restaurants to shame, particularly the Vietnamese hot pepper squid and virtually every roll we tried. My favorite, the rock 'n' roll, came wrapped in an extra layer of fish.*   —John Rosenthal, New York City

---

As its name implies, this cafe, on "restaurant row" between Centre and Hamilton streets, is a blend of bookstore and bistro. Staffed by artists and musicians, this unusual eatery is decorated with paintings by local talent and an eclectic blend of furniture, with chamber music emanating from the background. Dinner entrées include crab cake platter, vegetable stir-fry, crab and shrimp casserole, steaks, and "Chestertown Chicken," white meat marinated in a curry, garlic, and lemon sauce. Lunch features creative salads (such as artichoke and feta with spinach) and sandwiches. There is live solo or duo classical music every night.

✪ Women's Industrial Exchange Tea Room

333 N. Charles St. ☎ **410/685-4388.** Main courses $3.95–$6.95. MC, V. Mon–Fri 7am–2:30pm; lunch counter 10:30am–2pm; bakery 8am–3:30pm. Closed major holidays. AMERICAN.

Carrying on a 19th-century Baltimore tradition, this restaurant is in the back room of a craft shop/bakery run by the Women's Industrial Exchange, a foundation designed to help needy women and men of the city by consigning their handmade goods. It is housed in an 1815 building of fine Flemish bond work, wrought-iron railings, and marble steps. The restaurant setting is rich in Old Baltimore atmosphere, with historic wall murals, black-and-white tile floor, ceiling fans, fireplace, and motherly and grandmotherly waitresses. (In the movie *Sleepless in Seattle*, part of which was filmed here, waitress Miss Marguerite made her acting debut at age 92.) And the menu is simple—homemade soups, salads, sandwiches, omelets, meat or fish platters, and luscious desserts (charlotte russe is a specialty). After a light meal or snack at the restaurant, take time to browse in the shop and examine the many samples of local handiwork. If you're in a hurry, there is also a lunch counter in the building's basement (entrance from Pleasant Street).

FELLS POINT/LITTLE ITALY
EXPENSIVE

Chiapparelli's

237 S. High St. ☎ **410/837-0309.** Reservations required. Main courses $10.95–$22.95; lunch $5.95–$14.95. AE, CB, DC, MC, V. Mon–Thurs 11am–11pm, Fri–Sat 11am–midnight, Sun 3–11pm. ITALIAN.

In the heart of Little Italy, at Fawn Street, this restaurant is a longtime favorite. Southern Italian dishes are the trademark here, with special plaudits for Mom Chiapparelli's raviolis (stuffed with spinach and ricotta). Dinner is the main event, and veal is the star of the menu, cooked at least a dozen different ways, along with tasty chicken dishes and such classics as lobster fra diavolo, shrimp parmigiana, and steak Italiana.

Da Mimmo

217 S. High St. ☎ **410/727-6876.** Reservations required. Main courses $15–$35; lunch $8–$12. AE, CB, DC, MC, V. Mon–Thurs 11:30am–11:30pm, Fri 11:30am–1am, Sat 11am–1am, Sun 2–11:30pm. ITALIAN.

If you like music with your meal, head to this small candlelit Little Italy restaurant with piano entertainment nightly in the Roman-style lounge. The varied menu features everything from chicken cacciatore, lobster pizzaiola, and filet mignon to an award-winning butterflied veal chops and the Mimmo seafood special for two (shrimp, clams, calamari, and mussels in marinara sauce and on a bed of linguine). Lunch is also available here, with sandwiches, pastas, and seafood dishes.

Foster's Restaurant

606 S. Broadway. ☎ **410/558-3600.** Reservations recommended for dinner. Main courses $15–$21; lunch $5–$16. AE, CB, DC, DISC, MC, V. Mon–Thurs 11:30am–4pm and 5–10pm, Fri–Sat 11:30am–4pm and 5–11pm, Sun 11am–3pm and 4–10pm. AMERICAN/SEAFOOD.

Situated across from the Old Broadway market in Fells Point, this restaurant is housed in a historic building, with a decor of tall skylit ceilings, colored glass, old prints, and a fireplace. The menu focuses on seafood, with choices such as oyster stew, bouillabaisse, crab imperial, crab cakes, shrimp Creole, lobsters from the tank, and baked rainbow trout stuffed with scallops and fresh mushrooms and served with tomato-leek cream. The menu also offers some unique entrées such as antelope venison with shiitake mushrooms and sun-dried cherry demiglaze; grilled golden corvina, set atop warm black-bean-and-corn relish, with spicy cilantro-pesto cream; alligator chili; grilled wild boar sausage; and corn and crab crepes.

✪ Obrycki's

1727 E. Pratt St. ☎ **410/732-6399.** Reservations accepted only for lunch or for dinner parties of 10 or more. Main courses $13.95–$24.95; lunch/light fare $5.95–$9.95. AE, CB, DC, MC, V. Mon–Sat noon–11pm, Sun noon–9:30pm. Closed Dec–Mar. SEAFOOD.

East of Little Italy is Fells Point, the waterfront neighborhood where Baltimore began—and one of the best areas for seafood. Without a doubt, the benchmark of all the eateries here is Obrycki's, situated between South Broadway and South Register streets. Food connoisseurs Craig Claiborne and George Lang rave about this place, and so do we. The decor is particularly charming, with stained-glass windows, brick archways, and wainscoting along the walls.

But the big attraction is the fresh seafood, especially if you enjoy crabs. This is the quintessential crab house—where you can crack open steamed crabs in their shells and feast on the tender, succulent meat to your heart's content. There's crab soup, crab cocktail, crab balls, crab cakes, crab imperial, and soft-shell crabs. The rest of the menu is just as tempting—shrimp, lobster, scallops, haddock, flounder, and steaks. Among the lunchtime choices are seafood salads and sandwiches. The service is extremely attentive.

EXPENSIVE/MODERATE

✪ Haussner's

3244 Eastern Ave. ☎ **410/327-8365.** Reservations accepted only for lunch. Main courses $7.95–$24.95. AE, DC, DISC, MC, V. Tues–Sat 11am–10pm. INTERNATIONAL.

Established in 1926 by Bavarian-born William Henry Haussner, this landmark restaurant is firmly ensconced in the ethnic enclave of east Baltimore known as Highlandtown. Moved to its present location in 1936, the restaurant is still carried on by the founder's widow, Frances, and family. A Baltimore institution that you have to see to believe, this is not only a great place to go to for good value and good food (the main dining room seats 500), it is also an art and antique gallery, with paintings, porcelains, sculptures, clocks, and figurines. Everywhere you look there is art, collected over the years by the Haussners; even the menu features sample paintings.

It is the cuisine, however, that is the pièce de résistance, with more than 100 entrées, all fresh and delicious daily. The menu, which is the same all day but changes every day, offers all kinds of meats and seafoods as well as frogs' legs, finnan haddie, lobster tails, sweetbreads, baked rabbit, Wiener schnitzel, roast loin of boar, and pigs' knuckles. With its own bakery on the premises, Haussner's is also known for its desserts (more than 30 varieties, from strawberry pie and apple strudel to honey almond cake). Lighter choices include salads, omelets, and sandwiches.

Sabatino's
901 Fawn St. ☎ **410/727-9414.** Reservations required. Main courses $9.95–$23.95; lunch $5–$12. AE, MC, V. Daily noon–3am. ITALIAN.

Both northern and southern Italian cuisine are featured at this Little Italy restaurant with a plain stucco facade and a colorful interior, at the corner of High Street. This is a particularly good late-night dining spot since it is open every day until 3am. Dinner entrées include shrimp scampi, calamari marinara, beef pizzaiola, lobster fra diavolo, and two dozen pastas such as spaghetti with broccoli and anchovy sauce.

MODERATE

Bertha's
734 S. Broadway. ☎ **410/327-5795.** Reservations accepted only for parties of six or more. Main courses $7.95–$19.95; lunch $4.95–$11.95. MC, V. Sun–Thurs 11:30am–11pm, Fri–Sat 11:30am–midnight. INTERNATIONAL/SEAFOOD.

Don't miss this Fells Point landmark known for its mussels and music. The decor is a blend of yesteryear, with original brick walls, antique prints, old wine bottles, and nautical bric-a-brac. You'll also see musical instruments fashioned into chandeliers and wall hangings, a reminder that traditional and folk music or jazz are performed here on many weekend nights. Mussels headline the menu throughout the day, with a choice of a dozen different preparations, from simple mussels in garlic butter, to mussels in sour cream and scallions or mussels with anchovy, tomato, and garlic butter. Other specialties include Bertha's shrimp, broiled in tomato, lemon, and garlic sauce with scallions; shellfish royale, a medley of shrimp, oysters, scallops, mussels, and Smithfield ham in a cream sauce with sherry; chicken staccato, boneless breast with kumquats and peanuts; and a hearty paella with chicken, shrimp, scallops, Spanish sausage, and of course, mussels (it's made to order, so allow 30 minutes wait time). Lunch choices include salads, omelets, sandwiches, and burgers. Afternoon tea, Scottish style, is also served daily from 3 to 5pm except Sunday (reservations required).

Piccolo's
1629 Thames St. ☎ **410/522-6600.** Reservations recommended for dinner. Main courses $8.95–$19.95; lunch $6.95–$12.95. AE, CB, DC, DISC, MC, V. Mon–Thurs 11:30am–11pm, Fri–Sat 11:30am–midnight, Sun 11am–10pm. TUSCAN/ITALIAN.

Located at the foot of Broadway on the waterfront in Fells Point, this wide-windowed restaurant offers great water views and a choice of indoor or outdoor seating, conveying a little bit of the flavor of Venice minus the gondolas. The menu offers an array of Americanized pastas and pizzas with varied toppings and accompaniments. Entrées at dinner range from standard veal and beef dishes to house specialties such as Pollo alla Piccolo, chicken stuffed with spinach and mozzarella, and prosciutto; or sea scallops Conca d'Oro, a sauté of scallops with spinach, sun-dried tomatoes, pine nuts, and scallions. The lunch menu also offers salads and sandwiches.

INEXPENSIVE

Adrian's Book Café

714 S. Broadway. ☎ **410/732-1048.** All items $3.95–$6.95. AE, DISC, MC, V. Sun–Thurs 11am–11pm, Fri–Sat 11am–midnight.

Situated in the heart of Fells Point, this ground-floor bookstore and upstairs cafe provides a bit of tranquillity amid the bustle of Broadway. It is named after New York artist Adrian Rappin, whose paintings line the walls. The menu is simple: pastas, salads, sandwiches, quiches, chilis, and desserts, all made fresh daily on the premises.

5 Attractions

Although much of Baltimore's business activity takes place along Charles Street, the focus of the city for visitors is on the Inner Harbor, home of the Baltimore Convention Center and Festival Hall Exhibit Center, the Baltimore Area Visitors Center, the National Aquarium and other museums, and the Pier 6 Concert Pavilion.

It is also the site of historic and working ships, a host of major hotels, dozens of restaurants and shops, and the new Orioles baseball stadium, in Camden Yards.

And the centerpiece of it all is Harborplace, positioned right on the waterfront. It occupies a full two blocks along Light and Pratt streets, and has been the keystone to the revitalization of Baltimore as a tourist mecca. Designed to duplicate the look of an early steamship pier headquarters, Harborplace is made up of two pavilions, named after the streets they occupy: the Light Street Pavilion and the Pratt Street Pavilion.

Built in 1981, Harborplace is to Baltimore what Station Square is to Pittsburgh, Faneuil Hall to Boston, South Street Seaport to New York, or Ghirardelli Square to San Francisco—a historic setting transformed into a contemporary, bright, and airy complex of restaurants, food markets, curiosity shops, and trendy boutiques, side by side in a milieu of music, camaraderie, and good times. Shops are open Monday through Saturday from 10am to 10pm, Sunday from noon to 6pm, with later hours for restaurants and entertainment.

INNER HARBOR AREA

Babe Ruth Birthplace and Museum/Maryland Baseball Hall of Fame

216 Emory St. ☎ **410/727-1539.** Admission $5 adults, $3 seniors, and $2 children 5–16. Apr–Oct, daily 10am–5pm (until 7pm on Orioles home game days); Nov–Mar daily 10am–4pm. Closed Easter, Thanksgiving Day, Christmas Day, and New Year's Day.

Baseball fans will want to make a pilgrimage to the house where the great player was born on February 6, 1895. Located two blocks west of the Orioles' playing fields at Camden Yard, this restored house and adjoining museum contain personal mementos of George Herman ("Babe") Ruth, the Sultan of Swat. The exhibits focus on the Baltimore Orioles and Maryland baseball as well as the great Babe. You can reach out and touch the Babe's own hats, bats, and gloves; there is also an audiovisual presentation on the Babe, World Series film highlights, the Orioles, and more.

Baltimore and Ohio (B&O) Railroad Museum

901 W. Pratt St. ☎ **410/752-2490.** Admission $6 adults, $5 seniors, $3 children 5–12; children 4 and under free; train rides $2 per person. Museum daily 10am–5pm; train rides Sat–Sun at 11:30am, 12:30pm. 2:30pm, 3:30pm. Closed major holidays.

A trailblazer in American railroading, this city is also the setting of a fascinating railroad museum, situated 10 blocks west of the Inner Harbor. Often called a railroad university, this museum has hundreds of exhibits, from double-decker stagecoaches on iron wheels and early diesels to steam locomotives and the 1830 Mount Clare Station, the nation's first passenger and freight station, as well as the 1844 roundhouse with the original B&O tracks and turntable. Peter Cooper built and tested his famous Tom Thumb on this site, and Samuel Morse strung his first telegraph wires through this depot. On weekends a steam train will also chug you along on a 150-year round-trip through the annals of American train travel.

Baltimore City Life Museums

800 E. Lombard St. ☎ **410/396-3523.** Admission (covers all Museum Row sites) $5 adults, $3.50 seniors, children 4–18. Year-round, Tues–Sat 10am–5pm, Sun noon–5pm.

This is a collection of museums and historic sites, four of which are clustered together on "Museum Row," northeast of the Inner Harbor. The other two museums, the H. L. Mencken House and the Peale Museum, are located elsewhere in the city and must be toured separately (see Charles Street/Mt. Vernon Area, below).

"Museum Row" also includes Brewers' Park, site of a 1783 brewery. An outdoor interpretative display shows the position of the original buildings, from the warehouse and malt houses, to the brewer's houses, kitchen, and privy. Access to the park is unrestricted and no admission is charged.

The following four attractions can be visited together for one all-inclusive price:

Carroll Mansion. Filled with decorative arts and furnishings, this house illustrates the lifestyle of a wealthy 19th-century Baltimore family. It has special significance because it was used for a dozen years (1820–32) as the winter quarters of Charles Carroll of Carrollton, the Maryland patriot and last surviving signer of the Declaration of Independence.

Center for Urban Archaeology. This exhibit features a life-size excavation pit, showing archaeologists at work. Items recovered from the dig include ceramics and glassware from 18th- and 19th-century homes and shops that stood on this site.

1840 House. This reconstructed row house, once the home of a middle-class wheelwright and his family, features living history dramas that the illustrate the lifestyle and social issues of mid-19th-century Baltimore.

The Shot Tower. Located several blocks to the north of Museum Row, at 801 E. Fayette St., this 215-foot-tall brick structure is a local landmark, built in 1828 for the production of lead shot ammunition and is one of the nation's few

Baltimore Attractions

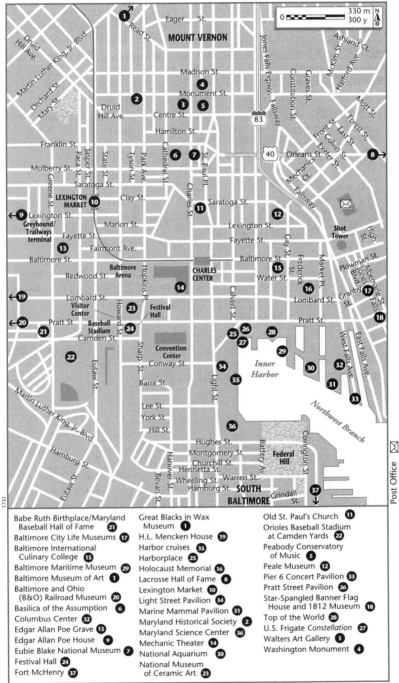

remaining shot towers. It contains a sound-and-light show that illustrates the story of how gun shot was made here until 1892, by pouring molten lead through perforated pans from "dropping stations" high up in the tower.

✪ Baltimore International Culinary College (BICC)

206 Water St. ☎ **410/752-4983.** Admission $10 per person per course. Mon–Thurs 10am–12:30pm and 2–3:30pm; Wed 5–7:30pm.

Learn to cook or at least learn a few of the basics by attending a minicourse at the demonstration theater of this prestigious culinary center. Each day is a new topic, from salads and spa cuisine to shellfish and starches, as well as Oriental, Greek, and regional French cooking. There are also courses in kitchen equipment basics and entertainment cooking, and lessons in working with fish, beef, pork, lamb, veal, vegetables, crepes, herbs and spices, and hot or filled desserts. Purchase tickets in advance at the BICC bookstore, 204 Water St.

Baltimore Maritime Museum

Pier 4, Pratt St. ☎ **410/396-3453.** Admission $4.50 adults, $4 seniors, $1.75 children age 5–12, free for children under 5. Mon–Fri 10am–5pm, Sat–Sun 10am–7pm.

This outdoor complex is the home of the U.S. Coast Guard cutter *Taney*, the last ship still afloat that fought in Pearl Harbor; the submarine USS *Torsk*, which sank the last enemy ship in World War II; and the lightship *Chesapeake*, a floating lighthouse built in 1930. The vessels are moored to the dock and are open to visitors.

Columbus Center

Piers 5 and 6, Pratt St. ☎ **410/547-8727.** Admission not available at press time. Opening hours not available at press time.

With a striking steel-and-glass futuristic facade, this $160 million building, slated to open in the spring of 1996, stands out along the harborfront as the highly touted new national center for marine biotechnology research. It is connected to Pier 4 and the rest of the Inner Harbor attractions by a unique 135-foot-wide pontoon-style pedestrian bridge, the first-ever floating bridge in Baltimore. There are four major units at the new attraction:

Center of Marine Biotechnology. This will be the scientific nucleus, a unit of the University of Maryland Biotechnology Institute, with state-of-the-art research laboratories and equipment.

Center for Marine Archaeology. A facility involved in the recovery and preservation of marine artifacts, using old and new technologies of underwater archaeology such as diving, preservation chemistry, robotics, sonar, computer mapping, and fiber-optic communications.

Hall of Exploration. A 23,000-square foot exhibition space that will allow the public to observe and experience the various phases of the ongoing scientific research in a "hands-on" manner.

Science and Technology Education Center. This component of the center includes classrooms, wet laboratories, and a computer-assisted lecture hall designed to give the public direct access to the Columbus Center researchers and their discoveries.

Eubie Blake National Museum & Cultural Center

34 Market Pl. ☎ **410/625-3113.** Admission free, but donations welcome. Mon–Fri noon–4:30pm.

Within walking distance of Haborplace, this museum is dedicated to Baltimore-born ragtime and vaudeville great James Hubert ("Eubie") Blake. It showcases photos, sheet music, manuscripts, letters, and newspaper clippings reflecting on the 100-year-long life of this great pianist and songwriter, as well as an art gallery with ever-changing exhibits of current interest. (*Note*: At press time there were plans to relocate this museum to its original site, at 409 N. Charles St. Call in advance to check.)

✪ Fort McHenry National Monument and Historic Shrine

E. Fort Ave. ☎ **410/962-4290.** Admission $2; visitors under 17 and seniors 62 and over admitted free. Day after Labor Day to mid-June, daily 8am–5pm; mid-June to Labor Day, daily 8am–8pm. Closed Christmas Day and New Year's Day.

Our national anthem was born here. The sight of our flag flying over this star-shaped fort during the 1814 Battle of Baltimore inspired Francis Scott Key to write the words of "The Star-Spangled Banner"; the American forces were successful against the British and the fort never again came under attack. It remained an active military base for many years, however, until 1925, when it became a national park. To assist visitors in touring the fort, there are historical and military exhibits, a 15-minute film shown every half hour, explanatory maps; during the summer months, guided activities are regularly scheduled.

Holocaust Memorial

Corner of Water, Gay, and Lombard sts. ☎ **410/752-2630.** Admission free. Open daily 24 hours.

Nestled in the heart of downtown near the Inner Harbor, this open-air memorial center and sculpture stand as a stark reminder of the six million Jews murdered by the Nazis in Europe between 1933 and 1945.

Jewish Heritage Center

15 Lloyd St. ☎ **410/732-6400.** Admission $2 per person. Tues–Thurs noon–4pm, Sun noon–4pm and by appointment.

For insight into Baltimore's Jewish history, stop at this museum, located a couple of blocks north of E. Pratt Street and Little Italy. It consists of two restored 19th-century synagogues—the Lloyd Street Synagogue, built in 1845 and the oldest in Maryland, and the B'nai Israel Synagogue, built in 1876 and still in active use as Baltimore's only downtown synagogue. In addition, there are two exhibition galleries featuring rotating displays on Maryland's Jewish connections.

Maryland Science Center

601 Light St. ☎ **410/685-5225.** Admission $8.50 adults, $6.50 seniors and children 4–17, free for children under age 4. Weekdays 10am–5pm, weekends 10am–6pm, with extended hours in summer.

Situated on the edge of the Inner Harbor, this center features hundreds of hands-on activities, live demonstrations, and interactive displays ranging from a simulated space station control center to experiments revealing the properties of sight, sound, magnetism, light, and mechanics. In addition, there are film presentations in the five-story IMAX movie theater and scientific shows in the Davis Planetarium.

✪ National Aquarium

501 E. Pratt St. ☎ **410/576-3800.** Admission $11.50 adults, $9.50 seniors, $7.50 children 3–11, free for children under 3. July–Aug Sun–Thurs 9am–6pm, Fri–Sat 9am–8pm; Mar–June and Sept–Oct Sat–Thurs 9am–5pm, Fri 9am–8pm; Nov–Feb Sat–Thurs 10am–5pm, Fri 10am–8pm.

A spectacular five-level glass and steel structure, this aquarium is the centerpiece of the Inner Harbor, stretching over Piers 3 and 4. It contains more than 5,000 specimens of mammals, fish, rare birds, reptiles, and amphibians. All the creatures are on view in settings that re-create their natural habitats, including a South American rain forest; a 335,000-gallon Atlantic coral reef exhibit that gives a "diver's eye" view of thousands of tropical fish from the Atlantic's coastal waters; and a 225,000-gallon Open Ocean Exhibit that showcases species of sharks, from sand tigers and nurses to lemons, plus a small-tooth sawfish. Moving belts and ramped bridges carry visitors from one exhibit level to the next.

In addition, the Marine Mammal Pavilion is home to Atlantic bottlenose dolphins, in a carefully controlled environment that enables visitors literally to go dolphin-watching indoors. The mammals are housed in a 1.2 million-gallon complex of four pools, surrounded by the world's largest acrylic windows and a 1,300-seat amphitheater. Visitors not only have an opportunity for close-up observation of dolphin behavior, but they also can attend an ongoing program of 20-minute educational talks, presented by aquarium trainers. In addition, there are nature films, plus a gallery of exhibits, an aquatic education resource center, and an animal care and research complex.

Star-Spangled Banner Flag House and 1812 Museum

844 E. Pratt St. ☎ **410/837-1793.** Admission $4 adults, $3 seniors, $1 students 13–18, free for children 6–12. Apr–Oct Tues–Sun 10am–4pm; Nov–Mar Mon–Sat 10am–3:15pm. Closed major holidays.

A national historic landmark, this Federal-style house (1793) was once the home of Mary Pickersgill, the seamstress who made the 30-by-42-foot red, white, and blue Fort McHenry flag that inspired Francis Scott Key to write the poem that was to become our national anthem. It is full of period furnishings and a collection of Early American art. Adjacent to the house is a museum of 1812 military artifacts commemorating the defense of Baltimore. Outside is an unusual garden featuring a map of the continental United States made of stones native to each state.

Top of the World

401 E. Pratt St. ☎ **410/837-4515.** Admission $2 adults, $1 children 5–15 and seniors over 60. Mon–Sat 10am–5pm, Sun 11am–5pm.

For a sweeping overview of the whole harbor and city, head for this sky-high observatory on the 27th floor of the World Trade Center, the world's tallest pentagonal building, just opposite Harborplace. In addition to a look at the cityscapes below, you can acquire a bit of background about Baltimore from the sky-high exhibits, hands-on displays, and multimedia presentations at this facility.

CHARLES STREET/MOUNT VERNON AREA

Baltimore Museum of Art

Art Museum Dr., N. Charles St., and 31st St. ☎ **410/396-7100.** Admission $5.50 adults, $3.50 seniors and students, $1.50 children 7–18. Wed–Fri 10am–4pm, weekends 11am–6pm.

Located on the northern edge of the city near Johns Hopkins University and about 3 miles from the Inner Harbor, this is the largest museum in Maryland, with exhibits of art from all periods, most notably an Impressionist collection and two outdoor sculpture gardens. In late 1994, a new $10 million modern art wing as added, housing 16 galleries for a diverse collection of 20th-century art including the largest ensemble of paintings by Andy Warhol outside of the Andy Warhol Museum in Pittsburgh, as well as the works of more than 75 other American and European artists of the post-1945 period.

✪ Basilica of the Assumption

Cathedral and Mulberry sts. ☎ **410/727-3564.** Admission free, but donations welcome. Mon–Fri 7am–5pm, Sat–Sun 7am–6:30pm.

Dating from 1806, this was the first metropolitan cathedral in the United States, and the mother church for Baltimore's Catholic population. A fine example of neoclassical architecture, it was designed by Benjamin Henry Latrobe, the same architect who designed the nation's capitol. Highlights include a grand organ dating from 1821, a high altar from 1822, stained-glass windows installed between 1943 and 1947, and paintings that were gifts from European kings. The remains of Bishop John Carroll, America's first Catholic bishop, are also interred here. Guided tours are conducted every Sunday at noon or by appointment.

Edgar Allan Poe House

203 N. Amity St. ☎ **410/396-7932.** Admission $3 adults, $1 children under 13. Apr–July and Oct to mid-Dec, Wed–Sat noon–3:45pm; Aug–Sept Sat noon–4pm. Closed mid-Dec to Mar.

The tiny house where Edgar Allan Poe wrote many of his great works is located in the heart of Baltimore. Poe lived here for three years (1832–35) while courting his cousin, whom he later married. The building contains Poe memorabilia, plus period furniture, ever-changing exhibits, and a video presentation of leading Poe works.

✪ Great Blacks in Wax Museum

1601–03 E. North Ave. ☎ **410/563-3404.** Admission $5.50 adults, $5 seniors and college students, $3.50 children 12–17, $3 children 2–11. Jan 15–Oct 15, Tues–Sat 9am–6pm, Sun noon–6pm; Oct 16–Jan 14, Tues–Sat 9am–5pm, Sun noon–5pm. Closed Mon except during Black History Month (Feb).

Nestled in the northeast corner of the city, this is the nation's first and only wax museum dedicated to famous black heroes and historical legends. Displays are in chronological order, and each highlights a period in African American history, from ancient Africa to slavery and the Civil War to the civil rights era. The people portrayed include black inventors, pilots, religious and education leaders, scientists, and more.

H. L. Mencken House

1524 Hollins St. ☎ **410/396-3523.** Admission $2 adults, $1.50 seniors and children aged 4–18. Year-round, Sat 10am–5pm, Sun noon–5pm.

For nearly 70 years, this 19th-century row house, located in historic Union Square on the city's west side, was the home of author, journalist, and literary critic Henry Louis Mencken, the "Sage of Baltimore." Now one of the City Life Museums, the house has been restored to include many of Mencken's original furnishings and belongings, among them his Tonk baby grand piano and a life mask of Beethoven. An audiovisual presentation highlights Mencken's life and career.

Lacrosse Hall of Fame Museum

113 W. University Pkwy. ☎ **410/235-6882.** Admission $2 adults, $1 students. June–Feb, weekdays 9am–5pm; Mar–May, Mon–Fri 9am–5pm, Sat 10am–3pm.

Located in the Johns Hopkins University milieu, this unique museum presents 350 years in the history of lacrosse, America's oldest sport. The displays include rare photographs and photomurals of men and women at play, art, vintage equipment and uniforms, sculptures, trophies, memorabilia, and a trivia game. A nine-minute audiovisual show captures the thrill of playing the game.

Maryland Historical Society

201 W. Monument St. ☎ **410/685**-3750. Admission $4 adults, $2.50 seniors, $3 children 5–17. Tues–Fri 10am–5pm, Sat 9am–5pm, Sun 1–5pm.

Nestled beside Mount Vernon and Antique Row between Park Avenue and Howard Street, this society was established in 1844. It houses many of the city's treasures, such as the original "Star-Spangled Banner" manuscript and silver from America's largest 19th-century silver collection, as well as more than 3,000 maps, 4,500 prints, 45,000 relics and artifacts, 55,000 books, and 200,000 photographs, all depicting Maryland in permanent and changing exhibits. In addition, there are antique dolls, toys, furniture, and clocks.

Old St. Paul's Church

Charles and Saratoga streets. ☎ **410/685**-3404. Admission free, but donations welcome. Weekdays 11am–1pm, Sun 8:30am–12:30pm.

Opened in 1856, this church is the sixth of a parish dating from 1692 and it is the mother church for the Episcopal diocese of the city of Baltimore. Designed by Richard Upjohn in the basilica style, it is noted for its Tiffany windows and inlaid mosaic work including marble reliefs of Moses and Christ dating from 1812. Don't miss a chance to hear the church bells ring; they are part of a carillon given by the people of Baltimore to the church. The choir of men and boys, one of the most notable in North America, sings every Sunday (September to May) at 10:30am.

Peale Museum

225 Holliday St. ☎ 410/396-3523. Admission $2 adults, $1.50 children 4–18. Year-round, Sat 10am–5pm, Sun noon–5pm.

Built in 1814 by American portrait painter Rembrandt Peale, this site is reputed to be the oldest museum building in the United States. It served as Baltimore's first city hall. A member of the City Life Museums, it houses a fine collection of historical photographs, prints, and paintings of Baltimore and the Peale family. The garden is enhanced by 19th- and 20th-century relief carvings and sculptures.

✪ Walters Art Gallery

600 N. Charles St. ☎ **410/547**-9000. Admission $4 adults, $3 seniors, free for children 18 and under, free before noon on Sat. Tues–Sun 11am–5pm.

Designed in an Italianate palazzo style, this museum houses more than 30,000 works of art, spanning some 5,000 years. The collection includes Asian, Egyptian, Greek, Roman, Byzantine, medieval, Renaissance, baroque, romantic, Impressionist, and art nouveau works. In addition, there are exhibits of historic jewelry, medieval armor, and illuminated manuscripts.

Washington Monument and Museum

Mount Vernon Place. ☎ **420/396**-0929. Donation $1 per person. Wed–Sun 10am–4pm.

This monument, 178 feet tall, stands as the country's first major architectural memorial to George Washington. Begun in 1815, it was designed by Robert Mills, who also designed the Washington Monument (begun in 1848) in Washington, D.C. To learn the whole story, step inside this building and have a look at the exhibit "The Making of a Monument." Those who are physically fit can also climb the 228 steps to the top of the tower and see why this spot is often called the best view in Baltimore.

ESPECIALLY FOR KIDS

Baltimore Museum of Industry

1415 Key Hwy. ☎ **410/727-4808.** Admission $3.50 adults, $2.50 students and seniors. Wed 7–9pm; Thurs–Fri and Sun noon–5pm; Sat 10am–5pm.

Housed in an 1865 oyster cannery, this museum illustrates the industrial history of the city through a series of 19th-century workshop settings—from a machine shop and a print shop to a clothing factory and cannery works. Kids can learn how machines work and how various industries helped Baltimore to develop into the city it is today.

Baltimore Zoo

Greenspring Ave., Druid Hill Park. ☎ **410/396-7102.** Admission $6.50 adults, $3.50 seniors and children 2–15, free for children under 2. Daily 10am–4pm.

The third-oldest zoo in the United States, this is a natural expanse of 150 acres of grassy slopes, tree-topped hills, and mountain caves. It provides an agreeable habitat to more than 1,200 animals, birds, and reptiles from seven continents, from bears to black-footed penguins. For young visitors, there's also an eight-acre interactive children's zoo.

6 Organized Tours & Cruises

WALKING AND BUS TOURS

Baltimore City Life Tours

800 E. Lombard St. ☎ **410/396-3279.** Admission $7–$10 for walking tours, $20 for bus tours. Sat–Sun, times vary.

Baltimore's City Life Museums sponsor occasional walking and bus tours, focusing on different historical, social, and cultural aspects of the city, from row houses and neighborhoods to cemeteries, Christmas decorations, and the Great Fire of 1904. The topics change monthly, so check in advance; duration is from $1^1/2$ to 4 hours, depending on the topic and itinerary. Reservations are required.

Baltimore Heritage Walking Tours

$11^1/2$ W. Chase St. ☎ **410/625-2585.** Admission $10 per person. Sat or Sun 10am.

This organization offers two-hour guided walking tours of the city's unique neighborhoods and historic areas. Tours begin at various sites and itineraries change monthly, so phone ahead to see what will be covered at the time of your visit. Reservations are necessary.

✪ Baltimore Trolley Tours

Various locations. ☎ **410/752-2015.** Admission $12 adults, $4.50 children 12 and under. Apr–Oct, daily 10am–4pm; Nov–Mar, reduced schedule.

Conducted in a colorful motorized trolley, this is really two activities in one: a narrated tour of major Baltimore sights and a means of transportation between all the sights. You can stay on board and enjoy a complete tour for two hours or longer, or you can get off at one stop, linger a while, and then reboard at your leisure (trolleys operate at 30-minute intervals for each stop). One ticket entitles you to reboarding privileges throughout the day, at a total of 20 different stops (at hotels and attractions). You can start your tour at any of the trolley boarding points, clearly posted, all over the city. Tickets are available from the driver, at certain hotels, and at the Inner Harbor ticket booth on Light Street.

Oriole Park at Camden Yards Tours

333 W. Camden St. ☎ **410/685-9800.** Tour admission $5 adults, $4 seniors and children 12 and under. Tours, Mon–Fri at 1pm; Sat at 11am and 2pm; Sun at 12:30pm and 2pm.

Situated between two 19th-century landmarks—the Baltimore and Ohio Railroad Warehouse and Camden Station—this is Baltimore's new "old-fashioned" ballpark, seating up to 48,000 spectators. It's a tourist attraction in itself. Behind-the-scenes tours of the facility are given daily, except when the Orioles play an afternoon game. Tickets can be purchased, on a first-come basis, at the Orioles Ticket Office.

CRUISES & BOATING TOURS

Baltimore Patriot

Constellation Dock, Pratt St. ☎ **410/685-4288.** $6 adults, $3.30 children under 12. Apr and Oct 11am, 1pm, and 3pm daily; May–Sept hourly departures 11am–4pm daily.

Maryland Tours operates this 300-passenger, two-deck boat on a 16-mile, 1¹/₂-hour narrated route around the Inner Harbor and Patapsco River.

✪ *Bay Lady/Lady Baltimore*

301 Light St. ☎ **410/727-3113.** Lunch $21.95; dinner $33.50–$44.50; moonlight cruise $17.95. Lunch daily at noon (boarding at 11:30am); dinner daily at 7pm (boarding at 6:30pm); moonlight cruise Fri–Sat at 11:30pm (boarding at 11pm).

Harbor Cruises operates three different cruises on board these two 450-passenger, three-deck luxury cruise ships, all departing from the Light Street dock next to Harborplace. The program includes a two-hour lunch, a three-hour dinner, and a 2¹/₂-hour moonlight excursion. The prices for the lunch and dinner trips include a narrated tour, seated meal, and entertainment. Special theme cruises, such as Sunday afternoon bull roasts, Friday lobster or crab nights, and holiday observances, are also held throughout the year. In addition, on selected dates, there are cruises to Annapolis, St. Michaels, and along the C&D Canal for fall foliage.

Clipper City

720 Light St. ☎ **410/539-6277.** Afternoon sail $12 adults, $2 children under 12; calypso and reggae sail $20 adults; Sun brunch $30 adults. Afternoon sail Tues–Sat noon and 3pm, Sun 3pm and 6pm; calypso and reggae sail Fri–Sat 8pm; Sun brunch 11am.

This sleek 149-passenger topsail schooner is a replica of an 1854 vessel and one of the largest tall ships licensed in the United States to carry passengers. It offers two-hour afternoon excursions, three-hour evening trips with live calypso and reggae music, and three-hour Sunday champagne brunch sails, all departing from the dock next to the Maryland Science Center.

Nighthawk

1715 Thames St. ☎ **410/327-7245.** for information or 410/276-7447 for reservations. Moonlight sail $32.50 per person; champagne brunch $32.50 per person; murder mystery cruises $45 per person. May–Sept, moonlight sail Wed and Fri–Sat 7:30pm; champagne brunch Sun 11am; murder mystery, check for schedule.

Sailing from Fells Point, this 82-foot, 49-passenger windjammer offers three-hour excursions into the waters of the Inner Harbor and Patapsco River. The schedule includes moonlight sails with buffet dinner and live music and afternoon champagne brunch sails with live music. Occasional "murder mystery" cruises are also offered.

Spirit of Baltimore

801 Key Hwy. ☎ **410/523-7447.** Lunch cruise $19.95–$23.50; dinner cruise $33.95–$41.35; moonlight cruise $17.75. Lunch cruise Mon–Sat at noon (boarding at 11:30am), Sun at 1pm (boarding at 12:30pm); dinner cruise daily at 7pm (boarding at 6:30pm); moonlight cruise Fri–Sat at 11:30pm (boarding at 11pm).

Departing from the Harborview dock, this three-deck, 500-passenger luxury cruiser offers two-hour lunch and dinner cruises and three-hour moonlight cruises in the waters of the Inner Harbor and beyond. Price includes buffet meal, narration, and entertainment.

7 Spectator Sports & Outdoor Activities

BASEBALL From April to October, when the Baltimore Orioles play ball, the city is obsessed with "Oriole fever"—everyone wants to go to the games and everyone talks about the results. If there's a game on in town during your visit, do whatever you have to do to get a ticket: It's a real Baltimore experience. The team plays at Oriole Park at Camden Yards, 333 W. Camden St. (☎ 410/685-9800). Afternoon games are usually at 1:35pm and evening games are slated for 7:35pm. Ticket prices range from $5 to $28.

HORSE RACING Maryland's oldest Thoroughbred track and the site of the annual Preakness Stakes is Pimlico Race Course, Park Heights and Belvedere avenues (☎ 410/542-9400), about 5 miles from the Inner Harbor on the city's northwest side. The full racing season extends from mid-March to the end of May and early August to early October. Post time is 1pm, and admission charges are $3 for the grandstand and $5 for the clubhouse, plus $1–$3 per car for parking. Pimlico is also the home of the National Jockey's Hall of Fame, open from 9 to 11am during the racing season, free of charge.

WATER SPORTS Trident Electric Boats (between the World Trade Center and Aquarium Dock, Pratt Street, ☎ 410/539-1837) rents electric-powered boats by the half-hour ($10 for a two-passenger boat, $15 for a two- to three-passenger boat). It's open May through September, Sunday through Thursday 10am to 10pm, Friday and Saturday 10am to midnight.

8 Shopping

THE SHOPPING SCENE

For visitors, Baltimore's prime shopping scene is centered around the Inner Harbor. **Harborplace,** Pratt and Light streets (☎ 410/332-4191), is the benchmark of the city's quintessential shopping experiences. It is an attractive waterside complex of two glass-enclosed bilevel shopping malls, known as the Light Street Pavilion and the Pratt Street Pavilion, featuring more than 135 shops, markets, craft vendors, restaurants, and cafes. You'll find everything from bonbons and books to scrimshaw and silks. To add to the ambience, from April through September free concerts are staged in the amphitheater in front of the pavilions. Open Monday through Saturday, from 10am to 9pm, and Sunday from 10am to 6pm.

Across the street is the **Gallery at Harborplace,** Pratt and Light streets (☎ 410/332-4191), an outgrowth of the original Pratt and Light Street pavilions. Opened in 1987, this is a four-story brass and mahogany atrium-style shopping mall of more than 70 fine shops, including Banana Republic, Brooks Brothers, Ann

Taylor, and the Disney Store. Open Monday through Saturday, from 10am to 10pm, and Sunday from noon to 6pm.

In addition, there are hundreds of fine individual shops scattered throughout Baltimore. Certain parts of the city are known for specific types of shopping, such as "Antique Row" along North Howard and West Read streets, featuring more than 40 independently owned antique shops. Fells Point is rich in antique, art, souvenir, and craft shops.

SHOPPING A TO Z
ANTIQUES & COLLECTIBLES

Antique Galleria
853 N. Howard St. ☎ **410/462-6365.**

This two-story shop offers the wares of 35 different antique dealers, ranging from formal or country furniture to smaller items such as porcelain, silver, brass, quilts, linens, toys, antique prints, books, fountain pens, jewelry, Judaica and folk art, and Civil War memorabilia. Open Monday through Saturday from 11am to 5pm, and on Sunday from noon to 4pm.

Harris Auction Galleries
875 N. Howard St. ☎ **410/728-7040.**

Try this shop for small pieces of art and collectibles including watches, plates, prints, paintings, jars, jugs, and Oriental pieces. Auctions are often held on Sunday here; check in advance. Open weekdays from 9am to 5pm, Saturday from 10:30am to 2pm.

L. A. Herstein and Co.
877 N. Howard St. ☎ **410/728-3856.**

The specialty of this shop is antique Tiffany lamps and shades, including repairs and supplying missing parts. Open Monday to Tuesday from 11am to 4pm, Friday to Saturday from 11am to 5pm.

Wittman's Oriental Gallery
825 N. Howard St. ☎ **410/462-5159.**

This shop specializes in antiques and art from Japan and China including ceramics and paintings. Open Monday to Saturday from 11am to 4pm.

ARTS & CRAFTS

Angeline's Art Gallery & Boutique
1631 Thames St. ☎ **410/522-7909.**

Located in the Brown's Wharf complex of shops at Fells Point, this shop specializes in original paintings and drawings by local and national artists, especially Baltimore and Fells Point scenes. There are also batiks, prints, ceramics, exotic jewelry, curios, and sculpture. Open daily from 11am to 6pm.

A People United
516 N. Charles St. ☎ **410/727-4470.**

More than an average commercial enterprise, this nonprofit shop features a variety of goods made by women who are part of development cooperatives in India, Nepal, Thailand, Guatemala, Kenya, and other lands. You'll find a colorful selection of exotic clothing, jewelry, and accessories. Open from Monday through Saturday from 11am to 6pm and on Sunday from noon to 5pm.

Art Gallery of Fells Point
811 S. Broadway. ☎ **410/327-1271.**

A cooperative gallery featuring works by Maryland and regional artists, this shop is located in the heart of the Fells Point district. Art for sale includes oil paintings, watercolors, drawings, sculpture, photography, pastels, fibers, and jewelry. Open Tuesday to Sunday from noon to 5pm.

✪ Women's Industrial Exchange
333 N. Charles St. ☎ **410/685-4388.**

Founded in 1882, this enterprise aims to help the needy women and men of the city by selling their handiwork and giving them employment in the shop and adjacent restaurant (see "Dining," above). The crafts offered are often one of a kind, from knitwear, quilts, afghans, and needlepoint, to jewelry, original photo cards, woodwork, dolls, tableware, and baked goods. Open weekdays from 9am to 3:30pm.

GIFTS & SOUVENIRS

Brassworks Company
1641 Thames St. ☎ **410/327-7280.**

This Fells Point shop stocks a large selection of fine quality gifts, accessories, and decorative furnishings, from brass and copper items to lamps, candlesticks, and door and furniture hardware. Open weekdays from 8:30am to 5:30pm, Saturday from 10am to 6pm, Sunday from noon to 6pm.

Gift Ahoy
1625 Thames St. ☎ **410/558-1933.**

This shop specializes in gifts and souvenirs that have the colors, symbols, and motifs of the City of Baltimore, State of Maryland, and the Chesapeake Bay area, including the game Chesapeakeopoly. In addition, there are home furnishings, apparel, and art with a nautical theme. It's located at Brown's Wharf in Fells Point. Open May through September, Sunday to Wednesday from 10am to 6pm, Thursday to Saturday from 10am to 9pm; October through April, Monday to Saturday from 10am to 8pm, Sunday from noon to 6pm.

Grrreat Bears and Childhood Delights
1643 Thames St. ☎ **410/276-4429.**

This Fells Point shop is a treasure trove of teddy bear-related toys, stuffed animals, and books for the young and young at heart; plus cats, dinosaurs, dolls, puppets, puzzles, tractors, trucks, and collectible miniatures. Open Sunday to Tuesday from 10am to 5pm, Wednesday to Saturday from 10am to 9:30pm.

MARKETS

Baltimore Farmers' Market
Holiday and Saratoga sts. ☎ **410/752-8632.**

For a look at Old Baltimore, stop to see this weekly outdoor gathering, a great source for crafts, herbs, jams, jellies, baked goods, and smoked meats, as well as local produce and flowers. Open from late June through December, Sunday from 8am till sold out.

Broadway Market
S. Broadway between Fleet and Lancaster sts. ☎ **410/396-9780.**

Smell and taste the flavors of Baltimore's original seaport at this 200-year-old market, tucked in the heart of Fells Point. The market area consists of two large covered buildings, each staffed by local vendors selling fresh produce, flowers, crafts, and an assortment of ethnic and raw bar foods, ideal for snacking, a quick lunch, or a picnic. Open daily from 8am to 6pm.

✪ Lexington Market
400 W. Lexington St. ☎ **410/685-6169.**

Established in 1782, this Baltimore landmark claims to be the oldest continuously operating market in the United States. It houses more than 140 merchants, selling prepared ethnic foods (for eat-in or take-away), fresh seafood, produce, meats, baked goods, sweets, and more. It's a real slice of Baltimore, well worth a visit for the aromas, flavors, sounds, and sights, as well as good shopping. Open Monday to Saturday from 8:30am to 6pm.

9 Baltimore After Dark

Baltimore is the home of the Baltimore Symphony Orchestra, the Baltimore Opera Company, and many fine theaters. Check the arts and entertainment pages of the *Baltimore Sun* for daily listings and ticket information. Also, for latest developments check with the Baltimore Area Visitors Center at the time of your visit.

For tickets, you can contact individual box offices or go to the **City Life Ticket Kiosk,** Light Street (☎ 410/396-8342), between Harborplace and the Maryland Science Center on the Inner Harbor. This one-stop shop sells theater and concert tickets, as well as tickets to sports events, museums, attractions, tours, and cruises. Package tickets to several sites are also available at a one-price discount. It's open daily from 10am to 4pm or later.

CONCERT HALLS/PERFORMING ARTS CENTERS

Baltimore Arena
201 W. Baltimore St. ☎ **410/347-2000.** Tickets $10–$45. Events are usually slated for 7:30pm.

This facility, with a capacity of 16,000 people, is the setting for an ever-changing program of entertainment and sports events, including concerts, plays, circuses, ice shows, and soccer and hockey matches.

✪ Joseph Meyerhoff Symphony Hall
1212 Cathedral St. ☎ **410/783-8000.** Tickets $15–$45. Starting times vary with each presentation, but are usually at 7:30 or 8:15pm.

Famed for its acoustics, this 2,450-seat hall is the home of the Baltimore Symphony Orchestra and Baltimore Symphony Chorus. In addition to concerts by those two ensembles, it also presents visiting classical and pops artists.

Lyric Opera House
1404 W. Mt. Royal Ave. ☎ **410/685-0692.** Tickets $18–$75. 8pm evenings and 2pm matinees.

A replica of Germany's Leipzig music hall, this impressive facility is home to the Baltimore Opera Company, which performs the world's great operas from October to May.

Peabody Conservatory of Music
1 E. Mount Vernon Pl. ☎ **410/659-8124.** Most tickets are $10, but range $5–$16; some performances are free. Days and times vary; most evening shows at 7:30, 8, or 8:15pm; matinees at 3pm.

A division of Johns Hopkins University, this is America's oldest school of music, dating from 1866. From September through May, there are more than 60 events open to the public each year, featuring the Peabody Symphony Orchestra and student performers. Concerts take place in the Miriam A. Friedberg Concert Hall, and the repertoire ranges from orchestral and opera to solo recitals, choral, wind, jazz, ragtime, and dance ensembles, and from early music to electronic music.

Pier Six Concert Pavilion
Pier 6 (off Pratt St.), Inner Harbor. ☎ **410/837-4636.** Tickets $15–$30 for most shows. Days vary, starting time is usually 7 or 8pm.

Sitting right on the Inner Harbor, this facility is a newly constructed 4,300-seat concert pavilion, in the format of an open-air, six-point aluminum tent. It presents the top names of the music industry in live concerts from May through September.

THEATERS

Arena Players
801 McCulloch St. ☎ **410/728-6500.** Tickets $12–$15. Fri–Sun at 7:30 or 8:30pm.

A prominent black theater company, this ensemble presents contemporary plays and romantic comedies.

Center Stage
700 N. Calvert St. ☎ **410/332-0033.** Tickets $10–$35. Sept–June Tues–Sat at 8pm, Sun at 7:30pm.

Recognized as Maryland's resident professional theater and the state theater of Maryland, this restored building provides an intimate setting for first-rate repertory and original shows, from cabaret-style musicals, comedies, and classics, to modern and contemporary masterworks.

Fells Point Corner Theatre
251 S. Ann St. ☎ **410/276-7837.** Tickets $9–$10. Fri–Sat at 8pm, Sun at 2pm.

Situated in the Fells Point district of the city, this small theater presents contemporary and historic dramas.

Morris Mechanic Theatre
Hopkins Plaza, Baltimore and Charles sts. ☎ **410/625-1400.** Tickets $35–$45 for most shows. Tues–Sat at 8pm; matinees Wed and Sat at 2pm, Sun at 3pm.

An ultramodern showplace in the heart of downtown, this theater stages contemporary plays with original casts en route to or from Broadway.

Theatre Project
45 W. Preston St. ☎ **410/752-8558.** Tickets $8–$15. Wed–Sat at 8pm, Sun at 3pm.

This small theater presents a variety of new work by professional theater and dance companies from this country and abroad.

Vagabond Players
806 S. Broadway. ☎ **410/563-9135.** Tickets $9–$10. Fri–Sat at 8pm, Sun at 2 and 7pm.

Located in Fells Point, this theater group presents a variety of classics, contemporary comedies and dramas.

CLUBS/BARS

Baja Beach Club

55 Market Pl. (at E. Lombard St.). ☎ **410/727-0468.** No cover.

Located at the Brokerage, opposite Harborplace, this place presents progressive DJ dance music from Wednesday through Sunday from 8pm until 2am

Buddies Pub & Jazz Club

313 N. Charles St. ☎ **410/332-4200.** No cover.

This informal and lively place is known for its live jazz sessions on Wednesday through Saturday, with open mike night on Thursday. House drummer Bing Miller heads a trio that performs regularly. Music starts at 8:30 or 9:30pm and continues to midnight.

The Club at Spike and Charlie's

1225 Cathedral St. ☎ **410/752-8144.** Cover ranges from $5 to $8, depending on the talent.

Located across from the Meyerhoff Symphony Hall, this spot draws crowds to its jazz sessions on Friday and Saturday nights, from 9pm.

Comedy Factory

36 Light St. (at Lombard St.). ☎ **410/752-4189.** Cover $10.

Located above Burke's Restaurant, this club presents live comedy acts on Thursday at 8:30pm, Friday and Saturday at 8:30 and 10:30pm.

Louie's Bookstore

518 N. Charles St. ☎ **410/962-1224.** No cover.

This bookshop/bar/cafe presents live classical music every night until at least midnight, featuring local artists playing the lute, guitar, piano, or violin.

McGinn's Irish Pub

328 N. Charles St. ☎ **410/539-7504.** No cover.

If you're in a St. Patrick's Day mood on any weekend, come to this pub in the heart of the city for live Irish traditional or ballad music. Music usually starts at 9pm.

Annapolis 3

A gem of Colonial architecture, Annapolis is home to a historic district of more than 1,500 buildings. Situated at the confluence of the Chesapeake Bay and the Severn River, this picturesque port is also the capital of Maryland.

First settled in the mid-1600s, Annapolis was initially known as Providence; later it was called Anne Arundel Town, after the wife of Cecilius Calvert, the second Lord Baltimore, who sponsored the area's first English settlers. It was an Englishman, Francis Nicholson, who laid out the city's streets in 1695 according to a pattern of radiating thoroughfares. In 1694 the name of Annapolis was chosen, in honor of Princess Anne, who later became queen of England.

With all of its lofty connections, it is no wonder that Annapolis has led a charmed existence. A prosperous seaport because of the tobacco trade, Annapolis had its golden years from 1750 to 1790, as the commercial, political, and social center of Maryland. The first library in the colonies, as well as the first theater, is believed to have been founded in Annapolis during those years, as was St. John's College, one of the first public schools in America. Between November 1783 and August 1784, Annapolis was also the first peacetime capital of the United States. It was during that period that the city served as the site for the ratification of the Treaty of Paris, the document in which Great Britain formally recognized the independence of the United States, ending the Revolutionary War.

As you stroll down the streets of Annapolis today, you can't help thinking that not much has changed here since those glorious days. Except for the cars, it is almost as if time has stood still. The city is a vista of 18th-century mansions, churches, and public buildings. The original layout is still in place—narrow brick streets fanning out from two circular thoroughfares, State Circle and Church Circle. Colonial names are everywhere: King George Street, Duke of Gloucester Street, Compromise Street, and Shipwright Street, to cite a few.

This charming seaport city, with a population of about 35,000, does have newer claims to fame, of course. It is the home of the U.S. Naval Academy and the government of the state of Maryland. With 16 miles of waterfront, tiny Annapolis is also the pleasure-boating capital of the eastern United States and a tourist destination renowned for its landmark sights, historic inns and restaurants, convivial taverns, trendy shops, and relaxed atmosphere.

What's Special About Annapolis

Sightseeing
- Annapolis Historic District, with more than 1,500 18th-century private and public buildings.
- U.S. Naval Academy, a national historic site spread over 300 acres.
- Maryland State House, the oldest U.S. state capitol in continuous use.
- City Dock and Marina, a yachting hub with hundreds of craft of all sizes.
- Market House, a central farmers' market dating from 1784.

Activities
- Taking a guided tour of the U.S. Naval Academy.
- Enjoying a sightseeing cruise of Annapolis Harbor.
- Taking a walking tour with a Colonially costumed guide or on your own.

Events & Festivals
- Commissioning Week at the U.S. Naval Academy.
- U.S. Sailboat Show, the world's largest in-the-water boat show.
- U.S. Power Boat Show, the largest of its kind.
- Maryland Seafood Festival, three days of continuous entertainment and the best of Chesapeake Bay seafood.

Museums
- Maritime Museum, for a look at what the Annapolis waterfront was like between 1751 and 1791.
- Banneker-Douglass Museum, with exhibits on the historical and cultural experiences of African Americans in Maryland.

1 Orientation

ARRIVING

BY PLANE   Annapolis is served by **Baltimore-Washington International Airport.** More than 300 flights a day land at this northern Maryland gateway, located approximately 20 miles northwest of Annapolis. Minibus transfer services between the airport and the major hotels of Annapolis are operated by **BWI Shuttle Express** (☎ 410/859-0800). The fare is $14 one way and $22 round-trip. Transfer by taxi is approximately $25 to $35 one way.

BY CAR   Located in the center of Maryland's Chesapeake Bay coast, Annapolis is about 30 miles south of Baltimore (via I-97), and 40 miles east of Washington, D.C. (via Rtes. 50 and 301). Annapolis is also accessible from the east via the William Preston Lane Jr. Memorial Bridge, locally known as the "Bay Bridge."

BY TRAIN   Since there is no train station in Annapolis, take Amtrak to Baltimore, 20 miles to the north. From there, you can either rent a car, or take BWI Shuttle Express, a local airport minibus service to Annapolis (see above).

BY BUS   Annapolis has no bus station. However, buses do stop at the Navy/Marine Stadium on Rowe Boulevard. **Greyhound** (☎ 800/231-2222) offers service from the eastern seaboard, **Baltimore MTA** (☎ 800/543-9809) provides service from Baltimore, and **Dillon Co.** (☎ 800/827-3490) operates commuter buses to and from Washington, D.C., on weekdays.

VISITOR INFORMATION

For tourist brochures and maps of Annapolis, contact the **Annapolis and Anne Arundel Conference and Visitors Bureau,** 26 West St., Annapolis, MD 21401 (☎ 410/280-0445 or 410/268-TOUR).

CITY LAYOUT

The city layout is based on two central circles: State Circle and Church Circle. All other streets radiate from these two points. The U.S. Naval Academy is in its own enclave, east of State Circle.

2 Getting Around

BY PUBLIC TRANSPORTATION

BY SHUTTLE   For visitors and locals, **Annapolis Transit** (☎ 410/263-7964 on weekdays and 410/263-7994 on weekends) operates Trolley Shuttle, a shuttle-bus service using gasoline-powered trolleys between the historic/business district and the parking area of the Navy/Marine Stadium. Shuttles operate Monday through Friday from 6:30am to 7pm every half hour and every 15 minutes during rush hours. From April through October, there is a Special Weekend Shuttle Express departing from the Visitor's Center and making stops around the historic district, every 15 minutes. One-way fares for all shuttle services are 75¢.

BY BUS   From Monday through Saturday, **Annapolis Transit** also runs commuter bus service from the historic district to other parts of the city such as the Annapolis Mall or Eastport. Base fare is 75¢ and exact change is required. Buses run every half-hour, starting at 5:20am and continuing to 6:20pm.

BY CAR

RENTALS   Car rental firms represented in Annapolis include **Budget,** 2001 West St. (☎ 410/266-5030 or 410/266-8233); **Discount,** 1032 West St. (☎ 410/269-6645); and **Enterprise,** 1023 Spa Rd. (☎ 410/269-5252).

PARKING   True to its 18th-century style, midtown Annapolis is very compact, with lots of narrow streets; consequently, parking in the historic district is limited. Visitors are encouraged to leave their cars in a park-and-ride lot, located on the edge of town, off Rowe Boulevard, on the west side of the Navy/Marine Stadium.

BY TAXI

Once you are in town, if you need transport call **Arundel and Colonial Cab** (☎ 410/263-2555 or 410/263-4200); **Capital City Cab** (☎ 410/267-0000); or **Yellow Checker Cab** (☎ 410/268-3737).

BY WATER TAXI

From late May through Labor Day, the **Jiffy Water Taxi** (☎ 410/263-0033) operates from the City Dock to restaurants and other destinations along Spa and Back Creeks. It's a handy way of avoiding Annapolis auto traffic and a pleasant sightseeing experience as well. The fare ranges from $1 to $4, depending on destination. Hours are Monday through Thursday from 9:30am to midnight, Friday from 9:30am to 1am, Saturday from 9am to 1am and Sunday from 9am to midnight. Service is limited in early May and in September and October.

FAST FACTS: Annapolis

Area Code   The area code of Annapolis is 410.

Baby-sitters   Inquire at your hotel or guest house.

Car Rentals   See "Getting Around" earlier in this chapter.

Drugstores   A downtown branch of the national chain **Rite Aid** is located at 179 Main St. (☎ 410/268-0583).

Emergencies   Dial **911** for fire, police, or ambulance.

Eyeglasses   Several national optical chains operate in the Annapolis area, including **Sterling Optical** and **Visionworks.**

Hospitals   **Anne Arundel Medical Center** is at Franklin and Cathedral streets (☎ 410/267-1000).

Information   See "Tourist Information" earlier in this chapter.

Library   The **Anne Arundel County Library** is on West Street (☎ 410/280-1750).

Liquor Laws   Places serving alcoholic beverages may be open from 6am to 2am, except on Sunday and election days. The minimum age for buying or consuming alcohol is 21.

Newspapers and Magazines   Local daily newspapers include the *Annapolis Capital* and the *Anne Arundel County Sun.* The *Baltimore Sun* and the *Washington Post* are also widely available. The leading monthly magazine is *Annapolis.*

Photographic Needs   Convenient downtown shops are **A. L. Goodies' One-Hour Photo,** 112 Main St. (☎ 410/263-6919), and **Ritz Camera,** 138 Main St. (☎ 410/263-6050).

Police   Dial **911**.

Post Office   The main branch is at Church Circle and North West Street (☎ 410/263-9292).

Shoe Repair   Try **Royal Valet,** 32 West St. (☎ 410/268-2807).

Taxes   The local sales tax is 5%; the local hotel tax is an additional 7%.

Taxis   See "Getting Around," above.

Telegrams and Telex   Check at your hotel.

Transit Information   Call the **Annapolis Department of Public Transportation** (☎ 410/263-7964).

3 Accommodations

The main accommodation choices in Annapolis are concentrated in or near the downtown area. Consequently, most hotels and inns are within walking distance of the major attractions, shopping, and restaurants. Convenience is costly, however, and except for a few motels on the outskirts of town, it is hard to find a double-occupancy room in Annapolis under $100, and even more of a coup to find one under $75. To lessen the dent in your wallet, many properties offer packages at specially reduced rates; be sure to inquire if a package rate applies at the time you intend to visit.

Annapolis Accommodations & Dining

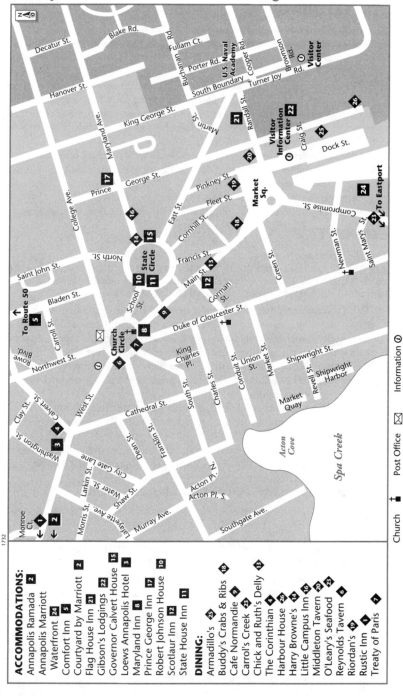

ACCOMMODATIONS:
Annapolis Ramada **2**
Annapolis Marriott
Waterfront **24**
Comfort Inn **5**
Courtyard by Marriott **2**
Flag House Inn **21**
Gibson's Lodgings **22**
Governor Calvert House **15**
Loews Annapolis Hotel **3**
Maryland Inn **8**
Prince George Inn **17**
Robert Johnson House **10**
Scotlaur Inn **12**
State House Inn **11**

DINING:
Armadillo's **25**
Buddy's Crabs & Ribs **18**
Cafe Normandie **9**
Carrol's Creek **23**
Chick and Ruth's Delly **13**
The Corinthian **4**
Harbour House **14**
Harry Browne's **16**
Little Campus Inn **20**
Middleton Tavern **23**
O'Leary's Seafood **6**
Reynolds Tavern **19**
Riordan's **1**
Rustic Inn **7**
Treaty of Paris

Church ⊠ Post Office ⊞ Information ⓘ

1732

VERY EXPENSIVE

Annapolis Marriott Waterfront

80 Compromise St., Annapolis, MD 21401. ☎ **410/268-7555** or 800/228-9290. Fax 410/
269-5864. 150 rms, 1 suite. A/C TV TEL. $120–$229 double; $450 suite. AE, CB, DC, DISC,
MC, V. Parking $10.

As the only waterfront hotel in Annapolis, this modern six-story property enjoys
an ideal location, beside the City Dock overlooking the Chesapeake Bay waterfront. Recently refurbished, the guest rooms are decorated in contemporary style,
enhanced by floor-to-ceiling windows. Most of the rooms have balconies facing the
harbor, and the rest overlook the historic district.

Dining/Entertainment: For meals or cocktails with a tropical island ambience,
try Pusser's Landing (see "Dining," later in this chapter), an indoor and outdoor
restaurant and lounge

Services: Room service, valet laundry service.

Facilities: Sundeck, 300-foot boardwalk, boat-docking slips, exercise room.

EXPENSIVE

✪ Loews Annapolis Hotel

126 West St., Annapolis, MD 21401. ☎ **410/263-7777** or 800/223-0888. Fax 410/
263-0084. 210 rms, 7 suites. A/C MINIBAR TV TEL. $95–$165 double; $200–$300 suite;
weekends $115–$155. AE, CB, DC, MC, V. Self-parking $7; valet parking $10.

With a handsome red-brick facade and a tree-shaded courtyard entrance, this modern six-story hotel sits within walking distance of Church Circle and the heart of
the historic district. Recently renovated, it has a spacious pastel-toned lobby and
skylit public areas including a unique conference center that was formerly the
Washington/Baltimore and Annapolis Power Substation. Guest rooms, furnished
in light woods, brass fixtures, quilted floral prints, and nautical art, offer views of
the city skyline and historic area.

Dining/Entertainment: The Corinthian Restaurant (see "Dining," later in
this chapter) offers full-service dining, and the Weather Rail Lounge serves light
food.

Services: Business center, notary public, valet laundry service, concierge, nightly
turndown, Federal Express drop-off in lobby, complimentary van transportation
within local area, child-care program.

Facilities: Fitness center, gift shop, hair salon, conference center.

MODERATE

Flag House Inn

26 Randall St., Annapolis, MD 21401. ☎ **410/280-2721** or 800/437-4825. 5 rms. A/C TV.
$85–$120 double. (Rates include full breakfast.) MC, V. Free parking.

With a gingerbread-trimmed front porch and colorful state and city flags flying
beneath a mansard roof, this lovely three-story Victorian house (ca. 1858) is nestled
on a quiet residential street between the City Dock and the main gate of the
naval academy. Inside, over the fireplace mantle, there is also a flag collection, with
flags from more than 40 states and 20 countries. The interior features Laura Ashley
prints and fabrics, antiques, and original paintings. Guest rooms have king-size
beds, period furnishings, handmade quilts, down pillows, and private baths in all
rooms. Innkeepers are Tom and Connie Tegen.

Gibson's Lodgings

110–114 Prince George St., Annapolis, MD 21401. ☎ **410/268-5555.** 18 rms, 2 suites. A/C TV TEL. $68–$85 with shared bath, $78–$98 with bath; $113–$125 suite with bath. (Rates include continental breakfast.) AE, MC, V. Free parking.

Operated by Claude and Jeanne Schrift, this three-building complex consists of two restored town houses and a modern three-story annex. The main building, the Patterson House (dating from 1760), is a Federal-Georgian house with a Victorian facade. It has five rooms, sharing three bathrooms, and two parlors where breakfast is served each morning. The adjacent Berman House, a tri-gable variation of a 19th-century stucco Homestead-style dwelling, has eight guest rooms with four adjoining baths and one room with private bath. The annex (or Lauer House), constructed in 1988 of brick to blend in with the older buildings, has two suites and four guest rooms, all with private bath, plus meeting and seminar rooms.

The bedrooms are furnished with antiques. A central garden and courtyard serves as a common ground for all three buildings, and there is plenty of off-street parking for guests. It's an ideal location if you want to be within walking distance of the harbor, the historic district, and the naval academy.

Wyndham Garden Hotel

173 Jennifer Rd., Annapolis, MD 21401. ☎ **410/266-3131** or 800/351-9209. Fax 410/266-6247. 190 rms, 7 suites. A/C TV TEL. $89–$139 double; $129–$209 suite. AE, CB, DC, MC, V. Free parking.

Totally renovated in 1995, this modern six-story brick-fronted hotel is located about 4 miles west of the historic district. Guest rooms are decorated in contemporary style. There is evening room service, valet laundry service, and a complimentary shuttle to the historic district. Facilities include a cafe, lounge, indoor/outdoor swimming pool, sauna, Jacuzzi, and gift shop.

MODERATE/INEXPENSIVE

Comfort Inn

76 Mill Bottom Rd. (Route 50/301, Exit 28), Annapolis, MD 21401. ☎ **410/757-8500** or 800/221-228-5150. Fax 410/757-1005. 60 rms. A/C TV TEL. $60–$100 double. AE, CB, DC, DISC, MC, V. Free parking.

A favorite lodging spot for families, this modern two-story motel is set back from the main road in a shady setting, conveniently located midway between downtown and the Bay Bridge. The guest rooms, accessible by computer-card keys, offer a choice of one king-size or two queen-size beds, with a decor of light woods and pastel fabrics; some units have pullout couches or whirlpool baths. On-site facilities include a (seasonal) outdoor pool.

⊛ Courtyard by Marriott

2559 Riva Rd., Annapolis, MD 21401. ☎ **410/266-1555** or 800/321-2211. Fax 410/266-6376. 149 rms. A/C TV TEL. $69–$99 double. AE, CB, DC, MC, V. Free parking.

Nestled in a quiet setting about 5 miles west of the historic district, this contemporary three-story facility is a favorite with business executives on weekdays and families on weekends. The rooms follow the usual Courtyard plan, with sliding glass windows and balconies or patios facing a central landscaped terrace. Guest units are spacious, with a separate sitting area, sofa, desk, and coffeemaking fixtures. Facilities include a restaurant, indoor swimming pool, whirlpool, and exercise room.

☉ Scotlaur Inn
165 Main St., Annapolis, MD 21401. ☎ **410/268-5665.** 10 rms. A/C TV TEL. $55–$75
double. (All rates include breakfast.) MC, V. Parking in adjacent public garage.

One of the best values in town is this inn, housed in a three-story brick building
in the heart of the historic district. The ground floor belongs to Chick and Ruth's
Delly, an Annapolis tradition for good food at reasonable prices. The eatery and
the inn are owned by the Levitt family, who are full of enthusiasm and offer a
warm welcome. The guest rooms are handsomely furnished in a turn-of-the-
century style, but require walking up one or two flights of stairs (no elevator).

FOUR HISTORIC INNS

Thanks to the efforts of a local preservationist and developer, Paul Pearson, five
of Annapolis's most historic buildings were purchased and saved from destruction
more than 20 years ago. With the guidance and encouragement of the nonprofit
group Historic Annapolis, Pearson has since turned the properties into four elegant
inns. Clustered around Annapolis's two key city circles, these landmark buildings
are now collectively known as the **Historic Inns of Annapolis.** To reserve a room
at any one of the locations, contact the central office of the Historic Inns of
Annapolis, 16 Church Circle (☎ 410/263-2641 or 800/847-8882).

Governor Calvert House
58 State Circle. ☎ **410/263-2641** or 800/847-8882. Fax 410/268-3813. 51 rms.
A/C TV TEL. $105–$195 double. AE, CB, DC, MC, V. Free parking.

Both a conference center and a hotel, this lodging is composed of several restored
and integrated Colonial and Victorian residences. Dating from 1727, one of the
public rooms, partially built on the site of the old Calvert family greenhouse,
contains an original hypocaust (a warm-air heating system), now covered with a
huge sheet of tempered glass and used as a museum display area. The bedrooms
are furnished with antiques. Facilities include underground parking and a sunny
ground-floor atrium.

Maryland Inn
16 Church Circle. ☎ **410/263-2641** or 800/847-8882. Fax 410/268-3813. 44 rms.
A/C TV TEL. $105–$195 double. AE, CB, DC, MC, V. Free parking.

Wedged into a busy triangular intersection, this impressive flatiron-shaped structure was built on "Drummer's Lot," so named because the town drummer
announced the daily news on this spot, and has been operating as an inn since the
1770s. It has been carefully restored and is now decorated in period furnishings
ranging from antique fireplaces, rush-seated chairs, lantern fixtures, and country
hunt prints to Queen Anne and Louis XIV pieces. Facilities include the Treaty of
Paris restaurant (see "Dining," later in this chapter) and a tavern.

Robert Johnson House
23 State Circle. ☎ **410/263-2641** or 800/847-8882. Fax 410/268-3813. 30 rms.
A/C TV TEL. $105–$195 double. AE, CB, DC, MC, V. Free parking.

Wedged between School and Francis streets and overlooking the governor's
mansion and the Maryland State House, this lodging consists of three adjoining
Georgian homes, dating from 1773. The artfully restored and furnished guest
rooms are individually decorated with four-poster beds and antiques; each unit also
has a private bath.

State House Inn

200 Main St. ☎ **410/263-2641** or 800/847-8882. Fax 410/268-3813. 9 rms. A/C TV TEL. $105–$195 double. AE, CB, DC, MC, V. Free parking.

Located between School and Francis streets off State Circle, this bed-and-breakfast inn occupies an 1820 four-story, mansard-roof building and offers nine rooms furnished with antiques. The Hampton House restaurant occupies the main floor, although it is operated by a separate management.

4 Dining

Annapolis is well known for its excellent restaurants, from Colonial dining rooms and taverns to romantic bistros and waterside seafood houses. Many choice dining spots are also located in the city's hotels and restored inns. In addition, for families and travelers on the go, Annapolis is home to a Restaurant Park, a fast-food and family style complex of eateries located at the intersection of Routes 50, 301, and 450, about 4 miles from downtown, opposite the Annapolis Shopping Plaza.

EXPENSIVE

The Corinthian

126 West St. ☎ **410/263-1299.** Reservations required. Main courses $16.95–$23.95; lunch $3.95–$14.95. AE, CB, DC, MC, V. Daily 11am–2pm and 5–10pm. INTERNATIONAL.

The main dining room of the Loews hotel, this restaurant draws people to Annapolis in its own right. The bright and airy decor is highlighted by floor-to-ceiling windows, indirect lighting, fish and waterfowl art, and a colorful assortment of plants and dried flowers.

The menu features a creative blend of ingredients in such dishes as lemon-baked crab cakes with angel-hair pasta; sautéed saffron and pistachio shrimp; pan-seared blue corn-breaded salmon; grilled rack of wild boar with blueberry puree; grilled vegetables with linguine; and various cuts of dry-aged steaks and prime rib. Four-course fixed-price dinners offer particularly good value (available Sunday through Friday).

Harry Browne's

66 State Circle. ☎ **410/263-4332.** Reservations recommended for dinner. Main courses $15.95–$21.95; lunch $5.95–$13.95. MC, V. Mon–Thurs 11am–3pm and 5:30–10pm, Fri–Sat 11am–3pm and 5:30–11pm; Sun 10am–3pm and 3:30–9pm. INTERNATIONAL.

A favorite haunt of legislators, this midtown eatery exudes an old-Maryland ambience, with nautical chandeliers, globe lights, and large framed mirrors. For a change of pace, there is also an Art Deco cocktail lounge upstairs and an outdoor brick-floored courtyard cafe. Entrées at dinner range from blackened swordfish, crab cakes, and grilled salmon to seared duck in cherry and port sauce, rack of lamb, and a variety of steaks. Lunch includes an interesting array of salads, quiches, croissant sandwiches, pizzas, and burgers.

Middleton Tavern

2 Market Space and Randall St. ☎ **410/263-3323.** Reservations not accepted. Main courses $11.95–$33.95; lunch $4.95–$9.95. DISC, MC, V. Mon–Thurs 11am–4pm and 5–10pm; Fri 11am–4pm and 5–11pm, Sat 10am–4pm and 5–11pm, Sun 10am–2pm and 5–10pm. AMERICAN.

Established in 1750 by Horatio Middleton as an inn for seafaring men, this restaurant had many prominent patrons, including George Washington, Thomas Jefferson, and Benjamin Franklin. Today, restored and expanded, this City Dock landmark offers dinner entrées such as crab cakes; char-grilled swordfish; lobster Luicci (lightly breaded lobster tails broiled in herbs and butter); filet of sole stuffed with crab, spinach, and mushrooms; as well as T-bone steaks, pizzas, pastas, fajitas, and chateaubriand for two. The lunch menu includes chili and fish and chips.

Treaty of Paris

16 Church Circle. ☎ **410/263-2641.** Reservations required for dinner. Main courses $16.95–$34.95; lunch $5.95–$11.95. AE, CB, DC, MC, V. Daily 11:30am–3pm and 6–9:30pm. AMERICAN.

Centrally located in the Maryland Inn, this cozy dining room exudes an 18th-century ambience with a decor of brick walls, Colonial-style furnishings, and an open fireplace, all enhanced by the glow of candlelight. The eclectic menu offers such dishes as sautéed rockfish, veal sweetbreads, smoked breast of duck, crab imperial, veal Oscar, blackened steaks, and beef Wellington.

MODERATE

Café Normandie

185 Main St. ☎ **410/263-3382.** Reservations recommended for dinner. Breakfast items $1–$8.95; main courses $13.95–$20.95; lunch $4.95–$9.95. AE, MC, V. Mon–Thurs 8am–10pm, Fri–Sat 8am–10:30pm. FRENCH.

This simple shopfront location is the next best thing to an authentic French country restaurant in the heart of Annapolis's historic district. It serves meals throughout the day, but it is especially worth a visit for dinner. Specialties include home-style and regional dishes such as shrimp Provençale, trout amandine, beef Bourguignon, duck with raspberry sauce, bouillabaisse, and an assortment of crepes. On many evenings, there are early bird specials from 5 to 6:30pm; check in advance.

Carrol's Creek

410 Severn Ave. ☎ **410/263-8102.** Reservations accepted only for indoor weekday lunches and dinners; priority seating on weekends. Main courses $12.95–$22.95; lunch $4.95–$9.95. AE, DC, DISC, MC, V. Mon–Sat 11:30am–10pm, Sun 10am–10pm. AMERICAN.

Sitting on the harbor in the Eastport section of the city, this festive red-trimmed restaurant offers some of the best views of the water and the Annapolis skyline. Seating is available indoors in a wide-windowed setting or on an umbrella-shaded outdoor porch. The menu features such creative choices such as Mediterranean flounder, baked on wilted spinach and topped with tomatoes, onions, black olives, and herbs; shrimp and scallops Tequila, with mixed peppers and garnished with jalapeño cornbread; southwestern blackened prime rib; and pastas such as wild mushrooms with sun-dried tomato linguine.

✪ Harbour House

87 Prince George St. ☎ **410/268-0771.** Reservations recommended for dinner. Main courses $12.95–$19.95; lunch $5.95–$8.95. AE, CB, DC, MC, V. Mon–Fri 11:30am–2:30pm and 5–10pm, Sat–Sun 11:30am–10pm. SEAFOOD.

The place to go for maritime views while you dine is this nautical-style restaurant overlooking the City Dock. Seafood dishes like crab quiche, salmon strudel, and seafood pie dominate the lunch menu, which also includes sandwiches and burgers. Soups, such as cream of crab with sherry or crab vegetable, are popular any time of the day. Dinner entrées include a host of crab creations and local fish specials, as well as steaks, prime rib, and pastas. In the summer months, meals are also served on an outside terrace.

Maria's
12 Market Space, City Dock. ☎ **410/268-2122.** Reservations recommended for dinner. Main courses $10.95–$20.95, lunch $4.95–$13.95. AE, MC, V. Mon–Thurs 11am–2:30pm and 4–10pm, Fri–Sat 11am–2:30pm and 4–11pm, Sun 11am–2:30pm and 4:30–10pm. SICILIAN.

Operated by Mama Maria and Pietro Priola, this restaurant is known for its authentic Italian cuisine. There is seating downstairs and upstairs, with the upper rooms providing a slightly more formal setting overlooking the dock area. Specialties of the house include home-baked stuffed pasta, deep-dish Sicilian pizzas, and standard thin-crust pizzas, as well as veal salitimbocca, chicken cacciatore, and a variety of traditional beef and seafood choices. Lunch offers part-portions of dinner items or a selection of sandwiches, subs, salads, and burgers.

✪ O'Leary's Seafood
310 3rd St. ☎ **410/263-0884.** Reservations not accepted. Main courses $10.95–$21.95. DC, MC, V. Mon–Thurs 5:30–10pm, Fri–Sat 5–11pm, Sun 5–10pm. SEAFOOD.

Located in the Eastport section of Annapolis, just over the Spa Creek Bridge, this spot has been synonymous with fine seafood for almost half a century. It is close to the water, but its paned windows really offer no sea views. The modern decor includes a timbered ceiling, light woods, potted palms, and table accessories made by the local pottery. The menu emphasizes fresh seafood, with each day's selections always posted on the blackboard. Each dish is prepared to order, either mesquite grilled, sautéed, poached, baked, or blackened. In addition, there is usually blackened gulf shrimp served with cucumber and sour cream sauce; mussels marinara; lump crabmeat baked in a cognac cream sauce with almonds; and backfin crab cakes. For meat-eaters, there is mesquite-grilled strip steak and chicken au poivre or chicken marinated in raspberry vinaigrette and topped with raspberry butter.

Pusser's Landing
80 Compromise St. ☎ **410/626-0004** or 410/268-7555. Reservations recommended for dinner. Main courses $8.95–$23.95; lunch $5.95–$13.95. AE, DC, DISC, MC, V. Daily 7am–11pm. BRITISH/WEST INDIAN.

With a Virgin Islands decor and nautical ambience, this restaurant is named after British Navy Pusser's Rum, a blend of five West Indian rums. Patrons of this restaurant today can taste the brew in a variety of cocktails while dining outdoors along the waterfront or in an indoor fireside setting. The menu offers West Indies dishes with a British influence, such as Pusser's Chicken Roti, the islands' equivalent of a burrito, with chicken, potato and onion stewed in a light curry sauce and wrapped in a shell of soft pastry; charcoal-grilled Jamaican jerk beef; as well as traditional shepherd's pie, fish and chips, and Cumberland sausage on a bed of mashed potatoes. Steaks and fresh seafood are also available. Lunch offers hot and cold sandwiches and build-your-own burger combinations.

Reynolds Tavern
7 Church Circle (at Franklin St.). ☎ **410/626-0380.** Reservations recommended for dinner. Main courses $12.95–$24.95; lunch $5.95–$7.95. AE, MC, V. Mon–Thurs 11:30am–2pm and 6–9pm, Fri 11:30am–2pm and 6–10pm, Sat 6–10pm, Sun 5:30–8:30pm. AMERICAN.

Tucked on the edge of the historic area, this restaurant is housed in one of the city's most historic sites. Built by William Reynolds in 1747, it first served as a hat business, then a tavern called the "The Beaver and Lac'd Hat," later a boarding-house, and finally it became a public library. Since restored, it still exudes a Co-lonial charm, with period furniture, stenciled walls, and lantern lights. In warm weather, there is also outdoor seating on a brick-walled courtyard terrace sheltered by boughs of 100-year-old magnolias and great Persian walnut trees and enhanced by the aromas of an adjacent herb garden.

The signature dish is the house-smoked "Reynolds Seafood Trio," a combina-tion platter of crabcake and two other seafood items, according to season. Otherwise the menu changes seasonally, but often includes choices such as shrimps en croûte, blackened tuna, or rack of lamb with mint-sage sauce.

⑤ Riordan's

26 Market Space. ☎ **410/263-5449.** Reservations recommended for dinner. Main courses $11.95–$19.95; lunch $5.95–$8.95. AE, DC, DISC, MC, V. Mon–Thurs 11am–2pm and 6–11pm, Fri–Sat 11am–2pm and 6pm–midnight; Sun 10am–1pm and 6–11pm. AMERICAN.

An Irish ambience prevails at this Early American tavern, as evidenced by an illuminated shamrock at the entrance and an Irish flag on the ceiling. The eclec-tic decor also includes Tiffany lamps, ceiling fans, vintage pictures and posters, and colorful stained glass. Light choices (overstuffed sandwiches, burgers, pastas, and salads) are available throughout the day. The regular dinner menu includes crab-stuffed flounder, prime rib, steamed shrimp, grilled marinated chicken, and steaks.

Rustic Inn

1803 West St. ☎ **410/263-2626.** Reservations recommended on weekends. Main courses $10.95–$21.95. AE, MC, V. Mon–Thurs 5–10pm, Fri–Sat 5–11pm, Sun 3–8pm. INTERNATIONAL.

With a suitably rustic decor, this restaurant is known for its fresh seafood, Iowa choice beef, and Provimi milk-fed veal. Entrées include scallops champignon (baked in Marsala wine with fresh mushrooms and grated Cheddar), lobster tails, crab imperial, veal (marsala, piccata, or francese), chicken Divan, and steak beéarnaise. It is located about 2 miles west of downtown at Admiral Drive.

MODERATE/INEXPENSIVE

Armadillo's

132 City Dock. ☎ **410/268-6680.** Reservations not accepted. Main courses $9.95–$16.95; lunch $4.95–$10.95. AE, MC, V. Mon–Sat 11am–11pm, Sun 11am–10pm. MEXICAN.

With a decor of Native American art and pottery, this busy two-story restaurant adds a south-of-the-border ambience to the waterfront area. The menu offers tacos, burritos, enchiladas, empanadas, tostadas, and chimichangas, as well as burgers, steaks, and seafood platters. For dessert, try the bananas sautéed with brandy and brown-sugar sauce. On Sunday afternoons, brunch is accompanied by live jazz music.

⑤ Buddy's Crabs & Ribs

100 Main St. ☎ **410/626-1100.** Reservations not accepted. Main courses $8.95–$16.95; fast-food items $3.95–$7.95; lunch buffet $5.95. AE, CB, DC, DISC, MC, V. Mon–Sat 11am–11pm, Sun 8:30am–10pm. AMERICAN.

Housed in a converted old building with a decor that includes an original tin ceil-ing, lots of leafy plants, big-screen TVs, and ceiling fans, this busy and casual restaurant is on the second floor overlooking the City Dock and Main Street. As the name implies, crabs are an important part of the menu, with all-you-can-eat steamed blue crab specials, as well as crab cakes and soft-shell crabs. Other favorites include barbecued baby-back ribs, fried shrimp, flounder amandine, and a variety of steaks, chicken dishes, sandwiches, burgers, and salads. The same menu is used at lunchtime, when a buffet is also available.

Griffin's

22–24 Market Space, City Dock. ☎ **410/268-2576.** Reservations accepted Mon–Thurs only. Dinner main courses $8.95–$19.95, lunch $4.95–$7.95. AE, DC, DISC, MC, V. Daily 11am–2am. AMERICAN.

Service is swift and attentive at this busy restaurant, almost in keeping with the rhythm of the rock music that blares in the background. It has a long turn-of-the-century-style bar, specializing in microbrews, and two dining areas with high vaulted ceilings, exposed brick walls, tile and marble flooring, mounted animal heads, and a unique collection of framed feathered masks, all surrounding several dozen small and tightly packed tables. Specialty dishes include Tuna Randell, a filet coated with Cajun spices and grilled with bell peppers; filet mignon Munoz, charcoal grilled with house port wine sauce; Charleston Porterhouse pork chops, marinated in juniper berries, peppercorns, and grilled; and Griffin's Penne Pasta, with chicken, broccoli, and sun-dried tomatoes.

⑤ Little Campus Inn

61-63 Maryland Ave. ☎ **410/263-9250.** Reservations recommended for dinner. Main courses $7.95–$15.95; lunch $3.95–$7.95. AE, MC, V. Mon–Sat 11am–3pm and 5–10:30pm. AMERICAN.

Conveniently situated, this midtown restaurant has been a favorite since 1923. The second generation of the Nichols family now runs the homey eatery, known for its hearty home-style food and decor of original brick, dark woods, and murals of early Annapolis. Lunch includes fried chicken, omelets, and breaded veal steak. Dinner selections include beef or lamb shish kebab; spaghetti with meatballs; chicken Kiev; baked, smoked, or fresh ham; shrimp and oyster gumbo; and seafood samplers (crab, lobster, scallops, shrimp, crab claw, fish filet, and clams casino).

Ram's Head Tavern

33 West St. ☎ **410/268-4545.** Reservations recommended for dinner. Main courses $5.95–$16.95, lunch $5.95–$10.95. Open daily 11am–11pm or later. AE, MC, V. INTERNATIONAL.

This informal shopfront pub/restaurant prides itself on serving more than 170 different beers from around the world. At press time, it is expanding into the adjacent house to allow for a new addition on the premises—the Fordham Brewing Company, billed as Annapolis's first microbrewery in 300 years. As a restaurant, it offers several different settings, ranging from cozy little rooms with brick walls and working fireplaces to an outdoor patio. The menu is the same all day, offering an assortment of local favorites like crab cakes, as well as barbecued ribs, London Broil, ale-marinated chicken, shepherd's pie, stir-fry dishes, salads, pastas, and curries.

INEXPENSIVE

All the Right Stuff

164 Main St. ☎ **410/626-0093.** All items $1.95–$6.95. No credit cards. Daily 7am–11pm. AMERICAN.

For a healthy lunch or snack, try this bright and airy spot in the heart of the historic district. Billing itself as a "fresh food cafe," it offers a variety of vegetable and fruit salads, soups, and veggie chilis, as well as quiches, stuffed potatoes, pizzas, and meatless entrées such as vegetable lasagne, spanikopita, gardenburger, and hot veggie casserole. There's also a sprinkling of tuna, chicken, and turkey dishes.

⊜ Chick and Ruth's Delly

165 Main St. ☎ **410/269-6737.** Main courses and lunch $2.95–$7.95. No credit cards. Daily 24 hours. AMERICAN.

To sample an Annapolis tradition, stop in at this ma-and-pa establishment that has been run by the Levitt family for more than 25 years. This small storefront deli/restaurant is famous for sandwiches named after either world political figures or local attractions, such as the Paris Glendenning (baked potato stuffed with broccoli and cheese), the Barbara Mikulski (open-face tuna with melted cheese on a bagel), Kathleen Kennedy Townsend (kosher hot dog, raw onion, and relish), and Main Street (corned beef and coleslaw). Platters, pizzas, and salads are also available.

Market House

City Dock. ☎ **410/269-0941.** All items $2–$8. No credit cards. May–Oct Mon–Thurs 9am–6pm, Fri–Sun 9am–7pm; Nov–Apr Mon and Wed–Sun 9am–6pm and Tues 9am–3pm. DELI/FAST FOOD.

Originally a central farmers' produce station built in 1784 and rebuilt in 1858, it still retains much of the flavor of a marketplace with open stalls and a variety of foods, although the wares now fall mostly into the fast-food category. Stroll around and order your pick of raw bar items, sandwiches, deli food, pizza, desserts, cheeses, salad bar, breads and pastries, espresso, and more. It's the ideal spot for a quick meal, to browse, or to stock up for a picnic.

5 Attractions

The entire midcity area of Annapolis is a National Historic District, with more than 1,500 restored and preserved buildings. Since the streets are narrow, the ideal way to see the sights is on foot. Several guided walking tours are described below; self-guided walking tour maps are also available free of charge from the various tourist offices.

Plan to spend some time around the City Dock along the Annapolis waterfront. This is a yachting hub, with hundreds of craft of all sizes in port. Various sightseeing cruises of the harbor are available in spring, summer, and fall. The City Dock is also home to fine seafood restaurants, lively bars, specialty shops, galleries, and a summer theater.

Banneker-Douglass Museum

84 Franklin St. ☎ **410/974-2893.** Admission free. Tues–Fri 10am–3pm, Sat noon–4pm.

Named after two prominent local black residents, Benjamin Banneker and Frederick Douglass, this museum presents arts and crafts, exhibits, lectures, and films, all designed to portray the historical life and cultural experiences of African Americans in Maryland. The site was formerly the Old Mount Moriah African Methodist Episcopal Church.

Charles Carroll House

107 Duke of Gloucester St. ☎ **410/263-1737.** Admission $4 adults, $3.50 seniors, $2 students aged 12–17; free for children under 12. Fri noon–4pm, Sat 10am–2pm, Sun noon–4pm.

Annapolis Attractions

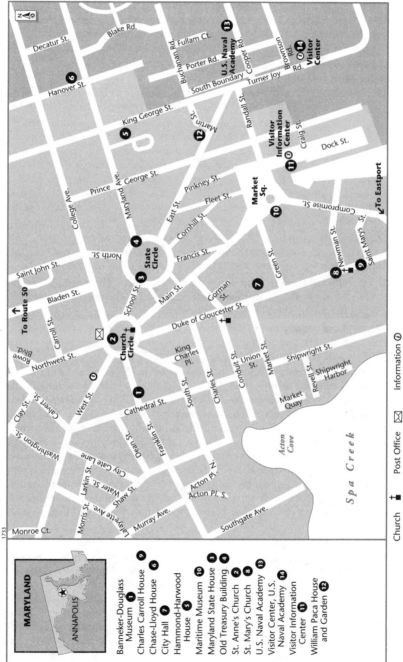

Banneker-Douglass Museum **1**
Charles Carroll House **9**
Chase-Lloyd House **6**
City Hall **7**
Hammond-Harwood House **5**
Maritime Museum **10**
Maryland State House **3**
Old Treasury Building **4**
St. Anne's Church **2**
St. Mary's Church **8**
U.S. Naval Academy **13**
Visitor Center, U.S. Naval Academy **14**
Visitor Information Center **11**
William Paca House and Garden **12**

Church ✝   Post Office ⊠   Information ⊙

Built in 1721 and 1722 and enlarged in 1770, this is the birthplace and dwelling of Charles Carroll of Carrollton, the only Roman Catholic to sign the Declaration of Independence. It sits on high ground overlooking Spa Creek, a block from the town dock. Visitors can tour the house plus the 18th-century terraced boxwood gardens and a 19th-century wine cellar.

Hammond-Harwood House

19 Maryland Ave. ☎ **410/269-1714.** Admission $4 adults, $3 children 6–18. Mon–Sat 10am–4pm, Sun noon–4pm. Closed New Year's Day, Thanksgiving Day, and Christmas Day.

Built in 1774, this house is one of the finest examples of Georgian architecture in the United States. It is also an outstanding example of the Maryland five-part plan that connects the central section by hyphens to semioctagonal wings. Famous for its center doorway of tall Ionic columns, the interior is a showcase of decorative arts and paintings as well as ornamentation and wood carvings. The house is named for its first and last owners: Mathias Hammond, a Maryland member of the Provincial Assembly, and the Harwood family, who owned the house before it became a museum.

Maritime Museum

77-79 Main St. ☎ **410/268-5576.** Admission free. Wed–Mon 9am–5pm, Tues 9am–3pm. Closed Thanksgiving Day and Christmas Day.

This historical trioramma is housed in the old Victualling Warehouse. The exhibit will give you an idea of what the waterfront looked like between 1751 and 1791, when the port of Annapolis was in its heyday.

✪ Maryland State House

State Circle. ☎ **410/269-3400.** Admission free. Daily 9am–5pm. Closed Thanksgiving Day, Christmas Day, and New Year's Day.

Located in the center of Annapolis, this is the oldest U.S. state capitol in continuous legislative use (built between 1772 and 1779). The building also served as the U.S. capital from November 26, 1783, to August 13, 1784. As you step inside the Old Senate Chamber, you'll be in the historic spot where George Washington resigned his commission as commander-in-chief of the Continental armies. This was also the setting for the ratification of the *Treaty of Paris,* which ended the Revolutionary War. The dome of this building, the largest of its kind constructed entirely of wood, is made of cypress beams and is held together by wooden pegs. You can stroll throughout the State House on your own, examining the various exhibits that depict life in Annapolis in Colonial times, or you can make use of the free guided tours that depart at 11am and 3pm from the Visitors Center on the first floor.

✪ U.S. Naval Academy

King George and Randall sts. ☎ **410/263-6933.** Admission free to grounds; visitor center (including walking tour) $5 adults, $4 seniors, $3 students. Mar–Nov daily 9am–5pm, Dec–Feb daily 9am–4pm. Closed New Year's Day, Thanksgiving Day, Christmas Day.

Founded in 1845, this national historic site is synonymous with Annapolis. It is the U.S. Navy's undergraduate professional college, spread over 338 acres along the Chesapeake Bay and Severn River on the eastern edge of town. To acclimate yourself, step into the new Armel-Leftwich Visitor Center at the Halsey Field House, a building just inside Gate 1. Here you can view a 12-minute orientation film and browse among the exhibits on the life of midshipmen. Among the attractions to see are the chapel and crypt of John Paul Jones and the U.S.

Naval Academy Museum in Preble Hall. It contains fascinating collections of nautical relics, paintings, ship models, and other historic items.

Commissioning Week, usually surrounding the last Wednesday in May, is a colorful time of full-dress parades; it is also a busy period for Annapolis hotels, as relatives and friends of the midshipmen pour into the city. Guided walking tours are available, departing daily from the Visitor Center (see "Organized Tours," later in this chapter).

✪ William Paca House and Garden

186 Prince George St. ☎ **410/263-5533.** Admission to tour house, $4 adults, $2 children 6–18; to tour garden, $3 adults, $1.50 youngsters 6–18. Mar–Dec, Mon–Sat 10am–4pm, Sun and holidays noon–4pm; Jan–Feb, Fri–Sat only, 10am–4pm.

Among the great historic residences in Annapolis is this former home of William Paca, a signer of the Declaration of Independence and a governor of Maryland during the Revolutionary period. Built between 1763 and 1765 and restored by Historic Annapolis from 1965 to 1976, it is a five-part structure, with a stalwart central block, hyphens and wings, and a total of 37 rooms. Guided tours of the house are available.

Another attraction of the Paca estate is the adjacent two-acre pleasure garden. The layout includes five elegant terraces, a fish-shaped pond, a Chinese Chippendale bridge, a summer house, and a wilderness garden. Combination packages, covering both the house and the garden, are $6 for adults and $3 for youngsters 6 to 18.

6 Organized Tours & Cruises

WALKING TOURS

To see all that is best about Annapolis, plan to take a **"Historic Annapolis Walk with Walter Cronkite,"** a self-guided audiocassette walking tour narrated by the famous TV news broadcaster. The Historic Annapolis Foundation is the sponsor of this comprehensive walking tour, which takes in 19 historic and architectural sites with a 45-minute commentary that can be completed at a leisurely pace in 1¹/₂ hours. It is available only at the Maritime Museum, 77 Main St. (☎ 410/ 268-5576), daily from 10am to 4pm. Cost per rental is $7.

Three Centuries Tours of Annapolis, 48 Maryland Ave. (☎ 410/263-5401), is known for its well-informed guides in Colonial costume. These tours, which provide the highlights of the historic district, the naval academy, and admission to the William Paca Garden, are two hours in length and are operated on a turn-up-and-go basis, with no reservations required.

Tours are operated daily, year-round, except for Christmas and New Year's Day, at 10:30am, departing from the Visitor Center at 26 West St. In addition, from April through October, there are two extra daily departures at 9:30am from the Annapolis Marriott lobby, and at 1:30pm from the City Dock Information booth. From November through March, there is an afternoon tour on Saturday only, at 2:30pm, departing from Gibson's Lodgings. The price is $7 for adults and $3 for students. Three Centuries Tours also offers preplanned and tailor-made tours by reservation, focusing on such topics as Colonial life (for young visitors), historic mansions, and bay cruises.

The **U.S. Naval Academy Walking Tours** depart from the Armel-Leftwich Visitor Center of the U.S. Naval Academy, Gate 1, King George and

Randall streets (☎ 410/267-3363), every day of the year except New Year's, Thanksgiving, and Christmas. From June through Labor Day, tours depart every half-hour on Monday through Saturday from 9:30am to 3:30pm and on Sunday from 12:30pm to 3:30pm; from September through November and March through Memorial Day, tours are hourly Monday through Friday from 10am to 3pm, and every half-hour on Saturday from 10am to 3:30pm and Sunday from 12:30pm to 3:30pm; and from December through February tours are Monday through Saturday at 11am and 1pm and on Sunday at 12:30pm and 2:30pm. The price is $5 for adults, $4 for seniors, and $3 for students.

The Annapolis Gardening School (☎ 410/263-6041) conducts **Gardens of Annapolis Guided Tours** every Saturday at 10am, Memorial Day weekend through Labor Day weekend. Tours depart from the Visitor Center at 26 West St.; cost is $6 for adults and $3 for children under 12.

CRUISES & BOATING TOURS

To see the sights of Annapolis from the water, **Chesapeake Marine Tours,** Slip 20, City Dock (☎ 410/268-7600), operates a variety of cruises along Annapolis Harbor and beyond. Choices include *The Harbor Queen,* a 297-passenger double-deck vessel offering a 40-minute narrated cruise that covers the highlights of Annapolis Harbor, U.S. Naval Academy, and Severn River; *Little Miss Anne I* and *II,* 24-passenger covered one-deck launches that provide 40-minute narrated tours focusing on the historic Annapolis harbor and residential waterfront along Spa Creek; *Providence,* a 140-passenger double-deck boat that offers 90-minute narrated trips, as well as luncheon cruises, around Annapolis Harbor, along the U.S. Naval Academy grounds, and through the Severn River; and *Annapolitan II,* a 102-passenger double-deck boat that provides a full-day cruise on the bay (7 1/2 hours), departing from Annapolis and cruising to St. Michaels, a historic fishing port on the Eastern Shore. Advance reservations are advised for this trip. In addition, a variety of "adventure cruises" are operated aboard the 48-passenger *Rebecca* ranging from eco-tours and bird-watching trips to cruising through nearby creeks to lighthouses or the Bay Bridge. Tours range from $6 to $35 for adults and $4 to $25 for children 11 and under. Sailings are daily from Memorial Day through Labor Day, with abbreviated schedules in the spring and fall.

7 Outdoor Activities

With the Chesapeake Bay and Severn River at its doorstep, Annapolis is considered the pleasure-boating capital of the eastern United States. The city offers many opportunities to enjoy sailing and water sports, as well as other outdoor activities.

BICYCLING   With its narrow streets, historic circles, and scenic dock frontage, Annapolis lends itself to touring by bicycle. You can rent a bike from Downtown Cycle, 6 Dock St. (☎ 410/267-7681), located on the City Dock behind the visitor information center. It's open Monday through Saturday from 10am to 7pm and on Sunday from noon to 5pm; rates start at $5 per hour or $21 per day.

A good place to bike is the Baltimore-Annapolis Trail (☎ 410/222-6244), a smooth 13.3-mile-long asphalt route that runs from Annapolis into the suburbs. Formerly a rail corridor, it's considered a "community sidewalk" by the locals and is ideal for biking, walking, jogging, roller-blading, or just meandering. It begins at Ritchie Highway, just outside of Annapolis at the Route 50 interchange and ends on Dorsey Road between Routes 648 and 3 at Glen Burnie. It's open daily from 7am to dusk.

SAILING SCHOOLS & SAILING TRIPS   Learn to sail at the oldest and largest sailing school in America: the **Annapolis Sailing School,** 601 Sixth St., P.O. Box 3334, Annapolis, MD 21403 (☎ 410/267-7205 or 800/638-9192). With more than 120 boats and a huge support staff, this facility offers a wide range of instructional programs for novice and veteran sailors. Courses range from a two-hour "sailing sample" from $25 per person to a weekend beginner's course for $225; or a five-day advanced course for bareboat (skipperless) charters, from $650 and up.

   Womanship, 410 Severn Ave., Annapolis, MD 21403 (☎ 410/267-6661), is a sailing program designed for women by women. Instruction is geared to all levels, from novice to advanced, in either daytime or liveaboard settings. Course duration ranges from two to seven days, priced from $298 to $1,050. There are also courses for mothers and daughters, families, and youth (ages 10 to 17).

   If you prefer to sit back and let a captain and crew take you out for a sailboat ride, you can board the 36-foot sloop *Beginagain,* 1056 Eaglewood Rd., Annapolis (☎ 410/626-1422) at the City Dock. Operating from May through September, this vessel offers three-hour trips, departing daily at 9am, 1pm, and 6pm (May through July) or 5pm (August and September). Cost is $40 per passenger.

   The 74-foot classic wooden yacht *Schooner Woodwind*, 301 Fourth St., Annapolis (☎ 410/267-6333), departs from the Marriott Hotel side of the City Dock, offering two-hour sailing trips. Departures are at 11am, 1:30pm, 4pm, and 6:30pm on Tuesday through Sunday and on Monday at 6:30pm during May through September; and at noon and 3pm Tuesday through Sunday in April, October, and November. Cost is $22 to $25 for adults and $12 to $15 for children under age 12. Overnight windjammer cruises are also available, as are "boat and breakfast" overnight accommodations on board the vessel.

WATER-SPORT RENTALS   To rent a sailboat, contact **Boat Rentals,** Pier 7, Edgewater (☎ 410/956-2288), located south of Annapolis. Rates are $20 to $30 an hour or $120 to $144 a day. You can also rent ski boats from $30 per hour. For speedboats, contact **Suntime Boat Rentals,** 2822 Solomons Island Rd., Rte. 2, Edgewater (☎ 410/266-6020). This company rents 17^1/$_2$-foot boats with 90- to 115-horsepower engines from $56 to $65 an hour or $325 to $375 per day; 19-foot boats with 195-horsepower engines from $75 an hour or $435 a day. Wave-runners are also available from $50 a half-hour or $70 per hour.

8 Shopping

Annapolis is a good shopping and browsing town. The historic district is lined with boutiques and shops of international and local appeal.

ANTIQUES

Walnut Leaf Antiques
62 Maryland Ave. ☎ **410/263-4885.**

   This shop specializes in period and oak furniture, European and Oriental porcelain, cut glass, vintage costume jewelry, nautical and optical antiques, and 20th-century collectibles. Open daily from noon to 5pm.

ART

Annapolis Marine Art Gallery
110 Dock St. ☎ **410/263-4100.**

Overlooking the City Dock, this gallery is devoted to marine and seabird art by living artists. It offers original paintings, graphics, ship models, scrimshaw, and sculptures. Open Monday to Thursday from 10am to 6pm, Friday to Saturday from 10am to 9pm, Sunday from noon to 6pm.

Gallery on the Circle
18 State Circle. ☎ **410/268-4566.**

The Maryland Federation of Art, a member's nonprofit cooperative organization, operates this gallery, showing traditional and contemporary original art in all media. It is housed in a historic 1840s building with brick walls and beamed ceilings, between School and Francis streets. Open Tuesday through Sunday from 11am to 5pm.

League of Maryland Craftsmen
54 Annapolis Ave. ☎ **410/626-1277.**

This gallery displays and sells the work of more than 60 Maryland artists, including paintings in oil, watercolor, and acrylic, as well as etchings, drawings, photographs, sculpture, and wood carvings. There are also works in fiber-silk, stained glass, porcelain, and pottery. Open daily 10am to 6pm.

Main Street Gallery
109 Main St. ☎ **410/280-2787.**

Situated near the City Dock, this is a cooperative effort by more than 50 Maryland artists who have pooled their energy, resources, and talents to create an innovative exhibition space and retail gallery. Open Sunday to Monday and Wednesday to Thursday from 10am to 6pm, Friday to Saturday from 10am to 8pm.

Whitehall Gallery
57 West St. ☎ **410/269-6161.**

This gallery specializes in antique prints and maps, nautical and duck art, Annapolis waterfront scenes, and prints of herbs and flowers. Open weekdays from 9am to 5pm, Saturday from 11am to 4pm.

BOOKS

Briarwood Bookshop
88 Maryland Ave. ☎ **410/268-1440.**

This shop specializes in bargain books, both new and used, including Maryland-related and naval history volumes. There is also a good selection of old prints. Open daily from 10 or 10:30am to 6 or 7pm.

CLOTHING

✪ Avoca Handweavers
141-143 Main St. ☎ **410/263-1485.**

This is the American branch of the Irish company founded in 1723. Soft and colorful Irish tweeds are the specialty here, with a wide selection of capes, coats, caps, suits, shawls, and sweaters, as well as Irish books, jewelry, glassware, and pottery.

Open daily in July and August from 10am to 8pm, and in September through June from 10am to 6pm.

CRAFTS & COLLECTIBLES

Annapolis Country Store
53 Maryland Ave. ☎ **410/269-6773.**

Claiming to be the oldest and largest wicker shop in Maryland, this shop also stocks pottery, mugs, candles, cards, jams, and kitchen accessories. Open Monday to Saturday from 10am to 6pm, Sunday from noon to 5pm.

✪ Annapolis Pottery
40 State Circle. ☎ **410/268-6153.**

As its name implies, this is a real working pottery as well as a shop. Potters work at the wheel almost every day and visitors are invited to watch and ask questions. The handmade items include vases, dishes, and plates, as well as one-of-a-kind pieces. Many pieces can be personalized with names or logos on request. Open Monday to Saturday from 10am to 6pm, Sunday from noon to 5pm.

Captain's Corner
126 West St. ☎ **410/280-2199.**

Although it is located off the lobby of the Loews Annapolis Hotel, this little enclave is far from the usual hotel sundry shop. It is a retail outlet for Providence Center, an organization that assists adults with developmental disabilities by giving them an opportunity to sell their handmade wares to the public. The products range from stuffed animals, toys, and doll furniture and clothes, to woodwork, needlepoint, knitwear, pottery, jewelry, mugs, wall hangings, note cards, wreaths, and crab-motif souvenirs. Open daily from 9am to 6pm.

The Nature Company
134 Main St. ☎ **410/268-3909.**

A branch of the environmentally conscious enterprise that began in California, this shop specializes in arts and crafts of indigenous peoples, as well as products developed to support the sustainable use of natural resources. The items on sale include rain forest shampoos and aloe moisture soaps; audiocassettes of environmental sounds; books on the environment; Native American arts and crafts; Earth Day symbols and recycled paper products. Open Sunday through Thursday from 10am to 6pm, Friday and Saturday from 10am to 7pm.

GIFTS & SOUVENIRS

Christmas Spirit
180 Main St. ☎ **410/268-2600.**

It's Christmas every day at this festive shop, in the heart of the historic district. The wares include lights and hand-crafted ornaments from around the world, angel tree tops, tree skirts, vintage Victorian decorations, candles, nutcrackers, character Santas, gift wrap, cards, and more. Open Monday to Saturday from 10am to 6pm, Sunday from noon to 5pm.

The Gift Horse
77 Maryland Ave. ☎ **410/263-3737.**

This is an emporium of unusual gift items, from glass, brass, pewter, and armetale (an alloy composed of 10 metals, similar to pewter), to oil lamps, figurines, prisms, mobiles, and paperweights. Open Monday to Saturday from 10am to 5:30pm, Sunday from noon to 5pm.

The Pewter Chalice
168 Main St. ☎ **410/268-6246.**

If you are fond of pewter and armetale, this is a great spot to browse or shop— pewter goblets, bowls, tankards, candelabra, pitchers, flagons, plates, teapots, candlesticks, cutlery, flasks, inkwells, jewelry boxes, vases, and much more. Open Monday to Friday from 10am to 5pm, Saturday from 10am to 6pm, and Sunday from noon to 5pm.

MALLS & MARKETS

Annapolis Harbour Center
2454 Solomons Island Rd. ☎ **410/266-5857.**

One of the area's newest shopping clusters, positioned west of downtown at the juncture of Routes 2 and 665, this mall is laid out like a maritime village, with more than 40 different shops, services, and fast-food eateries, as well as nine movie theaters. Open Monday through Saturday from 10am to 9pm and Sunday from noon to 5pm.

Annapolis Mall
Defense Highway and Route 178. ☎ **410/266-5432.**

If shopping on a big scale interests you, then head to this mall, situated off Route 50 between West Street and Bestgate Road. There are three department stores (Hechts, J. C. Penney, and Montgomery Ward) as well as more than 125 specialty shops. Open Monday to Saturday from 10am to 9:30pm, Sunday from noon to 5pm.

Pennsylvania Dutch Farmers Market
2472 Solomons Island Rd. ☎ **410/573-0770.**

Situated opposite the string of shops at Annapolis Harbour Center (see above), this market is an attraction in itself, run by Amish and Mennonite families from Lancaster County, Pennsylvania. The wares range from traditional sausages and pickled products to chemically free vegetables and fruits, as well as homemade jams, fudges, candies, cakes, pies, and soft pretzels, all ideal for a picnic or snack. There is also a section devoted to crafts such as handmade quilts, for which the Amish are widely known. Open Thursday 10am to 6pm, Friday 9am to 6pm, and Saturday 9am to 3pm.

MARITIME & NAVAL ITEMS

Peppers
133 Main St. ☎ **410/267-8722.**

This place offers a large selection of officially licensed navy clothing, from sweatshirts, T-shirts, and sweaters to hats and accessories. Open Monday to Saturday from 10am to 6pm, Sunday from noon to 5pm.

Save the Bay Shop
188 Main St. ☎ **410/728-5229.**

This is the retail outlet of the Chesapeake Bay Foundation, the largest nonprofit organization working to save the Chesapeake Bay. The products for sale range from books, videos, and environmental studies on the Chesapeake Bay to various gift items with the "Save the Bay" logo, from T-shirts and totes, to mugs, jewelry, note cards, and art posters. Open daily from 10am to 6pm or later.

The Ship and Soldier Shop
58 Maryland Ave. ☎ **410/268-1141.**

This is a good source for metal models and miniatures of the army, navy, and marines (and the Royal Canadian Mounted Police), as well as models of cars, ships, trains, and planes. Open Tuesday to Saturday from 10am to 5:30pm.

Sign of the Whale
99 Main St. ☎ **410/268-2161.**

Situated at Green Street across from the City Dock, this eclectic shop offers an assortment of naval and nautical crafts, as well as Chesapeake Bay–related art, glass sailboats, scrimshaw, ceramics, sculpture, and apparel. Open Monday to Saturday from 10am to 5:30pm, Sunday from noon to 5pm.

9 Annapolis After Dark

For up-to-date weekly listings of concerts and other entertainment events in the Annapolis area, check the "Entertainment" section of the *Capital* newspaper on Friday. *Inside Annapolis,* a bimonthly publication distributed free throughout the city, also gives a summary of entertainment venues and upcoming events and other information of help to visitors.

PERFORMING ARTS CENTER

✪ Maryland Hall for the Creative Arts
801 Chase St. ☎ **410/263-5019** or 410/263-5544. Tickets $10–$25. Nightly 7 or 8pm.

This hall presents performances by the Annapolis Symphony Orchestra, Annapolis Chorale, Annapolis Chamber Orchestra, and the Ballet Theater of Annapolis, as well as one-person shows and other guest stars.

THEATERS

Annapolis Summer Garden Theatre
143 Compromise St. (at Main Street.). ☎ **410/268-9212.** Tickets $7–$10. Memorial Day–Labor Day, Thurs–Sun at 8:30pm.

Established in 1966, this seasonal outdoor "theater under the stars" was once a blacksmith shop, and is ideally located across from the City Dock. It presents Broadway musicals, such as *Bye Bye Birdie* or *Annie.*

Chesapeake Music Hall
339 Busch's Frontage Rd. ☎ **410/626-7515.** Tickets $24.95–$27.95. Thurs, Fri, and Sat dinner at 6:30pm, show at 8pm; Sun brunch at 12:30pm, show at 2pm.

Located off Exit 29A of Route 50 between Annapolis and the Chesapeake Bay Bridge, this theater offers a year-round program of Broadway-style musicals and comedies. The price includes a full dinner or brunch.

Colonial Players Theater
108 East St. ☎ **410/268-7373.** Tickets $7–$10. Thurs–Sat at 8pm, Sun at 2:30 or 7:30pm.

Organized in 1949, this nonprofit community theater group performs in a 180-seat theater-in-the-round setting. It presents a variety of Broadway plays throughout the year, usually from September through June. The lobby displays the works of local painters, photographers, and artisans.

CLUBS & BARS

Armadillo's

132 Dock St. ☎ **410/268-6680**. Cover $2–$4. Music starts at 9pm on Wednesday through Saturday and at 6pm on Sunday.

This place offers a variety of live entertainment—jazz, blues, funk, classic rock, soft rock, and oldies.

Fran O'Brien's

113 Main St. ☎ **410/268-6288**. No cover. Music usually begins at 9pm.

Situated across from the City Dock, this popular place features live pop music and dancing Monday through Saturday and DJ music on Sunday.

✪ King of France Tavern

16 Church Circle. ☎ **410/269-0990**. Cover $3–$10, depending on the music. Music starts at 8 or 8:30pm.

The former Colonial kitchens of the Maryland Inn serve as the setting for this club, which is known for its jazz, as well as occasional programs of folk, classical, chamber music, and big bands. The Charlie Byrd jazz trio often plays here on Friday through Sunday nights.

Marmaduke's

301 Severn Ave. ☎ **410/269-5420**. Cover $3. Friday and Saturday nights at 8:30pm.

Located in the Eastport section of Annapolis at 3rd Street, this pub presents a singalong cabaret, with pianist and vocalist, performing show tunes upstairs. The ground floor is known for its seafaring decor and "yacht club" atmosphere.

Mums

136 Dock St. ☎ **410/263-3353**. No cover.

This two-story bar has alternative dance music with DJs from 10pm on Friday and Saturday; acoustic and other types of music are on tap other nights.

10 An Excursion to St. Mary's City

After you have seen the current capital of Maryland, you really should have a look at the state's first capital, **Historic St. Mary's City**, off Route 5, St. Mary's City (☎ 301/862-0990 or 800/SMC-1634), a National Historic Landmark situated about 80 miles southwest of Annapolis.

When you arrive in St. Mary's City (known originally as *St. Marie's Citty*), don't expect a panorama of colonial buildings like Annapolis. Don't even expect to find a city in the same format as we know it.

Nestled between the Potomac and the Chesapeake, this secluded corner of Maryland is almost as it was in 1634. That was the year *The Ark* and *The Dove* arrived from England with the first 140 colonists under a royal charter from Lord Baltimore. These stalwart settlers set up a community that served as the beginning of Maryland and the state's first capital until 1694. Among the many achievements of this early city was the enactment of the first laws recognizing religious tolerance.

Today's Historic St. Mary's City is a "living history" outdoor museum spread out over 850 acres of Tidewater landscape. Thanks to years of archaeological excavations, St. Mary's City has been authentically reassembled to show a typical tobacco farm plantation, a waterfront preserve, and woodland nature trails. The first State House has also been reconstructed as the *Farthing Ordinary*, a primitive tavern.

A tour of St. Mary's City starts at the Visitor Center. You'll see a five-minute introductory audiovisual presentation and exhibits that provide useful background on what life was like here more than 350 years ago. Plan to spend at least two hours outside to explore the Town Center, the *Woodland Indian Loghouse*, and other buildings, and to see the *Maryland Dove*, a replica of Lord Baltimore's square-rigged ship, as well as various gardens being cultivated in 17th-century style. The facilities include a cafe and a shop. Admission is $6.50 for adults, $6 for seniors, and $3.25 for children aged 6 to 12. It's open from late March to the end of November, Wednesday through Sunday from 10am to 5pm.

4 Maryland's Eastern Shore

A peninsula bordered on one side by the Atlantic and on the other by Chesapeake Bay, Maryland's Eastern Shore is almost an island. For centuries, this area was linked to the rest of Maryland's mainland only by a northeasterly spit of land closer to Wilmington than to Baltimore.

It wasn't until 1952, when the William Preston Lane Jr. Bridge was built from Annapolis over the Chesapeake Bay, that the Eastern Shore really became easily accessible to the rest of the state.

Back-to-back with Delaware and nudging Virginia's coastal strip, these eastern Maryland counties have developed a personality of their own, as part of the Delmarva peninsula. Some of the state's oldest towns and early shipbuilding centers are here. Much of James Michener's novel *Chesapeake* was inspired by the everyday lifestyle of these rural coastal communities.

Most of all, this part of the world is known for its good eating—a haven for crabs, oysters, and other seafood. Top-class restaurants line the shore, in settings ranging from picturesque Victorian buildings and converted crab shacks to wide-windowed marina decks. This part of Maryland is also one of the chief resting areas for migrating wildfowl along the Atlantic flyway and is famed for its bird-watching and duck and goose hunting.

SEEING MARYLAND'S EASTERN SHORE

The best way to reach the Eastern Shore from the west is via Route 50/301 and the bridge over the bay, crossing over Kent Island. Once you arrive, Route 301 swings northeast and leads toward Chestertown and Chesapeake City, while Route 50 takes you to Easton and other points south. If you are approaching from Delaware on the north or from the south via Virginia's coast, then Route 13 is the most direct road, connecting with Route 50/301. Route 13 and its offshoot, Route 413, will also bring you to Crisfield.

1 Kent Island

10 miles E of Annapolis, 40 miles SE of Baltimore, 55 miles E of Washington, D.C., 20 miles NW of Easton

Kent Island, or the "Isle of Kent," as it was originally named, was established in 1629 as a trading post by William Claiborne, an agent

What's Special About Maryland's Eastern Shore

Sightseeing
- Easton's historic district, the Eastern Shore's Colonial capital, with more than 40 preserved and restored buildings.
- St. Michaels Marina, attracting more than 20,000 pleasure craft a year.
- Wye Oak, largest white oak in the United States and Maryland's official state tree.

Activities
- Ride the Oxford-Bellevue ferry across the Tred Avon River, America's oldest privately operated ferry, dating from 1683.
- Cruise around St. Michaels on a "Patriot" boat, or to the offshore islands of Smith or Tangier from Crisfield.
- Fish the Chesapeake waters with Harrisons of Tilghman Island, the largest charter fleet on the bay.

Events/Festivals
- Waterfowl Festival, Easton, three days of waterfowl art, contests, auctions, workshops, and exhibits.
- Annual Hard Crab Derby and Fair, Crisfield, weekend of crab-themed feasting, frolic, and fun.

Great Towns/Villages
- Crisfield, crabbing center and "seafood capital of the world."
- Berlin, an inland town with eye-catching Victorian buildings and a dozen antique shops.
- Chesapeake City, a 19th-century canal town.
- Chestertown, an 18th- and 19th-century river town.

Museums
- Chesapeake Bay Maritime Museum, a waterside showcase of seafaring history, with a 110-year-old lighthouse, a skipjack, and a bugeye.
- Historical Society of Talbot County, a museum complex of 18th- and 19th-century buildings depicting Easton's rich heritage.
- Ward Museum of Wildfowl Art, largest of its kind.

Shopping
- Carvel Hall Factory Outlet, in Crisfield, for discounts on brand-name cutlery, glassware, pewter, and more.
- Dixon's Auction Sales, Crumpton, a unique weekly old-Maryland style furniture auction spread out over 15 acres.
- The antique and craft shops of Easton, St. Michaels, Oxford, Preston, Chesapeake City, and Chestertown.

of the Virginia governor. It is considered the first English settlement in Maryland under the 1631 patent from the king.

A relatively small area, it stands out today because of its geographic position—it is the first landfall of the Eastern Shore after crossing the William Preston Lane Jr. Bridge over the Chesapeake from Annapolis. It consists of a small island, just 15 miles long and less than 5 miles wide, mainly residential in character, and a narrow strip of land, appropriately known as Kent Narrows, connecting the island to the rest of the Eastern Shore. The chief towns are Stevensville, on the north of the island, Chester in the center, and Grasonville along the Narrows.

GETTING THERE　By Bus　Greyhound/Trailways stops in Stevensville on Route 18.

By Car　The best way to get to Kent Island is by car, via Route 50/301 from Annapolis.

ESSENTIALS　Area Code　The area code is 410.

Visitor Information　For brochures about the area, contact the Queen Anne's County Visitors Service, 107 N. Liberty St., Centreville, MD 21617 (☎ 410/ 827-4810).

WHAT TO SEE & DO

For many people traveling over the William Preston Lane Jr. Bridge from Annapolis, Kent Island and Kent Narrows are primarily a gateway to the rest of the Eastern Shore. It is here that the Route 50/301 splits, with Route 50 leading south to Easton and other bay resorts and east to Ocean City, and Route 301 wending its way north and east toward Chestertown, Chesapeake City, and other upper bay enclaves.

The Kent Island area is also a favorite for boaters, with four marinas: Mears Point, Piney Narrows Yacht Haven, Scott Marine, and Anglers, all offering boat slips, fuel, showers, ice, electric hookups, boat repairs, and marine supplies.

Besides the aquatic vistas and activities, the star attraction of the area is **Horseheads Wetlands Center**, 1 Discovery Lane, Grasonville (☎ 410/ 827-6694). Located off Exit 45B (Nesbit Road) of Route 50/301, this facility is operated under the auspices of the Wildfowl Trust of North America. Surrounded by more than 300 acres, it provides year-round opportunities to observe a variety of wildlife.

The visitors center serves as an orientation point and features seasonal exhibits. On the grounds, there are miles of walking trails meandering beside resident waterfowl habitats and natural areas. Visitors can see the birds and other species without disturbing them via enclosed observation blinds, raised platforms, and a boardwalk. Admission is $3 for adults, $2 for seniors, and $1 for children under 12. It is open daily year-round from 9am to 5pm.

The **Wildfowl Trust of North America** also operates a series of one- and two-day workshops, lectures, and guided walks and provides a free field guide outlining eco-touring opportunities for the entire Chesapeake Bay area. For more information, contact the Wildfowl Trust of North America, Ecological Tour Program, P.O. Box 519, Grasonville, MD 21628.

WHERE TO STAY

Comfort Inn/Kent Narrows

3101 S. Main St., Grasonville, MD 21638. ☎ **410/827-6767**, 800/828-3361, or 800/ 228-5150. 86 rms. A/C TV TEL. $75–$175 double. (Rates include continental breakfast.) AE, CB, DC, DISC, MC, V. Free parking.

Located off Exit 42 of Route 50/301, this modern four-story hotel sits amid a corridor of marinas and seafood restaurants. Guest rooms have light wood furnishings and sea art, plus extras such as a microwave oven, refrigerator, and coffeemaker. Many rooms have bay views and balconies. Facilities include an

Maryland's Eastern Shore

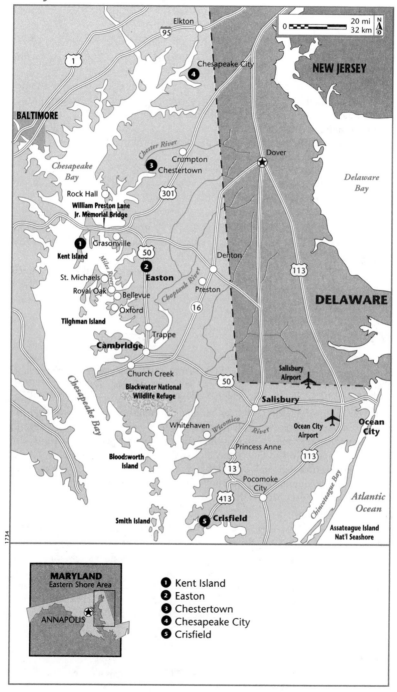

Elkton
95
Chesapeake City
4
NEW JERSEY
0   20 mi
     32 km
N

1
BALTIMORE

Chester River
Crumpton
3 Chestertown
Dover

Chesapeake
Bay
Delaware
Bay

Rock Hall
301

William Preston Lane
Jr. Memorial Bridge

1 Grasonville
50
Denton
Kent Island

Miles River
2 Easton
113

St. Michaels
Royal Oak   Bellevue
Choptank River
Preston
DELAWARE

Oxford
16

Tilghman Island

Trappe
Cambridge

Church Creek
50
Salisbury
Airport
Blackwater National
Wildlife Refuge
Salisbury

Whitehaven
Wicomico   River
Ocean City
Airport
Ocean
City

Bloodsworth
Island
Princess Anne
113

13
Chesapeake Bay
Pocomoke
City

413

Smith Island
5 Crisfield
Chincoteague Bay
Atlantic
Ocean

Assateague Island
Nat'l Seashore

1734

MARYLAND
Eastern Shore Area

ANNAPOLIS

1 Kent Island
2 Easton
3 Chestertown
4 Chesapeake City
5 Crisfield

indoor swimming pool, whirlpool, sauna, exercise room, game room, and guest laundry.

Kent Manor Inn

Kent Manor Dr., Stevensville, MD 21666. ☎ **410/643-5757**. 24 rms (all with bath). A/C TV TEL. $79–$159 double. AE, MC, V. Free parking.

Dating from 1820, this sprawling three-story Victorian-style inn exudes a southern plantation atmosphere, sitting on 226 acres of Kent Island farmland rimmed by a mile of Thompson Creek waterfront. The public areas are rich in antiques, original Italian marble fireplaces, and brass fixtures. Guest rooms, including some ground-floor units, have Victorian reproduction furniture, four-poster beds, and frilly fabrics, and most have verandas that overlook Thompson Creek. Facilities include a restaurant with a country manor ambience (see "Where to Dine," below), bar, and access to a nearby golf course. The highest rates prevail on weekends (Friday and Saturday). It is located off Route 8, Exit 37 of Route 50/301.

Sleep Inn

101 VFW Ave., Grasonville, MD. 21638. ☎ **410/827-8921** or 800/62-SLEEP. 50 rms. A/C TV TEL. $54.95–$79.95 double. (Rates include continental breakfast.) AE, DISC, MC, V. Free parking.

For bargain hunters, this modern two-story property is one of the newest hotels in the area. Set back from Route 50/301 (accessible by Exits 44A or 44B), it offers guest rooms with standard furnishings plus a refrigerator. An outdoor swimming pool and restaurants are nearby.

WHERE TO DINE

Annie's Paramount Steak House

500 Kent Narrows Way N., Grasonville. ☎ **410/827-7103** Reservations recommended for Mon–Thurs; accepted only for parties of 10 or more on Fri–Sun. Main courses $8.95–$19.95, lunch $5.95–$10.95. AE, DC, MC, V. Mon–Sat 11am–10pm, Sun 9am–9pm. AMERICAN.

Established in 1948, this restaurant has long distinguished itself for prime rib and steaks in an area otherwise known for seafood. The menu offers 12 types of steaks including Annie's famous "Bull in the Pan," top sirloin tips of beef marinated in herbs and spices. In addition, there are center cut pork chops, prime rib, French dip, trio of lamb chops, and smoked baby-back ribs. With a lovely wide-windowed setting overlooking the water, Annie's is also noted for some seafood items, especially the crab ball appetizers. It's located off Exit 42 of Route 50/301.

Harris Crab House

Kent Narrows Way N., Grasonville. ☎ **410/827-9500.** Reservations not accepted. Main courses $7.95–$16.95, lunch $1.95–$7.95. MC,V. Daily 11am–11pm. SEAFOOD.

This informal indoor-outdoor restaurant overlooks the Mears Point Marina. Heaping platters of fresh seafood are the specialty here, including crabs by the dozen, all-you-can-eat shrimp and crab, and various broiled, steamed, or fried combinations of hard and soft crabs, crab cakes, hard- and soft-shell clams, oysters, and scallops. In addition, the menu offers barbecued chicken and ribs. Lighter items, such as sandwiches and burgers, are popular at lunchtime. Get here early. It's off Exit 42 of Route 50.

Kent Manor Restaurant

500 Kent Manor Dr., Stevensville. ☎ **410/643-7716.** Reservations required. Main courses $14.50–$20.95, lunch $5.95–$11.95. AE, MC, V. Daily 11:30am–2:30pm and 5–9pm. INTERNATIONAL.

Overlooking more than 200 acres of farmland and waterfront on the east side of Kent Island, this historic manor house restaurant is an attraction in itself. It offers a choice of settings including four cozy candlelit Victorian dining rooms and an enclosed water-view solarium. Specialties of the house include local crab dishes and Black Angus steaks, as well as "veal California," a cutlet with artichoke hearts, sun-dried tomatoes, and proscuitto; seafood scampi, a trio of shrimp, scallops, and lobster over fettucine; and roast quail stuffed with apples, raisins, and pine nuts with an apple brandy glaze. It's located off Route 8, Exit 37 of Route 50/301.

2 Easton

40 miles SE of Annapolis, 60 miles SE of Baltimore, 110 miles SW of Wilmington, 76 miles NW of Ocean City, 70 miles SW of Dover

Once known as the Colonial Capital of Maryland's Eastern Shore, Easton is today a quiet little community (population 8,500), closely tied to nearby waters. Directly facing the center of the Chesapeake Bay, yet sheltered by the many coves of the Miles River and the Tred Avon River, Easton and neighboring towns were an ideal locale for shipbuilding in the 18th century, and now the area is equally perfect as a haven for those who love to savor the sea or to sample seafood.

The gateway to the rest of the Eastern Shore, Easton is also a hub leading to a trio of more secluded neighboring maritime retreats. We like to picture Easton as the inner core or heart of the area, with two arms stretching out toward the Chesapeake. The upper (and longer) arm takes you to the village of St. Michaels on the Miles River and to Tilghman Island, dangling right on the Chesapeake. The lower arm goes straight to Oxford, a sheltered town nestled along the shores of the Tred Avon River.

Named after the archangel, St. Michaels was one of the oldest settlements along the Chesapeake and flourished in Colonial times as a shipbuilding center (the birthplace of the illustrious Baltimore clipper). Today it is an aesthetic delight—no billboards or fast-food chains; just quiet tree-lined streets, rows of boutiques housed in graceful old restored buildings, and a marina so clean that it seems to sparkle. At least 20,000 boats a year pull into this idyllic harbor just 11 miles outside of Easton (via Route 33). Another 15 miles will bring you to Tilghman Island, an important base for fishermen of oysters, crabs, clams, and fin fish—an enclave with great seafaring atmosphere.

Oxford, also one of the oldest towns in Maryland, was the Colonial home of Robert Morris Jr., the man who befriended George Washington and then used his own savings to help finance the American Revolution. The Morris family home is now a first-rate inn and restaurant, which in itself is worth the 10 miles from Easton to Oxford (via Route 333). The most enjoyable way to reach Oxford, however, is to take the Tred Avon ferry across from the Bellevue section of St. Michaels. No matter how you come, don't miss Oxford—it's a town that time has hardly touched, with a pervasive quiet charm and views of the water at every turn.

GETTING THERE   By Plane   Easton Airport/Newnam Field (☎ 410/ 822-8560) is about 3 miles north of the city on Route 50. Among the carriers offering local charter service are Maryland Airlines (☎ 410/822-0400 or 800/ 451-5693), flying between Easton and Washington, D.C. In addition, Salisbury/ Wicomico County Airport, Airport Road, Salisbury (☎ 410/749-0633), is 60 miles southwest of Easton. The second-largest airport in Maryland, it is a gateway for scheduled passenger flights operated by USAir (☎ 800/428-4322).

By Bus   Greyhound offers regular service into its depot at the junction of Routes 50 and 309 (☎ 410/822-0280).

By Car   The best way to get to the Easton area is by car, via Route 50 from all directions.

ESSENTIALS   Area Code   The area code is 410.

Visitor Information   For complete lodging and restaurant information, maps, and brochures about Easton and environs, contact the Talbot County Chamber of Commerce, Tred Avon Square, Marlborough Road, P.O. Box 1366, Easton, MD 21601 (☎ 410/822-4606). This office is located just north of the historic district at the junction of Route 322; a second office is operated at the Talbot County Community Center, Route 50, across from the Hog Neck Golf Course.

GETTING AROUND   By Rented Car   If you haven't brought your own car to the Easton area, you can rent one from Avis, Easton Airport/Newnam Field (☎ 410/822-5040); or Hertz, Goldsborough Road and Route 50 (☎ 410/822-1676).

By Taxi   For local cab service, try Scotty's Taxi (☎ 410/822-1475) or Thomas's Yellow Top Cabs (☎ 410/822-1121).

By Ferry   For the trip between St. Michaels and Oxford or just for a scenic and satisfying experience, take the Oxford-Bellevue Ferry (☎ 410/745-9023). Established in 1683, this is America's oldest privately operated ferry. Crossing the Tred Avon River, the distance is just a mile, and seven minutes in duration. You can catch the ferry either from Bellevue, off Routes 33 and 329, near St. Michaels, or at Oxford (off Route 333). Operating year-round except from mid-December through February, with continuous service every 20 minutes, the ferry schedule is June 1 to Labor Day, on Monday through Friday from 7am to 9pm, and on weekends from 9am to 9pm; Labor Day to June 1, on Monday through Friday from 7am to sunset, and weekends from 9am to sunset. Rates for a car and two persons are $4.50 one way and $7 round-trip; extra car passenger, 50¢; walk-on passengers, $1.

WHAT TO SEE & DO
ATTRACTIONS

Start with a stroll around Easton's **historic district,** centered around Washington Street. Here you will find more than 40 beautifully restored and preserved public buildings, churches, and private homes, all dating back to the 18th and 19th centuries. Centerpiece of the district is the **Talbot County Courthouse,** on Washington between Dover and Federal streets. First built from 1710 to 1712, rebuilt in 1791, and remodeled in 1958, this impressive structure is the symbol of Easton. Among its claims to fame is the fact that its main portion was used as a subcapital of Maryland for the Eastern Shore. In addition, a document called the "Talbot Reserves," adopted on the courthouse grounds in May of 1774, was the first public airing of the sentiments that were later embodied in the Declaration of Independence.

Academy of the Arts
106 South St., Easton. ☎ **410/822-ARTS** or 410/822-0455. Admission free. Mon–Sat 10am–4pm, Wed 10am–9pm.

This is a regional arts center, with changing exhibitions of interest about the area and the entire Eastern Shore. Concerts are also periodically staged here.

✪ Chesapeake Bay Maritime Museum

Mill Street, Navy Point, St. Michaels. ☎ **410/745-2916.** Admission $7.50 adults, $6.50 seniors, $3 children 6–17, free for children under 6. June–Sept daily, 9am–6pm, Oct–Dec daily 9am–5pm; Jan–Feb Fri–Sun 10am–4pm; Mar–June, daily 9am–5pm. Closed Thanksgiving, Christmas, New Year's Day. Directions: At Mill Street, turn right, and follow signs to museum.

Dedicated to the preservation of maritime history and specifically to the Chesapeake Bay area, this waterside museum is a setting for the largest collection of Chesapeake Bay watercraft in existence (76 boats), located on 18 acres of land occupying 23 buildings, eight of which are open to the public. The comprehensive collection is comprised of many floating exhibits, including a skipjack and a restored log-bottom bugeye, as well as crabbing skiffs, workboats, and log canoes. Some of the other highlights include an authentic 1879 "screwpile" lighthouse, a working boatyard, an extensive waterfowl decoy collection, and a 4,000-volume library—a resource that James Michener relied upon when writing his best-seller *Chesapeake.* The newest addition, the Steamboat Building, opened in 1993, focuses on steam and mechanical propulsion on Chesapeake Bay.

✪ Historical Society of Talbot County

25 S. Washington St., Easton. ☎ **410/822-0773.** Museum, $2 adults, 50¢ children 6–17; guided tours of houses, $2 adults, 50¢ children 6–17. Tues–Sat 10am–4pm, Sun 1–4pm. Museum shop is open daily Mon 10am–4pm.

This society maintains eight historic buildings, five of which are open to the public. A focal point of the historic district, the buildings include an 1850s commercial building, the headquarters of the society and site of a modern museum with changing exhibits; the 1795 Joseph Neall House and the 1810 Joseph Neall House, both restored homes of Quaker cabinetmaker brothers; the partially restored 1670 Wenlocke Christison House, known locally as "The Ending of Controversie" House; and the 1810 Tharpe House, which now serves as a museum shop and library. The buildings surround a lovely Federal-style garden, also open to visitors. Guided tours of the houses are also available for an extra fee.

Orrell's Biscuits

14124 Old Wye Mill Rd. (Route 662), Wye Mills, MD 21679. ☎ **410/820-8090.** Admission free. Tues–Thurs; phone for hours.

The tiny community of Wye Mills is the home of a family enterprise producing a uniquely Eastern Shore biscuit that has been a tradition for more than 300 years. With their kitchen as a bakery, the Orrell family produces hundreds of biscuits every day. Following an original recipe that lacks baking powder or soda, the Orrells and their staff literally "beat" these doughy treats with the help of an electrically powered biscuit beater, and then shape each specimen by hand into the size of a walnut, producing a crusty biscuit with a soft center. Visitors are welcome to watch the baking process, sample the results, and purchase at the source, although the biscuits are also on sale throughout Maryland. They can also be ordered by mail.

Third Haven Friends Meeting House

405 S. Washington St., Easton. ☎ **410/822-0293.** Admission free, but donations welcome. Daily 9am–5pm.

Located in a tree-shaded residential area on the banks of the Tred Avon Creek, ³/₄ mile south of downtown, this structure is believed to be the oldest frame building dedicated to religious meetings in the United States and the oldest known building in Maryland. Made of pine and oak, and originally paid for in tobacco, it has been used continuously since the late 17th century. William Penn is said to have worshipped here. It has recently been restored under the auspices of the Maryland Historical Trust.

Wye Mill
Route 662, off Route 50, Wye Mills. ☎ **410/827-6909** or 410/685-2886. Admission free, but suggested donation is $2. Apr–Nov, Sat–Sun 11am–4pm, and by appointment.

The nearby town of Wye Mills, located about 12 miles north of Easton, is the site of this mill dating from the 17th century. Though the town is named for two mills, only one of these structures survives today. Owned and maintained by a nonprofit group known as Preservation Maryland, the mill is the earliest industrial-commercial building in continuous use in the state. In Revolutionary days, flour from this mill was produced for George Washington's troops at Valley Forge. Visitors today can see the mill in operation and sample some of the flour, whole wheat, or cornmeal.

While in Wye Mills, stop to see the huge tree that dominates the town—the Wye Oak, the largest white oak in the United States and Maryland's official state tree. Measuring $4^{1}/_{2}$ feet above its base, the Wye Oak is 37 feet in circumference and 95 feet high, with a crown spanning 165 feet, shading an area almost half an acre. The tree is believed to be more than 400 years old.

ORGANIZED TOURS

Historical Walking Tours of Easton's downtown area are conducted year-round by members of the Historical Society of Talbot County, 25 Washington St., Easton (☎ 410/822-0773). Tours last about an hour and cost $2 for adults and 50¢ for children aged 6 to 17. Tours are available daily at 11:30am and 1:30pm or by advance reservation.

For those who would like to see the highlights of the area by boat, **Patriot Cruises,** P.O. Box 1206, St. Michaels (☎ 410/745-3100), offers one-hour narrated cruises on board the *Patriot*, a 65-foot, two-deck vessel with indoor and outdoor seating. The cruise plies the waters of the Miles River and the shoreline off St. Michaels, passing historic homes, waterfowl, and watermen harvesting blue crabs, clams, and oysters. Operating from April through mid-December, the trip costs $8 for adults and $4 for children under 12. The boat sails from the dock next to the Chesapeake Bay Maritime Museum at 11am, 12:30pm, 2:30pm, and 4pm.

OUTDOOR ACTIVITIES

BICYCLE RENTALS   St. Michaels Town Dock Marina, 305 Mulberry St., St. Michaels (☎ 410/745-2400), rents bikes for $3 an hour, $5 for two hours, or $14 for a full day; tandems start at $6 an hour. Open April through November. You can also get two-wheelers of all sorts (from three-speeds to tandems) at **Oxford Mews,** 105 Morris St., Oxford (☎ 410/820-8222), daily except Wednesday, from $3.50 an hour with $7 minimum; $14 a day; or $75 a week.

FISHING   Fishing excursions along the Chesapeake are the specialty of **Harrison's Sport Fishing Center,** 21551 Chesapeake House Dr., Tilghman Island (☎ 410/886-2121 or 410/886-2109). This family enterprise, dating from more than 100 years ago, now comprises the largest charter fleet on the bay. Complete fishing packages are available from $135 to $150 a day, including all fishing, tackle, boat transport, a room at the nautically themed Harrison's Chesapeake House Country Inn, and meals (a boxed lunch, plus a huge fisherman's breakfast and dinner at the Harrison's Chesapeake House restaurant). Depending on the time of year, the catch often includes sea trout, blues, striped bass, croakers, spot, rockfish, or perch.

GOLF   There's plenty of room to swing at the **Hog Neck Golf Course,** 10142 Old Cordova Rd., Easton (☎ 410/822-6079), rated among the top 25 public courses in the United States by *Golf Digest.* Situated north of town off Route 50, between Route 309 and Rabbit Hill Road, it offers a par-72, 18-hole championship course and a par-32, 9-hole executive course. Rates for nonresidents are $28 for 18 holes, $10 for 9 holes; cart rental is $11 and $5.50 per person, respectively. Facilities also include a driving range, putting green, and a pro shop. Open February to December, weekdays from 7am to sunset, and weekends from 8am to sunset.

HUNTING   Maryland's Eastern Shore is considered by many to be the finest duck- and goose-hunting region on the Atlantic flyway. Every year, more than 500,000 migratory game birds winter on the fields, marshes, rivers, tidal flats, and waters of Maryland. More than 20 local organizations conduct regular guided waterfowl hunts for Canada geese (late November through late January), ducks (late November through mid-January), and sea ducks (early October through mid-January). Some quail and pheasant hunting is also available. Goose hunting for two people ranges from $300 to $400 a day plus licenses; and quail and pheasant rates are based on the number of birds caught. Three reliable sources for information are **Ray Marshall,** P.O. Box 83, Newcomb, MD 21653 (☎ 410/745-2060); **Bob Ewing,** 26532 Marengo Rd., Easton, MD 21601 (☎ 410/822-0272); and **Jay W. Tarmon,** P.O. Box 1201, Easton, MD 21601 (☎ 410/822-9334).

WATER SPORTS   Much of the focus of outdoor life in the Easton–St. Michaels–Oxford area is in and around the water. Whether you have your own boat or not, you'll always find lots of activity at **St. Michaels Town Dock Marina,** 305 Mulberry St., St. Michaels (☎ 410/745-2400). You can rent runabouts with outboard engines for $75 for the first two hours, $125 for four hours, or $185 per day. If you have your own craft, you can also dock it here. Overnight dockage charges are $1.50 per foot on weekdays and $2 per foot on weekends. Some smaller slips are also available, and there is hourly dockage, with a $5 an hour minimum.

   St. Michaels Harbour Inn and Marina Aqua Center, 101 N. Harbor Rd., St. Michaels (☎ 410/745-9001), also offers water-sports rentals. You can rent pedalboats by the hour for $10; canoes by the hour for $10 or by the day for $35; and aquabikes at $12 per hour.

SHOPPING A TO Z

The Easton–St. Michaels–Oxford area is full of craft and specialty shops. Antique hunters also flock to the town of Preston, 11 miles east of Easton via Route 331.

ANTIQUES

Country Treasures
200 Main St., Preston. ☎ **410/673-2603.**

   This shop is a favorite for antique seekers, stocking a great variety of home furnishings, from quilts to rolltop desks. Open Monday to Saturday from 10am to 5pm.

Hodgepodge

308 S. Talbot St., St. Michaels. ☎ **410/745-3062.**

Antiques, as well as a great variety of fabrics, accessories, baskets, decoys, afghans, and more fill this shop. Open Monday to Saturday from 10am to 6pm.

The Quaker Bonnet

202 Main St., Preston. ☎ **410/673-2322.**

Antique hunters visit this popular shop in the heart of Preston for old coins, jewelry, and dollhouse collectibles. Open Monday to Saturday from 10am to 5pm.

Books

✪ Rowen's Bookstore

14 N. Harrison St. and 8–19 Washington St., Easton. ☎ **410/822-2095.**

This is both a bookstore and a stationery store, with two entrances. It stocks a variety of books about the Eastern Shore, Chesapeake Bay, state of Maryland, sailing and nautical topics, waterfowl and wetlands, birds and bird-watching, ducks and decoys. In addition, there are stationery, artist's supplies, kites, prints, housewares, kitchen gadgets, gifts, and souvenirs with crab-design motifs. Open weekdays from 8am to 5pm, Saturday from 9am to 5pm.

Crafts, Gifts & Toys

Celebrate Maryland!

100 Talbot St., St. Michaels. ☎ **410/745-5900.**

As its name implies, this store is a treasure trove of items relating to Maryland—from books and posters, sports products and clothing, flags and windsocks, to home furnishings and kitchen supplies, as well as jewelry, pewter, mugs, and food products; plus all kinds of crab-decorated gifts and Christmas ornaments with a Maryland motif. Open daily from 10am to 6pm.

Crackerjacks

7 S. Washington St., Easton. Tel. **410/822-7716.**

This children's store stocks all sorts of books, toys, games, dolls, stuffed animals, pinwheels, crafts, and more. Open Monday to Saturday from 9am to 5pm.

Heavenly Miniatures

24 N. Harrison St., Easton. ☎ **410/822-1519.**

Small is beautiful in this tiny shop, which offers miniature dolls, dollhouses, doll furniture, animals, and more. Open May through October, Sunday and Tuesday to Saturday from 10am to 5pm; and November through April, Tuesday to Saturday from 10am to 5pm.

St. Michaels Candy Company

216 S. Talbot St., St. Michaels. ☎ **410/745-6060.**

For those with a sweet tooth, here is a shop stocked with handmade chocolates, truffles, novelty candies, gourmet ice cream and yogurt, and unique gift items such as chocolate crabs and oysters. Open Monday to Saturday from 9am to 6pm.

St. Michaels Pottery Warehouse

407 S. Talbot St., St. Michaels. ☎ **410/745-5919.**

In addition to pottery of all kinds, this shop offers a large selection of lamps, shades, brass, linens, porcelain, and wicker. Open Monday to Saturday from 10am to 5pm.

Silent Poetry
201 Tilghman St., Oxford. ☎ **410/226-5120.**

Inspired by a 4th-century Greek poet who declared that art is "silent poetry," this shop stocks an assortment of original paintings by regional artists, limited-edition etchings and prints, and decoys and carvings by local craftspersons. In addition, there are fragrances, candles, linens, china, scrimshaw, potpourri, books, seasonal decorations and one-of-a-kind gift wrap, plus herbs and seasonings. Open Monday and Thursday through Saturday from 10am to 5pm, and Sunday from noon to 5pm, with extended hours in summer.

SPORTS/OUTDOOR CLOTHES & GEAR

Albright's Gun Shop
36 Dover St., Easton. ☎ **410/820-8811.**

Located across from the Tidewater Inn, this shop stocks guns and accessories, as well as bow-hunting supplies, sport clothing and watches, canvas goods, and fishing tackle. Custom repair and gunsmithing are also done on the premises. Open weekdays from 9am to 5:30pm, Saturday from 9am to 3:30pm, Sunday from noon to 4pm, with extended hours in the waterfowl season.

✪ Cherry's
26 W. Dover St., Easton. ☎ **410/822-4750.**

Since 1926, this store has been a favored spot for ladies' and men's quality sportswear, outdoor wear, and casual shoes. Open Monday through Saturday from 9am to 5pm.

Harbour Dasher
100 S. Talbot St., St. Michaels. ☎ **410/745-3354.**

This specialty shop for men features traditional and contemporary sportswear, accessories, and gifts. Open Monday to Saturday from 10am to 6pm.

The Ship's Store
202 Bank St., Oxford. ☎ **410/226-5113.**

A wide selection of seafaring clothes and collectibles makes this one of the best-stocked chandleries on the Eastern Shore. The wares range from nautical necessities and yachting apparel to gifts and games. Open daily from 8am to 6pm. Closed Sunday in winter.

WHERE TO STAY

The Easton–St. Michaels–Oxford area offers a range of modern and old-world accommodations. Most of these fall into the moderate category, although suites and luxury rooms can be expensive. Rates on weekends are often subject to surcharges; summer prices are usually the highest. One exception to this is the waterfowl hunting season (October through January), when top rates can also apply at many places.

VERY EXPENSIVE

The Inn at Perry Cabin
308 Watkins Lane, St. Michaels, MD 21663. ☎ **410/745-2200** or 800/722-2949. Fax 410/745-3348. 20 rooms, 19 suites. A/C TV TEL. $175–$345 single or double room; $395–$525 suite. (Rates include full breakfast and afternoon tea.) AE, CB, DC, MC, V. Free parking.

Acquired by Sir Bernard Ashley of Laura Ashley Enterprises in 1990, this proper English country inn aims for the highest luxury standards and charges accordingly. No expense has been spared in the appointments or decor that, not surprisingly, showcase Laura Ashley designs and furnishings. Pampering, too, sets this place apart—from a full-time concierge to turndown services, fresh flowers in every room, morning newspaper at your door, and a complete afternoon tea in the drawing room each day. Set on the Miles River, this Colonial Revival manor dates from the early 19th century and was named after Com. Oliver Hazard Perry, a friend of the original owner. Over the years, Perry Cabin served as a private home and a riding academy before first opening its doors as an inn in 1980. Facilities include a restaurant, outdoor terrace, rose and herb garden, boat docking, an indoor heated swimming pool and fitness center, access to golf, fishing, horseback riding, hunting, and helicopter pad.

EXPENSIVE

✪ Robert Morris Inn
314 N. Morris St. and The Strand, P.O. Box 70, Oxford, MD 21654. ☎ **410/226-5111.** 34 rms. A/C. $70–$220 double. MC, V. Free parking.

The focal point of one of Maryland's loveliest towns, this inn is a standout along the Eastern Shore. Situated on the banks of the Tred Avon River, this historic building (1710) was once the home of the man who financed the Continental Army during Revolutionary times. It was constructed by ships' carpenters with wooden-pegged paneling, ships' nails, and hand-hewn beams, all of which remain today. The house also has much of its original flooring, fireplaces, and murals. The guest rooms, all of which have been restored and renovated, are spread out among the original house, a nearby lodge, and two cottages. Many rooms have river views, private porches, and sitting rooms; all rooms are non-smoking units. Facilities include a first-rate restaurant (see "Where to Dine," below).

St. Michaels Harbour Inn
101 N. Harbor Rd., St. Michaels, MD 21663. ☎ ☎ **410/745-9001.** Fax 410/745-9150. 8 rms, 38 suites. A/C TV TEL. $89–$379 double room or suite. AE, DC, DISC, MC, V. Free parking. From Route 33, turn right on Seymour Avenue or E. Chew Street, left on Meadow Street, to Harbor Road.

It's hard to beat this inn for views of the water and boats. Situated right along the marina, the modern hotel offers rooms and suites, all with sweeping views of the water and most with private balconies or terraces. Each room has contemporary furnishings with maritime-themed art, standard accessories, plus a coffeemaker. The suites also have kitchenettes, wet bars, and sitting rooms.

Other amenities include short-term berthing for guest boats on a 60-slip marina, an outdoor swimming pool, an exercise room, bike and water-sports rentals, guest laundry, a poolside bar, and a nautical-style restaurant overlooking the harbor. The restaurant is particularly romantic at dinner as the sun sets over the marina.

✪ Tidewater Inn

101 E. Dover St., P.O. Box 359, Easton, MD 21601. ☎ **410/822-1300** or 800/237-8775. Fax 410/820-8847. 112 rms, 7 suites. A/C TV TEL. $129–$160 double; $215–$295 suite. AE, DC, MC, V. Free valet parking.

If you want to stay right in the heart of Easton, this four-story brick-fronted inn is the ideal place. Built in 1949 in the tradition of old public houses of Colonial days, its decor features dark woods, arched doorways, hurricane lamps, electric candles, flagstone floors, open fireplaces, and paintings of 18th-century Easton. Bedrooms are furnished with reproduction pieces. Amenities include a swimming pool, valet service, entertainment on Saturday evenings, a hunting-theme restaurant, and a wildfowl-themed bar.

MODERATE

✪ Hambleton on-the-Harbour

202 Cherry St., St. Michaels, MD 21663. ☎ **410/745-3350.** 5 rms. A/C TV. $110–$125 double. (Rates include continental breakfast.) MC, V. Free parking. From Route 33, turn right on Cherry St.; the inn is on the right at end of street.

A turn-of-the-century atmosphere prevails at this bed-and-breakfast inn facing the harbor. Innkeepers Aileen and Harry Arader have completely renovated this historic antique-filled retreat and furnished each guest room with an individual style. All rooms have a view of the waterfront, private bath, and antique furnishings; some also have working fireplaces. An enclosed porch is also available for guests as a relaxing lookout from which to watch the boats go by.

Oxford Inn

510 S. Morris St., P.O. Box 627, Oxford, MD 21654. ☎ **410/226-5220.** 11 rms, 1 suite. A/C. $85–$135 double; $200 suite. (Rates include continental breakfast.) MC, V. Free parking.

Surrounded by a white picket fence, this three-story Victorian house sits beside the Town Creek. The guest rooms are individually furnished with antiques, quilts, armoires, dressing tables, and wicker or oak furniture. Many of the rooms have window seats and/or views of the water; six have private baths. Facilities include a nautically themed restaurant, Pope's Tavern, with indoor and outdoor seating; and a second-floor sitting room with bay windows overlooking the water, with telephone, TV, and VCR for guest use. Innkeepers are the Schmitt family.

✪ Wades Point Inn on the Bay

Wades Point Rd., McDaniel, St. Michaels, MD 21663. ☎ **410/745-2500.** 23 rms (16 with private bath, 7 with shared bath). $80–$125 in main house, $135–$175 in adjoining building, single or double. (All rates include continental breakfast.) MC, V. Free parking. Head 5 miles west of St. Michaels, off Route 33.

A long country road leads to this grand old house (ca. 1819), set on a curve of land overlooking Chesapeake Bay. Surrounded by a sprawling lawn and 120 acres of fields, woodlands, and nature trails, this inn offers seclusion, peace, and some of the best sunset views you'll ever see. Named after Zachary Wade who received a land grant here in 1657, the inn dates from the early 19th century. It was erected by Thomas Kemp, a shipbuilder credited with creating the Baltimore Clipper ships, including the famous *Pride of Baltimore*. It is now owned by caring and cordial innkeepers Betsy and John Feiler.

The main house today offers varied guest rooms (with private or shared baths), furnished with antiques and cooled by the cross-ventilation of bay breezes, ceiling fans and screened porches. For modern comforts mixed with reproduction furnishings and decor, request a room in the newer adjacent Kemp Building; these 12 rooms all have private baths, air-conditioning, and most have private porches or balconies; four have kitchenettes. Breakfast is served in a bright wicker-filled room in the main house overlooking the bay. A two-night stay required for weekends and holidays. Discounts available for stays of three days or more.

INEXPENSIVE

⑤ Comfort Inn

8523 Ocean Gateway, Easton, MD 21601. ☎ **410/820-8333** or 800/228-5150. Fax 410/ 820-8436. 84 rms. A/C TV TEL. $67–$90 double. (Rates include continental breakfast.) AE, CB, DC, MC, V. Free parking.

This two-story hacienda-style property is one of the newest lodgings in this area. Set back from busy Route 50 and surrounded by trees, it has a bright and airy lobby with lots of light woods and plants. The guest rooms, many of which surround a central courtyard, are furnished with pastel tones and waterfowl art. Facilities include an outdoor swimming pool and a small restaurant.

Days Inn

7018 Ocean Gateway (Rte. 50), P.O. Box 968, Easton, MD 21601. ☎ **410/822-4600** or 800/325-2525. Fax 410/820-9723. 80 rms. A/C TV TEL. $49–$79 double. (Rates include continental breakfast.) AE, CB, DC, DISC, MC, V. Free parking.

Set back from the main road in a shady setting between Easton and Oxford, this motel is a favorite with families. The guest rooms offer a well-maintained contemporary decor with a choice of bed sizes, coffeemakers, and standard furnishings. Facilities include a restaurant, lounge, and an outdoor swimming pool.

WHERE TO DINE

Seafood lovers, rejoice. The Easton area is the heart of Maryland's crab, oyster, and fish country. Crab is the prime attraction—whether it is served as "crab imperial" in a rich creamy sauce, rolled up in plump crab cakes, floating in crab chowder, as crab claws, soft-shell crabs, or the just plain hard-shell variety. Come and have your fill; the crab is plentiful and the price is right.

EXPENSIVE

Peach Blossoms

6 N. Washington St., Easton. ☎ **410/822-5220.** Reservations recommended for dinner. Main courses $17.95–$19.95; lunch $6.95–$8.95. MC, V. Wed–Fri 11:30am–2pm and 5:30–9pm; Sat 5:30–9pm. INTERNATIONAL.

Situated in the heart of Easton's historic district opposite the Talbot County Courthouse, this is a bright bistro-style restaurant and wine bar, with a decor of leafy plants and light caned furniture. Everything is made on the premises, from tangy salad dressings to breads, pastries, and desserts. The menu changes daily, but lunch usually features salads, sandwiches, omelets, and pastas. Dinner selections include imaginative and colorfully presented dishes such as molasses-glazed duck with green chili cornbread stuffing; grilled grouper with citrus salsa; and veal medaillons with balsamic glaze and hazelnuts.

✪ Robert Morris Inn

314 N. Morris St. and The Strand, Oxford. ☎ **410/226-5111.** Reservations not accepted. Dinner main courses $14.95–$29.95; lunch $4.95–$12.95. MC, V. Lunch Wed–Mon noon–3pm; dinner Wed–Mon 6–9pm. Closed Dec to mid-March. AMERICAN/SEAFOOD.

Dating from the early 18th century, the dining room and tavern of this old inn (see "Where to Stay," above) are attractions in themselves, featuring original woodwork, slate floors, and fireplaces. The murals of the four seasons were made from wallpaper of 140 years ago, which was printed on a screw-type press using 1,600 woodcut blocks carved from orangewood.

Crab is the specialty here, with such entrées as crab cakes, crab Norfolk (crab sautéed with butter and sherry), crab imperial, and baked seafood au gratin cakes (crab and shrimp with Monterey Jack cheese, Cheddar, and seasonings). Lunch items range from sandwiches and salads to omelets, burgers, seafood platters, and hot entrées. Jackets are required for men in the main dining room except from Memorial Day to Labor Day.

208 Talbot

208 N. Talbot St., St. Michaels. ☎ **410/745-3838.** Reservations required. Main courses $16.50–$21; fixed price 5-course $38; lunch $8.50–$12.50. MC, V. Tues–Fri noon–2pm and 5–10pm; Sat 5–10pm, Sun 11am–2pm and 5–9pm. AMERICAN.

Housed in an 1870s brick house and situated at the far end of town, this restaurant is on the busy main thoroughfare and offers no water views, but the food draws a crowd each night. The menu emphasizes indigenous Eastern Shore seafood, produce, and herbs. Entrées change often but usually include pan-seared rockfish with wild mushrooms and oyster cream sauce; grilled Atlantic salmon with smoked salmon dill cream and red lentils; roasted free-range chicken with garlic mashed potatoes and minted peas; and rack of lamb and steaks. The decor is relaxing, with exposed brick walls, crisp white linens, botanical and waterfowl prints, and an oyster plate collection. Dinner on Saturday night only is on a fixed price basis.

MODERATE

✪ Bay Hundred Restaurant

Route 33 and Knapps Narrows, Tilghman Island. ☎ **410/886-2622.** Reservations required for dinner on weekends. Main courses $12.95–$18.95; lunch $4.95–$9.95. AE, CB,DC, DISC, MC, V. Daily 11:30am–10pm or later. SEAFOOD.

Sitting on the east side of the bridge at the entrance to Tilghman Island, this restaurant overlooks the marina and all the local boating and fishing activities. Floor-to-ceiling windows dominate the decor, but there is also an assortment of local fishing memorabilia on the walls as well as nautical and wildfowl prints and shelves of books. There is also seating in the cozy bar, which has a wine cellar atmosphere.

The menu offers local favorites such as crab cakes and grilled shrimp as well as specialties such as shrimp Ella, with zucchini, peas, and tomatoes in a creamy basil-Parmesan sauce; Zuni stew, a bean, rice, and vegetable stew served with corn pone; oysters Donelda, with spinach, cashews, scallions, ginger, and oyster sauce, stir-fried and served over egg fettuccine; pan-roasted duck breast with maple sweet potatoes and cranberry and plum sauce; and fried oysters with filet mignon.

✪ Harrison's Chesapeake House

21551 Chesapeake House Dr., Tilghman Island. ☎ **410/886-2121.** Reservations recommended for dinner. Main courses $9.95–$17.95; lunch $1.95–$12.95. MC, V. Lunch daily 11am–4pm; dinner daily 4–9pm. SEAFOOD.

A tradition on the Eastern Shore dating from 1856, this nautically themed restaurant has been run by four generations of the Harrison family. It sits right on the water and the two dining rooms offer great views of the bay and fishing fleet. The menu includes all types of Chesapeake Bay seafood—prepared broiled, fried, au gratin, or sautéed. There is also pan-fried chicken, prime rib, and steaks. All dishes are cooked to order and served family style with lots of vegetables (be sure to try the mashed potatoes topped with stewed tomatoes).

Higgins' Crab House

1216 S. Talbot St., St. Michaels. ☎ **410/745-5151**. Reservations recommended for dinner. Main courses $11.95–$19.95; lunch $4.95–$6.95. AE, MC, V. Mon–Fri 11:30am–9:30pm, Sat–Sun 11:30am–10pm. SEAFOOD.

Although not perched right on the water, this restaurant's decor is thoroughly nautical. There is seating both indoors and out, depending on the weather. Lunch choices feature sandwiches, burgers, seafood salads, and soups (crab vegetable and cream of crab are local favorites).

Crab is the main focus at dinner; selections include an "all-you-can-eat crab feast," hard crab of all sizes (available April 15 to November 15 only), soft-shell crabs, king crab legs, crab imperial, Chesapeake surf-and-turf (two crab cakes and two pieces of fresh fried chicken), and oysters Chesapeake (stuffed with crab imperial). Different varieties of shrimp, scallop, and steaks and barbecued baby-back ribs are also on the menu. It is situated on the approach to St. Michaels from Easton on Route 33.

Legal Spirits

42 E. Dover St., Easton. ☎ **410/822-0033**. Reservations recommended for dinner. Dinner main courses $9.95–$18.95; lunch $4.95–$10.95. AE, MC, V. Sun–Thurs 11:30am–10pm, Fri–Sat 11:30am–11pm. AMERICAN.

Housed in the historic Avalon Theater complex dating from 1921, this tavern-style restaurant has a turn-of-the-century atmosphere. With a tin ceiling, stained-glass windows, and brass fixtures, it harks back to an era synonymous with silent movies, vaudeville, and Art Deco. The eclectic menu features Maryland seafood favorites from crab cakes to fried oysters, as well as steaks, pastas, and vegetarian choices such as wild mushroom stroganoff or vegetable tartar. Local favorites are "waterfowl fried noodles," with boneless duck breast and fresh berry sauce, and shrimp and mussel stir fry. Lunch items range from salads and sandwiches to burgers and soups.

Rustic Inn

Talbottown Shopping Center, Easton. ☎ **410/820-8212**. Reservations recommended for dinner. Main courses $10.95–$21.95; lunch $4.95–$14.95. AE, MC, V. Tues–Fri 11:30am–1:30pm and 5–10pm; Sat–Mon 5–10pm. INTERNATIONAL.

Established in 1984, this eatery is situated in the midst of a string of shops. Although it can easily be overlooked, it is a hideaway well worth finding, especially for families. The decor features early farm implements, fishing gear, tobacco-growing tools, and old newspapers, all surrounding a wood-burning fireplace. Entrées include surf-and-turf, lobster tails, crab and oyster imperial, veal (marsala, piccata, or scaloppini with sherry and mushrooms), chicken Divan, steak béarnaise, and "salty strip" (strip steak covered with freshly shucked sautéed oysters and mushrooms).

Schooner's Landing

Foot of Tilghman St., Oxford. ☎ **410/226-0160**. Reservations accepted only for parties of five or more. Main courses $10.95–$19.95; lunch $3.95–$5.95. MC, V. Sun–Thurs 11:30am–9pm, Fri–Sat 11:30am–10pm. Closed: Nov–Apr Tues–Wed. SEAFOOD.

Situated right on the marina, this informal spot is known for its wide-windowed views of the water, with seating both indoors and on an outside deck. The menu changes daily, depending on the latest catch, but usually includes such choices as hot steamed crabs in season, seafood pasta, crab cakes, crab imperial, jumbo shrimp scampi, soft-shell clams and crabs, mussels, and fried oysters, as well as steaks, prime rib, and barbecued or broiled breast of corn-fed chicken.

Town Dock Restaurant

125 Mulberry St., St. Michaels. ☎ **410/745-5577**. Reservations recommended for dinner. Main courses $12–$22; lunch $4–$9. MC, V. Daily 11:30am–1pm. AMERICAN.

Sitting on high ground overlooking the harbor, this spot dates from the mid-19th century when it was known as the White Manor House and later as the Longfellow Inn. There are two dining levels inside; meals are also served on an adjacent deck overlooking the water.

The chef/owner, Michael Rork, formerly chef of the highly touted Hamptons restaurant of the Harbor Court Hotel in Baltimore, endeavors to present a "new Eastern Shore" cuisine, with choices such as "chicken Chesapeake," grilled breast with crab imperial and saffron glaze; fishermen's crepes; or vegetable stew, a blend of seasonal vegetables in broth and served over orzo, as well as traditional crab cakes, fried oysters, and daily beef and veal specials. Lunch choices include stews, salads, sandwiches, quiches, and seafood platters.

Yesteryears

Easton Plaza, Marlborough Ave., Easton. ☎ **410/822-2433**. Reservations recommended on weekends. Main courses $9.95–$17.95, lunch $3.95–$8.95. AE, MC, V. Mon–Sat 11am–9:30pm. AMERICAN.

Don't judge this restaurant by its nondescript concrete exterior, wedged in a busy shopping center. Step inside and savor the decor designed to convey the ambience of Washington Street at the turn-of-the-century. The fittings incorporate genuine town memorabilia, from timbers salvaged from the old Dover Bridge, to mirrors from the 19th-century Brick Hotel. The menu presents American food with an Eastern shore accent, including items such as chicken pot pie and crab cakes, as well as prime rib, steaks, and barbecued baby-back ribs. In addition, there are several international favorites, including Italian pastas and teriyaki and cordon bleu dishes. There is also a large selection of salads, burgers, raw bar items, and tavern-style overstuffed sandwiches, such as "The Virginian" (hot ham and crab imperial with melted cheddar).

MODERATE/INEXPENSIVE

⑤ Crab Claw

Navy Point, Mill St., St. Michaels. ☎ **410/745-2900**. Reservations not accepted. Main courses $7.95–$18.95. No credit cards. Mid-Mar to mid-Dec daily 11am–10pm. SEAFOOD.

There is no air-conditioning, just ceiling fans and lots of bay breezes, in this casual indoor and outdoor eatery on the lower end of the waterfront. The emphasis on the all-day menu is on crabs, served from hot, steamed, and seasoned to fried hard crab, backfin crab cake, crab chowder, soft crab, "crab dogs" (on a stick), and crab imperial; other seafood and fried chicken are also available.

Morsels

205 N. Talbot St., St. Michaels. ☎ **410/745-2911**. Reservations recommended for dinner. Main courses $7.95–$17.95; lunch $3.95–$6.95. MC, V. Sun–Thurs 11am–3pm and 5:30–9pm, Fri–Sat 11am–3pm and 5:30–10pm. INTERNATIONAL.

The pink-and-white facade of this informal Victorian shopfront restaurant stands out along the main thoroughfare, as does its menu. Specialties include Moroccan chicken and almond pie; steak Eva, a grilled filet topped with mushrooms and béarnaise sauce; paella of chicken, shrimp, sausage, and mussels with Spanish beans and rice and spicy tomato-pepper sauce; and Basque seafood pasta, sautéed seafood in a roasted pepper sauce on spinach linguine.

St. Michaels Crab House

305 Mulberry St., St. Michaels. ☎ **410/745-3737.** Reservations recommended for dinner. Main courses $9.95–$15.95; lunch $4.95–$8.95. MC, V. Apr–Oct, Mon–Sat 11am–11pm, Sun 11am–10pm. SEAFOOD.

Located on the marina, this restaurant emphasizes casual dining, with a choice of indoor (air-conditioned) seating amid a nautical decor, and a large outdoor area lined with picnic tables and umbrellas. The building itself dates from the 1830s, when it was an oyster-shucking shed; the patio bricks outside were kilned in St. Michaels during the late 1800s.

The menu features all-you-can-eat steamed crabs and other crab dishes, from crab cakes and crab imperial to soft-shell crabs and snow crab legs. Other seafood choices include stuffed flounder, fried shrimp, and fried oysters. For landlubbers, there are steaks and barbecued or grilled chicken. Appetizers include an extensive raw bar. Lunch items range from soups and salads to sandwiches and burgers.

NEARBY EXCURSIONS

CAMBRIDGE

Don't leave this area without a short detour to **Cambridge,** a lovely old Eastern Shore town founded in 1684. Lying 15 miles south of Easton, off Route 50, it is situated on the Choptank River, just off the Chesapeake. With an active harbor, it is Maryland's second-largest deep-water port, supplying ocean-going vessels and coastal freighters with grain and seafood cargo. For visitors, Cambridge provides opportunities to stroll in grassy riverfront public parks or along **Historic High Street,** a two-block area lined with 18th- and 19th-century buildings. Gracious Victorian-style homes also rim the shoreline including a house originally built for Annie Oakley.

Cambridge's biggest draw, however, is positioned 12 miles southeast of town— the **Blackwater National Wildfowl Refuge,** 2145 Key Wallace Dr., Cambridge (☎ 410/228-2677), a 17,121-acre site of rich tidal marsh, freshwater ponds, and woodlands, used by huge flocks of Canada geese (approximately 33,000) and ducks (exceeding 15,000) as one of the chief fall migration and wintering areas along the Atlantic flyway. Established in 1933, the grounds are also the home of three endangered species: the bald eagle, the Delmarva fox squirrel, and the migrant peregrine falcon. Facilities include an observation tower, a 5-mile wildlife drive, and walking and biking trails. The visitor center is open Monday through Friday from 8am to 4pm, and on Saturday and Sunday from 9am to 5pm (except federal holidays and some summer weekends). The wildlife trail and other outdoor facilities are open daily, dawn to dusk. Entrance fee for the wildlife drive is $3 per vehicle and $1 for bicyclists and pedestrians.

SALISBURY

If you are heading from Easton to Ocean City, or vice versa, chances are that you'll encounter **Salisbury.** Situated approximately 60 miles southeast of Easton, Salisbury is a crossroads city on the Eastern Shore. Originally a settlement at the intersection of Indian trails on the banks of the Wicomico River, this "hub city" of today lies at the junction of Routes 13 and 50, almost equidistant between Easton and Ocean City. The largest city on Maryland's Eastern Shore, it is widely recognized as a major trade and transport center for the entire Delmarva Peninsula. As the home and business headquarters of Frank Perdue, Salisbury is also known as the "poultry capital of the world."

Like most of the Eastern Shore, Salisbury is positioned in the heart of waterfowl country and is the setting for the world's largest collection of contemporary and classic wildfowl art, the **Ward Museum of Wildfowl Art,** 909 S. Schumaker Dr. (☎ 410/860-BIRD or 410/742-4988). This museum sits on the southeast edge of the city, overlooking Schumaker Pond, amid a wildfowl sanctuary and habitat. It is a prime showcase for displays of antique decoys and contemporary carvings, as well as paintings and works on paper.

Interpretative galleries help visitors trace the development of the art form from hunters' tools to sculpture. The exhibits include an evolutionary history of decoy-making and a stylized re-creation of an early decoy-making workshop. Admission is $4 for adults, $3 for seniors and college students, and $2 for youths 5 to 18; free for children under 5. Open Monday through Saturday from 10am to 5pm, Wednesday from 10am to 8pm, and Sunday from noon to 5pm.

3 Chestertown

40 miles N of Easton, 55 miles E of Baltimore, 35 miles NE of Annapolis, 35 miles W of Dover, 70 miles NW of Salisbury, 70 miles NE of Washington, D.C.

Founded as the Port of Chester in 1706 on the Chester River off Chesapeake Bay, Chestertown was an important port in Colonial times. It was the economic, social, and religious hub of Kent County, vying with Annapolis in the 18th century as a major port on the Chesapeake Bay. Today the town is rich in well-preserved 18th- and 19th-century homes on Water Street, overlooking the river, and High Street, the main thoroughfare. Often called the "insider's Annapolis," Chestertown is also the home of Washington College, one of America's oldest colleges (established in 1782).

GETTING THERE The only way to get to Chestertown is by car. From Easton, follow U.S. Route 50 northward to Route 213 and then follow Route 213 north into Chestertown. From I-95 and U.S. Route 40, take the Elkton exit and follow Route 213 southward into Chestertown. From Dover and points east, follow U.S. Routes 13 and 301 to Route 213 and continue to Chestertown.

ESSENTIALS Area Code The area code is 410.

Visitor Information For a map and travel brochures about Chestertown and the surrounding area, contact the Kent County Chamber of Commerce, P.O. Box 146, 400 S. Cross St., Chestertown, MD 21620 (☎ 410/778-0416).

GETTING AROUND By Car Since there is no public transportation in Chestertown, the best way to see the area sights is to bring your car. High Street is Chestertown's main thoroughfare. To help you get your bearings, a self-guided driving tour brochure is available from the Kent County Chamber of Commerce.

On Foot A self-guided walking tour leaflet with a coded map is available from the Kent County Chamber of Commerce.

WHAT TO SEE & DO

The focal point of Chestertown is **High Street,** a wide thoroughfare lined with brick town houses and businesses including the Georgian-style **Court House,** built in 1860; the **White Swan Tavern,** 231 High St., established in 1733; and the **"Rock of Ages" House,** 532 High St., an unusual 18th-century house built entirely of massive angular stones.

Water Street, hugging the Chester River, is the setting for the **Customs House,** noted for its Flemish bond brickwork (ca. 1746), and **"Wide Hall,"** one of the town's most elaborate merchant's houses (ca. 1770). More than two dozen buildings throughout the town are identified with plaques and described in "A Walking Tour of Old Chester Town," a leaflet available free from the chamber of commerce. If you happen to be in town on a Saturday morning, don't miss the **Chestertown Farmers' Market** at Chestertown Park from 9am to noon.

The area around Chestertown is also worth exploring. About 15 miles southwest of town via Route 20 is **Rock Hall,** a boating and fishing center sitting where the Chester River meets the Chesapeake Bay.

About halfway between Chestertown and Rock Hall, off Route 20, is historic **St. Paul's Church** (☎ 410/778-3180), erected in 1713, making it one of the oldest continually used churches in Maryland. Among the notables buried in the church's oak tree-shaded graveyard is actress Tallulah Bankhead. The church is open daily from 9am to 5pm; there is no admission charge, but donations are welcome.

SHOPPING

Chester River Knitting Company
113 S. Cross St. ☎ **410/778-0374.**

Step inside this little shop and watch knitters Bill and Beth Ruckelshaus at work, producing hand-framed cotton, wool, and cashmere sweaters. Making use of wool from local farms, many of the sweaters bear distinctive designs, such as a crab or waterfowl motif or nautical symbols. Sweaters can also be knit to order. Unique straw hats are also for sale. Open Tuesday through Saturday from 10am to 5pm.

Creative Cookery
108 Cross St. ☎ **410/778-2665.**

This shop is a cornucopia for cooks, stocking all kinds of spices, sweets, condiments, teas, and herbs. There are also cookbooks of all kinds, canned Eastern Shore soups, and aprons and accessories with crab or clam designs. Open Monday from 10am to 3pm, Tuesday through Saturday from 10am to 5pm.

Dixon's Auction Sales
Rtes. 544 and 290, Crumpton. ☎ **410/928-3006.**

Located about 10 miles northeast of Chestertown, this unique auction complex has put Crumpton on the map. Weekly outdoor furniture auctions are spread over 15 acres. Bidders stand beside items they like, and Jesse Dixon swings by on a golf cart to lead the fast-paced auctioneer's chant. Smaller items, such as bric-a-brac, jewelry, and collectibles, are also up for auction, inside a large barnlike structure. Items range from rare antiques to a box full of brass doorknobs or 19th-century whaling harpoon, musical instruments, or records. Amish-made baked goods, smoked meat, cheese, and other foods are also for sale at an indoor lunch counter. Open every Wednesday from 10am to 6pm or later.

The Village House
103 Cross St. ☎ **410/778-5766.**

Wooden bird cages, needlepoint pillows, hand-painted plates and pottery, decorative candle holders, handmade wreaths, and lanterns fill this shop. In addition, there are household and garden accessories, and brass and cast-stone animal figurines. Open Monday through Saturday from 9:30am to 5pm.

WHERE TO STAY

✪ Brampton Inn
25227 Chestertown Rd., Chestertown, MD 21620. ☎ **410/778-1860.** 8 rms, 2 suites. A/C. $95–$155 single or double; $115–$145 suite. (All rates include full breakfast.) MC, V. Free parking.

A curving tree-lined driveway leads to this three-story red-brick inn, just over a mile southwest of town (off Route 20). Built in 1860 and listed on the National Register of Historic Places, it sits on 35 acres between the Chester River and Chesapeake Bay. Guests enjoy use of two gracious sitting rooms, a wide front porch, and extensive spruce-shaded grounds with lawn furniture. The guest rooms are furnished with authentic period antiques and canopy or four-poster beds; all have private baths and eight of the rooms have fireplaces. The suites have a sitting room and private TV. A two-night minimum is required on weekends and a three-night minimum on holiday weekends. The innkeepers are Michael and Danielle Hanscom.

✪ Imperial Hotel
208 High St., Chestertown, MD 21620. ☎ **410/778-5000.** Fax 410/778-9662. 11 rms, 2 suites. A/C TV TEL. $125 double room; $200–$300 suite. (All rates include continental breakfast.) DISC, MC, V. Free parking.

With a fanciful gingerbread-trimmed triple-porch facade, this three-story brick building is a focal point along the main street of this historic town. The interior includes a Victorian-style restaurant (see "Where to Dine," below), parlor and lounge/bar, a cellar-level coffee/bakery/wine shop, as well as a courtyard garden with a gallery displaying monthly exhibits of local and American art. Guest rooms are furnished with brass beds, period antiques, armoires, and colorful wallpapers. One suite is on the third floor with a private porch, parlor, and kitchen; and the other suite occupies the top floor of an adjacent 18th-century carriage house. Innkeepers are Barbara and Bob Lavelle.

Inn at Mitchell House
8796 Maryland Pkwy., Chestertown, MD 21620. ☎ **410/778-6500.** 6 rms. $75–$110 double. (Rates include full breakfast.) MC, V. Free parking.

If you are looking for a quiet old-world retreat surrounded by remote farmland and habitats for birds, migrating geese, white-tailed deer, and red fox, try this three-story, 1743 manor house with a screened-in porch. Nestled on 10 acres overlooking Stoneybrook Pond, it sits almost midway between Chestertown and Rock Hall off Routes 21 and 445; Tolchester marina is half a mile away. The guest rooms, named after historic people or places associated with the area, are furnished with four-poster beds, hook rugs, antiques, decorative wall coverings, and framed old prints. Most rooms have a fireplace or sitting area; all have private baths. On Friday and Saturday nights, dinner is also available to guests in the dining room (reservations are required 24 hours in advance). Innkeepers are Jim and Tracy Stone.

Lauretum Inn

954 High St. (Route 20), Chestertown, MD 21620. ☎ **410/778-3236** or 800/742-3236. 3 rms, 2 suites. $75–$85 with shared bath, $95 with private bath, single or double; $105–$115 suite. (Rates include continental breakfast.) DISC, MC, V. Free parking.

Sitting amid 6 acres on a shady knoll about a mile outside of town, this three-story 19th-century Queen Anne Victorian was named Lauretum, meaning "Laurel Grove" in Latin, by its first owner, Sen. George Vickers. Highlights of the interior include a formal parlor with painted ceiling medallion and fireplace, reading room, a screened porch, and a sweeping central staircase. Guests enjoy use of antique-filled sitting rooms and a screened-in porch. Two rooms share a bath; one room and the two suites have private baths. There is a two-night minimum on weekends, and three-night minimum on holiday weekends. Innkeepers are Peg and Bill Sites.

WHERE TO DINE

✪ Imperial Hotel

208 High St. ☎ **410/778-5000.** Reservations required. Main courses $18.50–$24; lunch $6–$12. DISC, MC, V. Tues–Sat 11:45am–2pm and 5:30–9:30pm; Sun noon–3pm. AMERICAN.

Housed in the center of the historic district, this inn offers fine cuisine and an elegant ambience reminiscent of bygone days. It has with two intimate Victorian-themed dining rooms: the Hubbard Room, dominated by hunt-green tones and tallyho prints, and the Leighton Room, with a rich claret-colored motif. Seating is also available on the outdoor garden patio in the summer months (with live jazz on Friday evenings). The menu changes seasonally, but house favorites often include pan-seared filet of salmon with sautéed shrimp, bell peppers, onions, and tomatoes; grilled marinated leg of lamb with rosemary, mustard, and garlic butter; and roast filet of monkfish with leek and watercress. Lunch items range from sandwiches and salads to pastas and quiches.

Old Wharf Inn

Foot of Cannon St. ☎ **410/778-3566.** Reservations accepted only for parties of 5 or more. Main courses $7.95–$17.95, lunch $2.95–$12.95. AE, MC, V. Mon–Sat 11am–9pm, Sun 10am–9pm. AMERICAN

For good value and good views, the locals congregate at this nautically themed restaurant, overlooking the Chester River, off Water Street. It has an informal "Old Chesapeake" atmosphere, with ships' wheels adapted into lighting fixtures, as well as captain's chairs, ceilings fans, and a row of paned windows overlooking the water. The menu features Eastern Shore traditions such as fried chicken, Smithfield ham, crab cakes, fried oysters, and a half-dozen kinds of shrimp dishes (from fried and coconut battered, to barbecued, stuffed, or Alfredo-style). Specials on Tuesday and Thursday nights offer "all-you-can-eat" steamed shrimp and on Friday there is a prime rib, seafood, and pasta buffet.

4 Chesapeake City

60 miles N of Easton, 70 miles NE of Annapolis, 43 miles NW of Dover, 40 miles SW of Wilmington, 25 miles NE of Chestertown, 125 miles NW of Ocean City

Sitting beside the banks of the Chesapeake and Delaware Canal (C&D) on the upper reaches of the Chesapeake Bay in Maryland's northeast corner, Chesapeake City is a picture-perfect specimen of a well-preserved Early American canal town.

Originally known as Bohemia Village because of its proximity to the Bohemia River, it dates from the 1780s, but did not begin to grow until after the construction of the C&D Canal in 1804. By 1824, it was one of the canal's thriving towns and aptly renamed Chesapeake City.

Although not as large as it was in its heyday, today it provides a good example of rural 19th-century architecture, from workers' cottages to merchants' residences and the homes of well-to-do farmers and local professionals. The remnants of a bygone era include an original canal lock pumping station with what is said to be the world's largest surviving water wheel and a set of Philadelphia-made Corless steam pumps with cast-iron Ionic columns. All in all, the town is a lovely maze of fine Victorian buildings, both on the north side and the south side of the canal. The south side, a National Register district, is the oldest part.

Surrounded by fertile farmlands, this area is also known for its horse farms. Equine greats Kelso and Northern Dancer were bred here.

GETTING THERE   The only way to get to Chesapeake City is by car. From Easton and other points in the southern Eastern Shore, take Route 301 northeast to Route 213, which leads directly into Chesapeake City. From I-95 or U.S. Route 40 take the Elkton exit and follow Route 213 south; from Dover, take U.S. Route 13 north to U.S. Route 301/310 westward, which connects with Route 213 into Chesapeake City.

ESSENTIALS   **Area Code**   The area code is 410.

Visitor Information   For travel brochures about the Chesapeake City area, contact the Cecil County Office of Economic Development, Tourism Department, 129 E. Main St., Room 324, Elkton, MD 21921 (☎ 410/996-5300 or 800/232-4595).

GETTING AROUND   **By Car**   Although the downtown area of Chesapeake City lends itself to walking, the best way to see the surrounding sights is by car. There is no public transportation.

On Foot   The Chesapeake and Delaware Canal (C&D) divides the city into a north and south side. The main commercial and historic area sits on the south side of the canal. It is a very walkable area, with one main street, Bohemia Avenue, where most of the shops and businesses are located. Pick up a copy of "Canal Town," a handy folder with a map, available free in all of the shops and public areas.

WHAT TO SEE & DO

A focal point of the town is the **C&D Canal Museum,** 815 Bethel Rd. (☎ 410/885-5622). Located on the waterfront at 2nd Street, it has a series of exhibits that depict the history and operation of the Chesapeake and Delaware Canal. It's open from April through October, Monday through Saturday from 8:15am to 4:15pm and Sunday from 10am to 6pm; from November through March, it's open Monday through Saturday from 8:15am to 4:15pm. Admission is free.

To soak up the ambience of this canal-side city, spend some time in **Pell Gardens,** a grassy parklike setting next to the museum and overlooking Back Creek on Rees Wharf at the end of Bohemia Street. There are lots of places to sit and relax, with over 40 wooden and iron benches and a gazebo.

A good way to get an overview of the area is to take a three-hour **"horse country tour,"** operated by a local agency, Hill Holidays Travel, 103 Bohemia

Ave., Chesapeake City, MD 21915 (☎ 410/885-2797 or 800/874-4558). The tours take you to the leading horse farms in the surrounding Cecil County area; to visit Mount Harmon, a 17th-century frontier tobacco plantation; and to three of the area's most historic churches—St. Augustine, St. Stephens, and Old Bohemia. Tours depart on Tuesday and Thursday at 9am, and on Tuesday, Thursday, and Sunday at 1pm. The price is $15 per person and reservations are required. All tours depart from the Hill Holidays Travel Centre; this agency can also arrange for sightseeing cruises on the canal ($5 to $20 per person, depending on the departure time and routing).

SHOPPING

Chesapeake City is a good shopping town, especially for arts and crafts.

Back Creek General Store
100 Bohemia Ave. ☎ **410/885-5377.**

Housed in a historic 1861 building, this shop features a variety of arts and crafts, from throw rugs and pottery, seagull-themed pewter, music boxes, prints, candles, soaps, scents, and books on the Eastern Shore and its birds. Open Monday through Tuesday from 11am to 5pm, Wednesday and Thursday and Sunday from 11am to 8pm, and Friday and Saturday from 11am to 9pm.

Canal Artworks
17 Bohemia Ave. ☎ **410/885-5083.**

Located in the Riley House, a building dating from 1831 next to the Bayard House, this shop/studio displays paintings of the Chesapeake City area by local artist Jon deVos, who can often be seen at work. Original prints, limited-edition prints, and note cards are for sale. Open on Wednesday, Saturday, and Sunday from 10am to 5pm and by appointment.

Maren's
200 Bohemia Ave. ☎ **410/885-2475.**

Horse-themed jewelry draws many people to this store, as does a wide array of local folk and wildlife art. There is also a Christmas Corner for Yuletide shopping year-round and Dickens Room for collectors. Open daily from 10am to 5pm or later.

WHERE TO STAY

The Blue Max
300 Bohemia Ave., Chesapeake City, MD 21915. ☎ **410/885-2781.** Fax 410/885-2809. 7 rms. A/C TV TEL. $75–$95 double. AE, MC, V. Free parking.

Built in 1844, this house was once occupied by author Jack Hunter at the time that he wrote his book *The Blue Max.* True to its name, this house has been furnished with an emphasis on blue-and-white decor, both inside and outside. The bedrooms are modern and large. Guests enjoy use of a cozy parlor with fireplace, dining room, and first- and second-floor porches overlooking the heart of the historic district. Innkeeper is Philip Braeunig, Jr.

Inn at the Canal
104 Bohemia Ave., P.O. Box 187, Chesapeake City, MD 21915. ☎ **410/885-5995.** 6 rms, 1 ste. A/C TV. $75–$105 double, $130 suite. (Rates include full breakfast and afternoon refreshments.) AE, DISC, MC, V. Free parking.

Situated on Back Creek Basin, a block from the Chesapeake and Delaware Canal in the heart of the historic district, this three-story Victorian house dates from 1870 and is known locally as the Brady-Rees House. Innkeepers Mary and Al Ioppolo have sought to preserve the house's 19th-century atmosphere by furnishing it with antiques and family heirlooms including a large collection of old baking and cooking implements on the fireplace wall of the kitchen. The guest rooms are individually decorated with antiques and quilts; half of the bedrooms have views of the water. Guests enjoy use of the turn-of-the-century dining room, guest parlor, and two wicker-filled porches where you can sit and watch the boats breeze by on the canal.

WHERE TO DINE

✪ Bayard House
11 Bohemia Ave. ☎ **410/885-5040.** Reservations recommended for dinner. Main courses $16.95–$24.95; lunch $8.95–$12.95. AE, DISC, MC, V. Mon–Fri 11:30am–3pm and 5–9pm, Sat 11:30am–3pm and 5–10pm, Sun 11:30am–2:30pm and 4–9pm. AMERICAN.

Few people come to Chesapeake City without stopping for a meal at this highly acclaimed restaurant, perched right beside the canal and considered to be the oldest building in Chesapeake City. It dates from the early 1780s when Samuel Bayard built a manor home on this site. As the city began to prosper, the house was converted into an inn and tavern; it was under various names and owners until finally reverting to its original name after a complete restoration in 1985. Two dining areas are offered: a glass-enclosed dining room with wide windows overlooking the water and an outdoor canal-side patio fanned by gentle breezes.

Featured dishes include tournedos Baltimore (twin petit filet mignons, one topped with a crab cake and the other with a lobster cake, served with Madeira-cream and seafood-champagne sauces); applewood-smoked duck with linguine, shiitake mushrooms, and tomatoes in a basil-cream sauce; salmon "painted desert" (on a palate of white-wine and shallot sauce and painted with red chiles and fresh herb purée); and macadamia-crusted tilapia.

Schaefer's Canal House
208 Bank St. ☎ **410/885-2200.** Reservations not accepted for Sat from Apr–Aug; otherwise recommended. Main courses $17–$32; lunch $7–$14; brunch $12.95. AE, MC, V. Lunch Mon–Sat 11am–4pm; dinner Mon–Sat 4–10pm, Sun noon–9pm; brunch Sun 11am–3pm. AMERICAN.

First opened in 1908 as a general store, this wide-windowed restaurant sits on the north side of the canal facing Chesapeake City's historic district. From June through August, seating is available outside on the dockside terrace. The menu offers a variety of meat and seafood dishes such as prime rib, breast of capon in lemon-lime champagne sauce, crab cakes, fried shrimp amandine, crab-stuffed flounder, and surf-and-turf as well as a vegetarian stir-fry.

5 Crisfield

119 miles southeast of Annapolis, 79 miles SE of Easton, 54 miles SW of Ocean City, 64 miles SE of Cambridge, 32 miles SW of Salisbury.

Legend has it that Crisfield is built almost entirely on oyster shells. It's a likely story, considering that this tiny town (population 2,900) has long laid claim to the title of "seafood capital of the world."

Tucked into the most southerly corner of Maryland's Eastern Shore along the Chesapeake, Crisfield has relied on the bay for its livelihood for more than 100 years.

Stroll the city dock or marina—you'll see everything from the fish-laden head boats to the crab-picking, oyster-shucking, and seafood-packing plants. Better still, breathe in the salty air and amble into one of the town's restaurants to taste the maritime bounty.

Although many types of seafood are caught in the waters off Crisfield, crab is unquestionably king in this port—there is even a crab derby festival staged here at the end of each summer.

GETTING THERE   By Car   Crisfield is accessible from all directions via Routes 413 and 13.

ESSENTIALS   Area Code   The area code is 410.

Visitor Information   For brochures, maps, and all sorts of helpful information about Crisfield and the surrounding countryside, contact the Somerset County Tourism Office, 11440 Ocean Highway (Route 13), P.O. Box 243, Princess Anne, MD 21853 (☎ 410/651-2968 or 800/521-9189); or the Crisfield Chamber of Commerce, J. Millard Tawes Museum, Somers Cove Marina, P.O. Box 292, Crisfield, MD 21817 (☎ 410/968-2500 or 800/782-3913).

WHAT TO SEE & DO

The **J. Millard Tawes Museum,** 3 Ninth St.(☎ 410/968-2501), on the Somers Cove Marina, was founded in 1982 to honor a Crisfield-born former governor of Maryland. The headquarters of the chamber of commerce offices, this museum is a good place to start a walk around the town. The exhibits will give you useful background about the history of Crisfield and the development of the city's seafood industry; there is also a fascinating wildfowl wood carving workshop on the premises. Open daily May through October 9am to 4:30pm; and Monday through Friday November through April 9am to 4:30pm. Admission charge is $1 adults, 50¢ children.

About 15 miles north of Crisfield on Route 13 is **Princess Anne,** a well-preserved Colonial town created in 1733. The highlight is the **Teackle Mansion** (☎ 410/651-1705), built in 1801 and patterned after a Scottish manor house. This was the residence of Littleton Dennis Teackle, an associate of Thomas Jefferson and one of the principal transoceanic shipping magnates of the 18th century. He also is credited with establishing Maryland's first public school system and the first public commercial bank on the American continent. With two entrances, one fronting the Manokin River and one facing the town, this grand house measures nearly 200 feet in length and is symmetrically balanced throughout. The house is open for guided tours year-round on Sunday from 2 to 4pm and from March to mid-December also on Wednesday from 1 to 3pm and Saturday from 11am to 3pm. Some of the things you will see include elaborate plaster ceilings, mirrored windows, a seven-foot fireplace, and a beehive oven, American Chippendale furniture, Della Robbia (fruit-designed) ceilings, a Tudor-Gothic pipe organ, an 1806 silk world map, and a 1712 family Bible. The admission and tour charge is $2 per person. For more information, call 410/651-3020 or 410/651-2238.

OUTDOOR ACTIVITIES

The **Somers Cove Marina** (☎ 410/968-0925), a $30 million development built on the site of a farm started in 1663 by Benjamin Somers, is one of the largest facilities of its kind in Maryland. The marina is ultramodern, able to accommodate all types of vessels, from 10 feet to 150 feet. There are 272 boat slips, boat ramps, deluxe tiled showers, a laundry room, a swimming pool, boat storage, electricity and water, and a fuel dock.

Head boats leave from the marina and from the nearby town dock each day on **fishing trips** in pursuit of flounder, trout, spot, drum, and blues. For further information, walk along the waterfront and talk with the various boatmen on duty or call any of the following: **Capt. Curtis Johns** (☎ 410/623-2035); **Capt. James Landon** (☎ 410/968-0177); **Capt. Joe Asanovich** (☎ 410/957-2562); and **Capt. Lionel Daugherty** (☎ 410/968-0947).

SHOPPING

Besides its copious crab, this area's other claim to fame is that it is the home of the **Carvel Hall Factory Outlet,** Route 413, Crisfield (☎ 410/968-0500). Carvel Hall was started in 1895 when a young blacksmith hammered out his first seafood-harvesting tools on a borrowed anvil. Today discounts of up to 50% are given on brand-name cutlery, made entirely in this Crisfield plant, plus hundreds of other nationally known gift items such as glassware, pewter, sterling silver, plated hollowware, brass, and crystal. Open daily from 10am to 6pm (closed major holidays).

WHERE TO STAY

Choosing where to stay is easy in Crisfield. There are only three motels in town, all in the moderate category with basic accommodations, as well as one good bed-and-breakfast.

✪ My Fair Lady

38 W. Main St., Crisfield, MD 21817. ☎ **410/968-3514** or 800/294-3514. 5 rms (all with private bath). A/C TV. $80–$90 double. (Rates include continental breakfast.) No credit cards. Closed Jan–Feb. Free parking.

With an inviting wrap-around porch, this beautifully restored Queen Anne Victorian bed-and-breakfast inn sits on the quiet residential end of Crisfield's main thoroughfare, at the corner of First Street. It offers a homey atmosphere and the aura of yesteryear while still providing modern comforts. Guest rooms are individually furnished with antiques and period reproductions, collected over the years by the attentive and enthusiastic innkeepers Jacqueline and Donald Brooks.

Paddlewheel Motel

701 W. Main St., Crisfield, MD 21817. ☎ **410/968-2220.** 19 rms. A/C TV. $35–$80 double. MC, V. Free parking.

Located in the heart of the town, this modern two-story motel is within walking distance of the City Dock and waterfront. Open April through December, the Paddlewheel offers rooms equipped with two double beds and standard furnishings.

Pines Motel

N. Somerset Ave., P.O. Box 106, Crisfield, MD 21817. ☎ **410/968-0900.** 40 rms. A/C TV. $40–$80 double. No credit cards. Free parking.

For more than 30 years, this motel has offered fine lodging in a quiet residential setting of tall pine trees. The modern ground-level units all have contemporary furnishings, two double beds, wall-to-wall carpeting, and views of the adjacent outdoor swimming pool and picnic area. Twelve efficiencies are available at $15 extra per room. Open all year.

Somers Cove Motel

R. R. Norris Drive, P.O. Box 387, Crisfield, MD 21817. ☎ **410/968-1900** or 800/827-6637. 40 rms. A/C TV TEL. $45–$80 double. MC, V.

Views of the water add to the setting of this modern two-story facility. Opened in 1979, the motel offers rooms with one or two double beds; each room also has a balcony or patio. Guest amenities include an outdoor heated swimming pool, patios, picnic tables, barbecue grills, boat-docking facilities, and ramps. Open all year. Seven efficiencies are available for $10 extra per room.

WHERE TO DINE

The focus of attention here is simply seafood, plenty of it. From crab omelets for breakfast and crab soup and crabwiches for lunch, to crab cooked in a dozen different ways for dinner, this is the place to have your fill of this tasty and succulent crustacean. Most all restaurants in town serve breakfast, with choices usually priced from $2 to $5, starting between 5:30 and 6am to cater to the resident and visiting fishermen. Beer, wine, and cocktails are available at most restaurants, unless noted otherwise.

Captain's Galley

1021 W. Main St. ☎ **410/968-1636.** Reservations recommended for dinner. Main courses $6.95–$18.95; lunch $2.95–$7.95. DISC, MC, V. Daily 11:30am–2:30pm and 5–10pm. SEAFOOD.

Overlooking the City Dock, this contemporary-style, wide-windowed restaurant is the ideal place to watch the boats moving in and out of the harbor. The dinner entrées range from a gargantuan "seafood feast" (soft crab, crab cake, fish filet, scallops, shrimp, and oysters) to crab cakes, crab imperial, crab au gratin, plus steaks and fried chicken. Lunch choices concentrate on sandwiches (such as crab cake, oyster fritter, crab imperial, soft crab, shrimp or tuna salad, as well as meats).

✪ Watermen's Inn

9th and Main sts. ☎ **410/968-2119.** Reservations recommended for dinner. Main courses $7.95–$18.95; lunch $2.95–$8.95. AE, DISC, MC, V. Mon–Sat 11:30am–2:30pm and 5–10pm, Sun 11:30am–2:30pm and 5–9pm. Closed Mon in winter. AMERICAN.

Although this eatery does not boast water views, the food here is the prime attraction—a little out of the ordinary, with an ever-changing menu of cooked-to-order dishes. Dinnertime choices focus on baked stuffed jumbo soft crabs, crab cakes, baked stuffed flounder, jumbo fantail shrimp, crab au gratin, fried chicken, imported baby-back ribs, charbroiled steaks, vegetarian plates, and a signature cream of crab soup.

AN EXCURSION TO SMITH ISLAND

Located 13 miles west of Crisfield in the midst of Chesapeake Bay's Tangier Sound, Smith Island is Maryland's only inhabited offshore island. The uninhabited southern tip of the island is intersected by the Maryland-Virginia state line.

Smith Islanders are the direct descendants of British colonists who first settled the island in the early 1700s. To this day, because of their separation from the mainland, they speak with a distinctive accent and speech pattern, said to be a holdover of the Elizabethan/Cornwall dialect. Smith Island is a world set apart—there are no sidewalks, beaches, convenience stores, boat rentals, movie theaters, liquor stores, bars, fast-food chains, boutiques, Laundromats, or taxi cabs. The people make their living primarily from the sea by crabbing and oystering.

There are three towns on Smith Island, each with a working harbor. The island's largest town is **Ewell,** sometimes referred to as the "capital" of Smith Island. It is the most visited destination and home of the majority of the island's seafood-packing houses. Homes in Ewell range from 1850s center-gabled two-story structures to Cape Cods or modular homes and trailers. The other two towns are **Rhodes Point,** situated a mile from Ewell and the island's center for boat repair, and **Tylerton,** Smith Island's most remote town, accessible only by boat from Ewell.

Passenger ferries depart year-round from Crisfield's City Dock or Somers Cove Marina for excursions to Smith Island. The trip takes approximately 35 minutes to one hour, depending on the route and time of year. The price of the trip averages from $20 to $25 for a round-trip boat ride or $30 to $35 for a round-trip that includes sightseeing on the island and a bountiful family style lunch at one of the local restaurants. Boats usually depart Crisfield around noon and return from the island around 5pm.

For exact schedules and reservations, inquire at the information booths at the City Dock or Somers Cove Marina or contact **Capt. Alan Tyler** (☎ 410/425-2771); **Capt. Otis Ray Tyler** (☎ 410/968-3206); **Capts. Terry and Larry Laird** (☎ 410/425-5931 or 410/425-4471); or **Capt. Wallace Thomas** (☎ 410/968-3571).

5

Ocean City

The narrow peninsula known as Ocean City is Maryland's star attraction along the Atlantic. A 10-mile strip of white sandy beach, Ocean City is a lively and well-developed vacationland, sandwiched in between the "quiet" Delaware resorts of Fenwick Island and Bethany Beach to the north and the equally tranquil Assateague Island and the Virginia border to the south.

In addition to its seafront side to the east, Ocean City is rimmed on its west by a series of picturesque bays with memorable names like Assawoman, Montego, Isle of Wight, and Sinepuxent. Ocean City's wide expanse of free beach is complemented by a 3-mile-long boardwalk, lined with hotels, restaurants, shops, and amusements. It's no wonder that the city's small resident population of 7,000 easily swells to more than 200,000 on July and August weekends.

Like other destinations in Maryland, Ocean City has a proud history. Officially opened as a beach resort on July 4, 1875, Ocean City was first reached by stagecoach from Salisbury, Philadelphia, and Baltimore. Turn-of-the-century sunseekers thought nothing of long train journeys from as far away as Wilmington to reach Ocean City's shores. In 1910, when the first permanent boardwalk was laid, its length was just five blocks; today it spans 27 blocks.

The beach itself has been developed to a 145-block length. The lower section, which was the original Ocean City, is home to the boardwalk, the amusement parks, and most of the older hotels. The upper section, from about 40th Street to 145th Street, is dominated by modern motels and rows of towering condominiums.

One road, Route 1 (otherwise known as Coastal Highway), spans the entire length of the beach from north to south. This road divides Ocean City into two halves, the oceanfront and the bay side. The city is connected to the Maryland mainland by two bridges, the Route 50 bridge (which crosses over into First Street at the southern tip of Ocean City) and the Route 90 bridge (which brings you midway into the city at 62nd Street).

1 Orientation

ARRIVING

BY PLANE The **Ocean City Municipal Airport,** Stephen Decatur Memorial Road, off Route 611 (☎ 410/213-2471), is

What's Special About Ocean City

Activities
- Swim along the 10-mile stretch of beach, or just lie on the sand. The beach will always remain Ocean City's prime attraction.
- Stroll the 3-mile-long boardwalk, lined with hotels, restaurants, shops, and amusements
- Ride the boardwalk tram, a nostalgic way to see the sights.
- Take a full-day's fishing trip along the ocean coast.
- Board a party boat and take a three-hour nature cruise to watch for dolphins, whales, sea turtles, pelicans, and seabirds.
- Sample harness racing under the stars at Delmarva Downs.
- Watch the sun rise over the Atlantic and set over Sinepuxent or Assawoman Bays.

Museums and Buildings
- Ocean City Life-Saving Museum, housed in an 1891 building, and focusing the history of the U.S. Life-Saving Service on the Eastern Shore of Maryland, Delaware, and Virginia.
- Berlin, a historic inland Victorian enclave.

Parks
- Assateague State Park, home to a band of wild ponies as well as a wide sandy beach and dunes reaching up to 14 feet in height.

located 3 miles west of town. This facility handles regularly scheduled commuter flights to and from Baltimore and other cities via **USAir Express** (☎ 800/ 428-4322).

BY CAR   From the west, use Route 50; from north or south, take Route 13.

BY BUS   **Greyhound/Trailways** has daily services into Ocean City from points north and south, stopping at Second Street and Philadelphia Avenue (☎ 410/ 289-9307).

VISITOR INFORMATION

Ocean City has a very active and enthusiastic tourist office that stocks all kinds of helpful information, maps, and brochures. It is located right in the heart of town and is open daily all year, with extended evening hours on summer weekends. Be sure to head for the **Ocean City Convention and Visitors Bureau,** 4001 Coastal Hwy., Ocean City, MD 21842 (☎ 410/289-8181 or 800/ OC-OCEAN).

CITY LAYOUT

A narrow strip of land, Ocean City stretches for 10 miles, with one main thorough-fare, Coastal Highway (Route 1), running north-south. Cross streets are designated by numbers (from 1st to 145th), with the lowest numbers on the southern tip of island. Attractions and businesses to the east of the highway are described as "oceanside" or "oceanfront" and places on the west of the highway are called "bay-side."

2　Getting Around

BY PUBLIC TRANSPORTATION

BY BUS　Regular daily bus services are operated up and down Coastal Highway (Route 1) by the **Ocean City Municipal Bus Service,** 65th Street and the Bay (☎ 410/723-1606 or 410/723-1607). In the summer months, the schedule is every 10 minutes, 24 hours a day. From October 1 until Memorial Day, buses run every half hour, except between 11pm and 7am, when service is hourly. The fare is $1 all day (24-hour period), and exact change is required.

BY BOARDWALK TRAIN　Starting at South First Street, a tram-type train runs along the 3-mile boardwalk every 20 minutes up to 27th Street. The trip lasts about a half-hour and is an ideal way to get an orientation to the hotels, restaurants, and shops along the boardwalk. You can also signal the conductor by raising your hand and then disembark at any point you wish before the end of the line. The fare is $1.50 and you pay as you board the train at the starting point. If there is room, the tram will also pick up new passengers along the route, but the fare remains the same. The train runs from Easter to first weekend of October.

BY CAR

RENTALS　The car-rental firms represented in this area include **Avis,** 1206 Philadelphia Ave. (☎ 410/289-6121); **Hertz,** Ocean City Airport (☎ 410/213-2400); and **Thrifty,** 5601 Coastal Hwy. (☎ 410/524-4222).

PARKING　Parking is difficult, particularly at the height of the season. Many public facilities, such as shopping centers and restaurants, usually offer ample free parking to patrons. There are also public parking lots in certain areas near the beach, such as the Inlet on South First Street. Otherwise, parking is by meter on the streets. Most hotels and motels have their own parking lots or garages and supply their guests with parking permits that usually allow one free parking space per room.

BY TAXI

If you need a ride, call **Ocean City Taxi** (☎ 410/289-8164) or **Coastal Resort Taxi** (☎ 410/250-5300).

FAST FACTS: Ocean City

Airports　See "Orientation," earlier in this chapter.

Area Code　Ocean City's area code is 410.

Car Rentals　See "Getting Around," earlier in this chapter.

Climate　See "When to Go" in Chapter 1.

Dentists　Emergency work is provided at Atlantic Dental Associates, 105 58th St. (☎ 410/524-0500); or 43rd Street Dental Center, 4306 Coastal Hwy. (☎ 410/289-8828).

Doctors　Ask for a recommendation from the Medical Referral Service (☎ 410/546-6400).

Ocean City

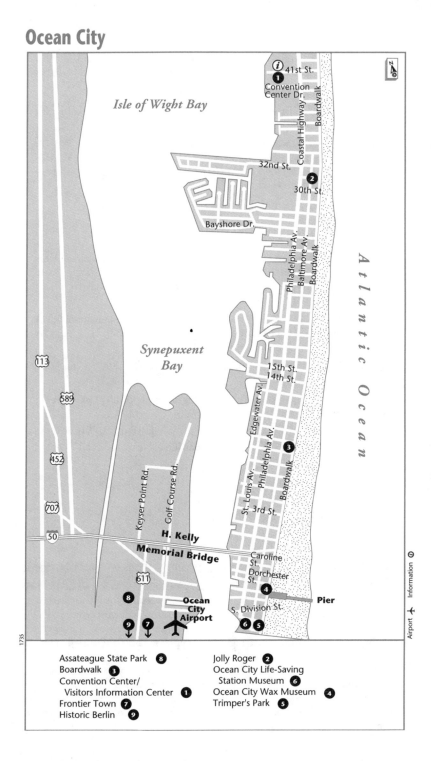

Isle of Wight Bay

Synepuxent Bay

Atlantic Ocean

41st St.

Convention Center Dr.

Coastal Highway

Boardwalk

32nd St.

30th St.

Bayshore Dr.

Philadelphia Av.

Baltimore Av.

Boardwalk

15th St.
14th St.

Edgewater Av.

Philadelphia Av.

St. Louis Av.

3rd St.

Boardwalk

Keyser Point Rd.

Golf Course Rd.

H. Kelly
Memorial Bridge

Caroline St.

Dorchester St.

Pier

S. Division St.

Ocean City Airport

1735

Airport ✈ Information ⊙

Assateague State Park **8**	Jolly Roger **2**
Boardwalk **3**	Ocean City Life-Saving
Convention Center/	Station Museum **6**
Visitors Information Center **1**	Ocean City Wax Museum **4**
Frontier Town **7**	Trimper's Park **5**
Historic Berlin **9**	

Drugstores   Try Bailey's, 8th Street and Philadelphia Avenue (☎ 410/ 289-8191); or Peoples Drug Store, 11905 Coastal Hwy. (☎ 410/524-5101).

Emergencies   Dial 911 for fire, police, or ambulance.

Eyeglasses   The local choice is Accurate Optical, 94th and Coastal Highway (☎ 410/524-0220).

Hospitals   Contact 75th St. Medical Center, 7408 Coastal Hwy. (☎ 410/ 524-0075); Atlantic General Hospital, 9733 Hathaway Dr., Berlin (☎ 410/ 641-1100); or Peninsula Regional Medical Center, 100 E. Carroll St., Salisbury (☎ 410/546-6400).

Information   See "Visitor Information," earlier in this chapter.

Library   The Ocean City branch of the Worcester County Library is at 14th Street and Philadelphia Avenue (☎ 410/289-7297).

Newspapers and Magazines   The *Daily Times* is the daily newspaper of Ocean City. The *Baltimore Sun* publishes "O. C. Tab," a supplement covering Ocean City events, weekly from April through October and on the first Sunday of each month during the rest of the year.

Photographic Needs   For camera repair, photo processing, or supplies, try Atlantic Color Lab, 11511 Coastal Hwy. (☎ 410/723-4687); or Ocean City Camera Shop, 3308 Coastal Hwy. (☎ 410/289-1135).

Police   Dial 911 or 410/641-3101 for state police or 410/289-7556 for beach patrol.

Post Office   The main post office is at 5th Street and Philadelphia Avenue (☎ 410/289-7819).

Radio   The local radio stations include WOCQ-104 FM and WKHI-99.9 FM for general programming, WETT-16 AM for Mutual News, and WETT-96 FM for rock.

Taxes   The state sales tax is 5%; the county tax, 3%.

Taxis   See "Getting Around" earlier in this chapter.

Transit Information   Dial 410/723-1607.

Weather   Dial 410/742-8400.

3 Accommodations

More than in any other part of Maryland, the lodgings in Ocean City depend on a short "high season." Summer (especially June through August) commands the highest rates, often with supplements on weekend nights as well. In many cases, minimum stays of two or three nights may apply, so check the rates in advance. Reservations are certainly a must.

In almost all cases, the larger hotels offer money-saving package plans, particularly in the late spring or early autumn seasons, when Ocean City can be equally as lovely as at the peak of summer (and a lot less crowded). Although it is a great treat to overlook the ocean, rooms with partial or no views of the water often cost considerably less than those with oceanfront views.

EXPENSIVE

Carousel

11700 Coastal Highway, Ocean City, MD 21842. ☎ 410/524-1000 or 800/641-0011. Fax 410/524-1286. 155 rms, 189 condo units. A/C TV TEL. June–Aug $89–$229, Sept–May $49–$149 rms; June–Aug $189–$289, Sept–May $99–$209 condos. AE, CB, DC, DISC, MC, V. Free parking.

Situated on the oceanfront between 117th and 118th streets, this hotel was considered a daring venture when it was launched in 1962 by Bobby Baker, Lyndon Johnson's confidante. It was built on the northern end of the beach amid the sand dunes, a full 5 miles north of the rest of the Ocean City action. It proved to be a trend-setter, however, spurring the development of many other hotel/condo complexes. Today it is most famous as the hotel with a year-round ice-skating rink, the only one in the area. In addition, there is an indoor heated swimming pool, weight room, saunas, whirlpool, basketball and tennis courts, game room, and the largest deck on the beach. Guest rooms, which are contained in a four-story hotel tower and a 22-story condo tower, have balconies overlooking the beach and most have kitchenettes. There is also a restaurant, two lounges, a cafe, and a deli.

✪ Coconut Malorie

Fager's Island, 201 60th St., Ocean City, MD 21842. ☎ 410/723-6100 or 800/767-6060. Fax 410/524-9327. 85 suites. A/C TV TEL. June–Aug $159–$350, Sept–May $69–$199 double. AE, CB, DC, MC, V. Free parking.

With a British Colonial name and ambience, this hotel stands out on the bay front. The lobby is palatial, with a waterfall, brass chandeliers, marble floors, palm trees and tropical foliage, and an eager staff attending to guests.

The guest rooms are equally distinctive—all decorated with a Caribbean flavor, including a collection of Haitian art. Each unit is a suite, comprised of a bedroom (often dominated by a four-poster bed) and a marble bathroom with whirlpool Jacuzzi tub, lighted makeup/shaving mirror, and hair dryer; plus a sitting and dining area, private balcony, kitchen, wet bar, refrigerator, microwave oven, and coffee- and teamaker. Facilities include an outdoor swimming pool and sundeck and a full-time concierge desk. This hotel is also connected by footbridge (and by the same ownership) to Fager's Island restaurant and lounge (see "Dining," below).

✪ Dunes Manor

2800 Baltimore Ave., Ocean City, MD 21842. ☎ 410/289-1100 or 800/523-2888. Fax 410/289-4905. 160 rms, 10 suites. A/C TV TEL. June–Aug $145–$210, Sept–May $39–$174 double; $85–$280 suite. AE, CB, DC, DISC, MC, V. Free parking.

With a pink-and-white Victorian facade, the Dunes Manor is situated on its own stretch of beach north of the boardwalk at 28th Street. The 11-story property is enhanced by a grand open porch (with rockers), rooftop cupolas, and a private miniboardwalk facing the ocean. Each of the bedrooms and suites has an oceanfront view, with balcony, two double beds, a decor of light woods and floral fabrics, a refrigerator, and microwave. The guest amenities include an indoor/outdoor pool, a Jacuzzi, an exercise room, a sundeck, and a Victorian-style restaurant and lounge. Afternoon tea is served in the lobby each afternoon. Open year-round.

Lighthouse Club

Fager's Island, 56th St. (in the Bay), Ocean City, MD 21842. ☎ 410/524-5400 or 800/767-6060. Fax 410/524-9327. 23 suites. A/C TV TEL. June–Aug $169–$269, Sept–May $89–$269 double (including continental breakfast). AE, DC, MC, V. Free parking.

Overlooking the Isle of Wight Bay and boasting an octagonal lighthouse exterior, this three-story inn sits on a patch of wetlands, surrounded by water. The library-style reception area has a homey atmosphere and the guest rooms are equally welcoming.

Each unit is a suite, comprised of a nautically themed bedroom and a marble bathroom with Jacuzzi tub, hairdryer, and lighted makeup mirror. There is also a sitting area, decorated with light woods and rattan furnishings. Eight of the units have gas fireplaces, double Jacuzzis, and balconies, and all are equipped with wet bar, refrigerator, ice maker, and coffee- and teamaker. Services include in-room continental breakfast, evening turndown, and VCR rentals. One drawback is the lack of an elevator between the lobby floor and the two guest floors. Facilities include an outdoor swimming pool and footbridge access to Fager's Island restaurant (see "Dining," below), under the same ownership.

Princess Royale Resort

Oceanfront (at 91st St.), Ocean City, MD 21842. ☎ **410/524-7777** or 800/4-ROYALE. Fax 410/524-7787. 310 one-bedroom suites, 30 two- and three-bedroom suites. A/C TV TEL. June–Aug $139–$269, Sept–May $79–$189 one-bedroom suite; June–Aug $150–$265, Sept–May $159–$199 two-bedroom suite; June–Aug $225–$315, $179–$219 three-bedroom suite. *Note:* From mid-June to Labor Day special inclusive weekly rates are available for two- and three-bedroom suites. AE, DC, DISC, MC, V. Free parking.

One of the newest deluxe hotels to be built on the ocean, this property consists of two five-story towers within a 10-story condominium layout. Guest rooms are furnished with light woods, nautical art, and sea-oat or surf-toned fabrics. Ideal for families or extended stays, one-bedroom suites can sleep two to six people, two-bedroom suites sleep six to eight, and three-bedroom suites sleep 8 to 10 people. Each unit has a full kitchen including dishwasher, garbage disposal, microwave, refrigerator, and ice maker.

Dining choices include an oceanfront restaurant, indoor atrium-style cafe, and outdoor deck eatery overlooking the ocean. Facilities comprise an indoor pool, health club, whirlpools, saunas, tennis, gift and jewelry shops, convenience store, guest laundry, game room, and shuffleboard.

Sheraton Fontainebleau

10100 Ocean Hwy., Ocean City, MD 21842. ☎ **410/524-3535,** 800/325-3535, or 800/638-2100. Fax 410/524-3834. 228 rooms, 22 suites. A/C TV TEL. June–Aug $130–$230, Sept–May $60–$150 double; June–Aug $205–$250, Sept–May $95–$170 studio; June–Aug 290–$295, Sept–May $150–$100 cabana suite. AE, CB, DC, DISC, MC, V. Free parking.

Of all the chain hotels in this beachfront community, this 16-story tower is in a class by itself. It is located right on the ocean, far from the boardwalk and in the midst of the residential high-rise condo section of Ocean City. It offers oversized rooms and suites, all with views of the ocean and bay. Each room also has its own private balcony, contemporary furnishings, coffeemaker, and refrigerator.

Amenities include a restaurant and two lounges overlooking the ocean, a beachside terrace, valet services, an arcade of shops, a video-game room, an indoor heated pool; and a complete spa with Jacuzzi, workout room, steam room, sauna, whirlpool, and sunrooms.

MODERATE

✪ Atlantic Hotel

2 N. Main St., Berlin, MD 21811. ☎ **410/641-3589.** Fax 410/641-4928. 16 rms. A/C TEL. June–Aug $73–$135, Sept–May $65–$135 double (Rates include continental breakfast).

MC, V. Free parking. From Ocean City, take Route 50 west to Route 113 (Main St.), a total of 7 miles.

Situated in the historic town of Berlin 7 miles southwest of Ocean City, this hotel offers a quiet old-world country inn setting within easy driving range of the beach and boardwalk attractions. Dating from 1895 and listed on the National Register of Historic Places, this Victorian three-story hotel has been updated with modern amenities, while still retaining its original 1895 charm. The guest rooms are individually furnished with local antiques and are rich in Victorian tones of deep green and burgundy, or delicate rose and aqua, with mahogany furniture, and accessories of lace, crochet, tassels, and braids. TVs are not usual fixtures in guest rooms, but they are available on request. Facilities include a reading parlor, outdoor balcony, and highly acclaimed restaurant (see "Dining," below) and lounge.

⑤ Brighton Suites

12500 Coastal Hwy., Ocean City, MD 19971. ☎ **410/524-1433** or 800/227-5788. Fax 410/250-7603. 57 suites. A/C TV TEL. June–Aug $99–$189, Sept–May $49–$129 double. AE, DISC, MC, V. Free parking.

Situated on the main highway, but within easy walking distance of beach or bay, this five-story, all-suite property is ideal for families or two couples traveling together. Each suite has a bedroom with two queen-size beds or a king-size bed with contemporary furnishings, and a large modern bathroom with hairdryer, plus a separate living room with pullout couch, wet bar, refrigerator-freezer, and a personal safe. Most units also have a private balcony. Facilities include an indoor heated swimming pool and secure underground parking.

Castle in the Sand

3701 Atlantic Ave., Ocean City, MD 21842. ☎ **410/289-6846** or 800/552-SAND. Fax 410/289-9446. 36 rms, 137 suites. A/C TV TEL. June–Aug $101–$149, Sept–May $55–$96 rms; June–Aug $122–$180, Sept–May $63–$122 suites. AE, DISC, MC, V. Free parking. Closed Nov–Mar.

Nestled on the beach north of the boardwalk at 37th Street, this modern property has a mock-castle exterior complete with turrets. Standard hotel rooms are offered, as well as oceanfront efficiencies with balconies. Outdoor amenities include an Olympic-size swimming pool, private beach, and oceanfront patio.

Comfort Inn Boardwalk

507 Atlantic Ave. (5th St. at the Oceanfront), P.O. Box 1030, Ocean City, MD 21842. ☎ **410/289-5155** or 800/228-5150. 84 efficiencies. A/C TV TEL. June–Aug $75–$169, Sept–May $39–$79 double. AE, CB, DC, DISC, MC, V. Free parking. Closed Nov–mid-Feb.

One of the newest chain properties to be built along the boardwalk, this is a modern five-story complex of two buildings, one directly on the boardwalk and the other next to it. All of the guest rooms are decorated with light wood furnishings and sea-toned fabrics, and each has a sleeping area, kitchenette, sitting area with sofa bed, and a private balcony. Facilities include a restaurant, heated outdoor and indoor pools, and boardwalk deck.

⑤ Comfort Inn Gold Coast

11201 Coastal Hwy., Ocean City, MD 21842. ☎ **410/524-3000** or 800/228-5150. Fax 410/524-8255. 202 rms. A/C TV TEL. June–Aug $84.95–$164.95, Sept–May $29.95–$124.95 double. AE, CB, DC, DISC, MC, V. Free parking.

Among the many chain properties, one of the best choices for good value and great location is this hotel set back from the main road on its own grounds overlooking the bay. Each room has a microwave oven, refrigerator, wet bar, and an ocean or bay view. Facilities include a glass-enclosed indoor pool, Jacuzzi, sundeck, convenience store, guest laundry, and fast-food restaurant, plus an adjacent lounge and movie theater.

⑤ Econo Lodge/Sea Bay Inn

6007 Coastal Hwy., Ocean City, MD 21842. ☎ **410/524-6100**, 800/888-2229, or 800/ 446-6900. Fax 410/524-1619. 92 rms. A/C TV TEL. June–Aug $89–$119, Sept–May $27–$94 double. AE, DC, DISC, MC, V.

On the bay side, this modern five-story property offers rooms with a balcony and at least a partial view of the bay. Each unit is equipped with a sitting area, table and chairs, sofa bed, refrigerator, microwave, and wet bar. Facilities include an outdoor pool and a cafe specializing in quick and healthful items.

Holiday Inn Oceanfront

6600 Coastal Hwy. (Oceanfront at 67th St.), Ocean City, MD 21842. ☎ **410/524-1600** or 800/638-2106. Fax 410/524-1135. 216 efficiencies. A/C TV TEL. June–Aug $129–$179, Sept–May $39–$159 limited view or ocean-view room; June–Aug $149–$189, Sept–May $49–$179 deluxe ocean-view, double. AE, CB, DC, DISC, MC, V. Free parking.

Located in the center of Ocean City, directly on the beach, this eight-story hotel is convenient to everything. Each room has a private balcony plus a fully equipped kitchen with microwave and dishwasher. Furnishings include dark woods, soft pastel fabrics, and wall art. Facilities include a gourmet restaurant, Reflections (see "Dining," below), plus a poolside bar, indoor and outdoor swimming pools, Jacuzzi, saunas, exercise room, tennis court, shuffleboard, and game room.

Phillips Beach Plaza Hotel

1301 Atlantic Ave., Ocean City, MD 21842. ☎ **410/289-9121** or 800/492-5834. Fax 410/ 289-3041. 60 rms, 36 apartments. A/C TV TEL. June–Aug $115–$145, Sept–May $40–$115 double; June–Aug $130–$165, Sept–May $50–$110 apt. AE, DC, DISC, MC, V. Free parking.

With an old-world ambience, this boardwalk hotel boasts an elegant Victorian lobby with crystal chandeliers, wrought-iron fixtures, open fireplace, and graceful statuary, plus a long open porch overlooking the ocean, a top-notch on-premises seafood restaurant, Phillips by the Sea (see "Dining" below), and a piano bar. The accommodations are housed in an attached modern four-story bedroom block with both rooms and apartments (with an elevator). The apartments have dining and/or living areas with full kitchens. It is situated between 13th and 14th streets.

MODERATE/INEXPENSIVE

Days Inn

4201 Coastal Hwy., Ocean City, MD 21842. ☎ **410/289-6488**, 800/325-2525, or 800/ 456-DAYS. Fax 410/289-1617. 162 rms. A/C TV TEL. June–Aug $60–$150, Sept–May $30–$120 double. AE, DC, DISC, MC, V. Free parking.

For value and convenience, this seven-story property is a good choice for families, particularly in the off-season. It is situated on the bay side of the highway one block from the beach or the Convention Center, and all rooms have balconies. The guest rooms, accessible by computer-card keys, are decorated with light wood furnishings and each has a sleep-sofa as well as one or two beds; some rooms have a microwave oven and refrigerator. Facilities include a fully equipped health center with glass-enclosed indoor heated swimming pool, game room, convenience shop, and guest laundry. Some units, with Jacuzzis or ocean views, cost extra.

Howard Johnson Oceanfront

1109 Atlantic Ave., Ocean City, MD 21842. ☎ **410/289-7251,** 800/926-1122, or 800/
654-2000. Fax 410/289-3435. 90 rms. A/C TV TEL. June–Aug $119–$179, Sept–May
$29–$149 double. AE, DC, DISC, MC, V. Free parking.

Situated on the boardwalk at 12th Street, this modern seven-story hotel has a welcoming lobby with fireplace. The guest rooms are decorated with light woods,
pastel-toned furnishings, and modern art prints. Each room has a private balcony
with full or partial ocean views. Facilities include a restaurant, indoor heated pool,
and gift shop.

Talbot Inn

Talbot St. (and the Bay), P.O. Box 548, Ocean City, MD 21842. ☎ **410/289-9125** or
800/659-7703. 36 efficiencies. A/C TV TEL $30–$85 double. MC, V. Free parking. Closed
Dec–Feb.

For good value on the bay side, this inn offers two adjacent three-story buildings,
one directly on the bay (bay front) and the other next to it (bay side). Each unit
accommodates four to six people and is decorated with light woods, floral fabrics,
and nautical art; the compact kitchenettes include microwaves, and most rooms
have balconies. Facilities include a marina, bar, and sportswear shop. There is a
three-day minimum on weekends in summer.

4 Dining

Understandably, seafood is a favorite here and, for the most part, a casual atmosphere prevails, although it is always wise to make a reservation in the better
restaurants and to check on the dress code.

During summer, restaurants are rarely closed. Some start as early as 5am, dishing
up hearty breakfasts for fishermen, and continue serving meals right through
until 10 or 11pm.

Most restaurants have full-bar facilities. Just to be safe, obtain a copy of the
Ocean City Visitor Bureau's guide to restaurants; it gives descriptions, hours of
opening, and price guidelines for at least 50 of the best eateries.

EXPENSIVE

✪ Atlantic Hotel Restaurant

2 N. Main St., Berlin. ☎ **410/641-3589.** Reservations required. Main courses $25.95–
$34.95. MC, V. April–Oct daily 6–10pm, Nov–Dec and Feb–Mar Tues–Sat 6–10pm. From
Ocean City, take Route 50 west to Route 113 (Main St.), a total of 7 miles. INTERNATIONAL.

One of Ocean City's best restaurants is not along the beach, boardwalk, or bay,
but a short 15-minute drive inland to the historic town of Berlin. The Victorian-
style dining room exudes a welcoming ambience, with eager and able waiters in
black tie, classical music in the background, a decor of rich colored glass, plush
velvet drapes, chandeliers with bell-shaped glass, and creative cuisine.

The dinner menu changes nightly, but often includes such specialties as veal
Wellington, chicken and scallops with orange-almond cream, roast duckling with
lingonberry sauce, salmon with basil sauce, Thai pork with peanut glaze, and rack
of lamb chèvre. In case you wish to linger, you may want to check into one of the
rooms upstairs at this charming inn (see "Accommodations," above).

Bonfire

71st St. and Coastal Hwy. ☎ **410/524-7171.** Reservations recommended on weekends. Main courses $11.95–$25.95. AE, DC, MC, V. May–Oct daily 4:30–11pm, Nov–April 5:30–10pm. INTERNATIONAL.

For more than 25 years, this bay-side restaurant has been drawing people for its charcoal-broiled steaks and cuts of aged prime rib, as well as surf-and-turf, lobster tails, jumbo shrimp, and veal dishes. A recent innovation is an additional menu of 25 Chinese dishes ranging from Szechuan shrimp and pepper steak to orange-flavored chicken. It is a large, elaborately decorated restaurant, with a choice of four different dining rooms. There is a huge oval bar in the center of the complex, and the eclectic furnishings include captain's chairs, plush leather banquettes, leaded- and etched-glass windows, gas lanterns, original oil paintings, and tree-size plants. A live band is featured on many nights during the summer. Open year-round.

✪ Fager's Island

60th St. (in the Bay). ☎ **410/524-5500.** Reservations recommended for dinner. Main courses $15.50–$24.50; lunch $4.95–$9.95. AE, CB, DC, DISC, MC, V. Daily 11am–10pm. AMERICAN.

Perched on the edge of the bay, this restaurant is surrounded by three outside decks, a pier, a pavilion, and a gazebo. With wide wraparound windows, Fager's Island is ideal for watching sunsets and is very popular at cocktail hour (when the "1812 Overture" is played). The dinner menu ranges from barbecued, blackened, or broiled shellfish and locally caught fish, to steaks and prime rib. House specialties are roast duck in orange sauce or a "mixed grille" of filet mignon, smoked pork chop, and chef's sausage. An award-winning wine cellar also offers more than 600 labels. Overstuffed sandwiches and heaping salads are available all day.

✪ Hobbit

101 81st St. ☎ **410/524-8100.** Reservations recommended for dinner. Main courses $14.95–$22.95; lunch $4.95–$8.95. AE, DISC, MC, V. Daily 11am–3pm and 5–10pm. Closed Christmas. SEAFOOD.

One of the loveliest places to dine while watching the sunset is this restaurant right on the bay. The emphasis is on Continental cuisine and there is seating on the outside decks; lacy tablecloths dominate the decor. Dinner entreés include flounder stuffed with lobster, rainbow trout stuffed with shrimp and crab, crab imperial, duck à l'orange, rack of lamb, and steaks. Lunch features raw-bar items, burgers, salads, stews, and sandwiches.

✪ Reflections

6600 Coastal Hwy. (67th and Coastal Hwy.). ☎ **410/524-5252.** Reservations required. Main courses $15.95–$26.95. AE, CB, DC, DISC, MC, V. Daily 5–10pm. CONTINENTAL/AMERICAN.

Located at the Holiday Inn Oceanfront, this classy restaurant draws a devoted clientele thanks to its Chaîne des Roîtisseurs affiliation, impeccable service, and incomparable food. The decor is reminiscent of a grand European palace, with arches, alcoves, and colonnades, enhanced by brick and mirrored walls, leafy plants, globe lights, and statues.

The menu, which changes daily, blends French table-side cooking with Eastern Shore ingredients. Specialties include "symphonia de la mer" (sauteéed shrimp, scallops, lobster, mushrooms, shallots, white wine, brandy, and cream); steak Diane sautéed with shallots, Dijon mustard, mushrooms, red wine, cream, and brandy; Tijuana tuna, charbroiled with jumbo shrimp flamed in tequila and tossed with freshly made salsa; and salmon Susan, charbroiled and served with sea scallops and a saffron hollandaise sauce.

EXPENSIVE/MODERATE

⑤ Phillips Crab House

2004 Philadelphia Ave. ☎ **410/289-6821.** Reservations not accepted. Main courses $9.95–$24.95; lunch $4.95–$9.95. AE, DISC, MC, V. Apr–Oct, daily noon–11pm. SEAFOOD.

The Phillips seafood restaurants that are so famous in Baltimore, Norfolk, and Washington, D.C., all owe their origin to a small crab carry-out started here by Shirley and Brice Phillips in 1956. That family enterprise is today an Ocean City tradition and the town's largest restaurant, seating 1,300 people in 11 different dining rooms. As on the menu of almost 40 years ago, seafood is the focus and crab is still king. Dinner entrées offer an extensive crab repertoire, including crab au gratin and imperial, crab cakes, soft-shell crabs, crab with Smithfield ham, and all-you-can-eat crabs. Lovers of salmon, shrimp, flounder, scallops, oysters, and lobster will also find their favorites here, prepared in a variety of ways, as well as steaks, filet mignon, and fried chicken. Lunchtime choices include sandwiches and salads.

MODERATE

Capt. Bill Bunting's Angler

Talbot St. (and the Bay). ☎ **410/289-7424.** Reservations recommended for dinner. Main courses $6.95–$20.95; lunch $3.95–$7.95. MC, V. May–Oct Daily 11am–4pm and 3:30–10pm. AMERICAN.

Since 1938 this has been a favorite eatery on the marina of Ocean City. With a rustic and nautical decor, this spacious restaurant features an air-conditioned main dining room plus an outdoor patio deck overlooking the bay. It's an ideal spot to see the boats sailing by or to watch the fishermen bring back their bounty. The extensive dinner menu revolves around a variety of daily fresh fish specials, each prepared seven different ways, plus steaks and seafood platters. In addition, a free evening cruise of the bay at 7 or 9pm is included as part of the dinner price. Lunch focuses on tempting raw bar selections, fishwiches, salads, and burgers. *Note:* For early risers, doors open at 5am for breakfast.

Hanna's Marina Deck

306 Dorchester St. ☎ **410/289-4411.** Reservations accepted only for parties of eight or more during May–Sept and six or more during Apr and Oct. Main courses $9.95–$19.95; lunch $3.95–$9.95. MC, V. Apr–Oct, Daily 11:30am–11pm. SEAFOOD.

Overlooking Sinepuxent Bay, the bilevel main dining room of this restaurant offers wide-windowed views of the water and passing boats, particularly memorable at sunset. There is also a smaller room facing the side street, so arrive early for a table with a view. The menu offers different "fresh catch" blackboard specials every day, prepared broiled, grilled, Cajun style, or blackened, as well as dishes such as crab-stuffed flounder; deep-fried crab cakes or soft-shell crabs; broiled lobster tails; and steamed, fried, or stuffed shrimp. Steaks, veal, and chicken dishes are also offered. Other specialties of the house include coconut muffins and tropical salads, much in demand at lunchtime.

✪ Harrison's Harbor Watch

Boardwalk South (overlooking Inlet). ☎ **410/289-5121.** Reservations recommended. Main courses $8.95–$19.95; lunch $4.95–$7.95. AE, DISC, MC, V. May–Oct daily 11:30am–11pm, Jan–April and Nov Thurs–Sat 5–10pm. SEAFOOD.

You'll get a spectacular full view of the ocean and nearby Assateague Island at this restaurant, situated at the boardwalk's southernmost point. It's a large complex (seating 400), with various levels of seating, tile floors, lots of leafy plants, and a Colonial-nautical decor. A bountiful raw bar is the focus of attention at dinner, followed by entreées such as hickory-barbecued shrimp, whole local lobster, lobster linguine, crab legs, swordfish with crab imperial, steaks, and fried chicken. Lunch emphasizes light fare (sandwiches and salads).

Higgins' Crab House

31st St. (and Coastal Hwy.). ☎ **410/289-2581.** Reservations accepted only for parties of eight or more. Main courses $10.95–$19.95. MC, V. May–Sept, Mon–Fri 4–10pm, Sat–Sun noon–10pm; Apr and Oct, Fri–Sun noon–10pm. SEAFOOD.

Owned and operated by the Higgins family, this busy spot is a sister operation to the restaurant of the same name in St. Michaels. The only difference is that this location just serves dinner. For a full description of the menu, see "Where to Dine," in the Easton section of Chapter 4.

MODERATE/INEXPENSIVE

Bayside Skillet

77th St. (and Coastal Hwy.). ☎ **410/524-7950.** Reservations not accepted. Main courses $4.95–$11.95. MC, V. May–Oct, daily 24 hours; Nov–Apr daily 7am–9pm. INTERNATIONAL.

If you tire of seafood or steaks, head to this chalet-style eatery on the bay side of the main highway at 77th Street. As its name implies, it specializes in crepes, omelets, and frittatas. House specialties range from a ratatouille omelet to a "steak-n-eggs" omelet (filled with prime rib and cheese), as well as crepes filled with seafood, bacon and spinach, or strawberries and cream. Burgers, sandwiches, nachos, and salads are also offered. This wide-windowed restaurant, offering some of the best sunset views along the bay, has a cheery decor of tall beamed ceilings, knotty-pine walls, pink linens, and hanging plants.

Charlie Chiang's

5401 Coastal Hwy. ☎ **410/723-4600.** Reservations recommended for dinner. Main courses $6.95–$17.95, lunch $5.95–$15.95. Mon–Thurs 11:30am–10:30pm, Fri 11:30am–11pm, Sat noon–11pm, Sun noon–10pm. AE, CB, DC, DISC, V. CHINESE.

Located on the bay side, at 54th Street, this restaurant is on the upper level of a two-story building, with a bright plant-filled conservatory-style decor, enhanced by Oriental screens and hangings. The menu features all the usual Chinese favorites, as well as some house specialties, such as "Charlie Chiang's chicken," deep-fried chunks of white meat sauteéd with broccoli, water chestnuts, and mushrooms, in a sweet-and-sour hot sauce; "Ma La pheasant," sauteéd in tangy sauce and garnished with watercress; "Treasures of the Sea," scallops and baby shrimp with onions, red and green peppers, and water chestnuts in ginger garlic sauce; and "Angel-Hair Noodles" with Taiwanese brown sauce or Singapore curry sauce.

INEXPENSIVE

⑤ Dumser's

12305 Coastal Hwy. ☎ **410/250-5543.** Main courses $6.95–$15.95; lunch $1.95–$6.95. MC, V. Mid-June to Labor Day daily 7am–1am; Sept to mid-June 7am–10pm. AMERICAN.

An Ocean City favorite since 1939, this eatery originally began as an ice-cream parlor but is now equally popular as a restaurant. Dinner entrées range from steaks and prime rib to crab cakes, stuffed flounder, fried chicken, and Virginia ham. And make sure to save room for dessert, especially the ice cream, made on the premises. Lunch choices include sandwiches, salads, subs, and soups. No liquor is served. A second location, **Dumser's Drive-In,** 49th and Coastal Highway (☎ 410/524-1588), is also open year-round, with a more limited menu.

Paul Revere Smorgasbord

2nd St. (and Boardwalk). ☎ **410/524-1776.** Buffet $7.99. MC, V. Apr to mid-Sept, daily 3:30–9pm. AMERICAN.

With eight Colonial-style dining rooms, this huge restaurant can accommodate up to 700 diners. One price prevails here for an all-you-can-eat buffet of more than 100 items, ranging from soups, salads, roast beef, turkey, fried chicken, ribs, seafood, and pasta to a tempting dessert bar. Beer and wine are served.

5 Attractions

To give yourself a proper feel for Ocean City, a stroll along the boardwalk is a must. You'll see lots of amusements and shops and some food concessions that have become traditions, like Dumser's Dairyland (since 1939), the Alaska Stands (since 1933), and Thrasher's French Fries (since 1929). Following are a few other sightseeing suggestions:

✪ Assateague State Park

Route 611, Assateague Island. ☎ **410/641-2120.** Admission Memorial Day–Labor Day, Thurs–Tues $2 per person; Wed $1 per person; rest of year, free. Year-round, daily dawn–dusk.

Situated on an island 10 miles south of Ocean City, this park is most famous for its bands of wild ponies, descendants of domestic stock that grazed here as early as the 17th century. They are small and sturdy and well adapted to the harsh seashore environment where marsh and dune grasses supply the bulk of their diet. Although they are a thrill to see, visitors are warned to keep a safe distance; these animals can kick and bite, and it is illegal to feed or touch them.

The state of Maryland owns 680 acres of this 32-mile-long island (a small part is under state of Virginia jurisdiction). The park has 2 miles of ocean frontage with a white-sand beach and dunes up to 14 feet high. Visitors can swim, surf, fish, and picnic, and there are more than 300 campsites for overnight guests. For information in advance, write to Assateague State Park, 7307 Stephen Decatur Hwy., Berlin, MD 21811-9741.

✪ Historic Berlin

c/o Berlin Chamber of Commerce, P.O. Box 212, Berlin, MD 21811. ☎ **410/641-4775.**

If it happens to rain or you'd like a change of pace from the beach and the bay, head inland about 7 miles southwest of Ocean City to the town of Berlin, a

Assateague State Park & Chincoteague N.W.R.

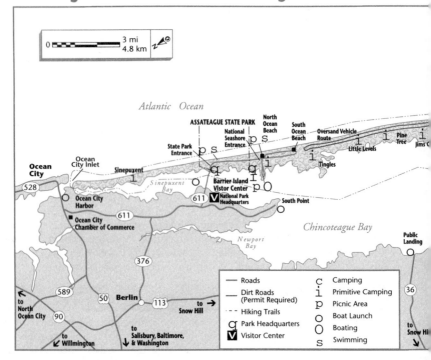

historic inland enclave with a turn-of-the-century charm. Enjoy a stroll along Main Street and visit some of the many antique shops and gift boutiques, as well as the recently restored Atlantic Hotel, a Victorian gem dating from 1895 and the centerpiece of the town (see "Accommodations" and "Dining," earlier in this chapter). For more information, including a self-guided walking tour map, contact the Berlin Chamber of Commerce.

Ocean City Life-Saving Station Museum

813 S. Boardwalk (at the Inlet). ☎ **410/289-4991.** Admission $2 adults, $1 for children under 12. June–Sept, daily 11am–10pm; May and Oct, daily 11am–4pm; Nov–Apr, Sat–Sun noon–4pm.

Perched on the southern tip of the boardwalk, this museum is housed in a building that dates from 1891. The exhibits focus on the history of the U.S. Life-Saving Service on the Eastern Shore of Maryland, Delaware, and Virginia and include some rare artifacts of the region. In addition, there are displays of dollhouse models depicting Ocean City in its early years; a pictorial history of the significant hurricanes and storms that have hit the mid-Atlantic coast; saltwater aquariums with indigenous sea life; a mermaid exhibit; and a unique collection of sand from around the world.

Ocean City Wax Museum

Pier Building, Boardwalk (at Wicomico St.). ☎ **410/289-7766.** Admission $4.95 adults, $3.95 seniors and youths 13–17, $2.95 youths 6–12. Apr–May, daily 10am–8pm; Memorial Day–Labor Day, daily 10am–midnight; rest of year, Sat–Sun 10am–6pm.

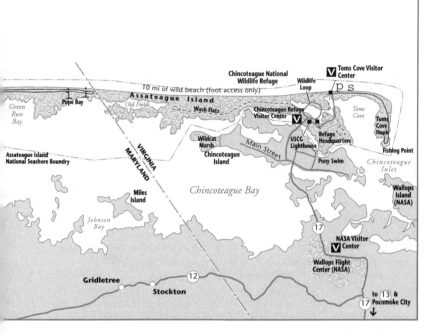

Touted as the largest of its kind on the East Coast, this museum displays more than 150 lifelike figures, all in settings enhanced by animation, high-tech lighting, and sound effects. The cast of characters ranges from Hollywood greats such as Charlie Chaplin, Marilyn Monroe, or Burt Reynolds, to music stars such as Elvis, Michael Jackson, and Dolly Parton. In addition there are scenes from classic movies and fairy tales, as well as great moments of history from the California Gold Rush to the first walk on the moon.

Ocean Gallery World
Boardwalk (and 2nd St.) ☎ **410/289-5300**. Admission free. Year-round daily 10am–midnight.

This three-story gallery is a standout along the boardwalk, with a mosaic-like facade of art from around the world. The interior is also chock-full of art posters, prints, and original oil paintings, all offered for sale at close-out prices.

ESPECIALLY FOR KIDS

Ocean City is home to several amusement parks and child-oriented activities. **Trimper's Rides and Amusement Park,** on the Boardwalk near the Inlet, between South Division and South First streets (☎ 410/289-8617), was established in 1887 and is the granddaddy of Ocean City's amusement areas. It has more than 100 rides and attractions for the whole family, including a water flume and a 1902 merry-go-round with all hand-carved animals. Most rides average $1.50, but a wristband, costing $8.50, allows the bearer to take unlimited rides between noon and 6pm on weekends and 1pm and 6pm on weekdays. The park is open daily, May through September, from noon or 1pm to midnight, and weekends February to April and October to November.

Jolly Roger, 30th Street and Coastal Highway (☎ 410/289-3477), is home to **SpeedWorld,** the largest go-kart racing complex of its kind in the United States, as well as two 18-hole miniature golf courses, a water park, and more than 30 rides and other attractions. Each attraction is individually priced. SpeedWorld rides cost from $3.50 to $5; miniature golf is $4.50 to $5; the water park is $10 per half-day or $12 a day; and individual rides are $1.20 to $2.40 each. The entire park is open daily Memorial Day through Labor Day, from 10am to midnight, and SpeedWorld and the miniature golf are also open in March through May and September through November, with slightly reduced hours.

Pier Rides, on the Pier near the Inlet (☎ 410/289-3031), is home to Ocean City's largest Ferris wheel and more than 50 other rides and attractions including a water park, and fishing pier. All rides and attractions are individually priced. Individual tickets are priced at 30¢, and each ride requires four to five tickets to enter. It is open daily May through September from noon to midnight.

Frontier Town and Rodeo, Route 1, West Ocean City (☎ 410/289-7877), is a western theme park. Set on 38 acres of woodland, this park includes a replica of a western town of the 1860s, genuine rodeos, cowboy and dance-hall shows, stagecoach rides, riverboats, a steam train, and a giant water slide. Children can also go trail riding and panning for gold, and visit a petting zoo. Open every day from 10am to 6pm, mid-June through Labor Day, the admission charge is $8 for adults, $7 for children aged 4 to 13, and free for children age 3 and under. To aid customers, a free van service is operated each morning and afternoon between the park and downtown Ocean City.

6 Outdoor Activities

BICYCLING   Ocean City is ideal for bicycling, particularly early in the morning before heavy traffic hours. Boardwalk biking is allowed between 6 and 10am. Rates vary according to the type of bike, but you can expect to pay between $4 and $6 an hour for a two-wheeler, $10 an hour for a tandem, and $15 an hour for a tri-tandem. Some of the best sources are **Continental Cycle,** 73rd and Coastal Highway (☎ 410/524-1313); **Pedal Pusher,** 609 N. Boardwalk (☎ 410/289-6865); **Mike's Bikes,** 1st Street (☎ 410/289-4637); and **Ocean Park Bike Rentals,** 17th Street and Boardwalk (☎ 410/289-7262).

HORSE RACING   **Delmarva Downs,** Route 50 at Route 589 (☎ 410/641-0600), located 4 miles west of Ocean City, features harness racing under the stars with 12 races slated each night. On Monday, Wednesday, and Thursday in season and on all nights during spring and fall, there is simulcast TV racing from other tracks. Admission is $2 to the grandstand, $4 to the clubhouse. Parking costs $1. It's open from early July to early September Tuesday and Friday to Sunday; post time is usually 7:30pm but sometimes varies (call to check).

SWIMMING   The entire 10-mile stretch of Ocean City beach is open to the public, free of charge. Beach chairs are provided on the beach at certain locations by the Town of Ocean City and private businesses, on a first-come basis. These chairs must be used within one block of where they are assigned and kept.

TENNIS   Local public courts are located at 41st, 61st, 94th, and 136th streets. From Memorial Day through Labor day, reservations are needed, on a three-day advance basis. The fees range from $5 to $7 for singles and $7 to $9 for doubles. For more information, call 410/524-8337.

WATER SPORTS   From April through October, Ocean City is a haven for all types of water activity, from jet-skiing and parasailing to sailboarding and windsurfing, or you can take to the seas in a motorboat, catamaran, or pontoon. Prices depend on type of equipment and duration of rental, but many boats can be rented from $30 to $70 an hour. Water skis and smaller equipment start at about $10 an hour, jet skis from $50 an hour. For full information, contact one of the following: **Advanced Marina Boat Rentals,** 122 66th St. and the bay (☎ 410/723-2124); **Bahia Marina,** 21st Street and the bay (☎ 410/289-7438); **Bay Sports,** 22nd Street and the bay (☎ 410/289-2144); or **Watersports Unlimited,** 142nd St. and the bay (☎ 410/250-2777).

GOLF

In recent years, the Ocean City area has blossomed as a golfing destination, frequently referred to as "The Myrtle Beach of the Mid-Atlantic." The following courses welcome visitors and can be contacted individually or through a golfing association known as **Ocean City Golf Getaway**, 6101 Coastal Hwy., Ocean City, MD 21842 (☎ 800/4-OC-GOLF).

Bay Club
9122 Libertytown Rd., Berlin. ☎ **410/641-4081** or 800/BAY-CLUB. Greens fees $42 per person including cart; rates are discounted after 4pm. Open year-round dawn–dusk.

This course, less than 10 miles from the boardwalk, offers traditional links and modern design in one 18-hole, par-72 championship course. Facilities include a club house, driving range, practice green, club rentals, and lessons.

Beach Club Golf Links
9715 Deer Park Dr., Berlin. ☎ **410/641-GOLF** or 800/435-9223. Greens fees $45 per person including cart. Open year-round, dawn–dusk.

Tee times are recommended at this 7,000-yard, 18-hole, par-72 championship semiprivate course. It has a clubhouse, pro shop, club rentals, driving range, and putting green. Tee times are recommended.

Eagle's Landing Golf Course
12367 Eagle's Nest Rd., Berlin. ☎ **410/213-7277** or 800/283-3840. Greens fees $35 per person including cart. Open year-round, dawn–dusk.

Overlooking Sinepuxent Bay less than 4 miles from downtown, this is a public resort course featuring an 18-hole, par-72 municipal championship course, driving range, club rentals, lessons, pro shop, practice facilities, and clubhouse restaurant. Tee times are recommended.

Ocean City Golf Club
11401 Country Club Dr., Berlin. ☎ **410/641-1779** or 800/422-3570. Greens fees $38–$40 per person including cart. Open year-round, dawn–dusk.

Founded in 1959, this club has two USGA-rated, 18-hole championship courses, a seaside par-73 and a bay-side par-72. There is a clubhouse, bar, and pro shop.

Pine Shore Golf
11285 Beauchamp Rd., Berlin. ☎ **410/641-5100.** Greens fees $30.50 per person with cart. Open year-round, dawn–dusk.

This public course, designed and built by Alan Janis, includes a 27-hole executive golf course, putting green, practice range, pro shop, and clubhouse with snack bar. Tee times are not accepted.

7 Bay Cruising/Fishing

Since Ocean City is surrounded by the waters of the Atlantic Ocean and four different bays, sightseeing by boat is especially popular, as is fishing. From Memorial Day through September, most vessels double as fishing boats by day and sightseeing boats in the evening, but a few specialize in sightseeing or fishing only. The fishing departures usually run from April to October.

The *Angler*
Talbot St. (and the bay). ☎ **410/289-7424.** Fishing $27 adults, $14 children under 12; $5 rod rental. Departure daily 7:30am. Sightseeing $6 adults, $3 children under 12. Departures daily 7 and 9pm. Nature cruises $12 per person. Departures daily 4pm.

This 97-passenger vessel offers 7-hour head-boat fishing excursions and one-hour sightseeing cruises that go through the Inlet and north along the ocean coast. In addition, there are two-hour nature cruises each afternoon.

The *Bay Queen*
Ocean City Fishing Center, Shantytown Pier, West Ocean City. ☎ **410/289-0926** or 410/213-0926. Sightseeing $6.50 adults, $3.50 children under 12. Departures daily 10:30am, 12:30pm, 2pm, 3:30pm, 7pm.

Day and evening cruises are operated on this 60-passenger boat, covering the harbor as far south as Assateague Island.

The *Captain Bunting*
307 Dorchester (and the bay). ☎ **410/289-6720.** Fishing $20 adults, $14 children under 13; rod rental included. Departure daily 8am and 1pm. Sightseeing $6 adults, $3 children under 13. Departure daily 7:30pm.

This 88-passenger boat offers half-day (4-hour) head-boat fishing trips and one-hour evening cruises through the Inlet and north along the ocean coast as far as 65th Street.

Judith M.
Bahia Marina, 21st St. (and the bay). ☎ **410/289-7438.** Fishing $20 adults, $17 children under 12. Departures daily 8am and 1:30pm. Sightseeing $7 adults, $5 children under 12. Departures daily 7:30pm.

Four-hour deep-sea fishing is available to 80 persons each day, followed by scenic ocean cruises for up to 150 passengers each evening on this new vessel, equipped with all electronics, snack bar, and air-conditioning.

The *Mariner*
Talbot St. Pier, Talbot St. (and the bay). ☎ **410/289-3503.** Fishing $20 adults, $15 children under 12; rod rental included. Departure daily 8am and 1pm.

This 95-passenger boat offers 4-hour head-boat fishing excursions each morning and afternoon.

Miss Ocean City

Route 50 and Shantytown Rd., Shantytown Pier. ☎ **410/213-0489** or 800/631-4848. Daytime fishing $20 adults, $15 children under 12, rod rental included. Evening fishing $25 adults, $18 children, rod rental included. Departure daytime daily 8am and 1pm; evening Tues–Thurs at 6pm.

Four-hour head-boat fishing is available each morning, afternoon and on some evenings on board this 150-passenger vessel.

Misty

Bahia Marina, 21st St. (and the bay). ☎ **410/289-7438.** Fishing $16 adults, $12 children under 12. Departures Mon–Fri 8am. Sightseeing $8.95 adults, $4.95 children under 12. Departures daily 2 and 4pm.

Sightseeing is the specialty of this 38-passenger craft, with 1½-hour narrated excursions to Assateague Island to see the wild ponies and the West Ocean City Harbor. In addition, bay bottom fishing for flounder is offered on weekdays.

O. C. Princess

Shantytown Pier (at Route 50 Bridge), West Ocean City. ☎ **410/213-0926.** Fishing $30 adults, $15 children under 12. Departure daily 7am. Sightseeing $18 adults, $8 children. Departure Tues–Sat 4pm.

One of the newest vessels to ply the waters around Ocean City, this 90-foot, 150-passenger party boat offers 7-hour daytime fishing trips and 3-hour evening nature cruises, with opportunities to observe marine life, from dolphins and whales to sea turtles, pelicans, and seabirds.

Sea Rocket

S. Division St. (next to coast guard station). ☎ **410/289-5887.** $8 adults, $5 children aged 7–10; free for children under age 7 with an adult. Departures mid-June–Sept 10am, 11am, noon, 2pm, 4pm, 6pm; mid-May to mid-June and Sept daily 11am, 1pm, and 3pm.

For sightseeing at top speed and splash, this 70-foot, 150-passenger open-top speed boat zooms along the waters of Ocean City and through the Assateague Island channel. It's a real fun ride for kids. The trip lasts about 50 minutes.

The Therapy

Ocean City Fishing Center, Shantytown Marina, West Ocean City. ☎ **410/213-0018.** Sightseeing $35 per person. Departures daily 9am, 1pm, 5:30pm.

Cruise in bay and ocean waters for three hours aboard a 38-foot sailboat, accommodating a maximum of six persons. The route passes by Assateague Island with a chance to see dolphins, wild ponies, shorebirds, and other wildlife. Reservations necessary.

The Tortuga

Bahia Marina, 21st St. (and the bay). ☎ **410/289-7438.** Fishing $16 adults, $12 children under 12, $4 rod rental. Departures daily 7am, noon, 5pm.

This 24-passenger boat offers 4-hour bay bottom-fishing trips for flounder in spring, summer, and fall.

6

Western Maryland

From the shores of the Potomac to the Allegheny mountaintops, western Maryland is a panorama of fertile farmlands and historic hillsides. Jutting out like a panhandle beyond Baltimore and wedged in between Pennsylvania and West Virginia, this land was the westward gateway of early Americans as they headed their covered wagons for Ohio and beyond. This area was also the path for the great feat of mid-19th-century ingenuity, the 184^1/$_2$-mile-long Chesapeake and Ohio Canal (the C&O) linking Georgetown to Cumberland.

Western Maryland is the home of Francis Scott Key and Barbara Fritchie and the site of Antietam National Battlefield, Fort Cumberland, and Fort Frederick. It is also the setting for Lily Pons Water Gardens; the "antiques capital of Maryland" at historic New Market; Camp David, the retreat of U.S. presidents since Franklin Roosevelt; and the Western Maryland Scenic Railroad excursions between Cumberland and Frostburg.

With an elevation ranging from 490 feet to 3,650 feet, this 225-mile stretch of land extends from the rolling hills of Frederick's horse country to the dramatic ski slopes of Wisp Mountain in Garrett County.

SEEING WESTERN MARYLAND

Alternate Route 40, the country's first National Pike, still meanders over the entire length of this countryside, connecting Frederick to Cumberland and other points east and west. In addition, a network of modern interstate highways will bring you to this relatively undiscovered corner of the Old Line State. I-70 runs from Baltimore to Frederick before it crosses the Pennsylvania border at Hancock just west of Hagerstown. I-270 connects Washington, D.C., to Frederick, and the new I-68 traverses the western part of the state—from Hancock to the West Virginia border—and intersects Route 219 heading south to Deep Creek Lake.

1 Frederick

33 miles S of Gettysburg, 148 miles SW of Philadelphia, 47 miles W of Baltimore, 45 miles NW of Washington, D.C.

The gateway to western Maryland, Frederick is just an hour's drive from Baltimore or Washington, D.C. It's in the heart of Maryland's prime horse country, the seat of one of America's richest agricultural counties.

What's Special About Western Maryland

Sightseeing
- Western Maryland Scenic Railroad, a 32-mile, round-trip scenic steam train ride between Cumberland and Frostburg.
- Antietam Battlefield, in Sharpsburg near Frederick, scene of the bloodiest day of the Civil War.
- Deep Creek Lake, a year-round recreational area and site of the Wisp Resort, Maryland's largest ski area.

Architectural Highlights
- Frederick Historic District, a 33-block showcase of 18th- and 19th-century mansions and town houses.
- Cumberland's Washington Street Victorian Historic District, a six-block-long section of mid-1800s mansions

Events/Festivals
- Deep Creek Lake's Autumn Glory Festival, a celebration of the area's fall colors.
- Rocky Gap Bluegrass/Country Western Musical Festival, a summer highlight near Cumberland.

For the Kids
- Rose Hill Manor Children's Museum, a hands-on experience of Early American life.
- Catoctin Zoo Park, a wildlife and petting zoo in a forest setting.

Museums
- Barbara Fritchie House and Museum, replica of the home of Frederick's fabled Civil War heroine.
- History House of Cumberland, a museum of Victoriana.

Religious Shrines
- National Shrine of St. Elizabeth Ann Seton, in Emmitsburg, home of America's first canonized saint.

Frederick is also a city of beautifully preserved 18th- and 19th-century town houses, landmark church spires, and gracious Victorian gardens. Perhaps Frederick is best known, however, as the birthplace of Francis Scott Key, the author of our national anthem, and Barbara Fritchie, legendary heroine of the Civil War. It also lies in the shadow of the Catoctin Mountains, the home of Camp David, the presidential retreat.

Named for Frederick Calvert, sixth Lord of Baltimore, this proud city was founded in 1745 by English and German settlers. Initially as a frontier settlement en route to the West, then as a Colonial crossroads on the National Pike, and later, during the Revolutionary and Civil wars, Frederick always played a pivotal role in our nation's progress. Today, with a population of 35,000, Frederick is a shining example of a prosperous 20th-century city that melds its history into everyday life. Horse-drawn carts still pass by Frederick's squares and courtyards; rows of craft shops and antique galleries line the streets. Old brick homes are enjoying a second life as trendy restaurants, and abandoned factories have been recycled into chic shopping boutiques.

GETTING THERE   By Bus   Greyhound operates regular services to Frederick into its depot on East All Saints Street (☎ 301/663-3311), between South Market and Carroll streets.

By Car   From the south and east, use I-70 and I-270; from the north, I-95 and I-70; from the west, I-70 and I-68.

ESSENTIALS   Area Code   The area code is 301.

Visitor Information   The Tourism Council of Frederick County operates an efficient, helpful visitor center at 19 E. Church St., Frederick, MD 21701 (☎ 301/663-8687). This office not only supplies maps, brochures, and listings of accommodations and restaurants, but will also arrange walking tours of the historic district. Tourist information booths are also located in the rest areas of the Frederick exits of I-70 east and U.S. 15 south. All of these facilities are open daily from 9am to 4:30pm.

GETTING AROUND   By Bus   Locally, the Frederick City Bus Transit Service (☎ 301/694-2065) connects major downtown points to the various shopping malls for a flat fare of $1.

By Taxi   Taxis do not cruise the city, but are available by phone; two reliable firms are Citycab (☎ 301/662-2250) and Bowie's Taxi (☎ 301/695-0333).

By Rented Car   Rent-a-Honda has an office at 5904 Urbana Pike (☎ 301/662-8888); and Hertz is at 511 W. South St. (☎ 301/662-2626).

WHAT TO SEE & DO
ATTRACTIONS

The focus of Frederick is its 33-block **Historic District**. Not only have many of the buildings been carefully restored, but the streetscape today is much as it was in the early days. With Court House Square and Old Frederick City Hall at its heart, this city is a showcase of stately mansions and elegant brick town houses. The vista also include 18th- and 19th-century church spires, graceful Victorian parks and gardens, and the oldest and largest ginkgo tree in the United States. The Frederick Visitor Center, 19 E. Church St. (☎ 301/663-8687) distributes a map of the district and also coordinates a program of walking tours. Tours depart from the Visitor Center each Saturday and Sunday, April through December, at 1:30pm. The price is $4.50 for adults, $3.50 for seniors, and free for children under 12.

Barbara Fritchie House and Museum
154 W. Patrick St. ☎ **301/698-0630.** Admission $2 adults, $1.50 seniors and children under 12. Apr–Sept Mon and Thurs–Sat 10am–4pm, Sun 1–4pm; Oct–Nov Sat 10am–4pm, Sun 1–4pm. Closed Dec–Mar.

This house is a replica of the home of Frederick's premier heroine during the Civil War. At age 95 Barbara Fritchie bravely waved the Stars and Stripes in the path of Confederate soldiers and was immortalized in a poem by John Greenleaf Whittier as the "bravest of all in Frederick-town." A visit to the house includes a video presentation of her life and times; a first-hand look at a collection of mementos including quilts and linens made by Barbara; her caps, shawls, and dresses; and her desk, tables, chairs, and china.

Western Maryland

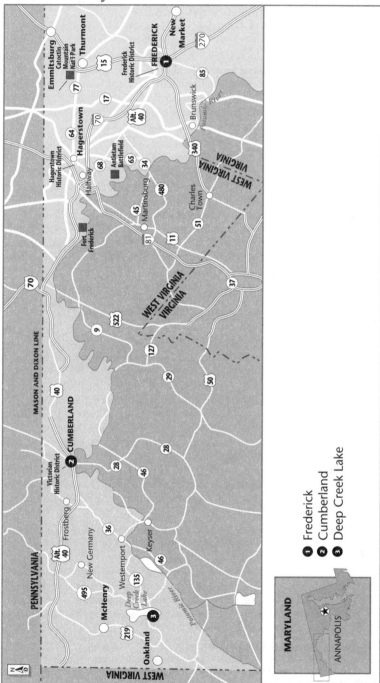

✪ Frederick County Historical Society Museum

24 E. Church St. ☎ **301/663-1188.** Admission $2 adults; free for children under 17. Mon–Sat 10am–4pm, Sun 1–4pm. Guided tours available year-round.

This Federal-style landmark (ca. 1820) is a good place to broaden your knowledge of area history. Main exhibits focus on local heroes, such as Roger B. Taney, chief justice of the U.S. Supreme Court and author of the Dredd Scott Decision; Francis Scott Key, author of the "Star-Spangled Banner"; Thomas Johnson, first governor of Maryland; and Barbara Fritchie, heroine of John Greenleaf Whittier's poem. There are also a genealogical library and formal garden.

✪ Schifferstadt

1110 Rosemont Ave. ☎ **301/663-3885.** Donation $2 adults. Apr to mid-Dec, Tues–Sat 10am–4pm, Sun noon–4pm. Closed mid-Dec through Mar, Easter, Thanksgiving Day.

On the western edge of town near U.S. 15 is the oldest standing house in Frederick, one of America's finest examples of German Colonial architecture. Built in 1756 by the Brunner family, who named it for their homeland in Germany, this house is made of stone walls more than two feet thick and hand-hewn beams of native oak pinned together with wooden pegs. Unusual original features include an enclosed winder stairway, a vaulted cellar and chimney, wrought-iron hardware, and a perfectly preserved five-plate jamb stove.

Guided tours are given throughout the day. A gift shop, featuring arts and crafts, is adjacent in a 19th-century addition to the house.

NEARBY ATTRACTIONS

✪ Antietam National Battlefield

Route 65, north of Sharpsburg. ☎ **301/432-5124.** Admission $2 adults, free for children under 16. Daily Jun–Aug 8:30am–6pm and Sept–May 8:30am–5pm. Closed major holidays.

Civil War buffs flock to Antietam Battlefield, the site of the bloodiest single-day battle of the Civil War, located about 20 miles southwest of Frederick. More than 23,000 men were killed or wounded here when Union forces met and stopped the first Southern invasion of the North on September 17, 1862. Abraham Lincoln issued the Emancipation Proclamation as a result of this victory. Clara Barton, who was to found the American Red Cross 19 years later, attended to the wounded at a field hospital here. A visitor center at the battlefield offers historical exhibits, a film shown on the hour, and a slide show on the half-hour. The staff provides free information and literature and can suggest tours of the battlefield and cemetery.

Lily Pons Water Gardens

6800 Lilypons Rd., Buckeystown. ☎ **301/874-5133.** Admission free. Mar–Oct daily 9:30am–5:30pm, Nov–Feb Mon–Sat 9:30am–4:30pm. Closed Easter. Thanksgiving, and Dec 24–Jan 2.

If you want to stop and smell the lilies, visit these beautiful gardens named after the famous opera singer Lily Pons, who visited here in 1936. One of the largest suppliers of ornamental fish and aquatic plants in the world, this site has acres of water lilies and goldfish ponds. The lilies are in bloom from Memorial Day to Labor Day.

✪ National Shrine of St. Elizabeth Ann Seton

333 S. Seton Ave., Emmitsburg. ☎ **301/447-6606.** Admission free; donations welcome. Daily 10am–4:30pm. Closed Mon (Nov–Mar), Christmas, New Year's, Thanksgiving, and last two wks of Jan.

For peace and tranquillity in the Catoctin Mountain Valley, visitors flock to this secluded sylvan setting, once the home of this country's first native-born canonized saint, Elizabeth Ann Seton (1774–1821). Located less than a half-hour's drive north of Frederick (22 miles), this site includes a splendid basilica-style shrine that contains the relics of the saint, plus the Stone House (ca. 1750), a building in which she established her religious community in 1809, and the White House, where she began America's Catholic parochial school system in 1810. The complex also offers a small museum about the life of Mother Seton, a 15-minute slide show of historical background, and two small shops, one stocking religious items and books and the other selling handiwork and crafts, much of which is made in-house by the nuns in residence, carrying on a tradition started by Mother Seton. Visitors are welcome to take a self-guided tour of the grounds.

OUTDOOR ACTIVITIES

Of the many parks in the Frederick area, **Catoctin Mountain Park,** Route 77, Thurmont (☎ 301/663-9388), is the most famous because it is adjacent to Camp David, the presidential retreat. Located 3 miles west of Thurmont and about 15 miles north of downtown Frederick, off Route 15, this 5,769-acre park is administered by the National Park Service. Facilities include hiking trails, fishing, cross-country skiing, camping, cabin rentals, and picnic sites. An information center is operated daily, Monday through Friday, from 10am to 4:30pm, Saturday and Sunday from 8:30am to 5pm. Admission is free.

ESPECIALLY FOR KIDS

A "touch and see" theme prevails at the **Rose Hill Manor Children's Museum,** 1611 N. Market St. (☎ 301/694-1646). Built in the 1790s, this Georgian mansion was the home of Maryland's first governor, Thomas Johnson. Now a museum of state and national heritage, it is designed to let children experience Early American life: combing unspun wool, throwing a shuttle on the loom, and adding a few stitches to a quilt. Other activities include soap-making, candle-dipping, quilting bees, barn raisings, and apple-butter boiling.

More than 300 items are on display on over 43 acres in the authentic settings of a manor house, a carriage museum, a blacksmith shop, a log cabin, and a farm museum. Walk-in tours are conducted by costumed guides March through October, daily from 10am to 4pm, Monday through Saturday; and from 1 to 4pm on Sunday. During November, the museum is open only on weekends, and it is closed during December, January, and February. Admission is $3 for those aged 18 to 55; $2 for seniors, $1 for children.

Animal lovers of all ages enjoy the **Catoctin Zoo Park,** 13019 Catoctin Furnace Rd., Thurmont (☎ 301/271-7488), a wildlife, breeding, and petting zoo in a 30-acre woodland setting, and home to more than 500 animals, including big cats, monkeys, bears, and farmyard pets. Open daily from 9am to 6pm throughout the summer months, and from 9am to 5pm after September. Admission is $6.50 for adults and $4.50 for children 2 to 12; children under 2 are admitted free.

SHOPPING

For many years, West Patrick Street (Route 40) has been known as the "Golden Mile," because of its many stores, shopping malls, and commercial enterprises. The continuing restoration of downtown, however, has also led to a renewed shopping interest along the city center streets. Today Frederick is home to dozens of antique and specialty shops in the mid-city historic district and throughout the county. Because Frederick county is also such a fertile area, it's an ideal place to shop for local produce, fruits, jams, jellies, ciders, baked goods, and more.

Catoctin Mountain Orchard
15307 Kelbaugh Rd., Thurmont. ☎ **301/271-2737.**

Situated on Route 15 north of Frederick, this farm sells a wide variety of locally grown fruits and vegetables, as well as canned fruits, preserves, maple syrups, apple and jelly packs, honey, salad dressing, relishes, and sugar-free products. Berries and cherries are also sold on a pick-your-own basis. Tours of the farm and orchards are given by appointment. Open July through October daily from 9am to 6pm; November and December daily from 9am to 5pm; and January through April on Friday through Sunday from 9am to 5pm. Closed May and June.

Everedy Square & Shab Row
East St. and E. Church St., Frederick. ☎ **301/662-4140.**

Situated on the east end of town, Everedy Square is a pivotal shopping development in the downtown area. It's a $2^1/_2$-acre, nine-building complex, originally the site of the Everedy Bottle Capping Company (founded in 1920 and formerly one of the largest businesses in Frederick). More than $2 million was spent in the mid-1980s to transform these old industrial buildings into a cluster of courtyards, craft shops, boutiques, and galleries. The adjacent Shab Row, a string of 200-year-old buildings that were once the homes of local merchants and artisans, has also been restored as specialty shops and craft centers. Open Monday through Saturday from 9am to 6pm or later, and on Sunday from noon to 6pm or later.

Historic Cozy Village of Shoppes
Route 806, Thurmont. ☎ **301/271-4301.**

As its name implies, this cluster of specialty shops is laid out like a country village, offering antiques, gifts, flowers, collectibles, and crafts, with craftspersons on the premises. Open daily from 11am to 5pm or later.

McCutcheon's Factory Store
13 S. Wisner St., Frederick. ☎ **301/662-3261.**

Located downtown, off South Street, this is one of the longest established local enterprises, founded in 1938. It sells a full range of apples, nuts, and dried fruits, as well as apple butter, preserves, jellies, honey, mustards, salad dressings, relishes, hot sauces, ciders, and juices. There is also a mail-order service, if you prefer to ship your purchases. Open Monday through Friday from 8am to 5pm and some weekends.

Museum Shop
20 N. Market St., Frederick. ☎ **301/695-0424.**

Although not affiliated with any particular museum, this shop is a good source for museum-quality works of art and collectibles, especially original etchings by Whistler, Grant Wood, and other early 19th- and 20th-century artists, as well as Japanese woodcuts from the 18th and 19th centuries. In between are coffee mugs, greeting cards, classical music tapes, pottery, jewelry, and other souvenirs. It is owned by artist Richard Kornemann, who has had his works displayed in the Smithsonian Institution and the National Museum of American Art. Open Monday through Wednesday from 10:30am to 6pm, Thursday through Saturday from 10:30am to 9pm, and on Sunday from noon to 5pm.

Pryor's Orchard

13841 Pryor Rd., Thurmont. ☎ **301/271-2693.**

Located a half-mile west of Thurmont off Route 77, this place sells a complete selection of local fruits, vegetables, cider, nuts, pear and peach butters, honey, and
jellies, as well as pick-your-own berries and cherries. Open from June through
November daily from 9am to 6pm or later.

Trail House

9 S. Market St., Frederick. ☎ **301/694-8448.**

For those who love the outdoors, this shop offers clothing and equipment for back-
packing, camping, hiking, rock climbing, and other sporting pursuits. It also stocks
local and regional maps and books, handy for walkers, too. Open Monday through
Thursday from 9:30am to 7pm, Friday from 9:30am to 8pm.

WHERE TO STAY

The hotels and motels of Frederick are primarily located on major roads (Routes
40, 15, and 85) leading into the city; most of the inns are found in the surrounding
countryside.

EXPENSIVE

Inn at Buckeystown

3521 Buckeystown Pike (Route 85), Buckeystown, MD 21717. ☎ **301/874-5755** or 800/
272-1190. 3 rms, 3 suites, 1 cottage. A/C. $225 room; $250 suite; $300 cottage. (Rates
include breakfast and dinner for two.) AE, MC, V. Free parking. Closed Mon–Tues.

Situated in a quiet country village setting on the Monocacy River about 4 miles
south of Frederick, this restored three-story mansion dates from 1897. It is rich
in Italianate Victorian details, with a wraparound porch, widow's walk, gables, bay
windows, and ornate trim. It operates as a country inn in the true tradition, providing bed and board (breakfast and dinner) to guests. All arrangements are by
advance phone reservation, and drop-in guests are not encouraged.

The interior decor is rich with antiques, Oriental rugs, chandeliers, and
hand-embroidered fabrics; there are five working fireplaces. Accommodations
consist of five rooms and suites (one suite has TV, VCR, and balcony; another
suite has a fireplace and a front bay window) in the main house; and two other
buildings, one a former church (1884) and the other a small cottage. These have
in-room telephones, TVs, VCRs, and fireplaces; the former church has a large
redwood hot tub and a grand piano. Dinner is served on Victorian china with
period silver and glassware. Innkeepers are Daniel Pelz, Chase Barnett, and Rebecca
Smith. *Note:* Rates include tax and service charge.

Tyler-Spite House

112 W. Church St., Frederick, MD 21701. ☎ **301/831-4455.** 6 rms. A/C. $95–$200
double. AE, MC, V. Free parking.

Located in the heart of Frederick's historic district opposite City Hall, this
three-story Federal mansion dates from 1814. It was built by Dr. John Tyler for
the sole purpose of preventing the city from building a thoroughfare through the
property, and hence the word *Spite* was added to the name. The house's interior
has 13-foot-high ceilings with intricate moldings; elaborate woodwork; raised paneling; and eight working fireplaces, many of which have carved marble mantels.
The guest rooms, four of which have private baths, are individually furnished with

antiques, down comforters, and Oriental carpets. Facilities include a parlor, library, music room, walled garden, and an outdoor swimming pool with adjacent patio. Rates include afternoon high tea and a horse-drawn carriage ride. Innkeepers are Bill, Andrea, and Annalee Myer.

MODERATE

⊗ Cozy Country Inn

103 Frederick Rd. (off Route 806), Thurmont, MD 21788. ☎ **301/271-4301.** 30 rms. A/C TV TEL. $52–$79 premium room; $75–$125 executive room. (Rates include continental breakfast.) AE, MC, V. Free parking.

Located about 15 miles north of Frederick at the base of the Catoctin Mountains, this motel has long been a popular place with families. Founded in 1929, it has recently been refurbished and upgraded, with rooms individually decorated to commemorate the style and influence unique to the presidents, political dignitaries, or news agencies that have visited Camp David and the inn. Rooms classified as "premium" have extras such as coffee/teamaker, refrigerator, hair dryer, towel warmer, and some have a VCR and wet bar. Rooms designated as "executive" all have wet bars and VCRs, all the components of the premium rooms, plus gas fireplace and Jacuzzi. Facilities include the Cozy Restaurant (see "Where to Dine," below), pub, bakery, and a village of shops.

Holiday Inn

I-270 at Route 85 (at Francis Scott Key Mall), Frederick, MD 21701. ☎ **301/694-7500** or 800/HOLIDAY. Fax 301/694-0589. 155 rms. A/C TV TEL. $69–$85 double. AE, CB, DC, MC, V. Free parking.

Situated off Hermitage Drive adjacent to the Francis Scott Key Mall, this hotel is in a landscaped garden setting. It is a favored location for business travelers or vacationers who enjoy shopping. The modern two-story brick structure offers rooms with a dark reproduction furniture and a colorful decor. Facilities include a restaurant, lounge, indoor pool, whirlpool, sauna, and fitness center, as well as a game room and miniature golf.

Spring Bank

7945 Worman's Mill Rd., Frederick, MD 21701. ☎ **301/694-0440.** 5 rms. $75–$90 double. (Rates include continental breakfast.) AE, DISC, MC, V. Free parking.

Dating from 1880 and listed on the National Register of Historic Places, this sprawling red-brick Italianate and Gothic Revival bed-and-breakfast inn exudes a homey feeling. Its three stories are bedecked with gables, cupolas, double porches, bay windows, and a fish scale–patterned slate roof. Inside are high ceilings with frescoes, intricate stenciling, faux-marble mantles, and antique furnishings and William Morris wallpaper. One of the five rooms has private bath. The inn is situated north of downtown Frederick, just off Route 15, in a country setting on 10 acres of grounds. Innkeepers are Beverly and Ray Compton.

INEXPENSIVE

Comfort Inn

420 Prospect Blvd., Frederick, MD 21701. ☎ **301/695-6200** or 800/228-5150. Fax 301/ 695-7895. 118 rms. A/C TV TEL. $49–$69 double. (All rates include continental breakfast.) AE, CB, DC, DISC, MC, V. Free parking.

Located 1 mile southwest of Frederick at the Jefferson Street exit of the I-270 and Route 15 interchange, this modern, two-story, brick-fronted hotel offers good value for standard accommodations. Facilities include a cafe, outdoor pool, guest Laundromat, and exercise room.

Hampton Inn

5311 Buckeystown Pike, Frederick, MD 21701. ☎ **301/698-2500** or 800/HAMPTON. 160 rms. A/C TV TEL. $64–$75 double. (All rates include continental breakfast.) AE, CB, DC, DISC, MC, V. Free parking.

Located 2 miles south of downtown Frederick at Exit 31B off I-270 at Route 85, this modern six-story hotel is a former Quality Inn with a brick facade—not the customary Hampton architecture. It is nestled beside an artificial lake and is connected by footbridge to a replica of a lighthouse that serves as an informal crab restaurant in the summer months. Many of the guest rooms also overlook the lake. Facilities include a lounge, outdoor pool, exercise room, and Jacuzzi.

WHERE TO DINE

Downtown Frederick is a mecca for fine food; the area around Market and Patrick streets alone boasts more than 20 good restaurants.

EXPENSIVE

Red Horse Restaurant

966 W. Patrick St. ☎ **301/663-3030.** Reservations recommended for dinner. Main courses $13.95–$19.95, with lobster, $18.95–$29.95; lunch $2.95–$12.95. AE, CB, DC, MC, V. Mon–Fri 11:30am–3pm and 4:30–10pm, Sat 4:30–10:30pm, Sun 4–9pm. AMERICAN.

If you crave a good cooked-to-order steak or sliced-to-order prime rib, this place is undisputedly the best in Frederick. Set along the busy Route 40 corridor west of downtown, this restaurant draws a mixed clientele of business executives, local families, and travelers. The decor is rustic and comfortable, consisting of two large dining rooms with stone fireplaces, and one with a glass-enclosed open kitchen where you can watch the chefs at work. In addition to beef, entrées include lamb and pork, as well as a local seafood and hefty cold-water lobster tails. Lunch focuses on sandwiches, burgers, and salads, although steaks are much in demand here at midday too.

MODERATE

Alpenhof Restaurant

137 N. Market St. ☎ **301/662-2866.** Reservations recommended for dinner. Main courses $8.95–$16.95; lunch $4.95–$10.95. AE, MC, V. Tues–Sat 11:30am–3pm and 5–10pm; Sun noon–8pm. SWISS/GERMAN.

Located in a shop-front setting, this restaurant brings an Alpine atmosphere to the historic district. Specialties include Wiener schnitzel, roast pork loin, sauerbraten, goulash with spaetzle, wurst platter with sauerkraut, breast of chicken paprika, steaks, and seafood. Lunch items include hot and cold sandwiches, Swiss cheese pie, and foot-long frankfurters. As befits a restaurant of this genre, there is also a wide selection of imported beers and rich desserts such as apple strudel and Black Forest cake.

✪ Brown Pelican

5 E. Church St. ☎ **301/695-5833.** Reservations recommended for dinner. Main courses $12.95–$19.95; lunch $4.95–$9.95. AE, MC, V. Mon–Thurs 11:30am–3pm and 5–9:30pm; Fri 11:30am–3pm and 5–10pm, Sat 5–10pm, Sun 5–9:30pm. INTERNATIONAL.

Situated on the corner of Market Street in the heart of the historic district, this basement restaurant is decorated in a nautical style of vibrant sea tones, driftwood, and yachting collectibles. Dinner includes a variety of dishes such as "veal Brown Pelican" (with ham, mushrooms, and cream); salmon with lemon Dijon sauce; stuffed shrimp with crab imperial; and roast duckling. Lunch offers sandwiches, soups, and salads.

Bushwallers

209 N. Market St. ☎ **301/694-5697.** Reservations recommended for dinner. Main courses $9.95–$16.95; lunch $4.95–$7.95. MC, V. Mon–Sat 11:30am–3pm and 5–10pm, Sun 3–10pm. INTERNATIONAL.

This restaurant is housed in an 1840s building that was used variously as a private home, a drugstore, and a dry-goods shop. Retaining its 19th-century atmosphere, the decor incorporates many Frederick family mementos as well as old pictures, newspaper front pages, and turn-of-the-century political cartoons. Dinner entrées focus on seafood dishes such as yellowtail flounder filets; swordfish steak; crab cakes; and shrimp scampi; as well as meat choices ranging from veal scaloppini alla Marsala and steak Diane, to a house specialty of "chicken Bushwallers," with garlic, mushrooms, and white wine. Lunch items include salads, pasta, chili, sandwiches, burgers, and raw-bar items.

Di Francesco's

26 N. Market St. ☎ **301/695-5499.** Reservations recommended for dinner. Main courses $11.95–$16.95; lunch $4.95–$9.95. AE, MC, V. Tues–Fri and Sun 11:30am–3pm and 5:30–10pm; Mon and Sat 5:30–10pm. ITALIAN.

Decorated like a country villa, with whitewashed walls and lots of leafy plants, this restaurant exudes the flavors and ambience of Italy. The dinner menu offers more than a dozen pastas available in full or half-orders, such as fettuccine with smoked salmon, spaghetti with anchovies and garlic, cannelloni, and lasagne. Entrées include veal saltimbocca, shrimp marinara or scampi, seafood with linguine, veal alla Marsala, chicken cacciatore, seafood and meat mixed grill, and filet mignon. Lunch features salads, omelets, pizzas, and pastas.

✪ Province

131 N. Market St. ☎ **301/663-1441.** Reservations required. Main courses $11.95–$17.95; lunch $4.95–$7.95. AE, CB, DC, MC, V. Mon 11:30am–3pm, Tues–Thurs 11:30am–3pm and 5:30–9pm, Fri–Sat 11:30am–3pm and 5:30–10pm, Sun 11am–2:30pm and 4–8pm. INTERNATIONAL.

One of Frederick's oldest houses (ca. 1767) is the setting for this restaurant, consisting of a small bistro-style front room and a bright brick-walled room in the rear. The latter overlooks the herb garden, which produces ingredients for the kitchen. The furnishings range from snowshoe chairs to handmade quilt hangings and paintings by local artists.

Dinner entrées change daily, but a few favorite dishes are lamb chops Dijon, Parisian poulet (chicken with mushrooms and dry sherry), scallops with Irish Mist, and herb-scented filet mignon. Lunchtime selections focus on salads, quiches, omelets, crab cakes, and creative-combination sandwiches. There is also a bake shop on the premises.

Tauraso's

6 East St. (at Everedy Square). ☎ **301/663-6600.** Reservations recommended for dinner. Main courses $6.95–$23.95; lunch $4.95–$9.95. AE, CB, DC, MC, V. Sun–Thurs 11am–4pm and 5–10pm, Fri–Sat 11am–4pm and 5–11pm. ITALIAN/AMERICAN.

Bright and busy, this restaurant is the main dining choice at the Everedy Square shopping complex. There are three settings: an indoor dining room, an outdoor patio, and a pub, but the menu is the same throughout. Entrées range from Italian choices such as pastas, Tauraso's original seafood sausage, and Italian bouillabaisse, to international favorites such as crab cakes, charcoal-grilled chicken, steaks, and duck à l'orange. Lunch items focus on sandwiches, frittatas, pastas, and salads. Pizzas made in a wood-burning oven are also featured throughout the day.

INEXPENSIVE

⑤ Cozy Restaurant

103 Frederick Rd. (Route 806), Thurmont. ☎ **301/271-7373.** Reservations recommended on weekends. Main courses $8.19–$14.99; lunch smorgasbords $5.19–$7.39; dinner buffets $7.39–$13.99. MC, V. Mon–Thurs 11am–8:45pm. Fri–Sat 11am–9:15pm; Sun 11:45am–8:45pm. AMERICAN.

Since 1929, this family run enterprise has been a tradition in the Frederick area. Over the years, it has grown from a 12-stool lunch counter to a 675-seat full-service restaurant with a Victorian atmosphere. Known for its plentiful luncheon smorgasbords and evening buffets, it also offers à la carte dining. Entrées include such items as country-fried chicken, roast turkey, baked ham, fried shrimp, crab cakes, surf-and-turf, lobster tails, and seafood platters. All entrées entitle you to unlimited trips to the "groaning board," a hefty table of soups, salads, breads, relishes, desserts, and cheeses.

The Province Too

12 E. Patrick St. ☎ **301/663-3315.** All items $1.50–$6. MC, V. Mon–Fri 7am–5pm, Sat 9am–4pm, Sun 8am–3pm. AMERICAN.

For breakfast or lunch or to stock up for a picnic, this spot offers a wide variety of freshly made baked goods, stews, soups, sandwiches, and creative combination salads, plus gourmet teas and coffees.

FREDERICK AFTER DARK

In June, July, and August there are free open-air concerts at the **Baker Park Bandshell,** Second and Bentz streets (☎ 301/662-5161, ext. 247). Concerts are scheduled for 7:30pm on Sunday evenings, and feature a variety of local and military bands.

Throughout the year, the **Weinberg Center for the Arts,** 20 W. Patrick St. (☎ 301/694-8585), presents drama, dance, and concerts. This old-world theater is the home of the Fredericktowne Players and also welcomes visiting troupes. Tickets average $15 to $20 and can be obtained at the box office Tuesday through Friday from 10am to 5pm, Saturday from 10am to 2pm, and one hour before all shows.

AN EXCURSION TO NEW MARKET

Six miles east of Frederick is historic **New Market,** founded in 1793 as a stop for travelers on the National Pike. Today this beautifully preserved Federal-style town (population 300) is listed on the National Register of Historic Places and is known as "the antiques capital of Maryland." More than 40 different antique shops line both sides of the half-mile-long main street. Unless noted otherwise, shop hours are usually Saturday and Sunday from 1 to 5pm, and at other times by appointment. The New Market Antique Dealers Association publishes a free, handy guide/map that's available throughout the town.

The Browsery

55 W. Main St. ☎ **301/831-9644.**

Handcrafted furniture and accessories are the focus of this shop.

Fromer's Antiques

52 W. Main St. ☎ **301/831-6712.**

Antique woodworking tools, Victorian furniture, Maxwell Parrish prints, china, and glassware are the attractions here.

Grange Hall Antiques

1 S. Eighth Alley (off E. Main St.). ☎ **301/865-5651.**

Housed in a former Grange Hall, this shop offers an eclectic variety of graniteware, jewelry, tools, and country primitives, as well as fishing and sporting antiques. Open Tuesday through Sunday from 11am to 5pm.

Maria's Chalet Antiques

2 E. Main St. ☎ **301/865-5225.**

This homey shop features German steins, teddy bears, old rugs, and clocks.

Mymanor

25 W. Main St. ☎ **301/865-3702.**

Browse in this shop for 19th- and 20th-century sporting-art and antiques.

New Market General Store

26 W. Main St. ☎ **301/831-6645.**

This is the quintessential country store, with jars of rock candy, condiments, local honey and preserves, as well as potpourri, herbs, and baking meals and mixes. There is also a take-out food counter as well as a fine selection of antique toys. Open Tuesday to Sunday from 10am to 6pm.

Shaw's of New Market

22 W. Main St. ☎ **301/831-6010.**

Try here for vases, chandeliers, grandfather clocks, china dolls, and brass lamps.

Thomas' Antiques

60 W. Main St. ☎ **301/831-6622.**

This is the place for oak furniture, brass and copper items, and equine and canine collectibles.

Victorian Manor

33 W. Main St. ☎ **301/865-3083.**

This place specializes in antique and estate jewelry and silver.

WHERE TO STAY

✪ National Pike Inn

9–11 Main St., P.O. Box 299, New Market, MD 21774. ☎ **301/865-5055.** 5 rms (3 with bath), 1 suite. A/C. $75–$125 double; $120–$160 suite. (Rates include full breakfast.) MC, V. Take Exit 62 off I-70; 6 miles east of Frederick. Free parking.

There's always a particularly warm welcome at this bed-and-breakfast named after the famous road that passes through the town. Meticulously restored and opened as a B&B in 1986 by Tom and Terry Rimel, this sturdy Federal house was built in the early 1800s; a unique widow's watch was added in 1900. The rooms are charmingly decorated with reproductions and local antiques. Guests also enjoy the use of the family rooms and a landscaped courtyard, as well as Terry's enthusiastic guidance about touring the local area.

Strawberry Inn

17 Main St., P. O. Box 237, New Market, MD 21774. ☎ **301/865-3318.** 5 rms (all with bath). A/C. $75–$95 double. (Rates include full breakfast.) No credit cards. Free parking.

Opened in 1973, this lovingly restored 120-year-old bed-and-breakfast home, run by innkeepers Jane and Ed Rossig, offers cheerful, antique-furnished rooms. Each room is individually decorated according to a special theme, such as the Strawberry Room or the 1776 Room. Ground-floor rooms are available.

WHERE TO DINE

Mealey's

8 W. Main St. ☎ **301/865-5488.** Reservations recommended for dinner. Main courses $9.95–$19.95; lunch $4.95–$9.95. MC, V. Mon–Thurs 5–9pm; Fri–Sat 11:30am–2:30pm and 5–9pm; Sun noon–8pm. AMERICAN.

Even if you don't stay in New Market, it's worth a trip to dine at this restaurant tucked in a handsome three-story Federal-style brick building dating from 1793. Like a Colonial house, the restaurant offers several small parlor-size rooms as well as the Pump Room, a large main dining room built around a wooden water pump that dates from 1800. The decor includes exposed brick walls, stone fireplaces, brass fixtures, and lanterns. Dinner entrées feature a blend of Maryland favorites including crab imperial, crab cakes, and fried chicken, as well as universal favorites such as prime rib and New York strip steak.

Village Tea Room

81 W. Main St. ☎ **301/865-3450.** All items $3.75–$6.95. AE, CB, DC, MC, V. Tues–Fri 11:30am–3pm, Sat–Sun 11:30am–5pm. AMERICAN.

Housed in a two-story Victorian house on the west end of town, this delightful eatery offers homemade soups, salads, sandwiches, beaten biscuits, and more. It's ideal for lunch or for afternoon tea. Save room for dessert—22 kinds of pie, sold whole or by the slice. There is also a shop on the premises that offers period lighting, furniture, and estate jewelry.

2 Cumberland

137 miles W of Baltimore, 135 miles W of Washington, D.C., 109 miles SE of Pittsburgh, 134 miles SW of Harrisburg

The most westerly of Maryland's big cities, Cumberland lies between West Virginia and Pennsylvania along the shores of the Potomac and in the heart of the Allegheny Mountains. First known as Fort Cumberland (after the English duke of the same name), this part of the state served as a western outpost in Colonial times for generals like George Washington and Edward Braddock.

In the 1800s Cumberland's importance grew as a gateway to the American West. Not only was it chosen as a terminus for the first National Pike (also known as the Cumberland Road and now Alternate Route 40/144), but it also became a focal point for the Western Maryland Railroad and the Chesapeake and Ohio Canal.

Although the railroad and canal have diminished in commercial importance, they have reemerged as tourism assets. In particular, the railroading era is now showcased in the new Western Maryland Scenic Railroad, a steam train ride through 16 miles of valleys and mountains between Cumberland and Frostburg.

A city of 24,000 people, Cumberland is centered around a pedestrian downtown mall, lined with shops and commercial outlets, in a parklike setting of shade trees, flowers, benches, brick walks, and fountains.

GETTING THERE   By Plane   Cumberland is served by the Cumberland Regional Airport, Route 28, just over the border in West Virginia. Flights are operated by USAir Commuter (☎ 800/428-4322).

By Bus   Greyhound operates regular bus service into Cumberland, stopping at 201 Glenn St. (☎ 301/722-6226).

By Train   Amtrak operates limited passenger service through Cumberland from points east and west, stopping at a station on East Harrison Street. For full information, call 301/724-8890 or 800/872-7245.

ESSENTIALS   Area Code   The area code is 301.

Visitor Information   Walking-tour folders, maps, and brochures of Cumberland and the surrounding area are available from the Allegany County Visitors Bureau, Western Maryland Station Center, Canal Street, Cumberland, MD 21502 (☎ 301/777-5905 or 800/508-4748). Open Monday to Friday from 9am to 5pm, Saturday and Sunday from 10am to 4pm.

WHAT TO SEE & DO
ATTRACTIONS

The highlight of a visit to Cumberland is a stroll through the **Victorian Historic District,** primarily along Washington Street on the western side of town. This area includes the site of the original Fort Cumberland (now the Emmanuel Episcopal Church) and more than 50 residential and public buildings, built primarily in the 1800s when Cumberland was at its economic peak. Placed on the National Register of Historic Places in 1973, this street is a showcase of homes with elaborate stained-glass windows, graceful cupolas, and sloping mansard roofs. You'll see architectural styles ranging from Federal, Romanesque, Queen Anne, Empire, Colonial Revival, Italianate, and English Country Gothic to Georgian Revival, Gothic Revival, and Greek Revival. Most of the houses are not open to the public, but a self-guided walking tour of the neighborhood has been plotted out and is described in a brochure available free from the tourist information office.

C&O Canal Boat Replica
At North Branch of C&O Canal Park, PPG Rd. ☎ **301/729-3136** or 301/777-5905. Admission free, but donations welcome. June–Aug, Sun 1–4pm, and other times by appointment.

This 93-foot boat is a full-scale replica of a C&O canal boat like the ones that used to move along the 184 1/2-mile canal between Georgetown and Cumberland. The boat features a captain's cabin with furnishings from the canal era (1828–1924), a hay house where feed was stored for the mules, and an on-board mule stable. Canal lock no. 75 and a restored log-cabin lock house are located nearby. Guided tours are conducted by volunteers. It is located 5 miles south of Cumberland off Route 51.

C&O Canal National Historical Park
Canal St. ☎ **301/722-8226**. Admission free. Visitor center, Tues–Sun 9am–5pm.

The C&O Canal came to this area in 1850, after 184^1/$_2$ miles of ditch and tow-path had been constructed, originating near Washington at Georgetown. For more than 75 years it was an important transport line and had a big impact on the early development of Cumberland. Start a visit at the Canal Visitor Center, in the Western Maryland Station Center at track level, to see the background exhibits on the history of the canal and pick up a brochure on the canal. Then explore the tow-path, a nearly level trail for walkers, hikers, and bikers. There are remnants of locks, dams, lock houses, and other historical features along the way.

Emmanuel Episcopal Church
16 Washington St., Cumberland. ☎ **301/777-3364**. Services Thurs 10:30am, Sun 8am and 10am; open by appointment or prior arrangement at other times.

This church is built on the foundations of Fort Cumberland, where George Washington began his military career; earthworks from the fort (ca. 1755) still lie beneath the church. Although the Emmanuel parish dates from 1803, the corner-stone of the present native sandstone building was laid in 1849 and was completed in 1851. The church, which contains original Tiffany stained-glass windows from three different periods and a scale model of Fort Cumberland, is not normally open to the public except for services, by tour, or by appointment, but the grounds are part of the Fort Cumberland Walking Trail, signposted with plaques and detailed in a leaflet available from the visitors center.

George Washington's Headquarters
In Riverside Park, Greene St. (at the junction of Wills Creek and the Potomac River). ☎ **301/777-5905**. Admission free. Open by appointment and on certain holidays. Exterior viewing at all times.

This log cabin, believed to be the only remaining structure from the original Fort Cumberland, was used by Washington as his official quarters during the French and Indian War. The cabin is not open to the public, but does have a viewing window and a tape-recorded description that plays when activated by a push button.

History House
218 Washington St. ☎ **301/777-8678**. Admission $3 adults, $1 students over 12. May–Oct Tues–Sat 11am–4pm, Sun 1:30–4pm; Nov–Apr Tues–Sat 11am–4pm.

Originally built as a private residence in 1867 for the president of the C&O Canal, this house is now in the hands of the Allegany County Historical Society. The restored 18-room dwelling contains antique furnishings such as a Victorian courting couch and an 1840 square grand piano. Other features include a research room, an early 19th-century brick-walled garden, and a base-ment kitchen with authentic cooking utensils, fireplace, coal stove, dishes, and pottery.

Thrasher Carriage Museum
19 Depot St., Depot Center, Frostburg. ☎ **301/689-3380** or 301/777-5905. Admission $2 adults, $1.75 seniors, $1 children under 12. May–Sept Tues–Sun 11am–4pm; Oct Tues–Sun 11am–6pm; Nov–Dec and Apr weekends 11am–4pm.

Housed in a renovated warehouse opposite the steam-train depot, this museum displays an extensive collection of late 19th-and early 20th-century horse-drawn carriages: formal closed vehicles, milk wagons, open sleighs, funeral wagons, dogcarts, phaetons, and runabouts.

Toll Gate House

Route 40A (the old National Rd., at LaVale). ☎ **301/729-4938.** Admission free. May–Oct Sat–Sun 1:30–4:30pm, and by appointment.

Built in 1836, this historic tollgate house is the last of its kind to remain in Maryland. When this country's first national road was built, federal funds were used; ownership was then turned over to the states and tolls had to be collected.

✪ Western Maryland Scenic Railroad

Western Maryland Station Center, 13 Canal St. ☎ **301/759-4400** or 800/TRAIN-50. Tickets May–Sept and Nov–Dec, $13.75 adults, $8.50 children 2–12, $12.25 seniors over age 60; Oct, $15.75 adults, $9.50 children, $15.25 seniors. Reservations are required. May–Sept, Tues–Sun, 11:30am; Oct, Tues–Sun 10:45am and 3:30pm; Nov to mid-Dec, Sat–Sun 11:30am. From I-68, take the Downtown Cumberland Exit 43C (westbound) or the Johnson St. Exit 43A (eastbound) and follow signs to Western Maryland Station Center.

It's worth a trip to western Maryland just to board this vintage steam train and ride the 32-mile round-trip between Cumberland and Frostburg. A genuine delight for young and old alike, this excursion—enhanced by an informative live commentary—follows a scenic mountain valley route through the Cumberland Narrows, Helmstetter's Horseshoe Curve, Brush Tunnel, many panoramic vistas, and a 1,300-foot elevation change between the two destinations. All trains depart and terminate at Cumberland. The trip takes three hours, including a 1 1/2-hour layover in Frostburg for local sightseeing, including the Depot Center, which is composed of a carriage museum, complex of shops, restaurant, and an active turntable where the train engine is turned in full view of the public for the Cumberland-bound segment of the journey.

ORGANIZED TOURS

Shircliffe Express Tours, P.O. Box 624, Cumberland, MD 21501 (☎ 301/ 759-0510), designs individual guided sightseeing tours to suit visitors' interests. Tours are conducted in a van or horse-drawn carriage by Ansel Shircliffe, a knowledgeable local tourism official who often dons a Revolutionary War uniform to enhance the flavor of an itinerary. Specialties include local history, Colonial and Victorian landmarks, craft shopping, fall foliage, and more. Tours operate year-round, with prices averaging $15 per hour, depending on exact requirements. Advance reservations are required.

ACTIVITIES

BIKING   The Cumberland area, nestled beside the scenic C&O Canal, is ideal for bicycling. **Allegany Adventures,** 14419 National Hwy., LaVale, MD 21501 (☎ 301/729-4719), operates one-day or weekend guided cycling tours along the canal towpath and wildlife areas from April through October. One-day trips, which last from four to six hours and include bike rental and a catered lunch, cost $25 to $40 per person; weekend trips, which provide bike rental, overnight camping accommodations, meals, and support vehicle, average $100 per person per day. Hiking/biking trips can also be booked. Advance reservations are required. If you prefer just to rent a bike and explore the area on your own, bike rentals can also be arranged for $5 per hour or $25 per day.

ART WORKSHOPS   With such sprawling mountain vistas, unique old buildings, and sylvan canal scenery, the Cumberland area is a natural setting to inspire artists. The **Haystack Mountain Art Workshops,** 120 Greene St., Cumberland,

MD 21502 (☎ 301/777-0003 or 800/286-9718), offer a series of year-round one-week or weekend adult art courses, based at the Inn at Walnut Bottom (see "Where to Stay," below), with classes conducted at a nearby art studio or outdoor locations by nationally known artists. Each course offers a different phase of art, from landscape and portrait painting to still life, florals, conceptual impression, watercolor, collage, and art for greeting cards. Fees, which include demonstrations, student painting time, individual and group instruction, plus accommodations, meals, field trips and activities, tours of local art galleries, and an evening at the theater, range from $275 to $395 per person for weekend courses to $630 to $880 per person for week-long courses. Advance reservations are required.

SHOPPING

Allegany Arts Council Artists Co-Op Gallery
13 Canal St., Cumberland. ☎ **301/777-ARTS.**

Housed in the Western Maryland Station Center, this gallery features the works of more than 30 western Maryland artists and craftspeople. The wares range from a wide selection of original oils, acrylics, and watercolors, to historic and limited-edition prints, wood carvings, stained glass, quilted items, and collectible Santas. Open Monday through Friday from 9am to 4pm and Saturday and Sunday from 10am to 3pm.

The Book Center
15–17 N. Centre St., Cumberland. ☎ **301/722-8344.**

Located just off the pedestrian mall, this shop has a large selection of books on Maryland and local history as well as volumes on railroading and canals. In addition, there are postcards, gifts, and out-of-state newspapers. Open Monday and Thursday from 8am to 9pm, Tuesday and Wednesday and Friday and Saturday from 8am to 6pm, and Sunday from 9am to 4pm.

Gallery on Greene
8 Greene St., Cumberland. ☎ **301/724-7936.**

Situated beside Wills Creek, this restored Victorian house features a gallery and working artist's studio with a selection of paintings by Maryland artists— landscapes, still lifes, florals, portraits, and local and historic scenes, plus stained glass and prints. Open Tuesday through Saturday from 11am to 4pm or by appointment.

Gateway Center
110 Baltimore St., Cumberland. ☎ **301/759-2821.**

This building, a former McCrory store, now houses several commercial enterprises including Yoder's Country Market and Kim's Khocolate Factory and Candy Store. Open Monday through Friday from 8:30am to 5pm and Saturday from 10am to 5pm.

Historic Cumberland Antique Mall
55–59 Baltimore St., Cumberland. ☎ **301/777-2979.**

Ensconced in a former department store in the center of the city's pedestrian mall, this antique emporium offers Victorian furniture, china, toys, decorated stoneware, glassware, primitives, clocks, jewelry, railroad and military memorabilia, quilts, brass, copper, tools, and more. Open daily from 10am to 5pm.

WHERE TO STAY

The Cumberland-Frostburg area offers an inviting blend of historic inns, modern hotels and motels, and homey bed-and-breakfast lodgings. Take your pick—most fall into the moderate price category and offer very good value.

Best Western Braddock Motor Inn

1268 National Hwy., LaVale, MD 21502. ☎ **301/729-3300** or 800/296-6006. Fax 301/729-3300. 108 rms. A/C TV TEL. $58–$95 double. AE, MC, V. Free parking.

A tree-shaded country setting adds to the rural atmosphere of this two-story motel, just off I-68 and east of the historic LaVale Toll Gate. Rooms are furnished in contemporary style. Facilities include a restaurant, lounge, indoor heated swimming pool, Jacuzzi, sauna, exercise room, and game room.

❸ Comfort Inn

State Route 36 N., Frostburg Industrial Park, Frostburg, MD 21532. ☎ **301/689-2050** or 800/228-5150. 100 rms. A/C TV TEL. $51–$73 double. (Rates include continental breakfast.) AE, DC, MC, V. Free parking.

Sitting on a hillside outside of town, with lovely views of the valley in all directions, this modern two-story inn is built in a hacienda style with a white brick exterior. Guest rooms have dark woods, pastel tone fabrics, separate sitting areas, and a choice of king- or queen-size beds. Facilities include a fitness center and sauna.

❍ Failinger's Hotel Gunter

11 W. Main St., Frostburg, MD 21532. ☎ **301/689-6511.** 17 rms. A/C TV TEL. $55–$80 double. (Rates include continental breakfast.) AE, DC, MC, V. Free parking.

Originally opened in 1897 as the Gladstone Hotel, this four-story landmark later came under the ownership and name of William Gunter and was for many decades the social center of Frostburg. After a stretch of lean times and disrepair, it was revived and restored several years ago by the present owners, the Kermit Failinger family. The guest rooms are masterfully done, as are the public areas and the main staircase, the centerpiece of the hotel. The restoration has added modern conveniences, like private baths in all rooms and an elevator, but it has not impinged on the hotel's Victorian style, nor its original oak doors and brass fixtures, clawfoot bathtubs, intricate wall trim, vintage pictures and prints, smoked glass lantern-style lamps, and delicate wall sconces.

The guest rooms are individually furnished, with canopy or four-poster beds, armoires, laces and frills, and pastel fabrics. The one exception is no. 307, decorated starkly in black and white, and named the Roy Clark Room, after the country-western entertainer who stayed in it during a 1990 visit. Throughout the corridors, there are collectibles, dried-flower assortments, and hanging plants. Facilities include a restaurant, lounge, and a unique basement area that houses a sports bar (which was once a gamecock fighting arena), and the remnants of an old jail.

❍ Inn at Walnut Bottom

120 Greene St., Cumberland, MD 21502. ☎ **301/777-0003** or 800/286-9718. 12 rms, 2 suites. A/C TV TEL. $65–$90 room; $95–$130 suite. (All rates include full breakfast.) AE, DISC, MC, V. Free parking.

Nestled in a quiet downtown residential area just a block from historic Washington Street, this bed-and-breakfast inn is composed of two restored 19th-century homes: the Cowden House (1820) and the Dent House (1890). It is furnished with antiques and period reproductions including four-poster and brass beds, tapestry rugs, and down comforters. The guest rooms are spacious, with high ceilings and large windows, and include some ground-floor accommodations. Ten rooms have private baths. Facilities include an independently operated restaurant, Oxford House (see "Where to Dine," below), two parlors, gift shop, and mountain-bike rentals. The inn is also the headquarters for a series of year-round art workshops; see "Activities," above. The innkeeper is Sharon Ennis Kazary.

WHERE TO DINE
EXPENSIVE

✪ Au Petit Paris
86 E. Main St., Frostburg. ☎ **301/689-8946.** Reservations required. Main courses $10.50–$31.50. AE, CB, DISC, MC, V. Tues–Sat 6–9:30pm. FRENCH.

The interior of this restaurant is delightfully Parisian thanks to French murals and posters and bistro-style furnishings. Established more than 35 years ago, this restaurant is a local favorite for such dishes as trout with almonds, frogs' legs, duck à l'orange, coq au vin, steak Diane or au poivre, chateaubriand, veal cordon bleu, and a signature dish of lamb noisettes with Madeira sauce.

MODERATE

❸ Giuseppe's
11 Bowery St., Frostburg. ☎ **301/689-2220.** Reservations recommended on weekends. Main courses $8.95–$15.95. AE, DISC, MC, V. Mon–Thurs 4:30–10pm, Fri–Sun 3pm–11pm. ITALIAN.

In the heart of town and a block from the Frostburg State University campus, this two-floor dining spot is popular for the college community and is staffed by many of the students and locals. The decor is eclectic, with colorful posters of herbs and plants, and the food is first-rate. Entrées include all the usual Italian favorites, such as pizza, pastas, chicken cacciatore, shrimp scampi, and sausage and peppers, and also a surprising array of nightly specials including fresh seafood, such as trout stuffed with crab imperial or orange roughy.

L'Osteria
Ali Ghan Rd., off I-68 (Exit 46E/W). ☎ **301/777-3553.** Reservations required. Main courses $10.95–$18.95. AE, MC, V. Mon–Sat 5–9pm, Sun 4–8pm. ITALIAN/INTERNATIONAL.

The ambience of "Old Cumberland" prevails at this mid-19th-century structure, said to have been erected as a tavern and located in a country setting east of downtown. The interior includes original woodwork and antiques, but the menu is thoroughly contemporary. Open for dinner only, the entrées include veal saltimbocca or pizzaiola, filet of beef au poivre, shrimp Parmesan, blackened red fish prepared following a Paul Prudhomme recipe, and chicken cacciatore with peppers and onions in tomato and wine sauce. More than a half-dozen pastas are also offered.

The Old Depot
19 Depot St., Frostburg. ☎ **301/689-1221.** Reservations recommended for dinner. Main courses $6.95–$15.95; lunch $2.95–$7.95. AE, MC, V. Daily 11am–11pm. AMERICAN.

Originally built in 1891 as the Cumberland and Pennsylvania Railroad Company passenger and freight station, this structure was abandoned after service was discontinued in 1973; it was then renovated and opened as a restaurant and lounge in 1989. With a decor and ambience that preserves the pace and din of a train station, it is a busy and informal dining spot, popular with students and faculty from the local university, as well as tourists who arrive via the excursion on the Western Maryland Scenic Railroad. Entrées range from steaks to barbecued pork ribs, grilled shrimp, barbecued chicken, and Mexican fajitas. Lunch items include sandwiches, burgers, wings, ribs, and other finger foods.

✪ Oxford House

118 Greene St. ☎ **301/777-7101**. Reservations recommended for dinner. Main courses $10.95–$14.95, lunch $3.95–$7.95. AE, DISC, MC, V. Tues–Thurs 11am–2:30pm and 5–9pm, Fri–Sat 11:30am–2pm and 5–9:30pm, Sun 10am–3pm. INTERNATIONAL.

Housed in the Inn at Walnut Bottom, this restaurant has three small dining rooms decorated with prints of the Cumberland area, floral linens, plants, and menu memorabilia; classical music plays in the background. The menu changes often, but reflects the culinary experience of the Swedish chef. Specialties include the Dent House Dinner (grilled ham with pineapple, topped with Cumberland sauce and served with roast potatoes), Delmonico or peppercorn steaks, crab imperial glazed with Dijon sauce, crab-stuffed flounder with shrimp Newburg sauce, chicken sautéed with Hungarian paprika and sour cream, and medaillons of pork stuffed with apples and prunes.

MODERATE/INEXPENSIVE

🅢 Mason's Barn

I-68 (Exit 46E/W). ☎ **301/722-6155**. Main courses $7.95–$14.95; lunch $3.95–$7.95. AE, DISC, MC, V. 7am–10pm. AMERICAN.

Established in 1954 as a small roadside diner 1 mile east of Cumberland, this dependable restaurant has been growing ever since, thanks to the friendly and attentive supervision of owners Ed Mason and his son, Mike. As its name implies, it offers an authentic barnlike setting, with a decor of farming tools, local antiques, and an eclectic collection of Maryland memorabilia. Entrées include steaks and seafood dishes as well as barbecued ribs, chicken, veal, and pasta items. Lunch choices range from salads and homemade soups to sandwiches (the crab-cake sandwich is a standout). Breakfast is also available. For those who favor charbroiled beef and seafood dishes, there is a saloon-style steak house downstairs.

Pennywhistle's

25 N. Centre St. ☎ **301/724-6626**. All items $3–$5.95. MC, V. Mon–Sat 11am–5pm. AMERICAN.

Situated just off the city's pedestrian mall, this is an ideal spot for a snack or lunch while browsing downtown. The menu offers a creative blend of soups, salads, and sandwiches. Sandwich specialties include roast beef with cream cheese and pepper jelly on a croissant; smoked turkey with cranberry relish; sprouts on whole grain bread; and a classic peanut butter with raisins, apple, nuts, and honey on croissant.

CUMBERLAND AFTER DARK

The **Allegany Arts Council,** Western Maryland Station Center, Canal Street (☎ 301/777-ARTS), publishes a bimonthly newsletter detailing upcoming concerts and cultural events in the Cumberland area. You can also stop by their office for an update on events when you are in town; hours weekdays from 9am to 4pm.

The **Cumberland Theatre,** 103 Johnson St. (☎ 301/759-4990), presents a June through November professional program of Broadway musicals and comedies as well as mysteries and dramas. Performances are slated Wednesday through Sunday, and tickets average $11 to $15.

3 Deep Creek Lake

50 miles SW of Cumberland, 190 miles W of Baltimore, 100 miles SE of Pittsburgh

Maryland's largest freshwater lake is Deep Creek, nearly 12 miles in length, with a shoreline of 65 miles and covering nearly 3,900 acres. Located in the heart of Garrett County, on the state's western border, Deep Creek is completely artificial, a 1925 work project of the Youghiogheny Electric Company, which sold it to the Pennsylvania Electric Company in 1942. It is now leased to the Maryland Inland Fish and Game Commission for the nominal fee of $1 a year, and is managed by the Maryland Department of Natural Resources.

Nestled in the heart of the Allegheny Mountains, and with an elevation of 2,462 feet, Deep Creek Lake has long been a popular year-round recreational area. Summer temperatures average 65.9°F. In the winter months, however, Deep Creek Lake really comes into its own, as Maryland's premier ski resort (with an average temperature of 28°F and a yearly snowfall of more than 80 inches).

The two principal towns in the area are Oakland, the county seat of Garrett County, and McHenry, named for Col. James McHenry of Baltimore, an aide to General Washington during the Revolutionary War and a signer of the Constitution.

GETTING THERE   By Car   You can reach Deep Creek Lake by heading westward along I-68 to Keyser's Ridge and then following Route 219 south. It's about an hour's drive from Cumberland.

ESSENTIALS   Area Code   The area code is 301.

Visitor Information   The Deep Creek Lake-Garrett County Promotion Council is in the Garrett County Courthouse, 200 S. Third St., Oakland, MD 21550 (☎ 301/334-1948). From mid-May through mid-October, an Information Booth is located on Route 219, at Deep Creek Lake, south of Deep Creek Lake Bridge (☎ 301/387-6171). In the winter, a telephone snow report service is operated (☎ 301/387-4000).

WHAT TO SEE & DO

A complete year-round resort, Deep Creek Lake is equally great in summer and winter.

OUTDOOR ACTIVITIES

BOATING   Summer activities focus on water sports, with every type of boat from sailboat to speedster on the lake. Nearly all marinas around the lake have craft for rent, seven days a week. Paddleboats or canoes average $6 an hour; fishing boats, $15 an hour; pontoon boats, from $20 to $30 an hour; ski boats and runabouts, from $16 to $32 an hour, depending on horsepower. Some of the leading firms at Deep Creek Lake along Route 219 are **Echo Marina** (☎ 301/387-BOAT); **Bill's Marine Service** (☎ 301/387-5536); **Crystal Waters** (☎ 301/387-5515); **Blue Anchor** (☎ 301/387-5677); **Deep Creek Outfitters** (☎ 301/387-6977) and **S&H Marina** (☎ 301/387-5616).

GOLF   The **Golf Club at Wisp,** Wisp Resort Golf Course, 290 Marsh Hill Road, Deep Creek Lake (☎ 301/387-4911), is an 18-hole championship facility nestled between the Allegheny Mountains and Deep Creek Lake. Open from April through mid-October, the course welcomes guests seven days a week. Greens fees and golf cart cost $48 per person for 18 holes and $30 for greens fees only. Rates are slightly lower after 4pm. There is a fully stocked pro shop on the grounds. In addition, the **Oakland Country Club,** Sang Run Road, Oakland (☎ 301/334-3883), invites visitors to play on its 18-hole championship course on weekdays. Greens fees are $20 to $25 for 18 holes. Golf carts are available for $18 per person for 18 holes.

SKIING   Deep Creek Lake is the home of Maryland's only ski area. With an elevation of 3,080 feet and a vertical rise of 610 feet, the **Wisp Resort** offers 23 ski runs and trails on 80 acres of skiable terrain. The longest single run is 2 miles. Slope fees range from $30 on weekdays to $37 on weekends, with reduced rates for night skiing, two-day tickets, early or late-season skiing, and children. The ski season opens at the end of November and closes in mid-March. The Wisp also operates an on-premises ski school, a rental service, and a ski shop. For full information, contact the Wisp Resort, 290 Marsh Hill Rd., Deep Creek Lake, MD 21541 (☎ 301/387-4911).

SWIMMING   Deep Creek Lake State Park, south of McHenry on State Park Road, features a 700-foot sandy beach with lifeguards on duty.

SHOPPING

The most unique shopping experience in the Deep Creek area is located en route from Cumberland about 25 miles northeast of the lake district at **Yoder's Country Market,** Route 669, Grantsville (☎ 301/895-5148). Started as a Mennonite family farm enterprise in 1932, it has grown from a one-room butcher shop to an extensive specialty market. It is known for a variety of fresh and natural food items such as jams, jellies, relishes, honey, maple syrup, molasses, fruits, nuts, baked goods, cereals and grains, meats, cheeses, herbs, and spices. In addition, there are cookbooks featuring Amish and Mennonite recipes and Pennsylvania Dutch crafts. It's open Monday through Saturday from 8am to 6pm.

WHERE TO STAY
MODERATE

Alpine Village
19638 Garrett Hwy. (at Glendale Rd.), Oakland, MD 21550. ☎ **301/387-5534** or 800/343-5253. 29 rms, 14 chalets. A/C TV TEL. $50–$80 double; $90–$150 chalet. AE, MC, V. Free parking.

Views of the lake and mountains are part of the charm at this inn nestled on 30 wooded acres. The facility offers a choice of lodge-style rooms and chalets. Rooms have queen-size beds and sundecks; many also have cathedral ceilings, fireplaces, and kitchenettes. The chalets, which have living rooms, patios, and complete kitchens, in addition to at least two bedrooms, can accommodate up to six people. Guests also enjoy docking facilities, beach swimming, and a heated outdoor pool (in summer).

✪ Wisp Resort
290 Marsh Hill Rd., Deep Creek Lake, MD 21541. ☎ **301/387-5581** or 800/462-9477. Fax 301/387-4127. 67 rms, 100 suites. A/C TV TEL. $65–$135 double. AE, DC, DISC, MC, V. Free parking.

A mecca for skiers in winter and golfers in summer, this resort is Deep Creek Lake's center of activity. In addition to an 18-hole championship golf course and a 23-trail ski area, the amenities include an indoor swimming pool and whirlpool, tennis court, and fitness center. The guest rooms have a queen-size bed, a sofa bed, and a small refrigerator. Some units also have small kitchenettes or fireplaces. Dining and entertainment facilities include a restaurant (see "Where to Dine," below), coffee shop/pizzeria, and two lounges.

MODERATE/INEXPENSIVE

Carmel Cove Inn

P.O. Box 644, Oakland, MD 21550. ☎ **301/387-0067.** 5 rms. A/C. $70–$100 double. (Rates include full breakfast.) MC, V. Free parking.

For off-the-beaten-path seclusion, head to this little bed-and-breakfast inn, tucked in a wooded area off Glendale Road and Route 219. It sits on the edge of a 53-acre residential community within walking distance of a private cove along Deep Creek Lake. With steeples, a clock tower, and a chapel-like facade, the inn is the former monastery of the Discalced Carmelite Fathers. The guest rooms are simply furnished and each has a private bath or shower. There are no telephones or TVs in the rooms, but a common parlor has a stacked stone fireplace and a TV for guest use. Innkeepers Peter and Mary Bender prepare hearty buffet breakfasts, often including items such as Belgian waffles, cheesy sausage mushroom quiche, and griddle cakes with Maryland maple syrup. Facilities for guest use include fishing poles, canoe, bikes, tennis court, and sundeck.

✪ Harley Farm

16766 Garrett Hwy., Oakland, MD 21550. ☎ **301/387-9050.** Fax 301/387-9050. 5 rms. $60–$80 double. (Rates include full breakfast.) MC, V. Free parking.

Located about 5 miles south of Deep Creek Lake and signposted off Route 219, this two-story bed-and-breakfast inn sits in a scenic valley surrounded by a 65-acre horse farm. The guest rooms, furnished in contemporary country style, are all in a newly built addition to the original brick farmhouse. Public areas include a downstairs gathering room with fireplace and a wraparound porch overlooking a wildflower meadow. Innkeepers are Wayne and Kam Gillespie.

Innlet Motor Lodge

Deep Creek Dr., P.O. Box 178, Deep Creek Lake, MD 21541. ☎ **301/387-5596** or 800/ 540-0763. 20 rms. A/C TV. $65–$75 double. AE, DC, DISC, MC, V. Free parking.

For a room with a view, try this dependable two-story motel facing Deep Creek Lake and the Wisp ski area. Each room has contemporary furniture with dark woods and rustic colors, and a balcony or patio; about half of the units have fireplaces. Facilities include a private beach, boat dock, and picnic tables.

Point View Inn

Route 219, P.O. Box 100, McHenry, MD 21541. ☎ **301/387-5555.** 22 rms. A/C TV TEL. $50–$75 double; $80–$95 efficiency. AE, DISC, MC, V. Free parking.

Right on the shores of Deep Creek Lake, this lodging offers motel-style rooms with porches or private terraces overlooking the lake. Most units have Victorian or antique furnishings, some with fireplaces. Facilities include a boat dock, a private beach, an informal cafe/lounge, and a full-service dining room that overlooks the lake.

Royal Oaks Inn

2704 Deep Creek Dr., McHenry, MD 21541. ☎ **301/387-4200** or 800/296-4209. 77 rms. A/C TV TEL. $55–$75 double. (Rates include continental breakfast.) AE, DC, DISC, MC, V. Free parking.

Situated a quarter-mile from the lake on the approach to the Wisp ski resort, this modern Victorian-style three- and four-story hotel is just off the main Route 219 corridor. Guest rooms are decorated in contemporary style, with dark wood furniture, mellow-toned fabrics, country art prints, imported marble floors, writing desks, and lighted luggage racks. Some rooms have individual Jacuzzi baths.

WHERE TO DINE

Note: Garrett County liquor regulations prohibit restaurants from selling or serving any alcoholic beverages, including wine, on Sunday.

EXPENSIVE/MODERATE

Deer Park Inn
Deer Park Hotel Rd., Route 3, Box 3270, Oakland. ☎ **301/ 334-2308.** Reservations required. Main courses $9.50–$20.50. AE, DISC, MC, V. Memorial Day–Labor Day Mon–Sat 5:30–9:30pm, September–May Thurs–Sat 5:30–9:30pm. FRENCH/COUNTRY.

For fine dining in an authentic turn-of-the-century atmosphere, it's hard to beat this lovely inn, originally built in 1889 as "Pennington Cottage," a 17-room summer home for a prominent Baltimore architect, Josiah Pennington, and his family. It sits on the grounds of the once-famous Deer Park Hotel, created by B&O railroad president John Garrett, but demolished in 1942. Although the cottage was left dormant for many years, it was restored several years ago and is now listed on the National Register of Historic Places. Furnished with Victorian antiques, many of which are original to the building and other nearby estates, it is now the setting for candlelight dining, prepared by chef-owner John Gonzales, formerly executive chef at the Watergate and Ritz-Carlton Hotels in Washington, D.C. House specialties include a mixed grill of jumbo shrimp wrapped in prosciutto, swordfish, and beef tenderloin; sautéed veal tenderloin with apples and calvados; warm salad of sea scallops, snow peas, and bell peppers on mixed greens with walnut vinaigrette; and roast rabbit on a bed of fresh fennel. The main drawback is that the inn is in the middle of nowhere, deep in the country but well-signposted, about 9 miles south east of the Deep Creek Lake Bridge, off Sand Flat Road and Route 135. If you want to stay overnight, the inn does offer three rooms with private bath upstairs (from $65 to $85).

MODERATE

Bavarian Room
290 Marsh Hill Rd., Deep Creek Lake. ☎ **301/387-4911.** Reservations recommended on weekends. Main courses $11.95–$18.95. AE, DC, DISC, MC, V. Sun–Thurs 5–10pm, Fri–Sat 5–10:30pm. INTERNATIONAL.

Part of the Wisp Resort, this restaurant offers an Alpine decor and old-world atmosphere with fireplace. The menu offers such varied dishes as barbecued ribs, charcoal-grilled steaks, and Wiener schnitzel, as well as design-yourself pasta dishes. Unlimited trips to the soup-and-salad bar go with the choice of entrée.

Dr. Willy's Great American Seafood Co.
178 Quarry Rd. (off Route 219), Oakland. ☎ **301/387-7380.** Reservations recommended on weekends. Main courses $9.95–$15.95. MC, V. June–Sept daily 5–9pm, Oct and Jan–May Sat–Sun 5–9pm. SEAFOOD.

When a restaurant has a seafood market on the premises, you can expect that the freshest of seafood is on the menu. Named after a legendary seafaring parrot, this rustic restaurant is a real find for fish lovers on this side of Maryland. The menu changes with the seasons but crab cakes and crab soup are usually available, as are other Maryland-seafood specialties, various kinds of shrimp, and fish shipped daily from afar. If you prefer a picnic, take-out is also available from the market. Although the original Dr. Willy is no longer around, owner Willy Hughes is ever-present and happy to answer any questions on the day's catch.

McClive's

Deep Creek Dr., McHenry. ☎ **301/387-6172.** Reservations not accepted. Main courses $8.95–$15.95. AE, DISC, MC, V. Sun–Tues 5–10pm, Fri–Sat 5–11pm. Closed Christmas and Thanksgiving. AMERICAN.

Perched on the lakefront, this modern restaurant offers panoramic views from its indoor dining room or on the outside deck. The menu presents a wide choice of seafood dishes such as blackened roughy, soft-shell crabs Dijon, garlic scallops, mussels Provençale, applewood smoked trout, shrimp and scallops Florentine, and mesquite-grilled swordfish or salmon. In addition, there is blackened prime rib, lemon chicken, lamb and pork chops, and a variety of pastas. Nightly specials offer particularly good value.

✪ Silver Tree

Glendale Rd., Oakland. ☎ **301/387-4040.** Reservations not accepted. Main courses $9.95–$19.95. AE, MC, V. Mon–Thurs 5–10pm, Fri–Sat 5–11pm, Sun 4–10pm. ITALIAN.

This lakefront restaurant has an 1890s decor of knotty-pine walls, beamed ceilings, colored-glass lamps, and open fireplaces. Wide picture windows add a contemporary touch, framing views of the lake and surrounding woodlands. The specialty here is Italian food—veal parmigiana, spaghetti with a choice of sauces, lasagne, and manicotti. In addition, there is a wide range of seafood entrées, ranging from crab imperial and crab soufflé to seafood Newburg and fish combination platters; prime rib and charbroiled steaks are also on the menu. In summer, light fun-food meals are also served at Silver Tree Harbor, a lakeside seafood bar on the restaurant grounds.

MODERATE/INEXPENSIVE

Uno Restaurant

19814 Garrett Hwy., Deep Creek Lake. ☎ **301/387-4866.** Reservations not accepted. Main courses $5.95–$14.95. AE, MC, V. Mon–Thurs 11am–midnight, Fri–Sat 11am–1am, Sun 11am–11pm. AMERICAN.

Situated in a beautiful lakefront setting on Route 219, this is one of the few chain operations in the Deep Creek area. The layout includes a central fireplace, booth seating on two levels, and framed posters of theater and movie personalities. In warm weather there is additional seating on an outdoor deck. The menu, which is the same all day, specializes in multi-ingredient pizzas and pastas. Burgers, soups, sandwiches, salads, wings, and ribs are also available.

NEARBY DINING

✪ Penn Alps Restaurant and Craft Shop

125 Casselman Rd., Grantsville. ☎ **301/895-5985.** Reservations not accepted. Main courses $7.95–$11.95; lunch $3.25–$6.95. MC, V. Nov–day before Memorial Day, Mon–Thurs 7am–7pm, Fri–Sat 7am–8pm, Sun 7am–3pm; Memorial Day–Oct 31, Mon–Sat 7am–8pm, Sun 7am–3pm. Closed several days at Christmas. PENNSYLVANIA DUTCH.

Don't leave the mountainous countryside of western Maryland without a stop at this welcoming oasis. Situated between an 18th-century gristmill and an old stone arch bridge along Alt. Route 40, this unique restaurant-cum-shop is housed in a remodeled log stagecoach inn dating back to 1818. There are five dining rooms, all with an old-world atmosphere, serving Pennsylvania Dutch–style cooking such as roast pork and sauerkraut and hickory smoked ham, as well as roast beef, fried chicken, steaks, and seafood. Lighter items are also available, including sandwiches, soups, salads, and burgers.

The adjacent shop offers dozens of unique handcrafts and baked goods produced largely by the neighboring Amish-Mennonite community north of Grantsville. In the summer months, a half-dozen rustic buildings in the nearby Spruce Forest serve as studios for a group of local artisans, including a spinner, weaver, potter, stained-glass worker, wood sculptor, and bird carver. Visitors are welcome to watch the craftspeople at work. The hours for the shop are the same as the restaurant, but schedules for the working craftspeople vary.

Introducing Delaware

7

A narrow strip of land wedged between the southeastern tip of Pennsylvania and the eastern rim of Maryland, Delaware is the second-smallest state in the nation, after Rhode Island. It's only 1,982 square miles, about the size of Yellowstone National Park or most individual U.S. counties. Yet, within its small area, Delaware contains a surprisingly large number of natural and other attractions, rivaling, in beauty and variety, those of its bigger neighbors. In addition to well-kept towns in picturesque settings and large cities with their landmark squares, historical museums, and public art treasures, it has stretches of unspoiled beaches, sylvan parks and meandering gardens, fertile farmlands, and abundant fishing shores.

Delaware is 96 miles long and from 9 to 35 miles wide. It has approximately 600,000 residents and is divided into three counties (New Castle to the north, Kent in the center, and Sussex to the south), prompting one wit to remark that when the tide is up the state is down to only two counties. The land, mostly at or near sea level, is flat, with the exception of the undulating hills of the Brandywine River valley in the north; about half of the land acreage is used for farming. Bounded by Pennsylvania on the north, Maryland on the west and south, and the Atlantic Ocean and Delaware Bay on the east (with New Jersey right across the bay), Delaware is within easy reach of the major metropolitan areas of the Northeast and the mid-Atlantic states. It has the distinction of being the only state to lie both north and east of the Mason-Dixon Line, which forms its western and southern borders.

1 Delaware Today

Delaware is known as the "First State," because in 1787 its citizens were the first to ratify the new Constitution of the United States. As a result, Delaware today takes precedence over all the other states at official functions and rosters.

Home of the Du Pont family, it is one of the world's major chemical centers. Other industries as well are located in Delaware, mostly in the northern part. Indeed, because of the state's lenient business tax laws, more than half of the companies on *Fortune* magazine's top 500 list are incorporated in Delaware. Similarly,

> ## ❓ Did You Know?
>
> - Three of America's oldest churches—Old Swedes (1698) in Wilmington, Old Welsh Tract (1703) near Newark, and Barratt's Chapel (1780) at Frederica—are still in use in Delaware.
> - In 1939 the Du Pont Company first developed and produced nylon at its plant in Seaford, which is now known as the nylon capital of the world.
> - A white cedar swamp in Sussex County is home to a rare curly grass fern, *Schizaeapusilla*, normally found only in scattered locations in Canada and Peru.
> - Delaware has the lowest average altitude of any state in the country—about 60 feet above sea level. Its highest point, just north of Wilmington, is only 447.85 feet above sea level.
> - Half of Delaware's 25-mile Atlantic coastline is devoted to wildlife refuges and parks.
> - A Dover mechanic and inventor, Eldridge Johnson, founded the Victor Talking Machine Company (1901), forerunner of the RCA Victor Company.
> - Sussex County, home of the Delaware beaches, is the number-one broiler chicken–producing county in the nation.
> - In 1880 the first beauty contest was held in Rehoboth Beach, to select "Miss United States." Thomas Edison was a judge.
> - The Nanticoke tribe, native to Delaware, still resides in Sussex County. Each September the members celebrate their heritage with a powwow in Millsboro.

because of novel tax incentives and the elimination of ceilings on interest rates, many new banks and financial service firms have established themselves in Wilmington, the largest city.

In contrast with the north, the rural south is chiefly agricultural, producing bountiful crops of soybeans, corn, tomatoes, strawberries, and asparagus. Chicken farming is also a big business.

Tourism is an important industry throughout the state, attracting some 5.5 million visitors and generating more than $800 million a year. Tourists take in the historical landmarks of the north as well as the natural attractions of the south. Because Delaware has no sales tax, it's a shopper's paradise.

Delaware's situation on the eastern seaboard has given the state its particular character. It shares a peninsula with Maryland and Virginia commonly known as "Del-Mar-Va." This broad finger of land between the Chesapeake Bay and the Atlantic Ocean is distinguished by a relaxed country lifestyle and down-home hospitality.

The seacoast extends some 25 miles; along its edge you'll find sandy and dune-swept beaches of all sizes and descriptions. Delaware also has 11 state parks, a dozen rivers, and 50 lakes, offering great opportunities for fishing, hiking, biking, water sports, and various other outdoor activities.

Because of its size and fertile soil, Delaware has been called, by Thomas Jefferson, the "Diamond State"—small but of great value.

2 A Look at the Past

EARLY EXPLORATIONS This tiny area was initially settled by the Lenni Lenape and Nanticoke Indian tribes. The first European to arrive was probably Henry Hudson, in 1609, when he sailed in from the Atlantic and along the neighboring bay (now known as Delaware Bay). He might have stepped off the *Half Moon* to explore, but the sight of dangerous shoals persuaded him to turn his ship northward, where eventually he discovered the Hudson River in New York.

The following year, an English sea captain, Samuel Argall, sailed into the same waters by accident while en route to Virginia. It is said that he named the body of water in honor of the governor of Virginia, Thomas West, Lord de La Warr (1577–1618). The name *Delaware* was later also assigned to the land around the bay.

FIRST SETTLEMENTS In 1631 a small group of Dutch fishermen settled on the curve of land between the bay and the ocean. They called their settlement Zwaanendael, or Valley of the Swans. But soon thereafter a misunderstanding arose between the Dutch and the Lenni Lenape Indians, and in the ensuing dispute the colonists were massacred. Now the town of Lewes (pronounced "*Loo*-is") lies at the site of their settlement.

In 1637 two Swedish ships, the *Kalmar Nyckel* and the *Vogel Grip,* sailed into Delaware Bay and continued northward almost 60 miles, entering a smaller river. The people on board named this new body of water the Christina River, after their queen, and in time they built a fortress and called their settlement New Sweden. The Swedes adapted well, using local trees to build log cabins, said to be the first in the New World. They also raised livestock and grew corn, a staple introduced to them by the Indians. Although the settlement prospered, it was not to remain under the Swedish flag for long. By 1655, the Dutch, led by Peter Stuyvesant, had succeeded in establishing a stronghold at Fort Casimir, 7 miles to the south. Anxious to extend their power, the Dutch sent warships and soldiers and forced the surrender of the Swedes, but they allowed them to keep their settlement near Fort Christina.

Dateline

- **1609** Henry Hudson explores Delaware Bay area.
- **1610** Delaware is named for the governor of Virginia, Lord De La Warr.
- **1629** Delaware's first town is settled by the Dutch.
- **1637** "New Sweden" is established at Wilmington.
- **1655** Peter Stuyvesant establishes Fort Casimir.
- **1664** The English rename Fort Casimir as New Castle and it becomes the first capital of Delaware.
- **1704** William Penn grants Delaware its own assembly.
- **1717** Wilmington is plotted as a city.
- **1776** The struggle for independence takes form.
- **1777** A Revolutionary War battle is fought near Newarkand, in the Brandywine Valley.
- **1787** The U.S. Constitution is drafted; Delaware is the first state to ratify the document, on December 7.
- **1792** Dover becomes the capital of Delaware.
- **1802** Du Pont chemical enterprises are established in America.
- **1829** The Delaware and Chesapeake Canal is completed.
- **1897** A new state constitution is adopted.
- **1940s** Route 13/Du Pont Highway is completed.
- **1981** Delaware enacts Financial Center Development Act.

THE COMING OF THE ENGLISH   The tides of history changed in 1664, when the English overpowered the Dutch and took over most of the Eastern seaboard, with settlements stretching from New England to Virginia. The English, like the Dutch, allowed all previous settlers to stay. They also made a few name changes, and Fort Casimir became New Castle. Because of its location, New Castle soon evolved into the first capital of Delaware and a major Colonial seaport.

Shortly afterward, William Penn crossed the Atlantic to claim extensive lands that were granted to him and his Quaker followers. He dropped anchor first at New Castle, in 1682, and then sailed farther up the Delaware River to found Philadelphia. At the time, Delaware's territory was considered part of Penn's lands, and so he divided the area south of Philadelphia into three counties: New Castle, Kent, and Sussex. As the three lower counties took shape, they also developed a sense of separateness from the rest of Pennsylvania. Recognizing this, Penn agreed to give them their own assembly in 1704.

As more English colonists poured into the counties, new cities and towns began to develop, including Wilmington (where Fort Christina once stood), named in honor of the earl of Wilmington, and Dover, plotted in 1717 according to a street plan devised by Penn. Dover would become the state capital 60 years later.

THE STRUGGLE FOR INDEPENDENCE   In 1776, as the colonies began their struggle for independence from England, Delaware assumed its part. At one point it was feared that a deadlock would develop in the vote for independence at the Continental Congress, but a Delaware man, Caesar Rodney of Kent County, rode through a storm-filled night on horseback for 80 miles from his Dover home to Philadelphia to cast his crucial vote.

As the Revolutionary War got underway, Delaware quickly raised an army of some 4,000 men, who became known for their blue uniforms. In their gear, some of the soldiers carried blue hen chickens (so called because of their blue-tinged feathers), which they used for cockfights. Today, the blue hen chicken is the official Delaware state bird.

The fighting of the war largely bypassed Delaware, except for a skirmish in 1777. A large army from England had landed near Elkton, Maryland, close to the Delaware border, and General Washington moved his forces into northern Delaware to meet it; a short encounter took place at Cooch's Bridge near Newark, southwest of Wilmington, after which the British headed north. They met Washington's army again at the Battle of Brandywine, one of the largest battles of the Revolutionary War, just north of the Delaware line in Pennsylvania.

STATEHOOD & EARLY GROWTH   The war ended in 1783 with independence from British rule, but a new country waited to take shape. In Delaware, as in the other former colonies, the citizens felt the need for a new form of government to replace the Articles of Confederation under which they had banded together to fight the war. In September 1787 a Constitutional Convention, meeting in Philadelphia, adopted a new Constitution and then submitted it to the states for approval. Delaware was the first to ratify the document, on December 7.

As the 19th century dawned, Delaware began to prosper, as did other states on the eastern seaboard that had fostered trade with Europe, including Britain. Early citizens of New Castle County were quick to harness the fast-flowing waters of the Brandywine River for milling, while the people of Kent and Sussex counties farmed their fertile lands. New immigrants from Europe arrived daily, among them a Frenchman, Eleuthère Irénée Du Pont, who started a black-powder (gunpowder) mill on the banks of the Brandywine in 1802. This establishment was the foundation of a family empire that was to become the largest chemical company in America and a powerful influence, to this day, on the state of Delaware.

Wilmington, fast growing into Delaware's largest city, soon became a hub of industrial development and a shipping center. With the coming of the railroads and the steamboat, farm products, from soybeans and corn to peaches, were moved ever more swiftly up from Sussex and Kent counties to northern markets. In 1829, the completion of the Delaware and Chesapeake Canal, a waterway that flows west to east across the entire state, provided a shortcut from Chesapeake Bay to the Atlantic. In the early 1900s, the Du Pont family, branching out into chemical and aerospace enterprises, also sponsored a new highway, Route 13, which runs the length of the state, from north to south.

MODERN MILESTONES   In recent times, the industrial northern part of the state has taken on an added dimension. The Financial Center Development Act of the 1980s freed banks from restrictions on credit-card interest rates and provided tax advantages for banks moving assets to the state. This legislation drew many of the nation's largest banks to Delaware, as well as other businesses, earning Delaware the title of "corporate capital of the world." Currently, thousands of businesses are incorporated in the state, including more than half of the companies on *Fortune* magazine's Top 500 list and more than a third of the companies listed on the New York Stock Exchange.

3 Visitor Information & Money

VISITOR INFORMATION   For a complete packet of information about Delaware, contact the Delaware Tourism Office, Delaware Development Office, 99 Kings Hwy., P.O. Box 1401, Dover, DE 19903 (☎ 302/739-4271, 800/ 441-8846, or in Delaware 800/282-8667; fax 302/739-5749).

PRICE GUIDELINES   In general, the lowest prices for hotel rooms in major cities, such as Wilmington and Dover, are available on weekends and in the summer months, when business travel is slow. In contrast, the best deals prevail at the beach resorts during weekdays, and especially in the off-season (October or November through April). Always inquire about package deals. Both city and country destinations frequently offer weekend or midweek packages that include accom-modations, some meals, and many extras. These packages not only save money and time but usually include some local highlights that you might miss otherwise.

In calculating the price categories within this book, we have used the following guidelines:

AREA CODE   All telephone numbers in the state of Delaware belong to the 302 area code.

SALES TAX   Although there is an 8% occupancy tax for lodgings in Delaware, there is no sales tax in the state, making Delaware an attractive place for dining out and shopping.

What Things Cost in Delaware

Deluxe room in the state's top hotel (Hotel Du Pont, Wilmington)	$119.00– 219.00
Moderate room in Wilmington suburb (Christiana Hilton)	$99.00–149.00
Budget room in Wilmington suburb (Fairfield Inn)	$49.95–54.95
Dinner for two at Wilmington's top restaurant (Green Room, Hotel Du Pont)	from $100.00
Dinner for two at a moderate Wilmington restaurant (Griglia Toscana)	from $60.00
Lunch for one at a downtown Wilmington budget restaurant (Govato's)	$5.00
18 holes of golf at a championship Wilmington golf course	from $16.00
Admission to the horse races at Delaware Park near Wilmington	$3.00
A ticket to a show at the Grand Opera House, Wilmington	from $10.00
Admission to Winterthur Museum and Gardens	$ 8.00
Room at a country inn in the Brandywine Valley (Brandywine River Hotel)	$119.00
Room at a Brandywine River budget motel (Abbey Green)	$45.00–59.00
Winery tasting tour at Chaddsford Winery	$5.00
Sunday brunch at Winterthur Museum	$18.95
Admission to the Old Court House, New Castle	Free
Room in Dover's top hotel (Sheraton Inn)	$82.00–115.00
Bed-and-breakfast room in Dover (Inn at Meeting House Square)	$48.00–65.00
Admission to Dover Air Force Base Museum	Free
Walking tour of Dover	$5.00
A day's headboat fishing from Lewes harbor	$32.00
Deluxe oceanfront hotel room at Rehoboth Beach (Boardwalk Plaza)	$100.00–395.00
Open-air music concert at Rehoboth Beach bandstand	Free
A day's bicycle rental on Fenwick Island	$10.00
Moderate motel room on Fenwick Island (Fenwick Islander)	$30.00–105.00
Pancake breakfast at Fenwick Island family restaurant (Libby's)	$3.95

Accommodations—The Average Cost of a Double Room, Excluding Tax: Very Expensive, $200 and up; Expensive, $125 to $200; Moderate, $75 to $125; Inexpensive, Under $75
Dining—Prices of Most Main Courses on the Menu: Very Expensive, Over $25; Expensive, $17 to $25; Moderate, $10 to $17; Inexpensive, Under $10

4   When to Go

THE CLIMATE   Delaware is always in season, with a climate that is moderate throughout the year. The average daily mean temperature for the entire state is 54°F (12°C). The state experiences four distinct seasons, with an average monthly temperature range of 31 to 76°F (0 to 24°C) and an average of 41 inches of annual precipitation.

DELAWARE CALENDAR OF EVENTS

January/February

- **Welcome Spring, Longwood Gardens,** Brandywine Valley. Conservatory displays featuring thousands of colorful, fragrant spring bulbs indoors. Late January through April.

March

- **Decoy Carving Workshop,** Dover. Demonstrations of the art of wooden waterfowl carvings at the Delaware Agricultural Museum and Village. Second-to-last weekend of March.

April

- **Great Delaware Kite Festival,** Lewes. Kite-flying demonstrations and competitions on the beach at Cape Henlopen State Park. Good Friday.
- **Ocean to Bay Bike Tour,** Fenwick Island. A bicycle marathon beside the beach. Last weekend of April.

May

- ✪ **Old Dover Days.** Dover's leading Colonial, Federal, and Victorian homes, mostly private residences and gardens, are all opened to the public. There's also a full program of parades, music, maypole dancing, refreshments, and craft demonstrations. Guides in period costumes greet visitors and answer questions.
  Where: The Green, Dover. **When:** First weekend in May. **How:** Tickets are $6 for house and garden tour. Contact the Friends of Old Dover, P.O. Box 44, Dover, DE 19903 (☎ 302/734-1736).
- **Winterthur Point-to-Point,** Winterthur. A fashionable annual event featuring five horse races, with a Grand Carriage Parade and a Tailgate Picnic Competition. First Sunday in May.
- **Tour Du Pont,** statewide. Some of the world's great cyclists compete in this annual 1,130-mile road race, setting out from Wilmington. First or second week of May.
- ✪ **A Day in Old New Castle.** For more than 70 years, the residents of this historic district have opened their doors for an open-house tour of the town. On this day, the town's private homes, public buildings, gardens, churches, and museums are all open to the public. Other events include maypole dancing, carriage rides, musical programs, and bell-ringing.
  Where: Historic New Castle. **When:** Third Saturday of May. **How:** Tickets are $10 for adults, $5 for children age 12 and under. Contact A Day in Old New Castle, P.O. Box 166, New Castle, DE 19720 (☎ 302/322-5744 or 302/328-2413).
- **Spring Sidewalk Sale,** Rehoboth and Dewey beaches. Townwide flea markets beside the sea. Third weekend of May.

June

○ **NASCAR Budweiser 500.** This two-day, action-packed stock-car racing competition draws dozens of top drivers from around the world to Dover Downs, nicknamed the "Monster Mile."

Where: Dover Downs. **When:** First weekend in June. **How:** Tickets range from $36 to $130. Contact the Dover Downs International Speedway, Rte. 13, P.O. Box 843, Dover, DE 19903 (☎ 302/674-4600 or 800/441-RACE).

○ **African American Heritage Festival.** Aiming to showcase the social, cultural, and educational achievements of African Americans in Delaware, this event features a day-long program of entertainment, artistic displays, fashions, and food.

Where: Downtown Dover and Mirror Lake. **When:** Last Saturday of June. **How:** Admission is free. Contact the Festival Committee, Inner City Cultural League, 109 Bertrand Dr., Dover, DE 19901 (☎ 302/736-0101).

• **Zwaanendael Heritage Garden Tour,** Lewes. A one-day tour of the historic houses and gardens of Zwaanendael Park and historic downtown Lewes. Fourth Saturday of June.

July

○ **Old-Fashioned Ice Cream Festival.** A refreshing Brandywine Valley event with major entertainment, band music, games, hot-air balloons, fashions from the past, a baby parade, an antiques show, Victorian crafts, and a chance to sample more than two dozen flavors of locally made ice cream.

Where: Rockwood Museum grounds. **When:** Second weekend of July. **How:** Tickets are $5. Contact Rockwood Museum, 610 Shipley Rd., Wilmington, DE (☎ 302/761-4340).

○ **Delaware State Fair.** The annual showcase for state and local produce, agricultural wares, and crafts, as well as stock car races, demolition derby, Paramutuel harness racing, rides, games, and concerts by top name entertainers.

Where: State Fairgrounds, Harrington. **When:** Third week of July. **How:** Admission is $3. Contact Delaware State Fairgrounds, Harrington, DE (☎ 302/398-3269).

• **County Pride Pops,** Winterthur. Annual outdoor concert by the Delaware Symphony Orchestra, along with hot air balloon displays and a finale of cannon fire with a rendition of the *1812 Overture.* Third Saturday of July.

August

○ **Rehoboth Beach Sandcastle Contest.** Held on the north end of the beach, this annual competition includes categories for both adult and child competitors in sand castle, whale sculpture, and free form.

Where: Rehoboth Beach. **When:** First Saturday of August. **How:** Free admission. Contact the Rehoboth/Dewey Beach Chamber of Commerce, 501 Rehoboth Ave., Rehoboth Beach, DE 19971 (☎ 302/227-2233 or 800/441-1329).

○ **Bethany Beach Boardwalk Arts Festival.** The major annual happening for the "Quiet Resorts" of Delaware's lower shore, this juried show attracts craftspeople, artisans, and spectators from near and far and takes up the entire length of the boardwalk. There are competitions for wood carving, photography, handmade jewelry, batik, metal sculpture, calligraphy, oil and watercolor painting, toys, dolls, and painted porcelain.

Where: Bethany Beach. **When:** Last Saturday of August. **How:** Free admission; varied fees for competitions. Contact the Bethany-Fenwick Area

Chamber of Commerce, P.O. Box 1450, Bethany Beach, DE 19930 (☎ 302/539-2100 or 800/962-7873).

September

- **Brandywine Arts Festival,** Wilmington. Held on the grounds of the Josephine Gardens, this event is a showcase for local craftspeople, artisans, and musicians. Second weekend of September.
- ✪ **NASCAR Split Fire Spark Plug 500.** This two-day stock-car racing competition, like June's NASCAR Budweiser 500 event, draws dozens of top drivers from around the world to Dover Downs and is action packed.

  Where: Dover Downs. **When:** Third weekend in September. **How:** Tickets range from $36 to $130. Contact the Dover Downs International Speedway, Rte. 13, P.O. Box 843, Dover, DE 19903 (☎ 302/674-4600 or 800/441-RACE).

October

- ✪ **Fall Sidewalk Sale.** Held along Rehoboth Avenue, adjacent to the boardwalk, this event draws a great display of arts, crafts, antiques, and collectibles.

  Where: Rehoboth Beach. **When:** First weekend of October. **How:** Free admission. Contact the Rehoboth/Dewey Beach Chamber of Commerce, 501 Rehoboth Ave., Rehoboth Beach, DE 19971 (☎ 302/227-2233 or 800/441-1329).
- **Coast Day,** Lewes. An "open house" day focusing on the marine environment of the Delaware coast, sponsored by the College of Marine Studies of the University of Delaware. First Sunday of October.
- ✪ **Rehoboth Beach Jazz Festival.** Some of the top names of international jazz gather for a weekend of oceanfront concerts at the boardwalk bandstand as well as continuous sessions at hotels, restaurants, clubs, and bars throughout the town.

  Where: Rehoboth Beach. **When:** Third weekend of October. **How:** Tickets range from free admission to $20. Contact the Rehoboth Beach Jazz Festival, P.O. Box 1055, Rehoboth Beach, DE 19971 (☎ 302/226-3844 or 800/29-MUSIC).
- **Sea Witch Festival,** Rehoboth Beach. A celebration of Halloween by the beach. Last weekend of October.

November

- **The World Championship Punkin' Chunkin',** Lewes. This contest offers a chance to break a world's record for pumpkin throwing, using handmade or professional catapults and centrifugal devices. First Saturday in November.
- ✪ **Yuletide at Winterthur.** Celebrate the holidays in 19th-century style, with a festive program at the Brandywine Valley's premier museum, featuring extensive decorations, entertainment, and guided tours.

  Where: Winterthur. **When:** Mid-November through early January. **How:** Admissions $8 adults, $6 seniors and students aged 12 to 18, and $4 children aged 5 to 11. Contact Winterthur, Rte. 52, Winterthur, DE 19735 (☎ 302/888-4600 or 800/448-3883).

December

- **Christmas at Rockwood,** Wilmington. Festive celebrations in Victorian style. End of November to January 1.

- **Yuletide in Odessa,** Odessa. Holiday decorations and observances in 18th-century style in a small town in central Delaware. Throughout December.
- **Christmas at Hagley,** Wilmington. See how the holidays were celebrated at a 19th-century mill village. Early December to January 1.

5 Getting There

BY PLANE Delaware does not have its own major airport for regularly scheduled passenger flights. The following airports, however, are located within easy reach: Philadelphia International Airport, 30 minutes from downtown Wilmington and $1^1/_2$ hours from Dover; Baltimore International Airport, approximately $1^1/_2$ to $2^1/_2$ hours to most points in Delaware; Washington/Dulles International Airport and Washington National Airport, approximately $2^1/_2$ to 3 hours to most points in Delaware. In addition, New Castle County Airport, about 10 miles south of Wilmington, serves private and corporate craft and some limited commercial flights.

BY TRAIN Amtrak offers convenient daily service to the downtown Wilmington Station, Martin Luther King Jr. Boulevard, and French Street.

BY BUS Buses from the Greyhound/Trailways system provide regular service into Wilmington, Dover, Rehoboth Beach, and Bethany Beach.

BY CAR I-95, the Eastern seaboard's major north-south link from Maine to Florida, runs right through Wilmington. The twin-span Delaware Memorial Bridge, peaking to a height of 441 feet over the Delaware River, connects the state to New Jersey. From the south, Route 13 brings you to Delaware via Virginia; and from the west, the best access is via Routes 50 and 301 from Maryland.

BY FERRY The Cape May-Lewes Ferry travels daily between southern New Jersey and the lower Delaware coast. This 70-minute crossing is operated on a drive-on, drive-off basis and can accommodate up to 800 passengers and 100 cars. Full details are given in the Lewes section of Chapter 11.

6 Getting Around

BY CAR The most practical way to see Delaware is by car. The north-south highway known as Route 13 runs the entire length of the state and is the major link between Wilmington and points south. It also provides a link to other roads, such as Route 1, which connects Wilmington to the beaches of Lewes, Rehoboth, Bethany, and Fenwick via a bypass around Dover. With the exception of the Delaware Memorial Bridge, the I-95 turnpike, and the new segments of Route 1, all roads in Delaware are toll free.

BY BUS Within the state, Blue Diamond Lines operates a bus service from Wilmington to Dover, with a connection to the beach destinations of Rehoboth Beach and Lewes.

Wilmington 8

Delaware's largest city, Wilmington dominates the bustling northeast corridor of the state—a nucleus of business, cultural, and social activity. The Delaware Memorial Bridge hangs over its eastern shore and I-95 cuts through its middle. A compact and cosmopolitan city, Wilmington is located in New Castle County, at the confluence of the Christina, Brandywine, and Delaware Rivers.

First settled some 350 years ago by Swedish colonists, who planted a permanent settlement at the mouth of the Christina River, this area was initially known as New Sweden until the Dutch conquered the colony and it became part of New Netherland. The English eventually claimed the land, and it evolved into prominence during Revolutionary times as Wilmington.

The city's ability to generate water power spurred its growth in the 18th century; by 1802, Wilmington had attracted a Frenchman named Eleuthère Irénée Du Pont de Nemours, who established a black-powder mill on the banks of the Brandywine. This establishment became the nucleus of the Du Pont Company, the largest chemical company in the United States.

Today, Wilmington is an industrial, financial, and banking center with an ever-changing skyline of sleek new buildings. It is also the gateway to the scenic and historic Brandywine Valley, home of some of America's greatest living history museums and art treasures.

A relatively small city (with a population of about 72,000), Wilmington has a compressed downtown area, easily walkable, and primarily commercial. It is almost equidistant from New York City and Washington, D.C.

1 Orientation

ARRIVING

BY PLANE   Most people flying into the northern Delaware area use the **Philadelphia International Airport** as a gateway. It is within a half hour's ride of downtown Wilmington, and many Wilmington hotels operate courtesy transfer services to and from the Philadelphia airport.

In addition, **SuperShuttle** (☎ 800/562-4094) operates a 24-hour transfer system between Philadelphia International Airport and any address in Delaware. The company has attended counters in all

What's Special About Wilmington

Sightseeing
- Market Street Mall, a five-block midcity pedestrian area of shops, museums, and restaurants.
- Wilmington Old Town Hall, depicting life in Delaware over the centuries.
- Old Swedes Church, one of the oldest churches in the United States.
- Delaware Art Museum, containing the largest collection of works by Brandywine School artist Howard Pyle.

Activities
- Tax-free shopping along 9th Street and the Market Street Mall.
- Spending a day at the horse races at Delaware Park.

Buildings
- Grand Opera House, one of the finest examples of cast-iron architecture in America.
- Hotel Du Pont, built in 1913, a landmark of lodging luxury and worth a stop even if you're staying elsewhere.

Parks and Zoos
- Bellevue State Park, the 270-acre former Du Pont family estate.
- Lums State Park, encompassing the state's largest freshwater pond.
- Brandywine Zoo, riverside habitat for animals from the Americas.

airport terminals and telephones located on courtesy phone boards at the airport. Rates per person range from $12 to $28, depending on pickup point. Departures are scheduled from the Philadelphia airport every 5 to 20 minutes between 6:30am and 11:30pm and every 10 to 40 minutes between 11:30pm and 6:30am.

BY CAR   The best way to drive to Wilmington is via I-95, which cuts across the city's center. The Delaware Memorial Bridge also connects Wilmington to the New Jersey Turnpike and points north. From the south, Route 13 will bring you into the city via Virginia and southern Delaware.

BY TRAIN   Wilmington is a stop on the main East Coast corridor of **Amtrak,** between Philadelphia and Baltimore. The Wilmington Amtrak station is located at Martin Luther King Boulevard and French Street (☎ 302/658-1515), on the city's southern edge, adjacent to the Christina River. This imposing structure, originally designed and built in 1907, has been recently restored to its former glory. Now on the National Register of Historic Places, it features terra-cotta window arches, red-clay tile roofing, and marble steps. There's a taxi stand outside the station.

Impressions

The Delaware ideal . . . is that life is best lived on a scale where everyone's hand leaves a print, and that a future without the best of the past isn't worth a darn.
                                    —Jane Vessels, *National Geographic,* August 1983

Downtown Wilmington

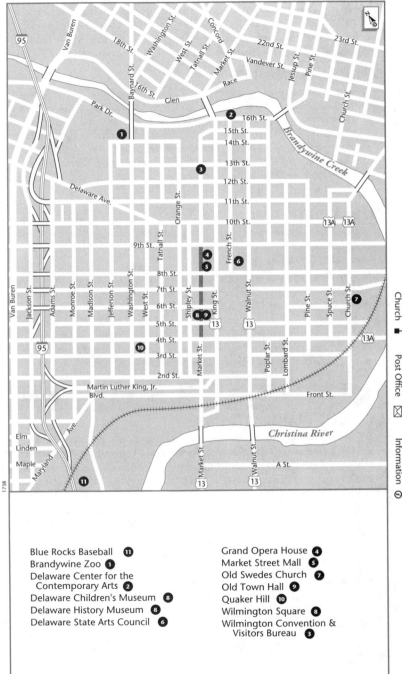

Church ✝ Post Office ⊠ Information ⊙

Blue Rocks Baseball ⑪
Brandywine Zoo ❶
Delaware Center for the
    Contemporary Arts ❷
Delaware Children's Museum ❽
Delaware History Museum ❽
Delaware State Arts Council ❻

Grand Opera House ❹
Market Street Mall ❺
Old Swedes Church ❼
Old Town Hall ❾
Quaker Hill ❿
Wilmington Square ❽
Wilmington Convention &
    Visitors Bureau ❸

BY BUS   Daily service is provided into the Wilmington Transportation Center, at 101 N. French St. (☎ 302/652-7391), by **Greyhound/Trailways** (☎ 302/655-6111). Weekday service from destinations within the state is provided into the same terminal by **Blue Diamond Lines** (☎ 302/577-6686 or 800/652-DART).

VISITOR INFORMATION

A complete selection of literature about Wilmington, the Brandywine Valley, and Historic New Castle is available from the **Greater Wilmington Convention and Visitors Bureau,** 1300 Market St., Suite 504, Wilmington, DE 19801 (☎ 302/652-4088 or 800/422-1181). In addition, for motorists passing through the area, the bureau maintains a **Visitors Information Center** on I-95 (☎ 302/737-4059). It is located just south of the city, in the service area between Routes 273 and 896, and operates from 8am to 8pm; at other times, an automatic hotel-reservation system is provided.

CITY LAYOUT

Wilmington is surrounded by three rivers: the Brandywine, the Christina, and the Delaware. The compact downtown area is laid out in an almost square grid system, less than 20 blocks wide or long.

MAIN ARTERIES & STREETS   Market Street runs from north to south in downtown Wilmington. The cross streets are numbered, from 1st to 16th, with the lowest number on the southern end of the layout; the streets running north to south bear the names of presidents, local heroes, and trees, in no definable order or system. Most streets are one way, except for Market and 4th streets. I-95 enters Wilmington via two main avenues: Delaware Avenue (Route 52) on the north end of the city and Maryland Avenue on the south end.

2   Getting Around

BY PUBLIC TRANSPORTATION

BY BUS   Wilmington has no subway, but it has an efficient bus system known as **DART (Delaware Administration for Regional Transit).** Blue-and-white signs indicating DART stops are located throughout the city, and regular routes can take you to hotels, museums, theaters, and parks, as well as such popular sights as Winterthur and New Castle. Exact fares, based on a zone system, are required; the minimum fare for one zone is $1.15. You may obtain complete information on schedules and applicable fares at most banks or by calling DARTLINE (☎ 302/655-3381).

BY SHUTTLE   The Delaware Department of Transportation operates the **Downtowner,** a free minibus shuttle service in Wilmington. Shuttles run from the Wilmington Amtrak station to Hercules Plaza, weekdays from 7:30am to 6pm. The route goes up Walnut Street north via Rodney Square and West Street to 13th Street and then down Market Street and King Street to the starting point. Service is provided every 20 minutes during off-peak hours (7:30 to 11am and 2 to 6pm) and every 10 minutes between the peak hours of 11am to 2pm.

BY CAR

Major car-rental firms represented in the Wilmington area include **Avis,** 903 Washington St. (☎ 302/654-0379); **Budget,** 100 N. Walnut St.

(☎ 302/764-3300); **Dollar,** 2100 Northeast Blvd. (☎ 302/655-7117); and **Hertz,** Front and French streets (☎ 302/428-1385).

BY TAXI

Taxi stands are located at the Du Pont Hotel, the Radisson Hotel, and the train station. If you wish to order a cab, call **Yellow Cab** (☎ 302/656-8151).

FAST FACTS: Wilmington

Airports   See "Orientation," earlier in this chapter.

Area Code   Wilmington's area code is 302.

Buses   See "Getting Around," earlier in this chapter.

Car Rentals   See "Getting Around," earlier in this chapter.

Climate   See "When to Go," in Chapter 7.

Dentists   Call the Wilmington Dental Referral Service (☎ 800/91-SMILE).

Doctors   Call the Medical Center of Delaware Physician Referral Service (☎ 302/428-4100) or the New Castle County Medical Society Physician Referral Service (☎ 302/658-3168).

Drugstores   A local chain with more than a dozen locations in the area is Happy Harry Discount Drugs; there are two downtown stores—900 Orange St. (☎ 302/654-1834) and Trolley Square Shopping Center, Delaware Avenue (☎302/655-6397).

Emergencies   Dial 911 for fire, police, or ambulance.

Eyeglasses   The most convenient downtown location is Wilmington Optical, 616 Market Street Mall (☎ 302/654-0530).

Film   See "Photographic Needs" below.

Hospitals   Wilmington Hospital, 14th and Washington streets (☎ 302/733-1000), or St. Francis Hospital, 7th and Clayton streets (☎ 302/421-4100).

Information   See "Visitor Information," earlier in this chapter.

Library   Wilmington Central Library is at 10th and Market streets (☎ 302/571-7415).

Newspapers and Magazines   The city's daily newspaper is the *News-Journal.* The best monthly magazine is *Delaware Today.*

Pharmacies   See "Drugstores," above.

Photographic Needs   For camera repair, supplies, or photo processing, try Lincoln Camera Shop, Delaware Avenue and Union Street (☎ 302/654-6241), or Ritz Camera, 108 W. 9th St. (☎ 302/655-4459).

Police   Dial 911.

Post Office   The main downtown post office branch is at Rodney Square Station, 1101 King St. (☎ 302/656-0196).

Taxes   There is no sales tax in Delaware, but an 8% lodging tax applies to stays at city hotels.

Taxis   See "Getting Around," earlier in this chapter.

Transit Information   Call DARTLINE (☎ 302/655-3381).

3 Accommodations

No matter where you go in Delaware, when you hear people refer to the "hotel," you can be sure they mean the Du Pont in Wilmington. For more than 80 years, this hotel has dominated the Delaware lodging scene. Consequently, there are relatively few other full-service hotels in downtown Wilmington. In recent years, however, as the Wilmington suburbs have grown, several new hotels and motels have sprung up in the surrounding areas.

Wilmington hotels, like other city hotels, charge top prices during the Sunday-through-Thursday period. The best way to save money is to reserve a one- or two-night weekend package (Friday and Saturday), which, in many cases, can represent a 50% reduction off normal midweek room rates.

DOWNTOWN
EXPENSIVE

✪ Hotel Du Pont
11th and Market sts., Wilmington, DE 19801. ☎ **302/594-3100** or 800/441-9019. Fax 302/656-2145. 206 rms, 10 suites. A/C TV TEL MINIBAR. $119–$219 double; $285–$385 suites. Weekend packages available. AE, CB, DC, MC, V. Parking $12.

Opened in 1913 and owned by E. I. Du Pont de Nemours and Company, this is the benchmark for all other Delaware hotels. Located in the heart of the city, the palatial 12-story, Italian Renaissance–style structure is a showcase of polished marble, elegant coffered ceilings, richly carved walnut, oak paneling, original artwork, and genteel service.

The guest rooms, recently refurbished and enlarged to the tune of $40 million, are in a class by themselves in this city, and have merited an International Gold Key Design Award. Each unit has mahogany reproduction furniture and built-in cabinetry, original artworks, and double-glazed windows; most of the fabrics, fibers, and fittings are made of the latest Du Pont products. Special amenities include a computer port in the phone system, voice-mail in three languages, a wall safe, and a videocassette player.

Dining/Entertainment: The hotel has two fine restaurants, the highly ranked Green Room (see "Dining," below) and the smaller Brandywine Room (see "Dining," below). In addition, the imposing old-world Lobby Lounge is a popular spot for cocktails, afternoon tea, or people watching.

Services: 24-hour room service, express checkout, concierge, turndown service, valet and laundry service, complimentary morning newspapers and shoeshine.

Facilities: Fitness center, bank, brokerage, barbershop, beauty salon, gift shops, jewelry shop, theater.

✪ Sheraton Suites
422 Delaware Ave., Wilmington, DE 19801. ☎ **302/654-8300** or 800/325-3535. Fax 302/654-6036. 230 suites. A/C TV TEL. $180–$210 double. Weekend packages available. AE, DC, DISC, MC, V. Parking $9.

In the heart of Wilmington's corporate and financial section, this contemporary, 16-story hotel is decorated with subdued Art Deco tones; the lobby is rich in columns, mirrors, and marble flooring. Each unit has a full bedroom and a separate living room, a large, well-lit bathroom with hair dryer and TV, and a dressing area. Amenities include two telephones with call-waiting services and computer access lines, a dining and work table, a desk, a wet bar, a coffeemaker, and a refrigerator with complimentary soft drinks.

Dining/Entertainment: The conservatory-style restaurant and lounge offer moderately priced food and drinks on the lobby level.

Services: Bell staff, morning and evening room service, dry-cleaning and valet service, baby-sitting, express video checkout.

Facilities: Indoor swimming pool, sauna, exercise room, gift shop, meeting rooms, self-service launderette, underground parking.

MODERATE

Ⓢ Guest Suites by Doubletree

707 King St., Wilmington, DE 19801. ☎ **302/656-9300** or 800/822-TREE. Fax 302/656-2459. 49 suites. A/C MINIBAR TV TEL. $99–$129 suite. (All rates include hot buffet breakfast. Weekend packages available.) AE, CB, DC, MC, V. Valet parking $7.50.

If you prefer a homey lodging in the heart of town, your best choice is this hotel adjacent to the historic Market Street Mall. Opened in 1987, it was created from a cluster of vintage three- and four-story brick buildings that were thoroughly renovated and then linked together with a central atrium and two elevators.

The result is a small all-suite hotel with a nouveau European decor. Each guest unit has a parlor, a bedroom, and a well-equipped bathroom, as well as a refrigerator, two TVs, and three telephones. On the ground floor, there's a small lobby with an open fireplace and a skylit sitting area. Facilities include a bistro-style restaurant and an exercise room.

Holiday Inn–Downtown

700 King St. (at Customs House Plaza), Wilmington, DE 19801. ☎ **302/655-0400** or 800/777-9456. Fax 302/655-5488. 217 rms. A/C TV TEL. $85–$95 double. Weekend packages available. AE, CB, DC, DISC, MC, V. Parking $6.

A modern glass-and-concrete facade fronts this nine-story structure just three blocks from the grandiose Hotel Du Pont. Conveniently located in the heart of Wilmington's business and financial district, the Holiday Inn is also a half-block from the opera house and the Market Street Mall. The rooms are decorated in a contemporary style, with colorful wall hangings; many units overlook a tropical indoor garden and patio with swimming pool. The restaurant, distinguished by its wall-length Brandywine Valley murals, serves meals and snacks all day. The hotel offers room service and laundry service. Its facilities include an indoor swimming pool, a whirlpool, and an exercise room.

MODERATE/INEXPENSIVE

Courtyard by Marriott/Wilmington Downtown

1102 West St., Wilmington, DE 19801. ☎ **302/429-7600** or 800/321-2211. Fax 302/429-9167. 126 rms. A/C TV TEL. $89 double. Weekend packages available. AE, CB, DC, DISC, MC, V. Parking $7.50.

Converted from a 10-story former office building, this hotel does not fit the usual mold of the Marriott chain. It has been recently (1993) refurbished, however, and offers good value for downtown. Guest rooms, accessible by computer-card keys, vary in size and configuration, but all have contemporary furniture, dark woods, a wet bar, a coffeemaker, a refrigerator, and a large desk; 18 rooms have a whirlpool bath and a microwave. The facilities include a restaurant/pub.

SUBURBS
EXPENSIVE

✪ Christiana Hilton Inn
100 Continental Dr., Newark, DE 19713. ☎ **302/454-1500** or 800/HILTONS. Fax 302/454-0233. 266 rms. A/C TV TEL. $99–$149 double. Weekend packages available. AE, CB, DC, MC, V. Free parking.

For a suburban location, the top choice is this hotel, nestled amid grassy grounds off Exit 4B of I-95. Located in a burgeoning area near Delaware's university at Newark and a variety of shopping malls, it boasts a modernized four-story, Victorian-style brick exterior, topped by a mansard-style roof and surrounded by English-style topiary gardens, with a brick-lined courtyard, a gazebo, and a swan-filled pond. The bedrooms are decorated in the Old Williamsburg tradition, with dark-wood reproduction furniture and Colonial prints and colors, combined with modern mirrored closets and tiled baths. The hotel provides concierge service, room service, same-day valet service, nightly turndown, free shuttle service to downtown Wilmington, and express checkout. Its facilities include two restaurants, a lounge, an outdoor swimming pool, a health and fitness room, and a gift shop.

Radisson Hotel Wilmington
4727 Concord Pike (U.S. Route 202), Wilmington, DE 19803. ☎ **302/478-6000** or 800/333-3333. Fax 302/478-6000. 149 rms. A/C TV TEL. $109 double. Weekend packages available. AE, CB, DC, DISC, MC, V. Free parking.

Popular with business travelers during the week and families on weekends, this modern, seven-story structure is on the busy Route 202 corridor, just north of downtown Wilmington and a few miles from the major historic museums and gardens. The bedrooms have a Brandywine Valley flavor, with dark reproduction furniture and local art. The facilities include two restaurants, an outdoor swimming pool, a fitness room, and a lounge with evening entertainment. There's a courtesy limousine service to downtown.

Wilmington Hilton
630 Naamans Rd. at I-95, Wilmington, DE 19703. ☎ **302/792-2700** or 800-HILTONS. Fax 302/798-6182. 193 rms. A/C TV TEL. $99–$136 double; $300 suite. Weekend packages available. AE, CB, DC, MC, V. Free parking.

Built in 1974, this modern, eight-story hotel is continually being improved (the latest refurbishment was done in 1995). It's a popular lodging spot for business travelers because of its handy location, 5 miles north of Wilmington and 12 miles south of Philadelphia Airport at Exit 11 off I-95, across from the Tri-State industrial complex; it's also next to the Brandywine Corporate Center. The contemporary rooms are designed in various configurations as bedroom and sitting areas, queen studios, and suites.

Among the amenities are a restaurant, a lounge, an outdoor swimming pool, an exercise room, a basketball court, and a volleyball court. The hotel provides room service, same-day valet and laundry service, and a daily shoe shine; it also offers a complimentary shuttle service to and from the airport or train station.

MODERATE

Best Western Brandywine Valley Inn
1807 Concord Pike (Route 202), Wilmington, DE 19803. ☎ **302/656-9436** or 800/537-7772. Fax 302/656-8564. 95 rms. A/C TV TEL. $69–$90 double. Weekend packages available. AE, CB, DC, DISC, MC, V. Free parking.

Situated north of downtown and at the gateway to the Brandywine Valley, this modern motor inn is next to a shopping center but set back from the main road. The lobby is particularly welcoming, with a Winterthur reproduction gallery, a collection of 15 furnishings commissioned by the nearby museum. A creative theme is carried through to the guest rooms, with Georgian-style furnishings and Andrew Wyeth prints. Many rooms face an outdoor swimming pool and gardens in a central courtyard.

Courtyard by Marriott

48 Geoffrey Dr., Newark, DE 19713. ☎ **302/456-3800** or 800/321-2211. Fax 302/456-3824. 152 rms, 12 suites. A/C TV TEL. $99 double; $109 suite. Weekend packages available. AE, CB, DC, DISC, MC, V. Free parking.

Opened in 1991, this four-story property was the first of the Marriott chain to open in the state. The layout follows the usual Courtyard plan, with sliding glass windows and balconies or patios facing a central landscaped terrace. Guest units—decorated in contemporary style—are spacious, with a separate sitting area, a desk, and coffeemaking fixtures. Hotel facilities include a restaurant, lounge, elevator, indoor swimming pool, and whirlpool.

INEXPENSIVE

⊛ Fairfield Inn

65 Geoffrey Dr., Newark, DE 19713. ☎ **302/292-1500** or 800/228-2800. Fax 302/292-1500. 105 rms. A/C TV TEL. $44.95–$54.95 double. (All rates include continental breakfast.) AE, CB, DC, MC, V. Free parking.

This three-story property offers comfortable and attractively furnished accommodations at low prices, in a very accessible location. There are three types of bedrooms: a compact one-bed room ideal for a single traveler, a standard double, and a larger room with a king-size bed. All units have a full-length mirror, a lounge chair, and reading light with a work desk. Complimentary coffee and newspapers are offered in the lobby. Facilities include an outdoor swimming pool, computer-card keys, and a meeting room.

Tally Ho Motor Lodge

5209 Concord Pike, Wilmington, DE 19803. ☎ **302/478-0300.** 100 rms. A/C TV TEL. $38–$48 double. AE, CB, DC, DISC, MC, V. Free parking.

Located on the busy Route 202 strip just south of Naamans Road, this modern, two-story motel is a popular choice for families. The rooms have standard furnishings and are equipped with one or two double beds or with a king-size bed; some rooms have a kitchenette. Among the facilities are an outdoor swimming pool and a guest Laundromat.

4 Dining

DOWNTOWN
VERY EXPENSIVE

✪ The Green Room

In the Hotel Du Pont, 11th and Market sts. ☎ **302/594-3154.** Reservations required. Jackets required for men. Main courses $21–$29, lunch $9.95–$16.95, brunch fixed price $27.50. AE, CB, DC, MC, V. Mon–Thurs 11:30am–2:30pm; Fri–Sat 11:30am–2:30pm and 6–10pm; Sun brunch 10am–3pm. FRENCH/CONTINENTAL.

Even if you can't spend a night at the Hotel Du Pont, treat yourself to a meal in this posh restaurant, known for its impressive decor of tall arching windows, walls of quartered oak paneling, and handcrafted golden chandeliers from Spain. To complete the tableau, tuxedoed waiters provide impeccable service and a classical harpist plays in the background.

Best of all, the chefs and the food are top rate. Entrées range from poached Maine lobster and sautéed Arctic char to rack of venison with portobello mushrooms or roast veal loin with sweetbreads. The prices are steep, but it's not an average restaurant—Delawareans consider this to be the state's top spot for a memorable meal. If you come for brunch, don't miss the "Good Morning America" omelet, filled with lobster, wild mushrooms, and smoked tomato sauce.

EXPENSIVE

✪ The Brandywine Room

In the Hotel Du Pont, 11th and Market sts. ☎ **302/594-3156.** Reservations required. Jackets required for men. Main courses $14.50–$24.50. AE, CB, DC, MC, V. Sun–Thurs 6–11pm. AMERICAN/REGIONAL.

This is the Hotel Du Pont's smaller and more clubby restaurant, with rich wood paneling, original artworks by three generations of the Wyeth family, and classical music playing in the background. Although the atmosphere here is slightly less formal than at the Green Room, the service is just as solicitous and the food equally outstanding. The emphasis is on local specialties, such as crab imperial with orange hazelnut Hollandaise sauce and veal Chesapeake, a thin scaloppini topped with jumbo lump crab and béarnaise sauce. For meat lovers, the Brandywine Mixed Grill offers a combination not often seen on menus—venison chop, sausage, and steak in juniper and rosemary juice; but our favorite is a succulent roast baby rack of lamb with a pecan crust.

✪ Columbus Inn

2216 Pennsylvania Ave. ☎ **302/571-1492.** Reservations recommended for dinner. Main courses $12.95–$26.95; lunch $6.95–$13.95. AE, DC, DISC, MC, V. Mon–Fri 11:30am–midnight; Sat 5pm–midnight, Sun 10:30am–2pm. AMERICAN/REGIONAL.

One of the city's oldest buildings, this stone house dates from 1798 and is set on a hill overlooking the main route (Route 52) to the Brandywine Valley at Woodlawn Avenue. The decor is a blend of dark woods, brick walls, book-filled shelves, brass fixtures, and photos of jazz stars—a perfect setting for live jazz sessions on Thursday through Saturday nights and on Sundays during brunch. It's a popular lunch spot for Wilmington businesspeople who enjoy the choice of hot beef and seafood entrées, salads, sandwiches, or burgers. The dinner menu includes several house specialties—among them "lobster scampi," lobster chunks sautéed in scampi sauce and served over linguine and spinach—as well as such regular fare as Dover sole, steaks, and rack of lamb. There are also a few dishes designed to promote the jazz-theme atmosphere, such as "linguine Ellington," veal chop "Fitzgerald," and "chicken Satchmo." This restaurant is also known for its snapper soup, doused with sherry, and its Caesar salad, prepared table side.

Constantinou's House of Beef

1616 Delaware Ave. ☎ **302/652-0653.** Reservations recommended for dinner. Main courses $17.95–$30.95; lunch $6.95–$15.95. AE, CB, DC, DISC, MC, V. Sun–Thurs 11am–10pm, Fri–Sat 11am–11pm. INTERNATIONAL.

For the best steak in town, head here. You'll also enjoy the Victorian decor, filled with original tankards, prints, and bric-a-brac from around the world. Flags of all nations, American eagles, gold-framed mirrors, and tuxedoed waiters add to the charm. Lunch includes prime rib and steak teriyaki, as well as seafood platters, salads, and hearty sandwiches. Aged tender beef takes center stage at night with a variety of cuts of prime Kansas steaks as well as cut-to-order prime rib. Other favorites include rack of lamb, surf-and-turf, lobster tails, shrimp scampi, and jumbo crab imperial. A raw bar is featured on Sunday, Monday, and Thursday evenings.

Shipley Grill

913 Shipley St. ☎ **302/652-77997.** Reservations recommended for dinner. Main courses $12.95–$23.95; lunch $5.95–$9.95. AE, CB, DC, DISC, MC, V. Mon–Thurs 11am–10pm, Fri 11am–11pm, Sat 5:30–11pm. INTERNATIONAL.

Situated just half a block from the Hotel Du Pont, this brick-fronted restaurant has an old-world atmosphere with banquette seats, dark woods, brass lighting fixtures, ceiling fans, and a round marble bar. Lunch items include soups, salads, sandwiches, burgers, and pastas. At dinnertime, the locals flock here for thick and juicy steaks or the signature dish, Shipley's Mixed Grill. Grilled salmon, served with a red onion confit and watercress mousse, is also popular, as is a unique vegetarian bouillabaisse, made with seasonal vegetables poached in an anise broth and served with grilled polenta.

✪ The Silk Purse & the Sow's Ear

1307 N. Scott St. ☎ **302/654-7666.** Reservations required. Main courses $15–$29. MC, V. Tues–Sat 6–9:30pm. INTERNATIONAL.

For many years, the Silk Purse has been heralded as one of Wilmington's best restaurants, drawing people north of downtown to an unlikely location, tucked in the middle of a quiet residential block in a private house. It presents an adventurous cuisine politely served amid a contemporary decor of fresh flowers, graceful glass lamps, framed gallery prints, and rattan furniture. About five years ago, the owners went one step further, adding the Sow's Ear upstairs, as a more informal and lower-priced extension. By early 1995, however, there was a merger, with both restaurants coming together to offer the same menu and the same prices. The menu changes daily, but it is never boring. Choices might include fried squid with spicy Vietnamese dipping sauce; seared sea scallops with leeks, tomatoes, and cream; and corn-coated oysters on salsa fresca with a chipotle cream—not to mention roasted garlic and goat cheese soufflé.

Waterworks Cafe

16th and French sts. ☎ **302/652-6022.** Reservations recommended for dinner. Main courses $13.95–$24.95; lunch $5.95–$14.95. AE, MC, V. Tues–Fri 11:30am–2:30pm and 5:30–10pm; Sat 5:30–10pm. INTERNATIONAL.

Overlooking the Brandywine, the trendy Waterworks Cafe is touted as Wilmington's only waterfront restaurant, housed in the former water-station buildings on the banks of the river. It has a colorful and contemporary decor; it also has an outdoor roofed deck and patio seating in good weather. Lunch includes a variety of fish and meat entrées, omelets, and cold platters (try the Great Oceans salad). At dinnertime the selections include roast duckling Brandywine, veal Oscar, chicken Marsala, prime rib, surf-and-turf, lobster tails, and Alaskan salmon steak.

MODERATE

⊛ Griglia Toscana

1412 N. Dupont St. ☎ **302/654-8001.** Reservations required. Main courses $9–$21; lunch $5–$12. AE, MC, V. Mon–Fri 11:30am–2pm and 5:30–11pm, Sat–Sun 5:30–10pm. TUSCAN/ ITALIAN.

Step into this restaurant and you know it has to be good, by the excited din of the customers, the bustle of the waiting staff, the piquant aromas flowing from the open kitchen and the wood-burning oven imported from Italy, and the constant attention displayed by the ever-present owner and chef, Daniel Butler, a native of Wilmington and graduate of the Culinary Institute of America. Even the name of this restaurant, translated as "Tuscan Grill," will whet the appetite of those familiar with the light and healthful cooking style of Tuscany, in northern Italy.

Specialties include charcoal-grilled veal chop with oregano and lime; Tuscan mixed grill of veal, sausage, chicken liver, and sage-seasoned chicken; and T-bone steaks grilled with a splash of lemon and Tuscan olive oil. Freshly made pastas and individual pizzas with exotic toppings are also on the menu. The restaurant is a little out of the way, at the Rockford Shops, 14th Street off Delaware Avenue, but there's rarely an empty table.

⊛ Kid Shelleen's

1801 W. 14th St. (at Scott St.). ☎ **302/658-4600.** Main courses $8.95–$16.95; lunch $2.95–$6.95. AE, MC, V. Mon–Sat 11am–midnight, Sun 10am–midnight. AMERICAN.

Tucked in a residential area on the city's north side, this lively indoor-outdoor restaurant is known for its casual atmosphere and open charcoal grill. The decor is highlighted by oil paintings of old Wilmington and New Castle on brick and wood walls. Entrées include grilled salmon, barbecued chicken, baby-back ribs, Black Angus strip steaks, and pastas. The bar here is known for its large-screen TV showing the latest sports action.

Tiffin

1210 N. Market St. ☎ **302/571-1133.** Reservations recommended for dinner. Main courses $15.95–$21.95; lunch $6.95–$10.95. MC, V. Mon–Thurs 11:30am–2:30pm and 5:30–10pm; Fri 11:30am–2pm and 5:30–11pm, Sat 5:30–11pm. AMERICAN.

Conveniently situated just two blocks north of the Hotel Du Pont, this trendy eatery has a bright and airy atmosphere, with pastel linens, light woods, wicker seats, mirrored walls, and lots of plants. For dinner, the menu offers several tempting choices, such as spicy cornmeal catfish; breast of duck with sautéed apples, honey, and cider vinegar; lump crab cake with lime and green-chile mayonnaise; and breast of chicken with rosemary; as well as steaks, grilled salmon, and tuna. Lunch items include sandwiches, burgers, omelets, and salads.

INEXPENSIVE

✪ Govatos

800 Market Street Mall. ☎ **302/652-4082.** Breakfast $2.95–$4.95; lunch $2.95–$7.95. MC, V. Mon–Fri 8am–3:30pm, Sat 8am–3pm. AMERICAN.

Established in 1894, this old-world–style eatery is a Wilmington tradition. It's an ideal choice in midcity for breakfast or lunch. The menu offers sandwiches, burgers, salads, and hot platters of Delaware favorites, such as honey-dipped chicken and shrimp in a basket. The main attractions, however, are the desserts and other confections, since this place produces Delaware's largest selection of homemade chocolates and candies. Govatos has a second restaurant located in the Talleyville Shopping Center (4105 Concord Pike, ☎ 302/478-5324).

Salad Works

831 Market St. ☎ **302/656-3277.** All items $3.95–$5.95. No credit cards. Mon–Fri 10:30am–4pm. AMERICAN/HEALTH FOOD.

Tucked in the middle of the Market Street Mall, this restaurant is a salad lover's paradise. The menu offers at least eight types of traditional and exotic salads; you can also create your own by selecting toppings and ingredients to match your appetite and tastes. Sandwiches, prepared to order, are also available, as are freshly made soups. A handy spot to know about, Salad Works offers table seating as well as take-out service.

Talkin' Turkey

907 Shipley St. ☎ **302/428-0665.** All items $1.95–$5.95. No credit cards. Mon–Fri 7am–4pm. AMERICAN/SELF-SERVICE.

This place is a haven for turkey lovers. Turkey is always on the menu, in a tempting variety of choices: Cajun turkey meat loaf, turkey chili, turkey hoagie, turkey Reuben, grilled turkey, and turkey pasta. There are also many combination sandwiches, salads, and omelets, with or without turkey. Table seating is available, but locals prefer to order food "to go" so as to enjoy a picnic along the nearby Market Street Mall. For morning snacking, the restaurant also offers bagels, muffins, and pastries.

Temptations

11A Trolley Sq., Delaware Ave. ☎ **302/429-9162.** All items $2.95–$6.95. AE, CB, DC, MC, V. Mon 10am–5pm, Tues–Thurs 10am–9pm, Fri–Sat 10am–10pm. AMERICAN/ICE CREAM.

If you have a sweet tooth, you'll want to try this ice-cream parlor and restaurant. It serves sandwiches, salads, and burgers in addition to an extensive selection of ice creams. The menu includes more than a dozen sundaes, among them the appropriately named "Original Sin"—a huge banana split, with fig leaves in season.

SUBURBS
EXPENSIVE

✪ Picciotti's

3001 Lancaster Ave. ☎ **302/652-3563.** Reservations required. Main courses $12.95–$25.95; lunch $5.95–$12.95. AE, CB, DISC, DC, MC, V. Mon 11:30–2pm and 5–9pm, Tues–Fri 11:30am–2pm and 5–10pm, Sat 5–10pm, Sun 5–9pm. INTERNATIONAL.

With a tradition that goes back some 60 years, this restaurant is known for outstanding beef. It was first established at 4th Street and Du Pont Street but moved to its present location, at the intersection of Cleveland Avenue, about 15 years ago. The exterior is unpretentious, but inside great culinary things happen. Most people come here for the filet mignon, touted as the best in Delaware and beyond; we heartily concur—Picciotti's filets are as tender and flavorful as any you'll find elsewhere. If beef, however, is not your dish, you may choose from a selection of other entrées, such as chicken cordon bleu, roast filet of lamb, calves' liver, baked salmon, grilled tuna, pastas, and a house specialty of crab cakes.

✪ Sal's Petite Marmite

603 N. Lincoln St. ☎ **302/652-1200.** Reservations required. Jackets required for men. Main courses $15–$29; lunch $8.95–$16.95. AE, CB, DC, MC, V. Mon–Fri 11:30am–2pm and 5–10pm; Sat 5–10pm. NORTHERN ITALIAN/CLASSICAL FRENCH.

Although tucked away in the heart of Little Italy, this restaurant is not a typical pasta and pizza spot. Founded more than 20 years ago by master chef Sal Buono, it is an elegant and award-winning culinary enclave with a country-club ambience, blending French and Italian cuisines amid a decor of rich leather furnishings. Great care is taken to obtain the freshest and best ingredients daily; all the tomatoes and herbs, for example, are grown in the owner's private garden.

Lunch focuses on salads and light entrées such as shrimp scampi, veal piccata, coquille St. Jacques, and fettuccine Alfredo. Dinner, more of an event, depends on what is in season but can often include salmon filet, whole Dover sole, frogs' legs, duckling flambé, beef Wellington, rack of lamb, and game dishes. The restaurant has a private parking lot.

EXPENSIVE/MODERATE

Feby's Fishery
3701 Lancaster Pike. ☎ **302/998-9501.** Reservations recommended for dinner. Main courses $10.95–$21.95; lobster dishes $22.95–$29.95; lunch $5.95–$14.95. AE, CB, DC, DISC, MC, V. Mon–Thurs 11am–9pm, Fri 11am–10pm, Sat–Sun 4–9pm. SEAFOOD.

Situated on the city's southwest side, just west of the junction of Route 100 South, this nautically themed restaurant also has a seafood market, a sure sign of fresh fish on the premises. The menu features a variety of crab, shrimp, lobster, and scallop dishes, as well as daily fish specials and creative combinations, such as salmon with tarragon sauce and crab imperial Florentine. The menu also offers Italian seafood dishes, such as cioppino—a stew of mussels, clams, oysters, shrimp, and fish in seasoned red sauce with fettuccine Alfredo. For landlubbers, it has filet mignon and Delmonico steak.

Ristorante Carucci
504–506 Greenhill Ave. ☎ **302/654-2333.** Reservations required. Main courses $13.95–$21.95; lunch $13.95–$18. AE, MC, V. Mon–Fri 11:30am–2:30pm and 5:30–midnight; Sat 5:30pm–midnight. ITALIAN.

This contemporary Art Deco–style restaurant is synonymous with music—piano tunes as background for lunch and opera arias performed by the waiting staff in the evening. The menu changes with the season, but it's always offered with a flourish: waiters present meats and fish on platters for you to inspect before selecting what you want and having it cooked to order. Wines are likewise introduced and described in detail before being chosen and uncorked. The cuisine is innovative, with the choices often including black shrimp ravioli and lobster sauce, baked red snapper with tomato and oyster mushrooms, braid of coho salmon and rainbow trout with tomato-basil cream sauce, rack of lamb, and homemade pastas.

MODERATE

⊜ DiNardo's
405 N. Lincoln St. ☎ **302/656-3685.** Reservations not accepted. Main courses $8.95–$21.95; lunch $3.95–$15.95. AE, CB, DISC, DC, MC, V. Mon–Sat 11am–10pm, Sun 3–10pm. SEAFOOD.

Crabs are the pièce de résistance at this small, casual, family-run Little Italy restaurant, a tradition in Delaware since 1938—and the place to go to if you enjoy cracking your own crustaceans. Crabs are flown in daily year-round from Louisiana and are served steamed or sautéed. Lunchtime choices include crab and shellfish platters, salads, and pastas. Dinner entrées, in addition to crabs in the shell, include a variety of other crab dishes—crab cakes, crab claws, crab legs, and crab imperial—as well as shrimp, lobster, flounder, scallops, oysters, and, for landlubbers, steaks. There are also combination platters.

Terrace at Greenhill
800 N. Du Pont Rd. ☎ **302/575-1990**. Reservations recommended for dinner. Main courses $7.95–$14.95; lunch $4.95–$7.95. AE, DC, DISC, MC, V. Mon–Thurs 11:30am–2:30pm and 5–9pm; Fri–Sat 11:30am–2:30pm and 5–10pm; Sun 10am–2:30pm and 4–8:30pm. INTERNATIONAL.

Situated west of downtown in a residential area off Pennsylvania Avenue (Route 52), this restaurant overlooks the Ed "Porky" Oliver Golf Course and is a favorite with local golfers. The decor is bright and airy, with light wood and rattan furnishings, lots of plants and greenery, and walls full of watercolors by local artists. Like the setting, the food is fun and varied. Lunch items range from southwest chicken sauté to turkey burger or salmon cake, as well as salads, soups, omelets, quiches, pizzas, crepes, and sandwiches. Dinner entrées include a selection of steaks and seafood, such as rainbow trout amandine or blackened red snapper, as well as several specialty items, among them jambalaya and chicken scampi.

5 Attractions

Much of Wilmington's waterfront beside the Christina River has been revitalized and is worth a visit. The central downtown area also offers major attractions. It revolves around Market Street Mall, a five-block pedestrian area of shops and restaurants on Market Street that stretches from 6th Street to 11th Street.

✪ Delaware Art Museum
2301 Kentmere Pkwy. ☎ **302/571-9590**. Admission $5 adults, $4 seniors and children over 6, free for children under 6. Tues–Sat 10am–5pm, Sun noon–5pm.

Renowned for its holdings of American art (from 1840 to the present), this prestigious museum is located just north of downtown in a residential area of the city. It houses the largest collection of works by Howard Pyle, the father of American illustration and founder of the Brandywine school of painting. It also contains outstanding examples of American sculpture, photography, and crafts, traditional and contemporary, as well as the largest display of pre-Raphaelite English art in the United States.

Delaware Center for the Contemporary Arts
103 E. 16th St. ☎ **302/656-6466**. Admission free. Tues–Fri 11am–5pm, Sat–Sun 1–5pm. Closed Aug.

Nestled beside the Brandywine, this impressive gallery focuses on contemporary visual arts that reflect everyday life, including controversial and provocative issues. The exhibits include paintings, drawings, sculptures, photographs, and crafts of various sorts by both national and local artists. The Center has more than two dozen exhibits a year, among them an Art Auction in early April, a kitchen tour in October, and a studio tour in November.

Delaware History Museum
504 Market St. ☎ **302/656-0637**. Admission free. Tues–Fri noon–4pm, Sat 10am–4pm.

Housed in a restored 1941 F. W. Woolworth Co. building, once the third-largest Woolworth store in America, this museum tells the story of Delaware. Operated by the Historical Society of Delaware, it features changing interactive exhibits on different phases of history and social development and permanent displays of regional decorative arts, paintings, children's toys, and items of local interest. The gift shop specializes in Delaware-handcrafted items and souvenirs.

Delaware State Arts Council

Carvel State Office Bldg., 820 N. French St. ☎ **302/577-3540.** Admission free. Mon–Fri 9am–4:30pm.

As the umbrella arts organization for Delaware and particularly for Wilmington, the Arts Council showcases local arts and crafts exhibits. It has two galleries, one on the mezzanine level and another on the first floor.

Kalmar Nyckel Foundation

1124 E. 7th St. ☎ **302/429-7447.** Admission $2 adults, $1 children 6–12, free for children under 6. Museum Mon–Sat 10am–4pm, boat building Tues–Sat 10am–4pm; Sun by appointment. *Note:* Parties of more than 5 persons need an appointment at any time.

Set on the shores of the Christina River near Old Swedes Church and Fort Christina Park, the Kalmar Nyckel Foundation, named after one of the ships that brought the first Swedish settlers to the New World in the 1630s, aims to re-create the story of their settlement in the Delaware Valley. It comprises a museum and a working 17th-century shipyard, with a full-scale working replica of the *Kalmar Nyckel.*

✪ Old Swedes Church

606 Church St. ☎ **302/652-5629**. Admission free, but donations are welcome. Mon, Wed, Fri, and Sat 1–4pm.

Located near the Christina River, this is one of the oldest churches in the United States. Erected in 1698, the church remains in its original form (with extensive genealogical records) and is still regularly used for religious services. Highlights of the interior include stained-glass windows installed from 1885 to 1897 and a church chest dating from 1713, as well as herringbone bricks in the main aisle and a black-walnut canopied pulpit, considered one of the oldest of its kind in the United States. The church yard, which predates the church by 60 years, was used as a burying ground for early settlers of Fort Christina and its community. A nearby reconstructed farmhouse depicts the everyday life of the early Swedish settlers.

Old Town Hall

512 Market St. ☎ **302/655-7161**. Admission free, but donations are welcome. Closed in 1995, but hours likely to be Tues–Fri noon–4pm, Sat 10am–4pm in 1996–97.

At press time, this landmark Georgian-style building in the heart of the city was closed for renovations, but plans called for it to be reopened to the public by 1997. The Town Hall was built from 1798 to 1800 and functioned as the center of political and social activities during the height of Wilmington's mercantile-milling economy. Operated by the Historical Society of Delaware, it features permanent and rotating exhibits depicting life in Delaware over the centuries. Recently, it put on displays of antique silver, furniture, and other objects of American craftsmanship. The basement contains restored jail cells.

ESPECIALLY FOR KIDS

The new **Delaware Children's Museum,** 601 Market St. (☎ 302/658-0797), is well worth a visit with young travelers. It presents a changing array of interactive and hands-on exhibits. Admission is $3 per person and $1.50 for children under three. Hours are Tuesday through Saturday from 10am to 4pm.

The **Delaware Children's Theater,** 1014 Delaware Ave. (☎ 302/655-1014), presents plays based on fairy tales and other stories familiar to children of all ages. Admission is $8.50, with performances on Saturday and Sunday at 1:30pm and 4pm. *Note:* For adult visitors without children, this ornate, three-story building is worth a look for its historic and architectural value. Listed on the National Register of Historic Places, it was designed in 1892 by a woman exclusively as a women's club. The building today continues to be owned and operated by women.

Children of all ages take delight in looking at the many exotic species of animals from North and South America on view at the **Brandywine Zoo,** 1001 N. Park Dr., Brandywine Park (☎ 302/571-7747). Open daily from 10am to 4pm. Admission is free from November to March; from April to October, there is a $3 charge for adults and $1.50 for seniors and children aged 3 to 12.

NEARBY ATTRACTIONS

Just under 15 miles southwest of Wilmington is **Newark**, New Castle County's second largest city (population about 24,000). It is a thriving center in its own right, although sometimes considered part of the greater Wilmington metropolitan area: Many suburban hotels have a Newark postal address.

Not to be confused with the city of the same name in New Jersey, this Newark is pronounced "New Ark" and is first and foremost a college town, the home of the University of Delaware. The university—which traces its origin as far back as 1743, with the Newark campus established in 1765—enrolls 15,000 undergraduates and more than 3,000 graduate students.

The best place to start a tour of the campus is at the Visitors Center, 196 S. College Ave., Newark (☎ 302/831-1557). Built in 1890 by Gilbert W. Chambers and originally known as the Chambers House, this Victorian-style structure is listed on the National Register of Historic Places. It houses an information center about the school and the surrounding area; among the publications it offers is a Visitors Guide with a map of the university grounds. Visitors may also view a video and take a one-hour guided tour of the campus. Tours are conducted by student volunteers Monday through Friday at 10am, 11:30am, and 2pm and Saturday at 10am and 11:30am. Admission and tours are free. Visitor Center hours are Monday through Friday from 9am to 4pm.

Nearby is the University Gallery, Main Street and N. College Avenue, Newark (☎ 302/831-8242). It is a repository of paintings, photo-documentaries, and other exhibits pertaining to the state of Delaware. Admission is free; hours are Monday through Friday 11am to 5pm and Saturday and Sunday 1 to 5pm.

In addition, take time to visit the university's Mineralogical Museum, Penny Hall, Academy Street. (☎ 302/831-8106). It contains an internationally recognized collection of minerals, crystals, gems, and stone carvings. It's open Monday through Friday from 9am to 4:30pm.

Local sights in the area include the **Welsh Tract Baptist Church,** the oldest primitive Baptist church in the United States, dating from 1703 (located west of Route 896), and **Cooch's Bridge**, the scene of the Battle of Cooch's Bridge, the only Revolutionary War engagement fought on Delaware soil. Tradition holds that the new 13-star flag, the Stars and Stripes, was unfurled during this encounter. The bridge is located on Route 4, east of Route 896.

One of the state's most unusual parks, **Fort Delaware State Park,** Pea Patch Island, Delaware City (☎ 302/834-7941), lies about 16 miles south of Wilmington. Located a mile offshore in the Delaware River, the park surrounds a massive five-sided granite fortress that served as a detention center during the Civil War. In addition to 19th-century cells, dungeons, and armaments, the current layout includes a museum and an audiovisual presentation about the history of the island. Other facilities include an observation tower for bird watchers (the island is a popular nesting spot for egrets, herons, and other marsh fowl) and an assortment of nature trails and picnic sites. You can visit the island by taking a 10-minute boat ride from Delaware City. The boat fare, which includes admission to the park, is $4.50 for adults and $3 for children 14 and under. The site is open from April through September, Wednesday through Friday from 11am to 4pm and Saturday and Sunday from 11am to 6pm.

6 Spectator Sports & Outdoor Activities

BASEBALL   When it comes to the national sport, Wilmington cheers for the **Blue Rocks,** 801 S. Madison St. (☎ 302/888-2015), a minor league baseball team first organized in the 1940s and revived with much fanfare in 1993. The team plays at the 5,400-seat Daniel S. Frawley Stadium, situated beside I-95, just south of downtown. Box seats cost $6 and reserved seats cost $5; general admission is $4 and admission for children and seniors is $2. Parking is free. Games are usually played Monday through Saturday at 7:05pm and Sunday at 2:05pm.

GOLF   The rolling hills around Wilmington make for challenging golf. Following are a few of the best clubs that welcome visitors:

Delcastle Golf Club, 802 McKennan's Church Rd. (☎ 302/995-1990), located southwest of the city near Delaware Park racetrack, offers an 18-hole championship course, a pro shop, a driving range, and a miniature golf course. Greens fees are $16 weekdays and $20 weekends; carts are $22. The club is open daily, dawn to dusk, except Christmas Day and New Year's Day.

Ed "Porky" Oliver Golf Course, 800 N. Du Pont Rd. (☎ 302/571-9041), is situated in a residential area west of downtown and off Route 52 (Pennsylvania Avenue). The club has an 18-hole championship course, a driving range, a pro shop, and a restaurant (see Terrace at Greenhill in "Dining," above); it also provides lessons and group clinics. Tee times are accepted by phone one week in advance. Greens fees are $16 on weekdays and $20 on weekends; a cart is $11 per person. The course is open daily, year-round, dawn to dusk.

The **Three Little Bakers Golf Course,** 3542 Foxcroft Dr. (☎ 302/737-1877), nestled in the Pike Creek Valley southwest of Wilmington, is a semiprivate, 18-hole, par-71 course open daily to the public except after 3pm on Thursday and Friday. Facilities include a pro shop, club rental, golf lessons, and bag storage. Greens fees are $25 weekdays and $29 weekends; carts rent for $11 per person.

HORSE RACING   For almost 60 years, racing fans have placed their bets at **Delaware Park,** Route 7, off I-95 Exit 4N, Stanton (☎ 302/994-2521), a picturesque setting with a tree-lined grove about 5 miles south of Wilmington. From April through November, there is daytime thoroughbred racing on various days of the week. Post time is 12:45pm; admission is $3 for adults, free for children under 12. During the rest of the year, Delaware Park offers simulcast races from other East Coast tracks.

WALKING & HIKING   Wilmington's playground is **Bellevue State Park,** 800 Carr Rd. (☎ 302/577-3390). Located on the northeast perimeter of the city, this 270-acre park was once the home of the William Du Pont family. Facilities include picnic areas, garden paths for walking, and fitness trails for jogging. Admission is free except from Memorial Day through Labor Day and weekends in May, September, and October, when the entrance fee is $5 for each out-of-state vehicle and $2.50 for each Delaware-registered car.

Southwest of Wilmington is **Lums Pond State Park,** 1068 Howell School Rd., off Route 71, Bear (☎ 302/368-6989). Stretching along the north side of the Chesapeake and Delaware Canal, this 1,757-acre park encompasses the state's largest freshwater pond, a home to several beaver colonies and waterfowl. For humans, the pond offers swimming and fishing; the surrounding parklands include hiking and walking trails, a nature center, picnic areas, and camping sites. Admission charges are the same as for Bellevue State Park, described above.

7 Shopping

THE SHOPPING SCENE

Wilmington has dozens of extensive malls and shopping centers, such as **Concord Mall,** 4737 Concord Pike (☎ 302/478-9271); **Christiana Mall,** 715 Christiana Mall, Route 7 at I-95 Exit 4S (☎ 302/731-9815); and **Independence Mall,** 1601 Concord Pike (☎ 302/656-2190). The downtown area also offers good shopping, particularly on **9th Street** and along **Market Street Mall,** a pedestrian area that runs from 6th Street to 11th Street.

SHOPPING A TO Z
ART

Hardcastle Gallery
1408 N. Dupont St. ☎ **302/655-5230.**

For original oil paintings and watercolors, as well as prints and sculptures, visit this gallery, located in the Rockford Shops shopping center. Open Monday to Wednesday and Friday from 10am to 6pm, Thursday from 10am to 8pm, Saturday from 10am to 4pm.

BOOKS

Encore Bookshop
827–829 Market Street Mall. ☎ **302/656-3112.**

In the heart of Wilmington's historic pedestrian mall, this shop carries a variety of discounted books on local history and sights. It also has a good selection of maps. Open weekdays from 9am to 6pm, Saturday from 10am to 6pm.

Ninth Street Book Shop
104 W. Ninth St. ☎ **302/652-3315.**

This shop offers a large selection of books on Delaware and local history, as well as travel books and maps. Other well-stocked categories include mysteries, children's books, and cookbooks, as well as a selection of books on African American history and culture. Open Monday through Friday from 8:30am to 5:30pm and on Saturday from 10am to 3pm.

CHOCOLATES & CANDIES

Govatos
800 Market Street Mall. ☎ **302/652-4082.**

Since 1894, this shop has been selling Delaware's largest selection of homemade chocolates and candies. All sweets are available by the piece or the pound. Open weekdays from 8am to 5pm, Saturday from 8am to 4pm.

FARM PRODUCTS

Wilmington Farmers Market
8th and Orange sts.

For local color and atmosphere, don't miss this open-air market featuring fresh produce and flowers. Open Wednesday and Friday to Saturday from 7am to 4pm.

FASHIONS

Handbags 'n Things
205 9th St. ☎ **302/654-5910.**

This little shop stocks ladies' hats, jewelry, and shoes. It's located on a street lined with art and antique shops and even a bank geared for talented customers— the Artisans Savings Bank. Open Monday to Saturday from 10am to 5pm.

Wright & Simon
911 Market Street Mall. ☎ **302/658-7345.**

A traditional haberdashery, this store carries fine suits and coats for men, including tailored and made-to-measure clothing. Open weekdays from 9am to 5:30pm, Saturday from 9am to 4:30pm.

JEWELRY & TIMEPIECES

The Jeweler, the Watchmaker
107 W. 9th St. ☎ **302/429-8463.**

As its name implies, a jeweler and a watchmaker have teamed up to run this inviting shop, known for unusual timepieces and jewelry created on the premises. Restoration and repair services for antique jewelry are also provided. Open weekdays from 8am to 4pm.

8 Wilmington After Dark

For the latest information about evening entertainment in the Wilmington area, consult the Friday edition of the Wilmington *News-Journal*. It publishes a weekend entertainment guide, "55 Hours." The city's monthly *Out & About* magazine also lists entertainment events. Both publications are available at newsstands. In addition, the **Delaware State Arts Council,** Carvel State Office Building, 820 N. French St. (☎ 302/577-3540), publishes *ARTLINE,* a free, bimonthly newsletter covering major arts events. It lists concerts, theater events, art exhibits, and cultural programs.

For most Wilmington performing arts events, tickets are available at **B&B Tickettown,** 322 W. 9th St. (☎ 302/656-9797), at the corner of West Street, behind the Sheraton Suites Hotel.

MAJOR PERFORMING ARTS CENTER

✪ The Grand Opera House
818 N. Market St. ☎ **302/658-7897** for information; box office 302/652-5577 or 800/37-GRAND. Tickets $10–$45 for most performances.

Much of Wilmington's nightlife is centered around this impressive restored Victorian showplace, nestled in the heart of the downtown pedestrian mall. Built in 1871 as part of a Masonic temple, this 1,100-seat facility is one of the finest examples of cast-iron architecture in America and is listed on the National Register of Historic Places. Recognized as Delaware's Center for the Performing Arts, it is home to OperaDelaware and the Delaware Symphony Orchestra. It also offers an ever-changing program of guest artists in ballet, jazz, chamber music, pop concerts, and theatrical productions. Schedule varies according to event; shows usually begin at 8pm.

CONCERT HALLS

Christina Cultural Arts Center
705 N. Market Street Mall. ☎ **302/652-0101.** Tickets $3–$5.

Founded more than 50 years ago, this center offers innovative programs that involve the community and celebrate the diversity of the city. It is best known for its weekly "Jammin' at Christina" sessions for musicians, comedians, vocalists, dancers, and poets, usually held on Thursdays from 7 to 11pm.

Delaware Center for the Contemporary Arts
103 E. 16th St. ☎ **302/654-7283.** Tickets $10–$12 for most events.

Chamber music and classical music concerts are often performed at this impressive arts center, situated beside the Brandywine Creek. A performance art series, often featuring music, dance, and video presentations, is also held throughout the year. Shows usually start between 7 and 8pm.

Wilmington Music School
4101 Washington St. ☎ **302/762-1132.** Admission free to some events; others $3–$10.

This facility offers frequent concerts and recitals by the Wilmington Community Orchestra and the Wilmington Festival Players. It also sponsors performances by faculty members, guest artists, and students. Days and hours vary, usually Friday or Saturday at 7:30pm.

THEATERS

Delaware Theatre Company
200 Water St. ☎ **302/594-1104;** box office 302/594-1100. Tickets $18–$33.

Situated at the foot of Orange Street, this is a modern, 389-seat, state-of-the-art facility; no seat is more than 12 rows from the stage. The theater is home to Delaware's only resident professional company, which presents an ever-changing program of classic and contemporary plays throughout the year. Evening shows are Tuesday through Saturday at 8pm; matinees Wednesday at 1pm, Saturday at 2 and 4pm, Sunday at 2pm.

The Playhouse
10th and Market sts. ☎ **302/656-4401.** Tickets $22–$50.

For more than 80 years, this theater has brought the finest of touring Broadway shows to downtown Wilmington. Located next to the Du Pont Hotel, it has a 1,239-seat capacity amid a vintage Victorian decor. Over the years, audiences have applauded stars from Sarah Bernhardt to Kathleen Turner; recent shows have included *Cats* and *Les Misérables*. In addition, local companies, such as the Brandywine Ballet, often perform in the Playhouse. Evening shows go on at 8pm

Tuesday through Saturday, matinees at 2pm Wednesday and Saturday and 3pm Sunday.

DINNER THEATERS

Candlelight Music Dinner-Theatre

2208 Miller Rd. ☎ **302/475-2313.** Tickets $23–$27.

A big red barn is the setting for the Candlelight, Delaware's first dinner theater, which started more than 25 years ago. Among its productions have been the musicals *Camelot, Gigi, My Fair Lady, Man of La Mancha,* and *Fiddler on the Roof.* The price of admission includes a buffet dinner, with members of the cast doubling as waiters and waitresses. The theater is located in the suburb of Arden, near the Hilton Hotel, and is signposted off Harvey Road. Open Thursday to Saturday, with buffet at 6pm and show 8:15pm; Sunday, buffet at 5pm and show at 7:15pm.

Little Bakers Dinner-Theatre

3540 Foxcroft Dr. ☎ **302/368-1616.** Dinner/show $23.95–$31.95.

Located southeast of Wilmington off Route 7, this suburban theater presents Broadway shows as well as celebrity specials featuring well-known stars and bands. Some of the productions put on here have been *The Sound of Music, Music Man, Evita,* and *West Side Story.* The price of admission includes a buffet dinner with French and Swiss pastries, dancing, and preshow entertainment. The theater is named after its three founders: Al, Nick, and Hugo Immediato, all originally bakers by profession. Open Wednesday, Friday, and Saturday, with dinner at 5:30pm and show at 8pm; Thursday and Sunday matinee, with buffet at 11:30am and show 2pm.

CLUBS & MUSIC BARS

The Wilmington music and dancing scene is centered largely on the big hotel lounges, such as **Copperfields** at the Radisson (☎ 302/478-6000) and **Whispers** at the Hilton (☎ 302/972-2701). In addition, there's nightly piano music at the **Lobby Lounge** of the Hotel Du Pont (☎ 302/594-3100) and the **Conservatory Lounge** of the Christiana Hilton (☎ 302/454-1500).

Bourbon Street Cafe

105 Kirkwood Sq., Kirkwood Hwy. ☎ **302/633-1944.** No cover or $3–$5 for some acts.

For a bit of New Orleans decor, atmosphere, and music in Wilmington, try this place, located next to the entrance of Delaware Park racetrack. It offers live jazz and blues every night except Monday.

Cavanaugh's

703 N. Market St. ☎ **302/565-4067.** Cover $2–$5.

Located in a historic building in the heart of the city, on the main pedestrian mall, this place offers a variety of music on most nights, from live jazz, blue grass, and rock to a sing-along piano bar.

Comedy Cabaret

1001 Jefferson St. ☎ **302/652-6873.** Cover $3–$10.

This club presents professional comedy shows on Friday and Saturday at 9:30pm.

Kelly's Logan House
1701 Delaware Ave. ☎ **302/652-9493.** Cover $2–$5.

Built in 1864, this place claims to be the oldest tavern in the city; it has the trappings of an old ale house, including tin ceilings and exposed brick walls. Kelly's takes its name from a famous Union army general, John A. Logan, who instituted Memorial Day; the "Kelly" part derives from the family that has owned the house since 1899. There's usually rhythm-and-blues music Thursday through Saturday night.

O'Friel's
600 Delaware Ave. ☎ **302/654-9952.** No cover for most sessions.

This the city's classic Irish pub, with beers from the "ould sod" on tap and traditional and contemporary Irish music on many nights. Every other Sunday, there is usually also a foot-tapping "session" of Irish traditional music at 6pm.

Porky's Dance Club
1206 N. Union St. ☎ **302/429-6633.** Cover $2–$5.

Dubbed Wilmington's "hottest over-30 dance club," this lively spot offers a variety of entertainment to appeal to different tastes: karaoke on Sunday, country dance lessons on Tuesday, "oldies" on Wednesday, contemporary live bands and DJ music on Thursday, Friday, and Saturday.

9

The Brandywine Valley & Historic New Castle

The Brandywine Valley is a great expanse of Delaware countryside at its best—sparkling river waters, rolling hills, lush landscapes, enchanting gardens, and great estates and museums. Historic New Castle, nestled beside the Delaware River, is a masterfully preserved 18th-century town—frozen in time, yet thriving in the 20th century. It retains the charm from the days when it was Delaware's original capital and a major Colonial seaport, with cobblestone streets, brick walkways, and Federal town houses. As well as being a vital part of the overall Wilmington experience, both the Brandywine Valley and Historic New Castle are outstanding travel destinations in their own right.

1 The Brandywine Valley

10 miles N of Wilmington, 35 miles W of Philadelphia, 115 miles SW of New York, 90 miles N of Baltimore, 120 miles N of Washington, D.C.

Meandering north from Wilmington, the scenic and historic Brandywine Valley embraces part of Delaware and part of Pennsylvania. Technically, the Brandywine starts as a creek in Philadelphia's western suburbs and ends 35 miles south, a full-scale tributary emptying into the Delaware River at Wilmington. The entire 15-mile-wide valley can be traversed by several routes, often crisscrossing and paralleling each other, and intertwining the attractions across state lines.

The Brandywine River itself has a long and storied history. To the Native Americans who inhabited the area first, the river was known as the Wawset or Suspecoughwit and was cherished as a bountiful shad fishing source. The Swedes and Danes who settled here also used the river for fishing, calling it the Fishkill. The Quakers and other English settlers, who renamed it Brandywine, used the river for power. This water power made the Brandywine an important milling center in the 18th and 19th centuries. At its peak, there were more than 100 water-powered mills along the Brandywine corridor, producing everything from flour, paper, and textiles to snuff and gun powder.

Today, the Brandywine Valley is a tourist mecca—a blend of historical museums, art galleries, idyllic gardens, welcoming inns, and gourmet restaurants. It is also a two-state visiting experience, stretching across the Delaware-Pennsylvania border, although, for

What's Special About the Brandywine Valley & Historic New Castle

Sightseeing
- Winterthur Museum and Gardens, the world's premier collection of American antiques and decorative arts.
- Hagley Museum, a re-creation of the original Du Pont family mills and mansion.
- Nemours Mansion and Gardens, a 102-room, French-style château.
- Rockwood Museum, a 19th-century, Victorian-style mansion filled with decorative arts.
- Old Court House at New Castle, Delaware's Colonial capital.
- Read House, a treasure trove of Federal-era memorabilia.

Activities
- Stroll around Historic New Castle's cobblestone streets and brick walkways.
- Sample the oak-aged vintages at the Chaddsford Winery.

Museums
- Brandywine River Museum, Chadds Ford, showcase for Brandywine River School and other American artists.
- Delaware Museum of Natural History, housing one of the largest shell collections in this hemisphere.
- Mushroom Museum, Kennett Square, a fun- and fungi-filled display.

Gardens and Parks
- Longwood Gardens, one of the world's most celebrated horticultural display.
- Brandywine Creek State Park, home of Delaware's first two nature preserves.

the most part, the most outstanding attractions and museums of the valley are in Delaware. To give you a well-rounded preview, however, of what the Brandywine Valley has to offer, we have included some Pennsylvania attractions, inns, and restaurants in this chapter.

GETTING THERE By Plane The nearest airport is Philadelphia International Airport, about 20 miles east of the Brandywine Valley. SuperShuttle operates a 24-hour, door-to-door transfer system between the airport and most communities in the Brandywine Valley. For reservations and schedules, call 800/562-4094.

By Train Amtrak provides regular service from major cities throughout the United States to Philadelphia and Wilmington. For more information, call 800/USA-RAIL.

By Bus From Philadelphia to various points in the Brandywine Valley, Southeast Pennsylvania Transportation Authority/SEPTA (☎ 215/574-7800) operates local bus service. From Wilmington, bus service is provided by Delaware Administration for Regional Transit/DART (☎ 302/655-3381).

By Car The Brandywine Valley is easily accessible via major routes, such as I-95, I-276, I-76, U.S. Route 1, U.S. Route 202, and the Pennsylvania and New Jersey turnpikes.

ESSENTIALS Area Code Like the rest of Delaware, the Brandywine Valley attractions located in the Wilmington suburbs have the 302 area code. Many neighboring sights, inns, and restaurants on the Pennsylvania side of the border, however, have the 610 area code.

Visitor Information For all types of helpful maps and brochures about the Brandywine Valley, contact the Greater Wilmington Convention and Visitors Bureau, 1300 Market St., Wilmington, DE 19801 (☎ 302/652-4088 or 800/422-1181), or the Brandywine Valley Tourist Information Center, Rte. 1 at the entrance to Longwood Gardens, P.O. Box 910, Kennett Square, PA 19348 (☎ 610/388-2900 or 800/228-9933).

WHAT TO SEE & DO

André Harvey Studio
101 Stone Block Row, Greenville, DE 19807. Mailing address: Box 8, Rockland Rd., Rockland, DE 19732. ☎ **302/656-7955.** Admission free. Mon–Sat 10am–5pm, Sun by appointment.

Housed in an 1814 stone mill building just downstream from the Hagley Museum gates, this studio features realistic bronze sculpture of people and animals by André Harvey. The museum also displays jewelry made in collaboration with goldsmith Donald Pywell. A separate gallery shows the different stages of casting.

Brandywine Battlefield
Route 100, P.O. Box 202, Chadds Ford, PA 19317. ☎ **610/459-3342.** Admission free to battlefield; house tour, $3.50 adults, $2.50 seniors, $1.50 youths 6–17. Sept–May Tues–Sat 9am–5pm, Sun noon–5pm; June–Aug Tues–Sat 9am–8pm, Sun noon–8pm.

Set amid 50 acres of rolling countryside, this is the site of a 1777 Revolutionary War battle, where Washington's troops fought with the British for control of strategic territory near Philadelphia. It is famous not because the Americans won, but because they lost. The revolutionaries' courageous stand in defeat helped convince the French to form an alliance with them, a union that turned the tide in favor of the Americans. The site includes a visitor center with exhibits and dioramas as well as two historic Quaker farmhouses that housed the officers during the battle.

Brandywine Creek State Park
Adams Dam Rd., Greenville, DE. ☎ **302/577-3534.** Admission Memorial Day–Labor Day and Sat–Sun in May, Sept–Oct, $2.50 Delaware registered cars, $5 out-of-state cars; other times, free. Open daily 8am–sunset.

Located 3 miles north of Wilmington, at the intersection of Routes 92 and 100, this 795-acre park, bisected by the Brandywine Creek, is home to a variety of flora and wildlife, including deer and an active bluebird population; hawks can be seen migrating over the valley from mid-September to mid-November. Originally a dairy farm owned by the Du Pont family, it contains rolling hills, mature woodlands, open fields, lush thickets, and marshlands. The park incorporates 12 miles of hiking trails and preserves, including Delaware's first two nature preserves: Tulip Tree Woods, a stand of 190-year-old tulip popular, and Freshwater Marsh, home to the elusive Muhlenberg bog turtle. There is also a visitors center with displays and picnic facilities.

✪ Brandywine River Museum
Routes 1 and 100, P.O. Box 141, Chadds Ford, PA 19317. ☎ **610/459-1900.** Admission $5 adults, $2.50 children 6–12. Open daily 9:30am–4:30pm.

The Brandywine Valley & Historic New Castle

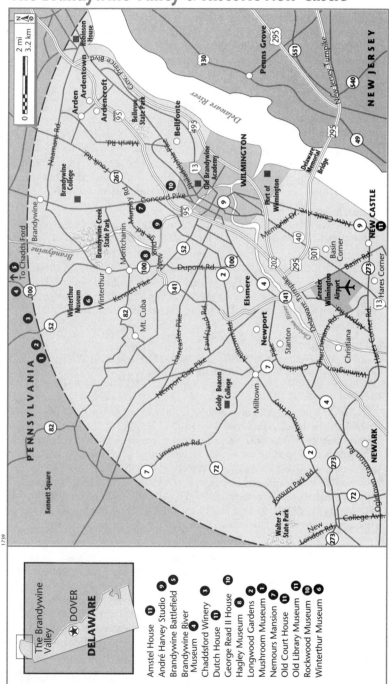

The Brandywine Valley

DELAWARE

DOVER

Amstel House ⑪
André Harvey Studio ⑨
Brandywine Battlefield ⑤
Brandywine River Museum ④
Chaddsford Winery ③
Dutch House ⑪
George Read II House ⑩
Hagley Museum ⑧
Longwood Gardens ②
Mushroom Museum ①
Nemours Mansion ⑦
Old Court House ⑪
Old Library Museum ⑩
Rockwood Museum ⑥
Winterthur Museum ⑥

Housed in a 19th-century restored gristmill, this museum is surrounded by a nature trail and wildflower gardens. The paintings on display reflect the best of Brandywine area artists, including Howard Pyle, Frank Schoonover, and three generations of Wyeths (N. C., Andrew, and Jamie), as well as works by other American artists and illustrators.

Chaddsford Winery

Route 1, Chadds Ford, PA 19317. ☎ **610/388-6221.** Admission free. *Note:* There is a $5 per glass fee to participate in a full tasting session. Mon–Sat 10am–5:30pm, Sun noon–5pm. Closed Mon (Jan–Mar).

Housed in a restored barn, this small winery produces some lovely oak-aged Chardonnays, Seyval blancs, and Cabernet Sauvignons, as well as table wines. Visitors are encouraged to tour, free of charge. Tours are conducted on the hour on weekends, between noon and 5pm, and at 1pm and 3pm on weekdays.

Delaware Museum of Natural History

Route 52 (between Greenville and Centreville), DE. ☎ **302/658-9111.** Admission $4 adults, $3 seniors and children 3–17, free for those under 3. Mon–Sat 9:30am–4:30pm, Sun noon–5pm.

Located on the main route between Wilmington and Winterthur, the Museum of Natural History houses more than 100 exhibits of birds, shells, and mammals from far and near, including displays of the Great Barrier Reef, an African water hole, and various Delaware fauna. For young visitors, there's a hands-on Discovery Room, as well as a continuous showing of nature films.

✪ Hagley Museum

Route 141, Wilmington, DE 19807. ☎ **302/658-2400.** Admission $9.75 adults, $7.50 students and seniors, $3.50 children 6–14, children under 6 free. Mar 15–Dec, daily 9:30am–4:30pm; Jan–Mar 14, Mon–Fri one guided tour at 1:30pm, Sat–Sun 9:30am–4:30pm. Closed New Year's Day, Christmas Day.

This is the spot where French émigré Eleuthère Irénée Du Pont de Nemours established a black-powder mill in 1802. The first of the Du Pont family developments in America, the mill was the forerunner of the large chemical companies developed by subsequent generations. Today, this 240-acre outdoor museum site re-creates the original 19th-century mill village through a series of restored buildings and gardens, as well as a series of displays and demonstrations of life back then. The highlight of the museum is Eleutherian Mills, the first (1803) Du Pont home in America, a Georgian-style residence furnished to reflect five generations of the Du Ponts.

✪ Longwood Gardens

Route 1, Kennett Square, PA 19348. ☎ **610/388-1000.** Admission $10 adults ($6 on Tues), $6 youths 16–20, $2 children 6–15, free for children under 6. Apr–Oct daily 9am–6pm; Nov–Mar daily 9am–5pm or later.

This is one of the world's most celebrated horticultural displays; more than 11,000 different types of plants and flowers thrive amid 1,050 acres of outdoor gardens and woodlands. On the grounds you'll find indoor conservatories, illuminated fountains, an open-air theater, and a huge pipe organ. Unique displays range from an indoor children's garden with a maze to an idea garden for home gardeners. Among recent additions are a completely restored Italian Water Garden, a new indoor Cascade Garden by the Brazilian landscape designer Robert Burle Marx, and an indoor Mediterranean Garden. Longwood's attractions include not only ever-changing seasonal plant displays but also more than 300 performing arts events each year.

Mushroom Museum at Phillips Place

Route 1, Kennett Square, PA 19348. ☎ **610/388-6082.** Admission $1.25 adults, 75¢ seniors and children 7–12. Daily 10am–6pm. Closed major holidays.

A good place to learn about mushroom farming is at this museum, where displays illustrate the history, lore, and development of mushrooms, from the ordinary to the exotic. There is also a shop selling fresh mushrooms and specializing in exotics and gift items with mushroom motifs.

✪ Nemours Mansion and Gardens

Rockland Rd., P.O. Box 109, Wilmington, DE 19899. ☎ **302/651-6912.** Admission $10 adults. May–Nov Tues–Sat tours at 9am, 11am, 1pm, and 3pm; Sun tours at 11am, 1pm, and 3pm.

This 300-acre estate was the home of Alfred I. Du Pont. Built in 1909 and 1910 and named after the Du Pont ancestral home in north-central France, it is a 102-room, Louis XVI–style château with landscaped gardens. It contains antique furnishings, oriental rugs, tapestries, and paintings dating from the 15th century, as well as personal items, such as vintage automobiles.

The gardens, which extend almost a third of a mile from the mansion, represent one of the finest examples of formal French-style gardens in America. Guided tours of the mansion and gardens take a minimum of two hours. Reservations are recommended; visitors must be over 16 years of age.

✪ Rockwood Museum

610 Shipley Rd., Wilmington, DE. ☎ **302/571-7776.** Admission $5 adults, $2 students 5–16, seniors $4; slightly higher for special events. Tues–Sun 11am–4pm (last tour at 3pm).

A Victorian theme prevails at this rural Gothic mansion, situated on 72 tree-filled acres between Route 202 and Marsh Road northeast of downtown. Inspired by an English country house, it was built in 1851 by Joseph Shipley, one of the city's early merchant bankers. The mansion was acquired in 1892 by the Bringhursts, a wealthy family, who furnished it with a lavish mélange of 17th-, 18th-, and 19th-century decorative arts from the United States, Britain, and Continental Europe. The elaborate conservatory features a brilliant array of Victorian flora that reflects the six acres of exotic foliage and landscape surrounding the manor. Among the outside buildings are a porter's lodge, a gardener's cottage, and a carriage house and barn. Seasonal programs include a summer concert series in May and June, a Victorian Ice Cream Festival in July, and a Christmas Pageant in December.

✪ Winterthur Museum and Gardens

Route 52, Winterthur, DE 19735. ☎ **302/888-4600** or 800/448-3883. Admission $8 adults, $6 seniors and students 12–18, $4 children 5–11, free for children 4 and under. One-hour tours available for $5 per person extra; two-hour tours from $13 extra. Mon–Sat 9am–5pm, Sun noon–5pm.

Named after a town in Switzerland, this nine-story mansion and country estate once comprised the country home of the late Henry Francis Du Pont. Today, it's the Brandywine Valley's star attraction, ranked as the world's premier collection of American antiques and decorative arts. Du Pont himself, a collector of furniture, made the initial acquisitions and the collection grew over the years. The objects, including Chippendale furniture, silver tankards by Paul Revere, and a dinner service made for George Washington, are displayed in more than 175 period rooms.

A tour of Winterthur starts either in the period rooms or in The Galleries, the new $20 million two-story pavilion that prepares visitors for a walk through the period rooms. The first of the galleries features a 10-minute audiovisual presentation and a series of interactive exhibits that provide background information about Winterthur's treasures. The second gallery, the Henry S. McNeil Gallery, offers an exhibition of tools and workshops used in furniture-making, while the third area, the Thomas A. Graves Jr. Gallery, houses rotating exhibitions.

Adding to the splendid aura of the house, the 980-acre grounds are meticulously landscaped with native and exotic plants. Access to the gardens, which can be toured on foot or by tram, is included in the admission charge.

The museum staff conducts several guided tours, including a one-hour general overview tour and a two-hour in-depth decorative arts tour that requires reservations. There is also an annual Yuletide tour, offered from mid-November through January. In addition, the estate serves as a venue for various events, including an amateur point-to-point steeplechase race on the first Sunday in May. Facilities include a restaurant (traditional afternoon tea is a special treat), a museum store, and a bookshop.

WHERE TO STAY

Most Wilmington-area hotels are convenient bases from which to tour the Brandywine Valley. In addition, there are a few nearby inns on the Pennsylvania side of the border.

⑤ Abbey Green Motor Lodge

1036 Wilmington Pike (Route 202), West Chester, PA 19382. ☎ **610/692-3310.** 18 rms. A/C TV TEL. $45–$59 double. AE, DC, DISC, MC, V. Free parking.

This family-run motel, situated just north of the Brandywine Battlefield Park and close to scenic Routes 52 and 100, is an excellent budget choice in the Brandywine region. Designed in a courtyard style, it's set back from the road on its own grounds, with picnic tables, a gazebo, and an outdoor fireplace. All rooms have a refrigerator; six units have their own fireplace. The owners also operate a gift shop on the premises.

✪ Brandywine River Hotel

Routes 1 and 100, P.O. Box 1058, Chadds Ford, PA 19317-1058. ☎ **610/388-1200.** Fax 610/388-1200, ext. 301. 40 rms, 10 suites. A/C TV TEL. $119 double; $140 suite. (Rates include "European Plus" continental breakfast.) AE, CB, DC, MC, V. Free parking.

Built to meld perfectly with this scenic and historic region, this hotel is perched on a hillside in the heart of the valley. Two stories high, with a facade of brick and cedar shingle, it is set beside a cluster of rustic shops, art galleries, and an artisans' cooperative. The historic Chadds Ford Inn restaurant is just a few steps away via a brick-lined path.

The lobby and reception area offers a huge stone open fireplace and a homey ambience. The guest rooms, half of which are on ground-floor level, are decorated with Colonial-style cherry wood furnishings, brass fixtures, chintz fabrics, and paintings in the Brandywine tradition; some of the suites have an individual fireplace and a Jacuzzi. Breakfast is served in an attractive "hospitality room" with a fireplace and old-world furnishings.

Longwood Inn

815 East Baltimore Pike (Route 1), Kennett Square, PA 19348. ☎ **610/444-3515.** Fax 610/444-4285. 28 rms. A/C TV TEL. $75–$85 double. (Rates include continental breakfast.) AE, MC, V. Free parking.

Situated half a mile southwest of Longwood Gardens, this inn is surrounded by beautifully landscaped flower beds and gardens. The accommodations are modern, almost motel style, with a Colonial reproduction motif and garden views. The facilities include a lounge and restaurant (see "Where to Dine," below).

Mendenhall Hotel

Route 52, P.O. Box 208, Mendenhall, PA 19357. ☎ **610/388-2100.** Fax 610/388-1184. 70 rms, 4 suites. A/C TV TEL. $99 double; $130–$175 suite with Jacuzzi. (Rates include continental breakfast.) AE, CB, DC, DISC, MC, V. Free parking.

Deep in the heart of the Brandywine Valley, this property is part of an original Penn Land Grant purchased by Benjamin Mendenhall in 1703. The current complex is a blend of old and new—the Mendenhall's 1796 lumber mill, which is now part of the restaurant structure, and an adjacent three-story complex of modern bedrooms with conference center.

The guest rooms have country-style furnishings, with pine headboards or four-posters, desks, armoires, and cabinets, and modern touches, such as hair dryers, bathroom telephones, and computer-card keys. The freestanding restaurant, traditionally known as the Mendenhall Inn, offers country French and American cuisine in five different dining rooms and a tavern setting for a more informal atmosphere. The hotel offers an exercise room and lovely gardens for strolling.

WHERE TO DINE
EXPENSIVE/MODERATE

♥ Chadds Ford Inn

Routes 1 and 100, Chadds Ford, PA. ☎ **610/388-7361.** Reservations recommended for dinner. Main courses $13.95–$22.95; lunch $5.95–$12.95. AE, CB, DC, MC, V. Mon–Thurs 11:30am–2pm and 5:30–10pm; Fri–Sat 11:30–2pm and 5–10:30pm, Sun 11am–2pm and 5–9pm. INTERNATIONAL.

Dating from the early 1700s, this sturdy stone building was first the home of the Chadsey family and then a tavern and a hotel. Although it's been renovated, the inn still retains much of its Colonial charm, with antique furnishings and century-old memorabilia. The walls display paintings by local artists, including works by Andrew and Jamie Wyeth. Salads, sandwiches, pizzas, burgers, and pastas make up the lunch menu. Dinner entrées include a variety of fish and meat dishes: baked salmon with potato-and-celery crust, Pennsylvania brook trout, shrimp and lobster sauté over pasta, roast free-range chicken, pork tenderloin with spaetzle, and herb-roasted prime rib.

Cuisines Restaurant

200 Wilmington–West Chester Pike (Route 202), Chadds Ford, PA. ☎ **610/459-3390.** Reservations recommended for dinner. Main courses $11.95–$23.95; lunch $4.95–$10.95. AE, MC, V. Mon–Fri 11am–2pm and 5:30–10pm; Sat 5:30–10pm. INTERNATIONAL.

Furnished with a relaxing blend of earth-toned fabrics, plush chairs, light wood trim, and plenty of glass and brass, Cuisines offers recipes from many lands: paella, sole buerre blanc, curry chicken, sirloin steak Creole, shepherd's pie, hot-pepper linguine and mussels with lemon-butter sauce, Black Angus steaks, and veal saltimbocca. Cuisines is located at the junction of Routes 202 and 491.

♥ Dilworthtown Inn

1390 Old Wilmington Pike and Brinton Bridge Road (off Route 202), West Chester, PA. ☎ **610/399-1390.** Reservations recommended for dinner. Main courses $13.95–$26.95. AE, CB, DC, MC, V. Mon–Sat 5:30–10:30pm, Sun 3–9pm. INTERNATIONAL.

Located on the road that was once the principal connection between Wilmington and West Chester, this establishment was built as a house by James Dilworth in 1758; because of its strategic position, it soon became a tavern. Restored in 1972, the restaurant now has 12 dining rooms, on two levels, including the house's original kitchen and an outside stable area for warm-weather dining. The decor consists of Early American furniture, hand-stenciled walls, 11 fireplaces, gas and candlelight lamps, and Andrew Wyeth paintings.

The menu features a gourmet medley of entrées, such as filet mignon Beaujolais and smoked chicken and lobster, as well as several delectable house specialties, such as Dilworthtown seafood sauté (shrimp and scallops sautéed in roasted garlic, oregano, spinach, and sundried tomatoes) and grilled breast of Lancaster County chicken with an apricot and ginger glaze. The extensive wine cellar offers 900 different labels.

Lenape Inn
Routes 52 and 100, West Chester, PA. ☎ **610/793-2005.** Reservations recommended for dinner. Main courses $12.95–$29.95; lunch $6.95–$12.95. AE, DC, DISC, MC, V. Lunch Tues–Sat 11:30am–3pm; dinner Tues–Sat 4:30–10:30pm, Sun 3–9pm. AMERICAN/CONTINENTAL.

Expansive views of the Brandywine River are the keynotes of this multilevel brick-facade restaurant with a modern decor. But views are not everything here—service is very attentive and the cuisine is artfully prepared. Evening selections include a house special of veal picante with prosciutto ham and shiitake mushrooms, salmon with golden caviar poached in court bouillon, duckling flamed in peach-brandy sauce, breast of capon with creamed leek and garlic sauce, rack of lamb, surf-and-turf, and prime western sirloin steaks.

✪ Longwood Inn
815 East Baltimore Pike (Route 1), Kennett Square, PA. ☎ **610/444-3515.** Reservations recommended for dinner. Main courses $10.95–$23.95; lunch $4.95–$10.95. AE, MC, V. Daily 11am–3:30pm and 4–9pm. AMERICAN.

Mushrooms are the specialty here, which is not surprising, since this is the heart of Pennsylvania's mushroom-growing country. Among the choices are mushrooms stuffed with crab imperial, mushroom strudel, mushroom omelets, mushroom burgers, and cream of mushroom soup, as well as mushroom-laden salads. Other dishes range from prime rib of beef and rack of lamb to shrimp Provençale, crab imperial, and low-calorie "cuisine minceur" platters of steamed vegetables and pastas. The decor is country style. The management also operates a gift shop and an adjacent 28-room motel.

MODERATE

✪ Buckley's Tavern
5812 Kennett Pike, Centreville, DE. ☎ **302/656-9776.** Reservations recommended for dinner. Main courses $6.95–$18.95; lunch $4.95–$8.95. AE, DC, MC, V. Mon–Wed 11:30am–2:30pm and 5:30–9:30pm; Thurs–Fri 11:30am–2:30pm and 5:30–10pm, Sat 11:30am–3pm and 5:30–10pm, Sun 11am–3pm and 5–9pm. AMERICAN.

Situated on the main road (Route 52) from Wilmington, this old house has a long history dating from 1817. It was first a private residence, then a stagecoach stop, with a tollgate in front. In the 1930s it became a taproom and bar, then an ice-cream store. In 1951 Dennis Buckley took over, gave the place his name, and turned it into a restaurant. Much of the decor retains an old-world country inn charm, with a fireplace, a plant-filled greenhouse room, and an outdoor porch.

The menu is an innovative blend of fresh ingredients: crab cakes with orange-and-dill sauce, shrimp ravioli with tarragon-rosemary cream sauce, chicken with artichokes and mushrooms, roast duckling with citrus glaze, and Delmonico steak with shiitake mushrooms. Lunch items range from sandwiches, salads, burgers, pastas, and pizzas to seafood stews.

✪ Garden Restaurant & Tea Room at Winterthur

Route 52, Winterthur, DE. ☎ **302/888-4600.** Reservations not required except for afternoon tea (required for parties of six or more). Most items $2–$7; Sun brunch $18.95 adults, $9.95 children 5–12; afternoon tea $9.50. AE, DC, DISC, MC, V. Tues–Sat 9am–3:30pm; afternoon tea Sat 2:30–4:30pm, Sun 3–4:30pm; brunch Sun 10am–1:45pm. AMERICAN.

With lovely garden views, this pavilion-style, self-service restaurant offers breakfast, lunch, and snacks. Afternoon tea is a special treat, with six types of tea, Victorian-style scones, traditional sandwiches (cucumber, smoked salmon, egg and watercress), pastries, and fresh fruits. Sunday brunch includes omelets cooked to order, Belgian waffles, leg of lamb, seafood Creole, chicken Mornay, desserts, and chilled mimosas or Champagne.

2 Historic New Castle

7 miles S of Wilmington, 40 miles SW of Philadelphia, 70 miles NE of Baltimore, 111 miles NW of Ocean City, MD

Located 7 miles south of Wilmington, New Castle was Delaware's original capital and a major Colonial seaport. First known as Fort Casimir, this area was purchased from the Indians as a Dutch settlement by Peter Stuyvesant in 1651. (It's said that Stuyvesant designed the town's central Green by "pegging it off" with his wooden leg.) Later captured by the Swedes and then the English, who named it New Castle, this stretch of land along the west bank of the Delaware River remains much the way it was in the 17th and 18th centuries. Original houses and public buildings have been restored and preserved, the sidewalks are made of brick and the streets of cobblestones.

Small and compact, New Castle is ideal for walking. In less than an hour, you can stroll past old homes and churches and such historic sights as Packet Alley, a well-worn pathway named after the many packet boats that used to travel to New Castle in the 18th and 19th centuries, as well as the green, the riverfront, and Battery Park.

GETTING THERE By Car From Wilmington take Route 13 south to Route 273 and then east to New Castle; or from Wilmington, take Route 9 south to New Castle.

ESSENTIALS Area Code The area code for all telephone numbers in New Castle is 302.

Visitor Information You can obtain brochures and information by writing to or calling in advance the New Castle Visitor's Bureau, P.O. Box 465, New Castle, DE 19720 (☎ 302/322-8411 or 800/758-1550).

WHAT TO SEE & DO
ATTRACTIONS

Amstel House

4th and Delaware sts. ☎ **302/322-2794.** Admission $2 per person (*note:* can be combined with a visit to the Dutch House for a reduced charge of $3.50). Mar–Dec, Tues–Sat 11am–4pm, Sun 1–4pm; Jan–Feb, Sat 11am–4pm, Sun 1–4pm.

Dating from the 1730s, this house is a fine example of 18th-century Georgian architecture. It was once the home of Nicholas Van Dyke, a state governor, and is furnished with antiques and decorative arts of the period.

Dutch House

The Green. ☎ **302/322-9168.** Admission $2 per person (*note:* can be combined with a visit to the Amstel House for a reduced rate of $3.50). Mar–Dec, Tues–Sat 11am–4pm, Sun 1–4pm; Jan–Feb, Sat 11am–4pm, Sun 1–4pm.

One of the oldest brick houses in Delaware, this building has remained almost unchanged since its construction around 1700. The early Dutch furnishings include a hutch table and a courting bench; on display is a 16th-century Dutch Bible. During various seasonal celebrations, the dining table is set with authentic foods and decorations.

Immanuel Episcopal Church

100 Harmony St., on the Green. ☎ **302/328-2413.** Admission free. Daily 9am–4pm.

Built in 1703, this was the first parish of the Church of England in Delaware. The church was burned in 1980, but it has been carefully restored. The adjoining graveyard has tombstones dating from 1707.

◎ Old Court House

211 Delaware St. ☎ **302/323-4453.** Admission free, but donations welcome. Tues–Sat 10am–3:30pm, Sun 1:30–4:30pm.

This building was Delaware's Colonial capitol and meeting place of the state assembly until 1777. Built in 1732, on the fire-charred remains of an earlier courthouse, it's been restored and modified over the years, always maintaining, however, its place as the focal point of the town. The building's cupola is at the center of a 12-mile circle that marks the northern boundary between Delaware and Pennsylvania. Inside the Court House you'll finds portraits of men important to Delaware's early history, the original speaker's chair, and excavated artifacts. Tours are conducted free of charge.

Old Library Museum

40 E. Third St. ☎ **302/328-2923.** Admission free. Mar–Dec, Thurs–Sun 1–4pm; Jan–Feb, Sat 11am–4pm, Sun 1–4pm.

This unique hexagonal building, erected in 1892 by the New Castle Library Society, is now used for exhibits by the New Castle Historical Society. The design of this house, a fine example of fanciful Victorian architecture, is attributed to noted Philadelphia architect Frank Furness.

◎ Read House and Garden

42 The Strand. ☎ **302/322-8411.** Admission $4 adults, $3.50 seniors and students, $2 children. Mar–Dec, Tues–Sat 10am–4pm, Sun noon–4pm; Jan–Feb, Sat 10am–4pm, Sun noon–4pm.

This 22-room house, built between 1791 and 1804 near the banks of the Delaware, is a fine example of Federal architecture in a garden setting. It features elaborately carved woodwork, relief plasterwork, gilded fanlights, and silver door hardware, all reflecting the height of Federal fashion. The surrounding $1^{1}/_{2}$-acre formal garden was installed in 1847. The Read House is named after a prominent lawyer who was the son of a signer of the Declaration of Independence.

SHOPPING

There is good shopping in New Castle, especially for antiques and collectibles.

Antique Co-Op of Historic New Castle

116 Delaware St. ☎ **302/328-6362.**

Staffed by individual dealers, this two-story emporium offers a wide variety of items: books, bric-a-brac, china, dolls and other toys, furniture, glass, jewelry, quilts, silver, watches and clocks, and New Castle memorabilia. Open Thursday to Sunday from 11am to 4pm.

✪ New Castle Farmers Market

Route 13. ☎ **302/328-4102.**

Located across from the New Castle County Airport, this vast market offers hundreds of new and used items, from diamonds and brass to auto parts, tackle, tools, furniture, and clothes. Fresh fruit and produce, pretzels, baked goods, spices, and a variety of fast food are also available. Open Friday to Saturday from 10am to 10pm, Sunday from 10am to 6pm.

Three Crowns of New Castle

1 E. Second St. ☎ **302/322-9011.**

This shop offers four rooms of imports from Scandinavia, including wildflower jewelry, stoneware, walking sticks, candles, glassware, chandeliers, prints, knits, mobiles, toys, papier-mâché masks, minibike sculptures, and Christmas items. Open daily from 10am to 6pm.

WHERE TO STAY

Since New Castle is only about 7 miles from Wilmington, many visitors choose to stay overnight or longer in this charming corner of Delaware. In fact, New Castle can even be a convenient base for touring the northern part of the state, including the Brandywine Valley.

For many years, the lodging and dining focal point of Historic New Castle was the **David Finney Inn,** consisting of two adjacent 17th-century brick buildings maintained in fine Colonial style. Unfortunately, a fire destroyed the inn in 1994 (plans, however, call for it to be totally restored and refurbished). As a result, lodging and dining choices within the historic district are currently very limited.

Ramada Inn—New Castle

I-295 and Route 13, P.O. Box 647, Manor Branch, New Castle, DE 19720. ☎ **302/ 658-8511** or 800/228-2828. Fax 302/658-3071. 130 rms. A/C TV TEL. $69–$99 double; weekend packages available. AE, CB, DC, DISC, MC, V. Free parking.

Close to the Delaware Memorial Bridge, wedged between I-295 and Route 13, this busy, two-story property sits on its own grounds, set back from the main roads but still within sight of constant traffic. Although not in the historic district, it is convenient for those in transit and is popular with a business clientele. The building is designed in a modernized Colonial motif; the rooms are decorated with watercolors of local attractions and reproduction furniture, including desks in work areas. Among the guest facilities are an outdoor swimming pool, a lounge, and a full-service restaurant.

Rodeway Inn

111 S. Du Pont Hwy., New Castle, DE 19720. ☎ **302/328-6246** or 800/321-6246. Fax 302/328-9493. 40 rms. A/C TV TEL. $45-$65 double. AE, DISC, MC, V. Free parking.

Positioned along the main highway outside of the historic district, this distinctive motel is laid out like a little village of individual cottage units, with Amsterdam-style tile roofs and facades, and front gardens. It's popular with seniors and families because of its homey atmosphere and because all rooms are ground-floor level, with car parking right outside each door. The facilities include a steak-house restaurant.

Terry House

130 Delaware St., New Castle, DE 19720. ☎ **302/322-2505.** 4 rms. A/C TV TEL. $60–$80 double (including continental breakfast). DISC, MC, V. Free parking.

Located in the heart of the historic district across from the courthouse, this three-story brick Federal town house dates from 1860; it was occupied by the Terry family for more than 60 years. The spacious guest rooms—which look out over either the Delaware River or the town square and courthouse—are furnished with antiques and reproductions; each room has a queen-size bed. There are two porches in the back of the house, which overlook Battery Park and the Delaware River. The innkeeper is Brenda Rogers.

WHERE TO DINE

The New Castle area is the site of a county airport and several commercial industries. Consequently, restaurants conveniently line the Du Pont Highway, otherwise known as Route 13.

Air Transport Command

143 N. Du Pont Hwy. ☎ **302/328-3527.** Reservations recommended for dinner. Main courses $12.95–$24.95; lunch $4.95–$12.95. AE, CB, DC, MC, V. Daily 11am–10pm. INTERNATIONAL.

Authentic air force memorabilia set the tone at Air Transport Command, appropriately located close to the runways of New Castle County Airport. The decor commemorates the flying heroes and heroines of World War II with old uniforms, newspaper clippings, pictures, and flying equipment. You can even pick up a set of headphones and listen to the ground-to-air instructions at the nearby control tower. Music from the 1940s adds to the vintage atmosphere.

Dinner entrées include veal saltimbocca, rack of lamb, prime rib, shrimp and lobster stir-fry, farmhouse chicken, and roast duckling.

Lynnhaven Inn

154 N. Du Pont Hwy. ☎ **302/328-2041.** Reservations recommended for dinner. Main courses $10.95–$26.95; lunch $5.95–$12.95. AE, DC, DISC, MC, V. Sun–Thurs 11am–10pm, Fri–Sat 11am–11pm. AMERICAN/SEAFOOD.

For more than 40 years, this restaurant has been winning raves from locals and travelers alike. The decor includes a changing collection of decoy and wildlife wood carvings and displays of ship models and nautical antiques. Lunchtime selections range from sandwiches and salads to burgers and hot seafood dishes. The dinner menu offers more than a dozen seafood selections, from local crab cakes, crab imperial, and crab-stuffed flounder to blackened redfish, shrimp Aegean (sautéed in butter sauce with oregano, garlic, tomato, green onions, and feta cheese), and imported warm-water lobster tails. Meat choices include steaks, prime rib, and veal dishes.

Dover 10

Dover is the capital of Delaware, the hub of local government and home to many historic sites. It's located at the state's geographic center.

Plotted in 1717 according to a charter rendered in 1683 by William Penn, Dover was originally designed as the courthouse seat for Kent County, a rich grain-farming area. By 1777, however, this agrarian community's importance had increased greatly, and the state's legislature, seeking a safe inland location as an alternative to the old capital of New Castle on Delaware Bay, removed itself to Dover. The city was declared the permanent capital in 1792. One of its claims to fame is that on December 7, 1787, the state's delegates, assembled at the Golden Fleece Tavern on the Dover Green and ratified the new Constitution of the United States, making Delaware the first state to do so.

Today, Dover, a city of approximately 30,000 people, continues to be a hub of state government and business. Its boundaries, however, have expanded far beyond the original historic district to a busy north-south corridor along Routes 13 and 113. The small agrarian community of the 18th century has grown to become a center of modern industry; at least 20 major companies—among them International Playtex, Scott Paper, and General Foods—are located here. Also located in the city's area is Dover Air Force Base, the largest airport facility on the East Coast. Yet, a glimpse of Dover's agrarian past can still be seen in the area's Amish community, which maintains the traditions, dress, and mode of transportation (horse and buggy) of the 19th century.

The area of Dover and central Delaware lies 45 miles south of Wilmington, 86 miles southeast of Baltimore, and 77 miles south of Philadelphia. It's easily accessible by air (from nearby Philadelphia), as well as by train and bus.

1 Orientation

ARRIVING

BY PLANE The closest major gateway for regularly scheduled flights from all parts of the United States is **Philadelphia International Airport,** 55 miles north of Dover. **SuperShuttle** operates a

What's Special About Dover

Attractions
- Delaware State House, built in 1792.
- Dover Air Force Base, home of one of the world's largest operational aircraft.
- Historic Houses of Odessa, a well-preserved 18th-century town.
- Bombay Hook National Wildlife Refuge, a 15,000-acre preserve.

Activities
- Dover Downs International Speedway, home of Budweiser 500 and Split Fire Spark Plug 500 auto races.

Events
- Old Dover Days, "open house" at the finest historic homes.

Museums
- Delaware Agricultural Museum, 200 years of farming heritage.
- Barratt's Chapel and Museum, the "cradle of Methodism" in America.

Parks
- Killens Pond State Park, a 950-acre state park.
- Silver Lake, just minutes from the sights of downtown, along whose shores visitors can swim, bike, or picnic.

Shopping
- The quilts and other handmade crafts at the Amish shops along Rose Valley School Road.

24-hour transfer system between Philadelphia International Airport and any address in Delaware (for full details, see "Arriving," in Chapter 8).

BY CAR   The best way to reach Dover from points north and west is to take I-95 or I-295 to Wilmington and then proceed southward via Route 1 or Route 13 to Dover. Route 13, which runs the entire length of Delaware, is also the best way to approach Dover from the south, via Virginia.

BY TRAIN   There is daily service from all parts of the United States via Amtrak into Wilmington (see "Arriving," in Chapter 8).

BY BUS   **Carolina Trailways** provides regular service into Dover, arriving at 650 Bay Court Plaza (☎ 302/734-1417 or 800/334-1590). Within the state, **Blue Diamond Lines** (☎ 302/577-6686 or 800/652-DART) operates weekday bus services to Dover's DelDOT Administration Building on Route 113 from Wilmington or from the beach destinations of Rehoboth Beach and Lewes.

VISITOR INFORMATION

Begin a visit to Dover at the **Delaware State Visitor Center,** 406 Federal St. at Duke of York Street, Dover, DE 19901 (☎ 302/739-4266). Centrally located near Dover's historic Green, this well-stocked office provides a wide range of literature on attractions of the city, Kent County, and the state. Hours are Monday through Saturday from 8:30am to 4:30pm, and Sunday from 1:30 to 4:30pm.

Eleven miles north of Dover en route to or from the Wilmington area, an excellent place to stop for brochures of the area is the **Smyrna Visitors Center,**

Dover

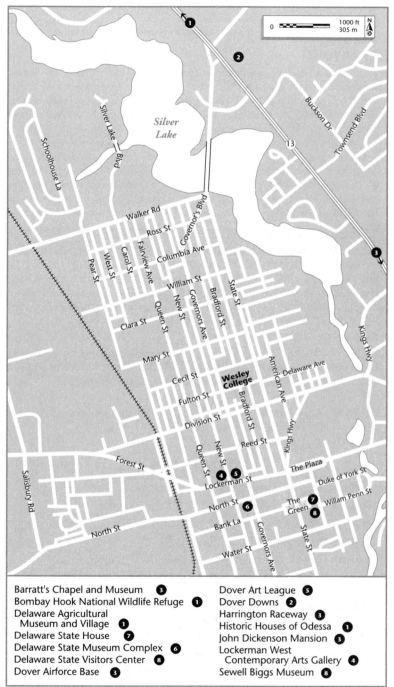

Barratt's Chapel and Museum	❸	Dover Art League	❺
Bombay Hook National Wildlife Refuge	❶	Dover Downs	❷
Delaware Agricultural Museum and Village	❶	Harrington Raceway	❸
		Historic Houses of Odessa	❶
Delaware State House	❼	John Dickenson Mansion	❸
Delaware State Museum Complex	❻	Lockerman West Contemporary Arts Gallery	❹
Delaware State Visitors Center	❽	
Dover Airforce Base	❸	Sewell Biggs Museum	❽

5500 Du Pont Hwy., off Route 13, Smyrna (☎ 302/653-8910); it's well stocked with restrooms, gardens, and picnic tables. The center is open 24 hours a day.

CITY LAYOUT

The downtown area is concentrated in a relatively small radius around the **Green,** a historic area where you'll find brick sidewalks and most of the government buildings and sightseeing attractions. You can park your car and explore easily on foot. **Division Street** is the dividing line between north and south and **State Street** divides the city for east-west addresses. North State Street, home of Wesley College, is particularly flush with well-preserved Victorian homes.

Dover's hotels and motels are concentrated east of the historic district, primarily along Route 13, otherwise known in Dover as Du Pont Highway. This strip, which is also home to the Dover Downs Raceway, Delaware Agricultural Museum and Village, Delaware State College, the Dover Shopping Mall, and the Dover Air Force Base, extends for several miles, so you'll need a car to get from place to place.

2 Getting Around

BY PUBLIC TRANSPORTATION   Central Delaware Transit (CDT), P.O. Box 1347, Dover, DE 19903-1347 (☎ 302/739-3278), a public bus system operating in the greater Dover area, provides service between posted stops within downtown and major residential, shopping, and college areas, Monday through Friday, from 7am to 6pm. The fare is 75¢ adults, 50¢ students, and 30¢ seniors. Exact change is required.

BY RENTED CAR   Some of the major car-rental agencies that have offices in Dover include **Avis,** 1615 S. Du Pont Hwy. (☎ 302/734-5550); **Hertz,** 650 Bay Court Plaza (☎ 302/678-0700); and **National,** Routes 13 and 113 (☎ 302/ 734-5774).

BY TAXI   City Cab of Dover (☎ 302/734-5968) operates a reliable taxi service, with 24-hour radio-dispatched vehicles.

FAST FACTS: Dover

Airports   See "Orientation," earlier in this chapter.

Area Code   Dover's area code is 302.

Car Rentals   See "Getting Around," later in this chapter.

Climate   See "When to Go," in Chapter 7.

Dentists   Contact the referral service of Dover Dental Associates, 63 N. Du Pont Hwy. (☎ 302/734-7634), or call the Dentist Information Service (☎ 302/ 736-1464).

Doctors   Contact the Health Link/Physician Referral Service of Kent General Hospital, 640 S. State St. (☎ 302/674-7042).

Drugstores   Contact Happy Harry Discount Drugs, Olde Oak Center, Route 13 (☎ 302/678-9820), or Rite Aid, 822 S. State St. (☎ 302/674-4211).

Emergencies   Dial 911 for fire, police, and ambulance.

Eyeglasses   Contact Horizon Optical, 1047 N. State St. (☎ 302/736-1302), or Vision Centre, 450 S. Du Pont Hwy. (☎ 302/678-3200).

Film   See "Photographic Needs," below.

Hospitals   The local hospital is Kent General, 640 S. State St. (☎ 302/674-4700).

Information   See "Visitor Information," earlier in this chapter.

Library   The City of Dover Public Library is located at 45 S. State St. (☎ 302/736-7030), and the Delaware State Library is located at the Edgehill Shopping Center, 43 S. Du Pont Hwy. (☎ 302/739-4740).

Newspapers and Magazines   The local daily newspaper is the Delaware State News; the Dover Post is published weekly on Wednesdays.

Pharmacies   See "Drugstores," above.

Photographic Needs   Try Cutler Camera, Dover Mall, Route 13 (☎ 302/678-9155).

Police   Dial 911.

Post Office   The main post office is at 55 The Plaza (☎ 302/734-5821).

Radio   Dover has three local radio stations: WKEN-AM 1600 for information and news, WDSD-FM 94.7 for country music, and WDOV-AM 1410 for news.

Taxes   There is no sales tax, but an 8% lodging tax applies to overnight accommodations.

Taxis   See "Getting Around," earlier in this chapter.

Transit Information   Call 302/739-3282 or 800/252-1600.

3 Accommodations

Dover doesn't boast grand or historic hotels. It has a few modern motels and motor inns, open year-round and set on their own grounds, with ample parking facilities. The major properties are on Route 13 (Du Pont Highway), a commercial strip.

The rates for accommodations, in general, are moderate. On some weekends, however, slightly higher prices are in effect, and surcharges as high as $30 a night can be levied during the May and September races at Dover Downs. It's best to check in advance, in case your planned visit coincides with a peak period.

⊛ Best Western Galaxy Inn
1700 E. Lebanon Rd., Dover, DE. 19901. ☎ **302/735-4700** or 800/528-1234. Fax 302/735-1604. 64 rms. A/C TV TEL. $50–$65 double. AE, DC, DISC, MC, V. Free parking.

Though situated across from Dover Air Force Base's north gate, at the junction of busy Route 113 and Route 10, this two-story motel is set back from the road on a small hillside. One of the newest lodgings in the area, its rooms are decorated in contemporary style with standard furnishings. The facilities include a lounge, an outdoor (seasonal) swimming pool, a Jacuzzi, and a meeting room. A choice of fast food restaurants is nearby. It's a popular motel for businesspeople and tourists interested in easy access to the air force base.

⊛ Comfort Inn of Dover
222 S. Du Pont Hwy., Dover, DE 19901. ☎ **302/674-3300** or 800/221-2222. Fax 302/674-3300. 94 rms. A/C TV TEL. $55–$70 double. (Rates include continental breakfast.) AE, DC, DISC, CM. V. Free parking.

Businesspeople and families are attracted to this motel, just off the Route 13 corridor at Loockerman Street. The closest motel to the city's historic district, the brick-fronted Comfort Inn is laid out in two adjoining bilevel wings. The decor and furnishings are typical of the Comfort chain. The facilities include an outdoor swimming pool and an exercise room. A branch of the TGIF restaurant chain is adjacent.

The Inn at Meeting House Square

305 S. Governors Ave., Dover, DE 19901. ☎ **302/678-1242.** 4 rms, 1 suite. A/C TV TEL. $48–$65 double; $60–$70 suite. (Rates include full breakfast.) AE, DC, DISC, MC, V. Free parking.

Housed in a building that dates from 1849, this well-maintained brick bed-and-breakfast is located in the heart of downtown (one block south of Loockerman Street) across from the State Museum, formerly the Old Presbyterian Church (ca. 1790), which stood on Meeting House Square. It exudes an old-Dover ambience. Guest rooms are furnished with antiques and reproductions; in contrast, on the third floor there's a loftlike suite with modern furnishings and a small kitchen with wet bar, minibar, microwave, and coffeemaker. The facilities include a plant-filled sun room, three heirloom-bedecked sitting rooms, and a small communal refrigerator and coffeemaker. Innkeepers are Sherry and Carolyn DeZwarte and Kathy Lee.

✪ Sheraton Inn and Conference Center-Dover

1570 N. Du Pont Hwy., Dover, DE 19901. ☎ **302/678-8500** or 800/325-3535. Fax 302/678-9073. 156 rms. A/C TV TEL. $82–$115 double. AE, CB, DC, DISC, MC, V. Free parking.

A favorite lodging spot for traveling business executives and conference attendees, this seven-story motor hotel is the most complete facility along the main north-south corridor. Guest rooms, revamped in 1994 and 1995, are furnished in a traditional motif with mahogany reproduction furniture, historically themed art, and such extras as coffeemaker and iron with ironing board. Dining and entertainment choices offer a full-service restaurant, a rooftop lounge for cocktails with a view of Dover, and a rock and roll–themed lounge and cafe for fast food and loud music. Facilities include an indoor swimming pool, a hot tub, and an exercise room.

4 Dining

EXPENSIVE/MODERATE

✪ The Blue Coat Inn

800 N. State St. ☎ **302/674-1776.** Reservations recommended on weekends. Main courses $8.95–$24.95; lunch $4.95–$8.95. AE, CB, DC, DISC, MC, V. Tues–Fri 11:30am–4pm and 4:30–10pm, Sat 11:30am–3pm and 4:30–10:30pm, Sun noon–9pm. AMERICAN/REGIONAL.

Nestled on Silver Lake just north of downtown in a garden setting, this Colonial-style restaurant was originally a private home. It's been a restaurant for more than 25 years, offering lovely waterside views. It takes its name from the uniform worn by the Delaware Regiment that marched from Dover Green in July 1776 to join General Washington's army. Four original stone fireplaces, weathered timbers, and antiques from the area enhance the interior. The names of the various dining rooms—Independence Room, Liberty Room, George Tavern—also reflect the Early American theme. At lunchtime there's an extensive menu of hot and cold entrées, including crab imperial, crab cakes, stuffed flounder, and filet mignon. Dinner entrées range from southern crab couplet (Maryland blue crab with Virginia Smithfield ham), shrimp Rockefeller, and prime rib to seafood combination platters. For after-meal browsing, there's an adjacent stable, which once housed thoroughbreds and has now been converted into a Gift Shoppe and Countrie Store.

Paradiso Ristorante

1151 E. Lebanon Rd., Route 10 Plaza. ☎ **302/697-3055.** Reservations required. Main courses $13.95–$22.95; lunch $6.95–$9.95. AE, DC, MC, V. Mon–Fri 11am–2pm and Mon–Thurs 5–10pm, Fri–Sat 5–11pm, Sun 1–9pm. SOUTHERN ITALIAN.

Tucked in a shopping center just west of the Dover Air Force Base, this place could easily be overlooked by visitors, but the locals beat a regular path to Paradiso. The interior features murals, paintings, and statuary reminiscent of a Roman palazzo. Be ready to spend a few hours here. Table-side service, which is a specialty, can be quite slow. Featured dishes include filetto Veneziano; filet mignon with wild mushrooms in Chianti wine; osso bucco alla Milanese, veal shank with Arborio rice; aragosta alla Genovese, egg-dipped lobster in lemon sauce; and saltimbocca alla Romano, medaillons of veal with prosciutto and cheese. There are also more than a dozen pastas made fresh daily, including a signature dish of tortellini Marco Polo con tonno, little hats with fresh tuna, capers, and olives in red sauce.

Village Inn

Route 9, Little Creek. ☎ **302/734-3245.** Reservations recommended for dinner. Main courses $12.95–$23.95; lunch $4.95–$7.95. DISC, MC, V. Tues–Fri 11am–2pm and 4:30–10pm; Sat 11am–10pm; Sun noon–9pm. SEAFOOD.

It's worth a slight detour about 4 miles east of Dover and past several cornfields to try this restaurant, situated in the town of Little Creek, on the Mahon and Little Rivers off Delaware Bay. Founded more than 20 years ago and still run by a local family named Roe, the restaurant has built its reputation on an ever-fresh seafood menu. Its specialty is fresh flounder, served in a variety of ways: stuffed with crab, breaded, poached, or however else you might want it. Other seafood entrées are oyster pot pie, crab cakes, crab imperial, stuffed butterflied gulf shrimp, and a steamed seafood pot containing king crab legs, clams, scallops, and shrimp. Steaks, chicken, veal, duck, and prime rib are also available. Lunch consists mainly of sandwiches, salads, chowders, and seafood platters. The interior is a cheery blend of nautical and floral decor, with local handcrafts and grapevine wreaths.

✪ W. T. Smithers

140 S. State St. ☎ **302/674-8875.** Reservations recommended for dinner. Main courses $10.95–$19.95; lunch $4.95–$6.95. CB, DC, MC, V. Mon–Fri 11am–2pm and 5–10pm, Sat noon–2pm and 5–10pm. INTERNATIONAL.

Housed in a Victorian-style building in the heart of Dover's historic district, W. T. Smithers is named in honor of a local hero who was, at various times, a baseball player, a lawyer, a member of the state's 1897 constitutional convention, and one of Teddy Roosevelt's Rough Riders. The interior offers a homey turn-of-the century atmosphere, with a choice of eight different dining rooms, including a library, a parlor, a tavern, a trophy room, an outdoor deck, and an "anniversary" room, ideal for special dinners for two to four persons. The menu at lunch features double-decker sandwiches, burgers, pasta, and vegetarian platters. Dinner entrées include steaks, surf-and-turf, crab imperial, shrimp scampi, blackened chicken, and pastas.

MODERATE/INEXPENSIVE

The Boondocks

Bayview Rd., Smyrna. ☎ **302/653-6962.** Reservations not accepted. Main courses $6.50–$15; lunch $3.50–$7. MC, V. Mid-Mar to Jan, Sun and Tues–Thurs 11am–9pm, Fri–Sat 11am–10pm; Feb to mid-Mar, Fri–Sun 11am–9pm. SEAFOOD.

Situated in the farming countryside about 15 miles northeast of Dover, off Route 6 and State Road 82, this rustic, shacklike structure is aptly named. It has a splendid view of an adjacent pond from its screened-in porch, but its main attraction is the food, especially steamed fresh hard crabs in season. The atmosphere is informal: picnic tables with plastic coverings, country music in the background, and paper towels for napkins. Besides crabs, the menu offers shrimp, clams, oysters, catfish, and flounder. Steaks, burgers, and chicken are also available. Accompaniments include hush puppies and sweet-potato sticks.

⑤ Captain John's

518 Bay Rd. (at Route 113). ☎ **302/678-8166.** Main courses $4.95–$14.95; lunch $2.95–$5.95; breakfast $2.95–$5.95. MC, V. Daily 6am–10pm. AMERICAN/SEAFOOD.

This nautically themed diner-style restaurant has long been a favorite for drop-in travelers and families en route to or from the Delaware beach corridor. Breakfast, served at all hours, includes an omelet bar, country platters, and pancakes and waffles. Lunch features sandwiches and burgers. Dinner entrées, which include a 75-item salad bar, feature fried chicken, seafood platters (shrimp, scallops, and flounder), crab imperial, steaks, and prime rib. On weekends an all-you-can-eat buffet is offered.

⑤ Sambo's Tavern

Front Street, Leipsic. ☎ **302/674-9724.** Reservations required on weekends for dinner. Main courses $5.95–$16.95; lunch $1.95–$5.95. No credit cards. Apr–Nov, Mon–Sat 11am–10:30pm. SEAFOOD.

Overlooking the Leipsic River northeast of Dover off Route 9, this informal restaurant-cum-tavern is a local favorite for heaping plates of steamed crabs and shrimp, served "in the rough." Other entrées are steaks, burgers, crab cakes, crab imperial, honey-dipped chicken, and seafood samplers (flounder, clams, shrimp, oysters, and scallops). Lunch items include burgers, sandwiches, and chowders.

INEXPENSIVE

⑤ The Blue Coat Inn Pancake House

950 N. State St. ☎ **302/674-8310.** Reservations not accepted. Breakfast $2.45–$6.95; lunch $2.95–$6.95; dinner $5.95–$9.95. No credit cards. Mon–Sat 6am–8pm, Sun 6am–3pm. AMERICAN.

Set overlooking Silver Lake on the edge of town, the Blue Coat Pancake Inn House, a sister operation of the more formal Blue Coat Inn next door, is a good choice for a hearty meal at a low price in a simple cottage setting. It is an ideal spot for pancakes—served in traditional style or with fruit and nut toppings—as well as for waffles and omelets. The restaurant also serves soup and sandwiches, as well as dinner entrées such as fried chicken, steaks, ribs, and traditional crab cakes. Take-out is available.

Bradford Street Cafe

150 S. Bradford St. ☎ **302/736-6200.** Breakfast $1.25–$4.95; lunch $1.95–$6.95. AE, MC, V. Mon–Sat 11am–3pm. AMERICAN/HEALTH.

A favorite with Dover office workers, this homey restaurant sits just north of Loockerman Street in the heart of the city. It presents fresh food prepared according to healthful recipes. Among the dishes offered are pizzas made from honey wheat crust, with fresh tomato sauce and choice of toppings; turkey and soy burgers; spinach-nut pâté; seafood strudel; lowfat chili; and steamed vegetable combinations. The house salad, a summertime favorite, consists of assorted greens, radicchio, escarole, carrots, beets, tomatoes, sprouts, and sunflower seeds. There is also a bakery on the premises.

McDowell-Collins Storehouse
408 S. State St. ☎ **302/734-5154.** All items $1.50–$4. No credit cards. Mon–Fri 7:30am–4pm. AMERICAN.

If you're looking for a quick snack or a light lunch in an old-Dover atmosphere, step into this 2¹/₂-story, early 19th-century frame house opposite the County Court House. Restored in 1975 as a museum by the Dover Heritage Trail, it has had a varied history including a stint as a general store from 1883 to 1907, operated by Robert Collins. The menu isn't fancy, just old-fashioned—BLT or tuna sandwiches, hot dogs, burgers, hearty soups, salads, and daily specials.

5 Attractions

Dover is centered around a parklike square, called simply the Green, which was laid out in 1722. From the beginning, it's been the site of public meetings, farmers' markets, and fairs. Most of Dover's landmark buildings surround the Green.

Barratt's Chapel and Museum
Route 113, Rd. 2, Box 25, Frederica. ☎ **302/335-5544.** Admission free, but donations are welcome. Sat–Sun 1:30–4:30pm and by appointment.

Listed on the National Register of Historic Places and one of Delaware's most significant religious sites, Barratt's Chapel is known as the "cradle of Methodism." A fine example of traditional Georgian architecture, it was erected in 1780 on land donated by Phillip Barratt. In 1784 Francis Asbury and Dr. Thomas Coke, an emissary of John Wesley, met here and formulated plans for the organization of the Methodist Episcopal Church in America. A reconstructed 18th-century vestry has been added to the complex.

✪ Bombay Hook National Wildlife Refuge
2591 Whitehall Neck Rd. (off Route 9), Smyrna. ☎ **302/653-9345** or 302/653-6872. Admission $4 per vehicle. Weekdays 8am–4pm, weekends 9am–5pm.

Eight miles northeast of Dover is the Bombay Hook National Wildlife Refuge. Created in 1937, it's one of the state's most important environmental resources and an essential link in the Great Atlantic Flyway, the chain of refuges that extends from the Gulf of Mexico to Canada. The site includes nearly 16,000 acres of salt marsh, swamp, freshwater pools, croplands, and woods. It attracts more than 250 species of migrating and resident birds—among them Canada and snow geese, great egrets, black-crowned night herons, and the bald eagle, which nests here from early December to mid-May—as well as white-tailed deer, foxes, otters, opossums, woodchucks, and muskrats. For human visitors, there are auto-tour routes, walking paths, nature trails, and 30-foot observation towers.

To get there, take Route 13 north of Dover to Route 42; travel east to Route 9 and then north on Route 9 for 2 miles to Route 85, which leads to the refuge's entrance.

❂ Delaware Agricultural Museum and Village

866 N. Du Pont Hwy. ☎ **302/734-1618.** Admission $3 adults, $2 seniors and children 10–17, $1 children 6–9, children under 6 free. Jan–Mar, Mon–Fri 10am–4pm; Apr–Dec, Tues–Sat 10am–4pm, Sun 1–4pm.

For insight into Delaware's rich agricultural heritage, this museum is well worth a visit. The large main building houses permanent and temporary displays, reflecting the last 200 years in the local poultry, dairy, and produce industries. The exhibits include more than 6,000 artifacts, from a 1941 crop-duster to an 18th-century log house, as well as harvesting and farm machinery. On the grounds behind the main building, there's a re-creation of an 1890s village, with a one-room schoolhouse, a church, a mill, a blacksmith shop, and a farmhouse. There's also a gift shop. Special events are often held on the grounds.

❂ Delaware State House

S. State St. ☎ **302/739-4266.** Admission free. Tues–Sat 10am–4:30pm, Sun 1:30–4:30pm.

Built in 1792, the State House was restored in 1976 as part of Delaware's bicentennial celebration. It contains a courtroom, a ceremonial governor's office, legislative chambers, and county offices. Although the state's legislature, the General Assembly, moved to the nearby Legislative Hall in 1934, the State House still remains Delaware's symbolic capitol.

❂ Delaware State Museum Complex

316 S. Governors Ave. ☎ **302/739-4266.** Admission free. Tues–Sat 10am–3:30pm.

Three important museums are housed in this complex. Two of them are Meeting House Gallery I, formerly a Presbyterian church, built in 1790 and now the home of rotating exhibits highlighting life in Delaware, and Meeting House Gallery II, a showcase for turn-of-the-century crafts. The third is the Johnson Victrola Museum, a tribute to Dover-born Eldridge Reeves Johnson, inventor and founder of the Victor Talking Machine Company, now known as RCA. This museum, located a block west of the other two buildings at Bank Lane and New Street and designed as a 1920s Victrola dealer's store, contains an extensive collection of talking machines, early recordings, and an oil painting of Nipper, the dog that made the RCA trademark, "His Master's Voice," a household name in the early 20th century.

Dover Air Force Base & Museum

201 18th St. (Route 113). ☎ **302/677-3379.** Admission free. Mon–Sat 9am–4pm.

Founded in 1941, this base, situated 2 miles south of the city, is the hub of strategic airlift in the eastern United States. With a 6,000-plus work force, it's also Dover's second-largest industry. The base is home to the 436th Air Lift Wing and to the giant C-5 Galaxy airplane, one of the world's largest operational aircraft—equivalent in size to an eight-lane bowling alley. Visitors are welcome to tour the base museum, which houses a fine collection of vintage aircraft and artifacts, among them C-47 Gooney Birds, used in the D-Day 1944 troop drop over Normandy, France, and one of the few surviving B-17Gs, a veteran of "flying bomb" operations. Unlike some other museums, this one encourages picture taking, even with flash equipment. The adjacent gift shop offers unique aviation-related books, posters, patches, and souvenirs.

Dover Art League Gallery
102 W. Loockerman St. ☎ **302/674-0402**. Admission free. Mon–Fri 11am–4pm, Sat 9am–3pm.

This long, narrow shop-front facility is composed of a gallery, a classroom, and an artists' work space. There's a new show every month.

✪ Historic Houses Of Odessa
Main St., Odessa. ☎ **302/378-4069**. Admission to one house, $4 adults, $3 seniors; two houses, $6 adults, $5 seniors; three houses, $7 adults, $6 seniors. Children 5–11 $3. Admission free to all houses for children under 4. Mar–Dec, Tues–Sat 10am–4pm, Sun 1–4pm.

Dating from the 17th century, Odessa, north of Dover, was settled by the Dutch and first named Appoquinimink, after the creek on which it lies. In 1731 it became known as Cantwell's Bridge, and in 1855 the name Odessa was adopted in honor of the Ukrainian seaport. Over the years, the town prospered as a grain-shipping port and peach grower. Today, Odessa is a good example of a rural American adaptation of urban Georgian architecture; its historic houses are the centerpiece of the town. Administered by the Winterthur Museum, the structures include the Corbit-Sharp House, a three-story brick home dating from 1774; the Wilson-Warner House, built in 1769; and the Brick Hotel Gallery, a Federal-style building from 1822.

John Dickenson Plantation
Kitts-Hummock Rd. ☎ **302/739-3277**. Admission free. Jan–Feb, Tues–Sat 10am–3:30pm; Mar–Dec, Tues–Sat 10am–3:30pm, Sun 1:30–4:30pm. Closed Mon and state holidays and Sun in Jan–Feb.

This is the boyhood home of John Dickinson, one of Delaware's foremost statesman of the Revolutionary and Federal periods. It is a fine example of Delaware plantation architecture, built around 1740 and furnished with period antiques.

Sewell C. Biggs Museum of American Art
406 Federal St. ☎ **302/674-2111**. Admission free. Wed–Sat 10am–4pm, Sun 1:30–4:30pm.

Housed on the second and third floors of the Delaware State Visitor Center, this museum has a large collection of American paintings, sculptures, and decorative arts. The majority of works are by artists from the Delaware Valley region, such as oil paintings by Frank Schoonover and Thomas Cole and cabinetry by the Janvier family. Named after a native of Middletown, Delaware, who assembled the collection, the museum also includes tall clocks by area craftsmen and historic pieces that once belonged to noted 18th-century Delaware families, such as the Reads, the Loockermans, and the Finneys.

ORGANIZED TOURS
An ideal way to get your bearings in Dover is to take a two-hour walking tour conducted by the knowledgeable guides of **Dover Heritage Trail**, P.O. Box 1628, Dover, DE 19903 (☎ 302/678-2040). Two different itineraries are available: One covers the Old Dover historic district and begins at the visitor center; the other covers the streets of Victorian Dover and departs from the Delaware Department of Natural Resources and Environmental Control, 89 Kings Hwy. Tours can be arranged by appointment, year-round. The historic tour also has regularly scheduled departures, May through October, on Thursdays at 10am. Rates are $5 for adults, $4 for seniors, and $2 for youngsters 5 to 17.

6 Outdoor Activities

CAR RACING   Without a doubt, Dover's biggest sporting activity is stock car racing. Fans from far and near flock to the "Monster Mile" at **Dover Downs International Speedway,** Route 13, P.O. Box 843, Dover, DE 19903 (☎ 302/ 674-4600 or 800/441-RACE for information, or in Delaware only 302/ 734-RACE for tickets), the home of two top auto races: the Budweiser 500 in June and the Split Fire Spark Plug 500 in September. These two 500-mile races draw 40 of the world's top stock-car drivers. Ticket prices for adults range from $25 for general admission on Saturday to $36 to $130 for reserved-seat tickets on Sunday. Mail orders are accepted. In addition, from November through March, this track is open for a full program of harness racing. Post time is 7:30pm Friday and Saturday and at 1pm on Sunday.

HORSE RACING   For horse racing, it's the **Harrington Raceway,** Route 13, Harrington (☎ 302/398-3269). The oldest pari-mutuel racing track in the United States, it's situated on the state fair grounds, about 15 miles south of Dover. Racing is scheduled September through November, Thursday through Sunday 7 to 11pm. Admission is free.

PARKS   Dover's beautiful **Silver Lake** is the core of a park-side recreation area in the heart of the city. Biking, swimming, and picnicking are among the activities available. The park is open each day from sunrise to sundown, with entrances on State Street and Kings Highway. Complete information is available from the **City of Dover Parks and Recreation Division,** P.O. Box 475, Dover, DE 19903 (☎ 302/736-7050).

   Some 13 miles south of Dover, about a half-mile east of Route 13, is Kent County's only state park, **Killens Pond State Park,** County Road 426, R.D. 1, Box 858, Felton (☎ 302/284-4526). Covering approximately 950 acres, with a 66-acre mill pond at its core, Killens Pond is a natural inland haven. Its facilities include picnic areas, a guarded swimming pool and wading pool, shuffleboard and horseshoe courts, hiking trails, volleyball courts, boat rentals, pond fishing, and camping sites. Admission is $2.50 for Delaware-registered cars, $5 for out-of-state vehicles.

7 Shopping

Since Delaware has no sales tax, many people travel here to shop. Among the major shopping centers in Dover are the sprawling Dover Mall and the Blue Hen Mall, both on Route 13.

   A highlight of the Dover shopping experience is provided by the local Amish community, one of Delaware's closely knit religious groups. The Amish operate several shops, well stocked with crafts made by members of the community. The Amish area is located about 5 miles outside of the historic district. To get there, drive west on Loockerman Street or Division Street (Forest Street) and follow Route 8 west to Route 198 (also known as Rose Valley School Road).

Bylers
Rose Valley Platz, Rose Valley Rd. (Route 8). ☎ **302/674-1689.**

   Situated at the gateway to the lands farmed by the Amish community, this is not a souvenir shop but a general store, patronized as much by the Amish themselves as by visitors. It's fun to browse here, if not for baked goods, smoked meats, spices, sweets, nuts, health foods, and groceries, then for Amish-made products, such as woodwork, quilts, baskets, and books. Open Monday through Thursday from 8am to 6pm, Friday and Saturday from 8am to 7pm.

Delaware Made
214 S. State St. ☎ **302/736-1419.**

Housed in a restored 18th-century house in the heart of Dover's historic district, this shop presents an array of arts, crafts, and gifts made in the state. Open Monday through Saturday from 9:30am to 6pm and, from May through September, additional hours on Sunday from noon to 5pm.

Dover Farmers' Market
Route 13 and Leipsic Rd. ☎ **302/736-5644.**

Situated next to Dover Downs and opposite the Delaware Agricultural Museum, this huge indoor market has more than 250 stalls, selling everything from baked goods and produce to baskets, books, furniture, shoes, tools, and T-shirts. For locals, it's a shopping focal point on weekends. Open Friday and Saturday from 10am to 9pm and on Sunday from 10am to 6pm.

Rose Valley Quilt Shop
175 Rose Valley School Rd. (Route 198). No phone.

This fine shop, located in the heart of Dover's farming countryside, is operated by Rachel Herschberger, a member of Dover's Amish community. Local Amish and Mennonite women handcraft the items on sale, from a dazzling array of colorful quilts in all sizes and patterns to place mats and baby booties. The shop operates a mail-order service and takes special orders. Open Monday through Wednesday and on Friday and Saturday from 9am to 5pm.

Spence's Bazaar
550 S. New St. ☎ **302/734-3441.**

Started more than 50 years ago, Spence's is a combination farm stand, flea market, and auction house—all housed in a big red building, formerly a tomato cannery. Local craftspeople and entrepreneurs gather here to sell, as do the Amish, who bring homemade breads, pies, cheese, and sausages. Open Tuesday and Friday from 8am to 9pm.

11

The Delaware Beaches

Nestled along Delaware's Atlantic coast, the beach communities of Lewes, Rehoboth, Dewey, Bethany, and Fenwick Island are in a class by themselves—28 miles of sandy and serene shoreline, clean and well kept, dune filled, and uncommercialized. Swimming, boating, fishing, and crabbing play a large part in the "good life" along the Delaware beaches. And each of the beaches is distinctive, with its own personality and ambience.

The five beach areas constitute the busiest segment of Sussex County, Delaware's most southerly county, ranked largest in size but smallest in population. During the summer season, however, the beaches quadruple in population as they draw visitors from all over Delaware and the surrounding states.

Sussex is the most rural of Delaware's three counties, with interior farmlands and orchards, nature preserves and wildlife areas, state parks and forests, bays and rivers. It yields bountiful supplies of grains, soybeans, corn, tomatoes, asparagus, strawberries, peaches, cantaloupe, and watermelon. It also produces more broiler chickens than any other county in the nation—more than 180 million a year.

1 Lewes

40 miles SE of Dover, 86 miles SE of Wilmington, 7 miles N of Rehoboth Beach, 34 miles N of Ocean City, 121 miles from Washington, D.C., 107 miles SE of Baltimore, 117 miles S of Philadelphia

Situated at the tip of Cape Henlopen, between the Atlantic Ocean, Delaware Bay, and the Lewes-Rehoboth Canal, Lewes (pronounced "*Loo*-is") is the northernmost of the beach communities. History plays a large part in the character of the town, touted as Delaware's oldest community.

Lewes was settled in 1631 by the Dutch. Although their settlement, Zwaanandael, lasted only a year, the Lewes area has since been recognized as Delaware's first European colony.

In later years, Lewes was known by various names (from "Whorekill" to "Port Lewes," after a namesake in England) and was ruled alternately by the Dutch and the English, until it finally came under William Penn's control in 1682. It evolved into a prosperous maritime town and seaport, occasional county seat, and leading fish-processing center.

What's Special About the Delaware Beaches

Sightseeing
- Zwaanandael Museum, in Lewes, replica of a Dutch town hall.
- Fenwick Island Lighthouse, one of Delaware shore's oldest landmarks, with beams that project 15 miles.
- Nanticoke Indian Museum, Millsboro, with exhibits on the area's first residents.
- Treasures of the Sea Exhibit, in Georgetown, containing gold, silver, and other artifacts from a 1622 shipwreck.

Activities
- Boat cruises on Delaware Bay from Lewes Harbor.
- Windsurfing or sailing at Dewey Beach.

Events
- Fishing tournaments at Lewes in late May to August and in October.
- Annual Rehoboth Beach Sandcastle Contest, for sandcastle and whale sculptures.

For the Kids
- Funland, Playland, and Sports Complex at Rehoboth Beach.

Parks
- Cape Henlopen State Park, 2,500-acre playground bordered by the Atlantic Ocean and Delaware Bay.
- Fenwick Island State Park, 3 miles of beaches and dunes and more than 300 acres of parklands, bay front, and wildlife areas.

Shopping
- Ocean Outlets, at Rehoboth Beach, a cluster of 70 factory outlets.

During the War of 1812, the British formed a blockade on Delaware Bay and began to bombard Lewes. The local militia, under Col. Samuel Boyer Davis, returned fire with a small group of cannons. No lives were lost and no homes were destroyed, but one house was hit with a cannon ball that lodged in its foundation. It is still referred to as the Cannon Ball House.

Today, Lewes, with a population of about 2,600, is still inseparably involved with the sea—as a beach resort, as a boating marina, and as a port for dozens of fishing fleets. Also located here is the College of Marine Studies of the University of Delaware, with its own shoreline park and harbor and two research vessels. In 1984, in the waters off Lewes, deep-sea divers discovered the fabled HMS *DeBraak,* a British brig that sank off the coast of Cape Henlopen in 1798.

GETTING THERE   By Plane   The closest gateways for regularly scheduled flights from all parts of the United States are Philadelphia International Airport and Baltimore International Airport. For commuter flights, the nearest gateways are Ocean City and Salisbury, Maryland.

By Train   There's daily service from all parts of the United States via **Amtrak** into Wilmington (see "Arriving," in Chapter 8).

By Bus   Carolina Trailways provides regular service into the Rehoboth Bus Center, 251 Rehoboth Ave., Rehoboth Beach (☎ 302/227-7223), about 5 miles south of Lewes. Monday through Friday, **Blue Diamond Lines** (☎ 302/577-6686 or 800/652-DART) operates service from Wilmington via Dover into Lewes, stopping at Savannah Road and at the Cape May–Lewes Ferry Terminal.

By Car   From points north or south, take Routes 113 and 13 to Route 1 and thence to Route 9 into town. From the west, take Route 50 to Route 1 or 9.

By Ferry   Many visitors come to Lewes via the Cape May–Lewes Ferry, a convenient, 70-minute Delaware Bay minicruise that connects southern New Jersey to mid-Delaware and saves considerable driving mileage for north- or south-bound passengers along the Atlantic coast.

In operation since 1964, this ferry service maintains a fleet of five vessels, each holding up to 800 passengers and 100 cars. Departures are operated daily year-round, from early morning until evening, with almost hourly service in the summer months from 6:20am to midnight.

Passenger rates are $4.50 for adults and $2.25 for children 6 to 12 per trip; vehicle fares, calculated by car length, range from $18 for most cars to $64 for large trucks, with reduced prices for motorcycle and bicycle passengers and off-peak reduced rates from January to March and in December. A drive-on, drive-off service is operated, so reservations are not necessary. The Lewes Terminal (☎ 302/644-6030) is next to the Cape Henlopen State Park entrance, about a mile from the center of town. For further information, call 800/64-FERRY for schedules or 800/717-SAIL for reservations.

ESSENTIALS   **Area Code**   The area code is 302.

Visitor Information   Contact the Lewes Chamber of Commerce, P.O. Box 1, Lewes, DE 19958 (☎ 302/645-8073). The chamber's offices are in the charming Fisher-Martin House at Kings Highway, next to the Zwaanandael Museum. Moved from its original location at Coolspring, this structure was once owned by Joshua Fisher, who is credited with charting Delaware Bay and River. This is one of almost 50 houses in Lewes, many transported from surrounding areas, that are now fully restored and in present-day use in the town. Summer hours are from 10am to 4pm on Monday through Friday and from 10am to 2pm on Saturday, with a reduced schedule during the rest of the year.

GETTING AROUND   **By Minibus or Bus**   The Seaport Shuttle of Lewes, 306 Savannah Rd. (☎ 302/645-6800), operates a minibus transfer service from the ferry terminal to the downtown area, meeting each arriving ferry and transporting passengers to the historic district. Passengers are free to remain in Lewes as long they desire, returning to the terminal on a later shuttle. The minibuses operate weekends only May to June and September to October and daily during July and August. The fare is free for those who have traveled over from Cape May on the ferry or $1 per person for other passengers.

By Rented Car   Cars can be rented from Hertz, 1101 Hwy. 1 (☎ 302/645-2846), and National, 700 Kings Hwy. (☎ 302/645-2622).

By Taxi   Local services are operated by Seaport Transportation, 306 Savannah Rd. (☎ 302/645-6800).

WHAT TO SEE & DO

Most visitors are drawn to Lewes by the beaches and marina, but you'll find many other intriguing attractions well worth a visit once you come to this friendly, historic town.

The Delaware Beaches

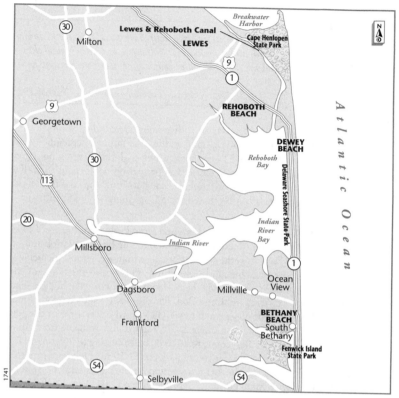

OUTDOOR ACTIVITIES

BICYCLING Lewes's historic streets and shoreline paths are ideal for cycling. You can hire a bike from the **Lewes Cycle Sports,** in the Beacon Motel, Savannah Road (☎ 302/645-4544). This shop also rents bicycles and tandems from 9am to 5pm seven days a week, June through Labor Day, and on weekends during the rest of the year. Charges average $9 to $14 for a day or $23 to $39 for a week.

FISHING With easy access to both Delaware Bay and the Atlantic, Lewes offers a wide variety of sportfishing opportunities. The fishing season starts when the ocean fills with huge schools of mackerel in late March through April; large sea trout (weakfish) invade the waters in early May and June; and flounder arrive in May and remain throughout the summer, as do bluefish and shark. As the ocean warms up in June, it is also time for offshore species such as tuna and marlin. Bottom fishing in the bay for trout, flounder, sea bass, and blues continues all summer, with late August through September often providing the largest catches. October and November also bring porgies, shad, and blackfish.

Head boat ocean and bay fishing excursions can be arranged at the **Fisherman's Wharf Fishing Center,** Anglers Road (☎ 302/645-8862). Full-day (eight-hour) trips are operated from early March through October daily departing at 7am, and in November, on Friday through Monday at 7am; the cost is $32 for adults, and

This expansive 25-mile coastline, more than half state parkland, seems to defy crowding, even when weekends lure as many as 90,000 sun seekers. Step beyond clusters of bodies and blankets, and the surf, gulls, and gentle dunes work their magic for an audience of one.

—Jane Vessels, *National Geographic*, August 1983

$20 children 12 and under. Half-day trips (five-hour) are conducted in May and October, on weekends at 8am and 1:30pm, and in June through September, daily at 8am and 1:30pm; the cost is $20 per person. Full-night trips (seven hours) go out in May and June, daily at 7pm; cost is $36 per person. Half-night trips (five hours) are operated during July and August, daily at 7pm; the cost is $21 per person. Conventional reels can be rented for $3, spinning reels $5; and bait is furnished.

SWIMMING & WALKING   Cape Henlopen State Park, 1 mile east of Lewes, is a 2,500-acre outdoor playground bordered on one side by the Atlantic and on another by Delaware Bay—just the spot for beach swimming, tennis, picnicking, nature trails, bay-shore crabbing, and pier fishing. This is also the home of the famous "walking dunes," most notably the 80-foot Great Dune, the highest sand dune between Cape Hatteras and Cape Cod. For those who enjoy a good climb, a refurbished World War II observation tower (115 steps) offers some of the best coastal views for miles. In addition, there are 155 campsites, available from April 1 through October 31, on a first-come, first-served basis, costing $10 per night for up to six people. Admission charges to the park are $2.50 for Delaware cars and $5 for all out-of-state cars. For further information on the park's attractions, contact the **Cape Henlopen State Park,** 42 Cape Henlopen Drive, Lewes, DE 19958 (☎ 302/645-8983).

WATER SPORTS   **If you prefer to pilot a boat yourself, contact **Rod-n-Reel Boat Rentals, Lewes Boatyard, Canal Street (☎ 302/644-2304). This company rents a variety of pontoon boats and runabouts, by the hour or by the day, for fishing, crabbing, or cruising. Rentals include safety equipment, tank of gas, and map of the bay.

The prices for runabouts are $35 for the first hour, and $7 each additional hour, or $75 per day; pontoon boats, $95 per hour, or $225 for eight hours. It's open daily from 8am to 5pm from Memorial Day to Labor Day; hours vary from March through May and September through November.

ATTRACTIONS

Throughout the streets of Lewes, you'll see beautifully restored 17th-, 18th-, and 19th-century structures functioning as private homes, shops, churches, and public buildings, such as the **visitor information center** at the **Fisher-Martin House** (ca. 1730). To guide you around, the Lewes Chamber of Commerce has designed a free, pocket-size brochure detailing a self-guided walking tour of the town.

The **Zwaanandael Museum,** Kings Highway and Savannah Road (☎ 302/645-1148), was built in 1931 to duplicate the architectural style of the town hall of Hoorn, Holland, in memory of Lewes's first Dutch settlers. The exhibits inside the Zwaanandael explore the rich and varied history of the area, from the original colony to the present, including a display on the HMS *DeBraak*. Open Tuesday through Saturday from 10am to 4:30pm and Sunday from 1:30pm to 4:30pm. Admission is free, but donations are welcome.

The **Lewes Historical Complex** is a cluster of a half-dozen buildings and a lightship administered by the Lewes Historical Society, Third Street and Shipcarpenter Street (☎ 302/645-7670 or 302/645-8719). The buildings include an early plank house, a country store, a doctor's office, and the Burton-Ingram House (ca. 1789). This house, known for its fine collection of Early American furniture, is constructed of hand-hewn timbers and cypress shingles; its cellar walls are made of stones and bricks once used as a ship's ballast. The entire complex is open from mid-June to Labor Day, Tuesday through Friday from 10am to 3pm and Saturday from 10am to 12:30pm. Admission charge, which includes a guided tour, is $5 for adults and free for children under 12. If you prefer to visit only a few houses at your own pace, admission to each building is $1.

SIGHTSEEING TOURS/CRUISES

A good way to see the Delaware Bay and the Lewes Canal harbor is to take a tour, either by land or by sea.

Fisherman's Wharf Cruises

Fisherman's Wharf, Anglers Rd. ☎ **302/645-8862.** Two-hour dolphin-watching cruise, $12 adults, $6 children 12 and under; four-hour whale/dolphin-watching cruise, $22 adults, $10 children 12 and under; two-hour sunset cruise, $10 adults, $5 children 12 and under; buffet dinner cruise $18.95 adults, $9.95 children 12 and under. Two-hour dolphin cruise, late June–Sept, daily 9am and 11:30am. Four-hour dolphin/whale cruise, late June–Sept, daily 2:30pm. Two-hour evening cruise, late May–late June, Fri–Sat 7pm; July–Labor Day, daily 7pm; Sept–Oct, Wed and Fri–Sat 7pm. Two-hour buffet cruise June–Aug daily 6pm.

This company operates a variety of narrated cruises around the historical harbor of Lewes and the Delaware Breakwater areas, including two-hour morning dolphin-watching cruises with Continental breakfast or midday snack; a four-hour afternoon whale- and dolphin-watching cruise; a two-hour sunset cruise; and a two-hour buffet dinner cruise.

The *Jolly Rover*

By the drawbridge. ☎ **302/644-1501.** Two-hour sail, $20 adults, $10 children under 12; three-hour sunset sail, $25 per person. Sat before Memorial Day through Labor Day daily 2pm and 6pm and Tues–Sat 10am; Sept daily 5pm.

Plying the waters of Delaware Bay, this topsail schooner offers two-hour sailing trips in the morning or afternoon and three-hour sailing trips at sunset. Advance reservations are necessary.

Queen Anne's Railroad

730 Kings Hwy. ☎ **302/644-1720.** Afternoon excursion, $7 adults, $5 children under 12. Evening dinner trip, $39.95 adults, $32.95 for children under 12. Excursion train, June Wed and Sat at noon; July–Aug, Wed noon and 3:30pm, Fri–Sat noon; dinner train, June–Sept, Sat 6pm; May–Apr and Oct–Nov schedule varies.

It's all aboard this vintage steam train for a ride in the Lewes countryside. This train line offers two types of excursions: 1-hour and 45-minute afternoon sightseeing trips and 2^1/$_2$-hour evening trips with sit-down dinner and entertainment. Reservations are not accepted for afternoon rides, but are required for the dinner departures.

SHOPPING

Lewes is a good town in which to shop for unusual crafts and collectibles.

For the Child in All of Us

142 2nd St. ☎ **302/645-5142.**

This is just the spot for dolls of all shapes and sizes, including miniatures, as well as dollhouse furniture. The shop also has stuffed animals, vintage Santas, Victorian cards and wrappings, music boxes, and Christmas ornaments. Open Monday to Saturday from 10:30am to 5pm, Sunday from 11am to 4pm.

Puzzles

111 2nd St. ☎ **302/645-8013.**

Intriguing games and puzzles of all kinds are on sale at this shop, including jigsaws, crosswords, brain-teasers, mazes, and metal and wooden puzzles. Open daily from 10am to 5pm.

✪ The Saxon Swan

101 2nd St. ☎ **302/645-7488.**

The Saxon Swan offers a potpourri of figurines, pottery, sculptures, ornaments, etchings, and watercolors. It also has an array of international Nativity scenes and Santas, as well as menorahs and Judaica collectibles. Open Monday to Saturday from 10am to 5pm, Sunday from 11am to 5pm.

The Stepping Stone

107 W. Market St. ☎ **302/645-1254.**

Traditional and contemporary American handcrafts are the focal point of this shop, including the work of many local artisans. The wares range from wooden ship models and unusual musical instruments to hand-painted scarves, pottery, jewelry, candles, and cards. Open daily from 10am to 5pm.

WHERE TO STAY

Lewes's choice of accommodations includes handsome downtown inns as well as traditional motels. Prices, in general, are in the moderate-to-expensive range in the summer months and in the moderate-to-inexpensive range at other times of the year. Check what rate is in effect at the time you plan to visit and whether any minimum-night stays are required. Reservations are required in the summer months and recommended at other times, since the total room capacity barely exceeds 300. All properties described below are clustered in the town near the canal and wharf areas, but not directly on the beach.

EXPENSIVE/MODERATE

✪ The Inn at Canal Square

122 Market St., Lewes, DE 19958. ☎ **302/645-8499** or 800/222-7902. 19 rms, 3 suites, 1 houseboat. A/C TV TEL. $65–$135 double, $125–$155 suites in main building; $175–$250 adjacent houseboat that sleeps four. (Rates include continental breakfast.) AE, DC, DISC, MC, V. Free parking.

Located in an ideal setting overlooking the marina, this four-story bed-and-breakfast hotel has a country-inn atmosphere. The guest rooms are extra large, and most have a balcony or porch overlooking the water. The decor includes designer fabrics, waterfowl art prints, live plants, and 18th-century reproductions of headboards, nightstands, armoires, brass lamps, and comfortable armchairs.

The modern bathrooms offer a contrast of sleek black-and-white marble and tile appointments, each with separate vanity area and hair dryer.

The facilities include a sitting room and parlor and a conference center. For those who may be looking for something different, the inn also rents a custom-designed, two-bedroom houseboat, permanently moored on the marina. The houseboat has a full galley and sleeps four adults.

✪ The New Devon Inn

142 Second St. (at 2nd and Market sts.), Lewes, DE 19958. ☎ **302/645-6466** or 800/824-8754. 24 rms, 2 suites. A/C TEL. $65–$120 double; $120–$155 suite. AE, DC, MC, V. Free parking.

Dating from the 1920s, this restored, three-story brick hotel sits right in the heart of Lewes. Guests relax in a modern sitting room with Art Deco tones and a baby grand piano, in the adjacent Music Room, or in the wicker and plant-filled Garden Room. The hotel facilities include a full-service restaurant and a half-dozen shops on the main and lower levels. On the second and third floors are the guest rooms, each individually furnished with local antiques, crystal or brass lamps, and fine comforters and linens. The bathrooms are modern and have a hair dryer.

Wild Swan Inn

525 Kings Hwy., Lewes, DE 19958. ☎ **302/645-8550.** Fax 302/645-8550. 3 rms (all with bath). A/C. $75–$120 double. (Rates include full breakfast.) No credit cards. Free parking.

Built in 1910 as a lightship captain's house, this bed-and-breakfast inn, with a well-tended garden and gazebo, is a standout for turn-of-the-century ambience and 1990s comfort. A classic example of Queen Anne Victorian style, it's rich in ornate gingerbread and fancy finials. The Victorian theme pervades the common rooms and guest rooms, with high ceilings and vivid colors, lavish wallpaper, antique brass lighting fixtures, and antique furnishings. They've been collected over the years by innkeepers Mike and Hope Tyler, who are antique buffs and old-house addicts. In honor of the house's name, they have also filled the rooms with swan-motif accessories, from china swans to swan toilet paper. The facilities include a wraparound veranda and an outdoor swimming pool; bicycles are available for guests. The Wild Swan is located a half-mile from town and a mile from the beach, opposite the Lewes Library on Adams Avenue.

MODERATE/INEXPENSIVE

❺ Angler's Motel

110 Anglers Rd. (at Market St.), Lewes, DE 19958. ☎ **302/645-2831.** 25 rms. A/C TV TEL. $55–$85 double. AE, CB, DC, MC, V. Free parking.

One of the oldest lodgings in the area, this well-kept motel is a favorite with fishing guests and families. Most of the rooms enjoy views of the wharf and marina, and there is a pleasant sun deck. All rooms have a kitchenette or refrigerator. A two-day minimum stay applies on summer weekends; reduced rates are in effect from mid-September to mid-May.

❺ The Beacon Motel

514 Savannah Rd., P.O. Box 609, Lewes, DE 19958. ☎ **302/645-4888** or 800/735-4888. 66 rms. A/C TV TEL. $45–$105 double. AE, MC, V. Free parking. Closed late Dec–Mar.

This motel, opened in 1989, occupies the top two floors of a three-story property, with the ground level devoted to shops and a reception area. The bright and cheery rooms feature standard furnishings and seashell art, plus a refrigerator and a small balcony with sliding glass doors. The facilities include an outdoor swimming pool and a sundeck.

Cape Henlopen Motel
Savannah and Anglers Roads, P.O. Box 243, Lewes, DE 19958. ☎ 302/645-2828 or 800/447-3158. 28 rms. A/C TV TEL. $40–$85 double. AE, MC, V. Free parking.

Located directly across from Fisherman's Wharf, this modern, two-story, L-shaped motel has fully carpeted and wood-paneled rooms; some have beach-style furniture. All second-floor rooms have balconies. There's a two-night minimum on weekends and a three-night minimum during holiday weekends in the summer. Open all year.

INEXPENSIVE

Savannah Inn
330 Savannah Rd. (Route 9), Lewes, DE 19958. ☎ **302/645-5592.** 7 rms (with shared baths). $40–$60 double. (Rates include breakfast.) No credit cards. Free parking. Closed Oct–late May.

The ambience of a bygone era is offered to guests by innkeepers Dick and Susan Stafursky. A gracious, semi-Victorian brick house with wraparound enclosed porch, this bed-and-breakfast is conveniently situated in the heart of midtown Lewes at the corner of Orr Street. Bedrooms are of varying size and decor, all with shared baths; the rates include a bountiful breakfast of local fruits, homemade breads or muffins and jams, and a choice of hot beverage. There's a two-night minimum on weekends and a three-night minimum on holidays. Some rooms can accommodate three or four persons, at a rate of $55 to $65. (*Note:* Rooms are available at reduced rates without breakfast during the off-season.)

WHERE TO DINE
EXPENSIVE

✪ Kupchick's
3 E. Bay Ave. ☎ **302/645-0420.** Reservations recommended for dinner. Main courses $15–$25; lunch $5–$14. AE, CB, DC, MC, V. Sun–Thurs 11am–4pm and 5–10pm, Fri–Sat 11am–4pm and 5–11pm. Closed early Jan–mid-Feb. INTERNATIONAL.

This beachfront restaurant, opened in 1985, carries on a tradition of fine food started in 1913 when the present owners' grandparents, immigrants from Romania, began the first Kupchick's in Toronto and later added a second restaurant in Montreal. There are two dining rooms on the ground floor, each with a European ambience and decor, and a more casual upper-level open deck for sea-view meals on warm summer days.

Diner entrées include crab imperial, shrimp scampi, chicken piccata, stuffed quail, lobster, fresh swordfish, chateaubriand, and certified Angus steaks. Kupchick's is also known for its chowder and desserts—Key lime cheesecake, chocolate walnut pie, and raspberry soufflé. Hours are slightly curtailed in winter.

MODERATE

Gilligan's
134 Market St., Canal Square. ☎ **302/645-7866.** Reservations recommended for dinner. Main courses $11.95–$19.95. Lunch $4.95–$9.95. AE, MC, V. Apr–Oct, daily 11am–11pm. SEAFOOD.

One of the unique dining spots in Lewes is Gilligan's, next to the Inn at Canal Square and right on the water. The restaurant consists of a refurbished diving boat anchored on the marina and attached to a renovated chicken coop on the dock. Although it sounds outlandish, the result is a charming harborfront structure with a trendy deck bar and a glass-walled dining room, all decorated in a tropical island motif.

Seafood dominates the dinner menu, with such choices as crab cakes, soft-shell crabs, tuna steak, lemon-pepper shrimp, and lobster tail. For landlubbers, there's also a variety of chicken, veal, pork, steak, and pasta dishes.

✪ Jerry's American Cafe

115 2nd St. ☎ **302/645-9733.** Reservations recommended for dinner. Main courses $8.95–$17.95; lunch/brunch $4.95–$9.95. AE, MC, V. Mon–Thurs 11am–4pm and 5–9pm, Fri–Sat 11am–4pm and 5–10pm, Sun 11am–2pm and 3–8pm. Closed Sun (Sept–May). AMERICAN.

Nestled in the heart of downtown, this shop-front restaurant offers no views of the water, but it does present creative cookery and a relaxing "Art Deco moderne" decor of peach and green tones, with walls full of framed international posters and seascapes by local artists. Specialties range from old-time favorites such as chicken potpie, Yankee pot roast, and crab cakes to concoctions of lobster-filled ravioli with Newburg sauce, catfish El Paso (pan-fried in olive oil with a piquant salsa), and poached salmon with yogurt-dill sauce.

⑤ La Rosa Negra

128 2nd St. ☎ **302/645-1980.** Reservations recommended for dinner. Main courses $6.95–$16.95, lunch $3.95–$6.95. AE, MC, V. Mon–Thurs 11:30am–2pm and 5–9:30pm, Fri–Sat 11:30am–2pm and 5–10pm, Sun 5–9:30pm. ITALIAN.

In a town known for seafood, this small shop-front restaurant is a pleasant change of pace. The decor is highlighted by a black rose (*rosa negra*) etched on stained glass in the front window; the table settings carry on the same theme with black-and-white linens and pottery. The white walls are enlivened by local art. Specialties include chicken Florentine Gorgonzola, scampi alle ceci (with chickpeas, black olives, and white wine over linguine), and sole puttanesca (with chopped olives, garlic, and tomatoes, over linguine pesto), as well as vegetarian dishes such as mushroom pasta primavera.

The Lighthouse Restaurant

Savannah and Anglers rds. ☎ **302/645-6271.** Reservations accepted only for parties of eight or more. Main courses $11.95–$24.95; lunch $3.95–$13.95. MC, V. Mar–Oct, Sun–Thurs 11am–4pm and 5–9pm, Fri–Sat 11am–4pm and 5–10pm. SEAFOOD.

Pleasant views of the marina and a nautical decor are featured at this restaurant with indoor and outdoor covered-deck seating. An all-day menu features soups, salads, sandwiches, and platters; especially worth trying are the seaside salads (greens topped with sautéed shrimp, scallops, and crab). The dinner menu emphasizes a selection of fish dishes, such as crab cakes, combination platters, and lobster, as well as steaks, ribs, and fried chicken.

Rose and Crown Restaurant and Pub

108 2nd St. ☎ **302/645-2373.** Reservations recommended for dinner. Main courses $8.95–$18.95; lunch $3.95–$7.95. AE, MC, V. Daily 11:30am–4pm and 5–11pm. INTERNATIONAL.

Housed in the historic 1930s Walsh Building, this restaurant offers a pub atmosphere in three separate eating areas: a bright, plant-filled front room with large windows overlooking busy Second Street; a clubby bar area with brass fixtures, skylit ceiling, and wall hangings from England and Ireland; and a cozy back room with dark wood trim, exposed-brick walls, and a tin ceiling. Lunch fare includes pub salads, homemade soups, quiches, shepherd's pie, Welsh rabbit, and fish and chips. Dinner features such entrées as London broil, English cottage beef pie, pork stew in cider, and crab imperial.

AN INLAND EXCURSION

If you tire of the waterfront activities, head west about 15 miles, via Route 9/404 to Georgetown, the county seat of Sussex since 1791. It's a delightful 18th-century town, with a center designated as the Circle, dominated by a redbrick Greek Revival courthouse (1839).

Every two years, Georgetown is the focus of statewide attention with the traditional celebration of **"Return Day,"** two days after Election Day. All candidates for office, victorious and otherwise, gather at Georgetown. The highlight is a reading of the election results, but the festivities include a parade that pairs winners and losers of all statewide and county races in horse-drawn carriages and antique autos, followed by speeches and revelry.

The newest attraction in the area is the **Treasures of the Sea Exhibit,** Route 18, Georgetown (☎ 302/856-5700). Located just west of the town and west of Route 113 at the Delaware Technical and Community College, this display presents a collection of gold, silver, and other artifacts recovered from the 1622 shipwreck of the Spanish galleon *Nuestra Senora de Atocha.* It's open year-round Monday and Tuesday 10am to 4pm, Friday noon to 4pm, and Saturday 9am to 1pm. Admission charge is $2 for adults, $1 for students and seniors, and free for children 4 and under.

Two other exhibits are also on view, free of charge, at Delaware Technical and Community College: the **Elsie Williams Doll Collection,** with hundreds of dolls from around the world (open year-round Monday through Thursday 8am to 10:30pm, Friday 8am to 4:30pm, and Saturday 8:30am to 1pm); and the **Trees of the States,** an outdoor arboretum exhibit displaying the official state trees from all 50 states and the District of Columbia (open year-round, dawn to dusk).

2 Rehoboth & Dewey Beaches

43 miles SE of Dover, 88 miles SE of Wilmington, 7 miles from Lewes, 27 miles N of Ocean City, 124 miles SE of Washington, D.C., 110 miles SE of Baltimore, 120 miles S of Philadelphia

Of all the Delaware beaches, the most popular is Rehoboth, a small year-round coastal community that swells from its normal population of approximately 4,000 in winter to more than 50,000 in the summer months. Though considered small by most standards, it's Delaware's largest Atlantic shore town.

Founded on strong religious traditions, Rehoboth traces its origin to 1873, when it was selected by the Methodist church as a site for summer camp meetings. It was an inspirational spot, with the ocean waves meeting the sandy shores amid groves of holly and pine. Even the name, Rehoboth, is biblical in origin, meaning "room enough."

Rehoboth's popularity owes much to its idyllic location—a pleasant tree-shaded strip of land, bordered on the east by the Atlantic, on the west by the Rehoboth-Lewes Canal, and on the south by a natural waterfowl refuge called Silver Lake.

The town is immaculately maintained, with many Victorian homes and turn-of-the-century cottages, tree-lined streets, up-to-date motels, fine restaurants, and all kinds of shops.

Neighboring Dewey Beach, named for Spanish-American War hero Adm. George Dewey, is a relatively new community. Nestled just south of Rehoboth Beach on the lower shore of Silver Lake, Dewey is an unusual stretch of real estate—only two blocks wide, divided in the center by Route 1 (also known as Highway 1 and Ocean Highway), with the Atlantic Ocean on the east and Rehoboth Bay to the west.

No matter where people walk at Dewey Beach, they always have views of the water. And the views can be mesmerizing—from the amber sunrise on splashing ocean waves in early morning to the golden sunset over the calm ripples of Rehoboth Bay each evening.

In contrast to Rehoboth Beach, Dewey is the shore's youngest town. Although there is no boardwalk, the entire strip along Route 1 is lined with motels, beach houses, apartments, restaurants, and fast-food establishments, all catering to a beach-going clientele. The beach is also a lively nighttime spot, making it a great favorite with young vacationers.

GETTING THERE   By Plane   The closest gateways for regularly scheduled flights from all parts of the United States are Philadelphia International Airport and Baltimore International Airport. For commuter flights, the nearest gateways are Ocean City and Salisbury, Maryland.

By Train   There is daily service from all parts of the United States via **Amtrak** into Wilmington (see "Arriving," in Chapter 8).

By Bus   Carolina Trailways provides regular service into the Rehoboth Bus Center, 251 Rehoboth Ave., Rehoboth Beach (☎ 302/227-7223 or 800/441-1329). **Blue Diamond Lines** (☎ 302/577-6686 or 800/652-DART), operates weekday service from Wilmington via Dover to Rehoboth Beach, stopping at Rehoboth Avenue at the Boardwalk.

By Car   From points north or south, take Routes 113 and 13 to Route 1.

By Ferry   See "Lewes," earlier in this chapter.

ESSENTIALS   Area Code   The area code is 302.

Visitor Information   Sightseeing brochures, maps, descriptions of accommodations, and restaurant listings are available from the Rehoboth Beach-Dewey Beach Chamber of Commerce, 501 Rehoboth Ave., P.O. Box 216, Rehoboth Beach, DE 19971 (☎ 302/227-2233 or 800/441-1329). The office is open year-round Monday through Friday, from 9am to 4:30pm; in addition, from Memorial Day through Labor Day there are Saturday and Sunday hours from 10am to 2pm.

GETTING AROUND   By Bus   From Memorial Day through Labor Day, Delaware Resort Transit/DRT (☎ 302/226-2001) operates daily bus shuttle service between Route 1 and the Rehoboth Beach boardwalk and other nearby beach points. The daily cost is $1 per person or $4 per car, which includes parking, with unlimited reboarding privileges.

By Trolley   Between Memorial Day and Labor Day, the Jolly Trolley (☎ 302/227-1197), an independent firm, also operates a shuttle service between Rehoboth Beach, starting at the Boardwalk and Rehoboth Avenue, to Dewey Beach. The service runs daily from 7am to 3am, on the hour and half hour; in May and

September it operates on weekends only. The cost is $1 per ride for adults and free for children under 12. You can board at any signposted stop along the route.

On Foot For walking on your own, the Rehoboth Beach Downtown Business Association publishes a handy "Downtown Rehoboth Beach Walking Guide," showing the main streets and arteries, the Boardwalk, and shops, restaurants, and businesses of interest to visitors. It's free and available at shops and from the chamber of commerce office.

By Car Parking in Rehoboth Beach can be difficult. Metered parking is in effect (30 minutes, hourly, and up to 12 hours, with the majority of machines programmed for the first two time limits). This system operates from 10am to midnight on weekends during May and seven days a week from June 1 to one week after Labor Day; head-in or parallel parking only is permitted. The number of spaces can rarely accommodate the demand; to ease the situation, most lodging places offer free parking to their guests and many people choose to park their car and leave it at the hotel or motel until departure for home. Rehoboth is small enough that walking usually proves to be the best way to get around.

WHAT TO SEE & DO

Most of Rehoboth Beach's activity emanates from the 1-mile-long Boardwalk and Rehoboth Avenue, the main street that runs perpendicular to the Boardwalk at its center point. The Boardwalk itself features the standard mix of amusements, games, fast-food concessions, and shops to be found at the beach. When the mood strikes, don't miss two unique Rehoboth experiences: Dolle's Taffy (established 1927) and Grotto's Pizza (operating since 1960).

Dewey Beach offers a wide and sandy Atlantic Ocean beachfront and a busy bay front overlooking Rehoboth Bay.

OUTDOOR ACTIVITIES

BICYCLING With its flat terrain and shady streets, Rehoboth Beach is ideal for bicycling. Bikes are allowed on the Boardwalk during the hours of 5am to 10am from May 15 to September 15. Two companies offers rentals to visitors. **Bob's Bicycle Rentals,** 30 Maryland Ave. (☎ 302/227-7966), located between Baltimore and Maryland Avenues, rents one-speed touring bikes ($2–$5 per hour, $7–$15 per day), mountain bikes ($2.50–$3 per hour, $8–$10 per day), and tandems ($3.50–$5 per hour, $10–$15 per day). Bob's is open Memorial Day through Labor Day, daily 9am to 6pm or later; hours vary the rest of the year. **Wheels Bicycle Shop,** 318 Rehoboth Ave. (☎ 302/227-6807), is conveniently situated on the main thoroughfare. This well-stocked shop rents a variety of cruising bikes. In the peak season, it also operates a rental station on the Boardwalk at Virginia Avenue (☎ 302/227-8520). The prices are $3 per hour, $12 per day; the hours are 9am to 6pm or later daily Memorial Day through Labor Day (they vary the rest of the year).

WATER SPORTS Swimming at Rehoboth's wide sandy beaches is one of the area's top activities. All the beaches have public access.

Bay Sports, 11 Dickinson St., Dewey Beach (☎ 302/227-7590), rents Windsurfers, Sunfish, and jet skis by the half hour or hour or by the day. Rates for a Windsurfer or Sunfish are $22 first hour, $32 for two hours, $42 for three hours; and jet skis are $30 to $60 for a half hour. Sailing and windsurfing lessons are also arranged.

For a selection of water sports, plan to visit the **Delaware Seashore State Park Inlet 850,** Route 1 (☎ 302/227-2800), located 2 miles south of Rehoboth Beach. This 10-mile-long beach paradise offers both the crashing surf of the Atlantic and the gentle waters of Rehoboth Bay. Its facilities include lifeguard-supervised swimming, surfing, and fishing. In addition, it has a full-service boating marina and a bay-shore campground with more than 300 sites for RVs and trailers. Admission to the park is $2.50 for Delaware cars and $5 for out-of-state vehicles.

ATTRACTIONS

If the weather turns cloudy or your skin turns too red, move off the beach and see what else Rehoboth has to offer.

Anna Hazzard Museum

17 Christian St. (on Martin's Lawn, off Rehoboth Ave.). ☎ **302/226-1119.** Admission free. Advance appointment only.

Named for a former owner and civic leader, this house is one of the original "tent" buildings erected during Rehoboth's camp-meeting era. It's a good place from which to gain a perspective on Rehoboth and its early days. (*Note:* As we went to press, the museum was undergoing renovation; it should be fully operational again by 1996. Call before you visit for an update.)

Rehoboth Art League

12 Dodds Lane. ☎ **320/227-8408.** Admission free; special events $1–$10. Oct and Feb–Apr, weekdays 10am–4pm; May–Sept Mon–Sat 10am–4pm and Sun 1–4pm.

Nestled in the Henlopen Acres section of town amid three acres of gardens and walking paths and an outdoor sculpture area, this facility includes three galleries, a teaching studio, and a restored mansion. It offers exhibits by local and nationally known talent, art classes, workshops, and cultural performances.

Rehoboth Railroad Station Visitors Center

501 Rehoboth Ave. ☎ **302/227-2233.** Admission free. Memorial Day–Labor Day, weekdays 9am–4:30pm, Sun 10am–2pm; rest of year, Mon–Fri 9am–4:30pm.

This recently restored building, located in Lighthouse Island Park, serves as the visitor center for the chamber of commerce. Erected in 1879, when there was regular train service to Rehoboth Beach, the station is a good example of late Victorian style and ornamentation. It was a focal point for the town for several decades, as locomotive trains brought visitors from faraway cities, but service came to an end in the late 1920s.

ORGANIZED TOURS

There's more to Rehoboth than its beach and Boardwalk, and the best way to see the town's highlights is to take a ride on the **Jolly Trolley** (☎ 302/227-1197), a 55-minute narrated sightseeing tour. Operating daily from Memorial Day through Labor Day and some weekends in September, the trolley departs from Rehoboth Beach and the Boardwalk at 10am, 1pm, and 4pm. Cost is $5 for adults, $3 for seniors and for students 12 to 18, and $1 for children 2 to 12.

ESPECIALLY FOR KIDS

Rehoboth Summer Children's Theatre is operated at the Epworth United Methodist Church, 20 Baltimore Ave. (☎ 302/227-6766). Curtain time is at 7:30pm on Tuesday, Wednesday, and Thursday. Prices range from $4 to $7, depending on the event. The repertoire includes *Snow White, Robin Hood,* and *Peter Pan.*

Rehoboth Beach has two summertime Boardwalk family amusement areas: **Funland,** situated between Brooklyn and Delaware Avenues, which has rides and games (opens at 1pm daily); and **Playland,** 101 S. Boardwalk, off Wilmington Avenue, which features video games for all ages (open from 10am to midnight). About $1^1/_2$ miles north of town there's also **Sports Complex,** Route 1 and Country Club Road (☎ 302/227-8121). This is a family-fun park with go-kart tracks, miniature golf, a water slide, bumper boats, kiddie canoes, and other outdoor rides. Open weekends May and September and daily from Memorial Day to Labor Day.

SHOPPING

Downtown Rehoboth Beach's streets are lined with shops. Some are clustered in minimalls such as **Gingerbread Square Mall,** 167 Rehoboth Ave.; **Village-by-the-Sea Mall,** 149 Rehoboth Ave.; **Rehoboth Mews,** 127–129 Rehoboth Ave.; and **Penny Lane Mall,** 42 Rehoboth Ave. On the outskirts of town, factory outlets, along Route 1, are the main attractions.

Christmas Spirit
129 Rehoboth Ave. ☎ **302/227-6872.**

It's Christmas year-round in this delightful shop, stocked full of trees, lights, handcrafted ornaments from around the world, angel tree tops, tree skirts, vintage Victorian decorations, candles, nutcrackers, character Santas, lighted villages and figurines, gift wrap, and more. Open daily from 10am to 6pm or later.

Mizzen Mast
149 Rehoboth Ave. ☎ **302/227-3646.**

Dedicated to the good nature in all of us, this shop features environmentally friendly and recycled products, such as Birkenstock footprint sandals, nature music, T-shirts, pottery, notepads, stickers, mugs, cards, posters, games, stuffed animals, and hand-painted birds. Open daily from 10am to 6pm or later.

Ocean Outlets—Bayside and Seaside
Route 1. ☎ **302/227-6860** or 302/227-4845.

Situated on both sides of the main highway, these two outlet complexes house more than 70 shops. Manufacturers represented include Aileen, American Tourister, Corning Revere, Eddie Bauer, Jockey, Izod/LaCoste, Oneida, Reebok, Totes, and Van Heusen. Open Monday to Saturday from 10am to 9pm and Sunday from 10am to 6pm, with extended hours from July to September.

Olde Salt Gift Shop
42 Rehoboth Ave. ☎ **302/227-1210.**

Tucked in the Penny Lane Mall, this shop stocks nautically themed gifts, such as books on Chesapeake Bay, illustrated maps, watercolors, and miniature lighthouses, as well as Christmas items, Dickens Village collectibles, and baking tools. Open January to March, Saturday to Sunday, from 11am to 5pm; April to Dec, daily from 10am to 11pm.

Sea Shell Shop
119 Rehoboth Ave. ☎ **302/227-6666.**

This shop is a treasure trove of seashell art, lamps, jewelry, and gifts, as well as loose shells, sponges, coral, and hermit crab souvenirs. Other locations are at Bellevue Street and Highway 1, Dewey Beach (☎ 302/227-6695) and Bethany Beach, 206 Garfield Pkwy. (☎ 302/539-6611). Open daily from 10am to 6pm or later.

Wild Birds Unlimited
49 Baltimore Ave. ☎ **302/227-5850.**

For nature lovers, this shop offers bird-themed stained glass, chimes, art, and books, as well as bird houses and bird-feeding equipment. Open June through August daily from 10am to 10pm, and September to May daily from 10am to 5pm; occasionally closed Tuesday through Thursday in January and February.

WHERE TO STAY

Most of the accommodations in Rehoboth and Dewey are moderate. In July and August, however, you may encounter difficulty finding any room (single or double occupancy) near the beach for under $100 a night; if you must be by the water, be ready to pay for it. You may want to travel here in May, June, September, or October instead. But if you come at the height of the summer, be prepared to accept lodgings on side streets without views of the water and with compulsory minimum stays. In any case, reservations are always necessary in the summer and strongly recommended at other times.

REHOBOTH BEACH
Very Expensive/Expensive

✪ Atlantic Sands Hotel & Suites
101 N. Boardwalk, Rehoboth Beach, DE 19971. ☎ **302/227-2511** or 800/422-0600. Fax 302/227-9476. 114 rms. A/C TV TEL. $60–$259 double. AE, DC, DISC, MC, V. Free parking.

Situated on the Boardwalk between Baltimore and Maryland Avenues, the five-story Atlantic Sands is Rehoboth's largest hotel and the only oceanfront property in town with an outdoor ground-level swimming pool. Besides an ideal location, it also offers newly refurbished guest rooms, all with a balcony and view of the water. Each unit is furnished with light woods or rattan furniture, brass fixtures, seashell art and accessories, silk and dried floral arrangements, and fabrics of sea, sky, and sand tones. Some rooms also have a Jacuzzi bath, a wet bar, and a refrigerator. In the summer months, the hotel operates a buffet-style restaurant, featuring all-you-can-eat breakfasts and dinners. Among the facilities are a hot tub, a rooftop sundeck, and a game room.

Boardwalk Plaza
2 Olive Ave., Rehoboth Beach, DE 19971. ☎ **302/227-7169** or 800/33-BEACH. Fax 302/227-0561. 33 rms, 39 suites. A/C TV TEL. $60–$300 standard room; $70–$350 ocean-view room; $100–$395 oceanfront deluxe room; $80–$360 ocean-view suite; $90–$390 oceanfront suite. AE, DC, DISC, MC, V. Free parking.

With a fanciful pink-and-white gingerbread facade, this four-story, Victorian-style hotel stands out on the Boardwalk. The Victorian theme is also evident inside, with an antique-filled lobby complete with live talking parrots in gilded cages, and guest rooms decorated with rich dark-wood reproduction furniture and frilly fabrics. Most of the rooms have a balcony, with a full or partial view of the ocean, a refrigerator, and a coffeemaker. Facilities include an oceanfront restaurant, an indoor and outdoor heated spa pool, a rooftop sundeck, and an exercise room.

Expensive/Moderate

✪ Brighton Suites Hotel
34 Wilmington Ave., Rehoboth Beach, DE 19971. ☎ **302/227-5780** or 800/227-5788. Fax 302/227-6815. 66 suites. A/C TV TEL. $59–$189 suite. AE, DISC, MC, V. Free parking.

For families or two couples traveling together, this all-suite hotel is a good choice, a short walk from the beach, at the corner of First Street. Each unit in this sandy pink four-story property has a bedroom with a king-size bed, a large bathroom, and a separate living room with sleep-sofa. Features include a wet bar, refrigerator, a safe, and a hair dryer. A three-night minimum stay applies for holidays and summer weekends. In the summer months, there is a child-care service on some evenings, and there is a heated indoor pool on the premises.

○ Henlopen Hotel

511 N. Boardwalk, Rehoboth Beach, DE 19971. ☎ **302/227-2551** or 800/441-8450. Fax 302/227-8147. 92 rms. A/C TV TEL. $55–$140 standard, $75–$170 studio, $95–$195 oceanfront. AE, CB, DC, MC, V. Free parking. Closed Nov–Mar.

Situated between Lake Avenue and Grenoble Place, on the north end of the Boardwalk, this beachfront hotel has a tradition dating from 1879, when the first Henlopen Hotel was built on this site. The present modern structure has 12 oceanfront rooms and 80 rooms with an ocean view, each with its own balcony. All rooms have a coffeemaker, and some come with a microwave and a refrigerator. Dining facilities include Rehoboth's only rooftop restaurant and lounge, overlooking the beach and the boardwalk. There are two-night minimums for all weekend bookings and three-night minimums for holiday weekend reservations.

Moderate

Admiral Motel

2 Baltimore Ave., Rehoboth Beach, DE 19971. ☎ **302/227-2103** or 800/428-2424. 66 rms. A/C TV TEL. $45–$139 double. AE, MC, V. Free parking.

In the heart of the beach district, this modern, five-story motel is a favorite with families—children under 11 stay free in their parents' room. It has an indoor-outdoor rooftop swimming pool and a sundeck with a Jacuzzi. All rooms have a partial ocean view, a refrigerator, and a coffeemaker; most units have a private balcony. There are three-night minimums in the summer and supplementary charges for some peak or holiday weekends.

Oceanus Motel

6 Second St., P.O. Box 324, Rehoboth Beach, DE 19971. ☎ **302/227-9436** or 800/852-5011. 38 rms. A/C TV TEL. $45–$139 double. (All rates include continental breakfast.) DISC, MC, V. Free parking. Closed Nov–late Mar.

This L-shaped, three-story motel lies two blocks from the beach and just off Rehoboth Avenue in a quiet neighborhood. Each room is outfitted with extra-length beds in a setting of nautically toned furniture, plus a refrigerator; most rooms have a balcony overlooking the pool. Guest facilities include an outdoor swimming pool and patio area. At certain times weekend supplements of $10 to $20 a night prevail.

Sandcastle Motel

123 Second St., off Rehoboth Ave., Rehoboth Beach, DE 19971. ☎ **302/227-0400** or 800/372-2112. 60 rms. A/C TV TEL. $42–$125 double. AE, MC, V. Free parking. Closed Jan–Feb.

Built in the shape of a sugary-white sandcastle, this unique, five-story motel is situated two blocks from the beach and right off the main shop-lined thoroughfare. Each of the large and well-laid-out rooms has a private balcony and a refrigerator. The motel's facilities include an enclosed parking garage, an elevated sundeck, and an indoor and outdoor swimming pool with lifeguard. Minimum stays apply during peak season.

DEWEY BEACH
Expensive/Moderate

Atlantic Oceanside
1700 Hwy. 1, Dewey Beach, DE 19971. ☎ **302/227-8811** or 800/422-0481. 60 rms. A/C TV TEL. $35–$109 double. AE, MC, V. Free parking. Closed Nov–Apr.

Situated between Dagsworth and McKinley streets, this modern, three-story structure is set on the main north-south beach highway and enjoys equal distance from the bay and the ocean (both about a block away). The rooms are of the standard motel variety, but each has a coffeemaker, a microwave oven, and a refrigerator. The facilities include an outdoor heated pool and a sundeck. A weekend surcharge is in effect at certain periods, and a three-night minimum stay is required for summer weekends.

✪ Bay Resort
Bellevue Street, P.O. Box 461, Dewey Beach, DE 19971. ☎ **302/227-6400** or 800/ 922-9240. 68 rms. A/C TV TEL. $45–$139 double. (Rates include continental breakfast.) DISC, MC, V. Free parking. Closed Nov–late Mar.

The ideal place from which to watch the sun go down on Rehoboth Bay is at this three-story motel complex, located on a strip of land between the bay and the ocean. Guest units, each with a small kitchenette and a balcony, face either the pool or the bay. The facilities include an outdoor pool, a water-sports center, a private beach, and a 250-foot pier on the bay. Depending on the time of year, there can also be a weekend surcharge of $15 to $25 per night and a three-night minimum on holidays.

ⓢ Best Western Gold Leaf
1400 Hwy. 1, Dewey Beach, DE 19971. ☎ **302/226-1100** or 800/422-8566 or 800/ 528-1234. Fax 302/226-9785. 76 rms. A/C TV TEL. $48–$178 double. AE, CB, DC, DISC, MC, V. Free parking.

Located one block from both the beach and the bay, this modern, four-story motel is situated across the street from the Ruddertowne complex. It offers bright, contemporary rooms with balcony and a view of the bay, ocean, or both. Rooms are also equipped with a refrigerator and a safe. Facilities include enclosed parking, a rooftop swimming pool and sundeck. There's a weekend surcharge and two- and three-night minimums in the summer. Complimentary coffee is provided for guests in the lobby. Open year-round, with reduced-rate packages November through March.

WHERE TO DINE
Some motels do not have restaurants, so here are the two best bets for a morning meal: **Royal Treat** (8 to 11:30am) and or the **Lamp Post** (7 to 11am). For addresses and telephone numbers, see below.

REHOBOTH BEACH
Expensive

Back Porch Cafe
59 Rehoboth Ave. ☎ **302/227-3674.** Reservations recommended on weekends. Main courses $20–$26; lunch $8–$10. MC, V. Apr–Oct, daily 11am–3pm and 6–11pm. INTERNATIONAL.

For more than 20 years, a Key West atmosphere has prevailed at this restaurant, where the emphasis is on fresh foods creatively prepared and presented.

The decor is a mix of indoor alcoves with three outdoor decks, all furnished with an eclectic collection of plants, stained glass, and handmade tables. Lunch items include various omelets, basil ratatouille, and sampler plates. Dinner entrées include rosemary-scented duck, spice-crusted tenderloin of beef, pan-seared salmon, grilled sweetbreads with artichokes and morel ragout, and roast rockfish in lemon champagne sauce.

Blue Moon

35 Baltimore Ave. ☎ **302/227-6515.** Reservations required. Main courses $16–$26. AE, DISC, MC, V. Mar–Dec, Mon–Sat 6–10pm; Sun 11am–2pm and 6–10pm. AMERICAN/ INTERNATIONAL.

Located off the main thoroughfare, between First and Second Streets, this restaurant is housed in an eye-catching blue-and-cream-colored beach cottage. The interior features curved banquettes, indirect lighting, exotic flower arrangements, and rotating art exhibits by local and international artists. California and Pacific Rim styles of cooking are featured, and the chef buys from a local grower who specializes in gourmet herbs. Entrées range from braided salmon and sole with saffron risotto in champagne sauce to Thai-seasoned duck breast with coconut-curry sauce. Seared beef tenderloin with a dry vermouth and Dijon mustard sauce and a variety of pastas are also available.

✪ Chez La Mer

210 Second St. ☎ **302/227-6494.** Reservations required. Main courses $15–$28. AE, DC, MC, V. June–Sept, Mon–Thurs 5:30–10pm, Fri–Sat 5:30–10:30pm; Apr–May and Oct–Nov, Wed or Thurs–Sunday 5–10pm. CONTINENTAL.

Although this area is full of good restaurants, Chez La Mer is the only one with French country inn decor, cuisine, and service; it's no wonder that the three intimate little dining rooms fill up quickly. The menu changes several times during the year, but specialties often include veal sweetbreads, soft-shell crabs, and a spicy bouillabaisse. All dishes are cooked to order, and special diets, such as low sodium, can be accommodated. Neat attire is a must.

Club Potpourri

316 Rehoboth Ave. ☎ **302/227-4227.** Reservations recommended on weekends. Main courses $15.50–$21.50. AE, DC, MC, V. Dinner June–Sept Mon–Thurs 5–11pm, Fri–Sat 5pm–midnight; Oct–April Wed–Sat 5–10pm. INTERNATIONAL.

A classy cafe ambience prevails at this restaurant, a mecca for fans of live jazz as well as good food. The decor blends brass, globe lanterns, skylights, mirrored walls, and lots of garden plants. The dinner menu ranges from jambalaya and Southwest grilled chicken to pan-roasted rib of veal, filet mignon, and rack of lamb. Early bird specials are featured from 5 to 7pm in the summer.

La La Land

22 Wilmington Ave. ☎ **302/227-3887.** Reservations required. Main courses $18–$24. CB, DISC, MC, V. May–Oct Sun–Thurs 6–10pm, Fri–Sat 6–11pm. INTERNATIONAL.

Located on a side street off the Boardwalk, this highly acclaimed restaurant specializes blending California influence with Asian and southwestern overtones. There's seating indoors in an art-filled pink, purple, and periwinkle-toned dining room and outdoors on a patio with a bamboo garden setting. The menu offers a variety of creative choices: cured salmon tartar with cucumbers, basil cream, and black olives; sautéed Norwegian salmon wrapped in rice paper; seared noisettes of lamb with wild-rice custard; striped bass sautéed in pine nuts; crisp-skin Canadian salmon; and mixed grill of rack of lamb with duck breast.

Expensive/Moderate

✪ Sea Horse

330 Rehoboth Ave. ☎ **302/227-7451.** Reservations recommended for dinner. Main courses $12.95–$26.95; lunch $4.95–$12.95. AE, CB, DC, MC, V. Mon–Thurs 11:30am–10pm, Fri–Sat 11:30am–11pm. INTERNATIONAL.

A mainstay for more than 25 years in Rehoboth Beach, the Sea Horse is hard to beat for quality food and hefty portions. The plush and welcoming dining rooms are filled with sturdy captain's chairs, copper lanterns, a huge stone fireplace, mirrored panels, carpeted walls, and floral prints. Lunch ranges from burgers to crab imperial. Dinner offers a wide selection of beef (from prime rib to chateaubriand) and seafood (gulf shrimp, crab cakes, snow crab legs, scallops Dijon, rock lobster tails, and many local fresh fish). The restaurant provides a large guest parking lot.

Summer House

228 Rehoboth Ave. ☎ **302/227-3895.** Reservations recommended on weekends. Main courses $9.95–$23.95; light fare $5.95–$8.95. AE, DISC, MC, V. Apr–Oct, daily 5–10pm. SEAFOOD.

Situated on the main thoroughfare next to the Rehoboth Public Library and across from the Convention Hall, this restaurant exudes a festive resort atmosphere in its Gazebo and Aspen dining rooms. The menu emphasizes seafood, with such choices as crab Rolande (lump crab with green and red peppers, mozzarella, hollandaise, and onion) and a house "treasure" consisting of broiled crab cake, shrimp, scallops, swordfish, and brandied clams casino. In addition, there are more than a half-dozen steak, filet mignon, and chicken dishes. Burgers, sandwiches, and other light items are also offered for more informal dining at lower prices.

✪ Sydney's

25 Christian St. ☎ **302/227-1339.** Reservations recommended on weekends. Main courses $14–$19; grazing portions $9–$11. AE, DISC, DC, MC, V. May–Oct, Sun–Tues and Thurs 5:30–10pm and Fri–Sat 5:30–11pm; Nov–April, Thurs–Sun 5:30–10pm. LOUISIANAN.

Located in an old schoolhouse and run by Sydney Arzt, a former schoolteacher, this restaurant is known for its nightly jazz and blues sessions as well as its unique grazing menu, allowing customers to sample more than one main course. Grazing entrées include jambalaya with andouille sausage, duck, chicken, and shrimp; shrimp and scallop stir-fry with spinach, pine nuts, and ginger over wild rice; filet of beef with caramelized red onions and angel-hair pasta pancake; and herbed Cornish hen with chicken sausage, sweet potato, and pink peppercorn sauce. The candlelit decor is also an attraction, with a skylit ceiling from which gold and silver mobile ornaments are suspended and black-and-white photos of Hollywood stars on the walls.

Moderate

Ann Marie's Italian and Seafood Restaurant

208 Second St. ☎ **302/227-9902.** Reservations not accepted. Main courses $7.95–$19.95. DISC, MC, V. June–Aug, Mon–Thurs 5–10pm, Fri–Sun 5–11pm; May and Sept–Oct, Thurs–Sat 5–10pm, Sun 4–10pm. ITALIAN.

Established in 1977, this beach-house restaurant is located on the corner of Wilmington Avenue, just off the main thoroughfare. Bringing the atmosphere and flavors of Italy to the beach, it offers a wide variety of freshly made pastas, especially homemade lasagne, a family recipe and a Rehoboth culinary icon for some

20 years. Other mainstays include veal (Parmesan, alla Marsala, and piccata), prime rib, lobster, surf-and-turf, shrimp and seafood cacciatore, shrimp and scallops in marinara sauce, and crab cakes.

☉ Lamp Post

Routes 1 and 24. ☎ **302/645-9132.** Reservations not accepted. Main courses $8.95–$25; lunch $3.95–$11.95; breakfast $2.50–$8.95. AE, DISC, MC, V. Sun–Thurs 7am–9pm, Fri–Sat 7am–10pm. SEAFOOD/STEAK.

Far from the boardwalk and the action of downtown Rehoboth, this restaurant sits along the main highway, 3 miles north of town, a convenient find for a change of pace from beachfront life or if you're in transit along the coast. Opened in 1953 as the Drexel Diner by award-winning restaurateur Ruth Steele, this friendly spot has been expanded by three generations of the Steele family. Tables are handcrafted from authentic hatch-cover tops from the Liberty ships of World War II. The menu focuses on fresh local flounder served in a variety of ways, including "Henlopen"-style (stuffed with shrimp, sea scallops, provolone cheese, and seasonings), as well as a half-dozen types of hand-cut steaks and prime rib (weekends only). House specials also include "Chicken Delaware" (sautéed breast of chicken topped with a grilled slice of ham, mushrooms, and melted cheddar cheese) and "shrimp sauté Rehoboth Beach" (shrimp with artichoke hearts, sun-dried tomatoes, onion, mushrooms, and Parmesan cheese).

Obie's by the Sea

On the Boardwalk (at Olive Ave.). ☎ **302/227-6261.** Main courses $4.95–$14.95. AE, MC, V. Daily 11:30am–1am. Closed Nov–Apr. AMERICAN.

You can't dine any closer to the ocean than at this restaurant, situated beside the Boardwalk between Virginia and Olive Avenues. A casual seaside atmosphere prevails here, with an all-day menu of sandwiches, burgers, ribs, salads, and "clam bakes" (steamed clams, spiced shrimp, barbecued chicken, corn on the cob, and muffins). There's DJ music and dancing on weekends.

Inexpensive

Dream Cafe

26 Baltimore Ave. ☎ **302/226-CAFE.** All items 75¢–$5.95. AE, DISC, MC, V. June–Sept, daily 7am–10pm; Mar–May, Fri–Mon 7am–6pm. AMERICAN.

Conveniently situated between the Boardwalk and First Street, this bright and airy cafe offers a fine selection of fresh-baked breads, baguettes, bagels, croissants, and pastries, as well as gourmet salads, sandwiches, pâtés, quiches, pastas, and tempting desserts. Exotic coffees and herbal teas are also available. Eat-in and take-out service is provided.

Grotto's Pizza

36 Rehoboth Ave. ☎ **302/227-3575.** Reservations not accepted. Main courses $4.95–$6.95; whole pizzas $6.95–$16.95. AE, DISC, MC, V. Daily 11am–11pm. PIZZA/FAST FOOD.

One of the great traditions in the area, this informal eatery specializes in pizzas of all sizes. The menu also offers salads, pasta, subs, burgers, and chicken. Other locations are at the Boardwalk, Rehoboth Beach (☎ 302/227-3601) and Route 1, Dewey Beach (☎ 302/227-3407).

Pierre's Pantry

First St. (at Wilmington Ave.). ☎ **302/227-7537.** All items $1–$8. No credit cards. Sept–May, Wed–Mon 7:30am–5pm; Memorial Day–Labor Day, daily 7am–9pm. AMERICAN.

Located in a shopping complex known as Times Square, this bright eatery offers a 50-seat indoor dining area and take-out service. Specialties include Brooklyn bagel sandwiches; vegetarian dishes; and creative homemade soups, such as tomato-basil walnut, red bell-pepper with yellow squash, and lentils with Italian sausage. Summer dinner items include baked local fish, vegetarian rice casserole, and signature dishes, such as Chicken Russell—chicken breast stuffed with smoked Havarti cheese and topped with raspberry melba.

Royal Treat

4 Wilmington Ave. ☎ **302/227-6277.** Reservations not accepted. All items $2–$7. No credit cards. May–Oct Breakfast daily 8–11:30am; ice cream daily 1–11:30pm. AMERICAN.

For breakfast and refreshing snacks, try this airy restaurant, a restored Rehoboth landmark, next to the Boardwalk, with an ice cream parlor ambience. Breakfast favorites include pancakes, French toast, and old-fashioned omelets.

DEWEY BEACH
Moderate

✪ Rusty Rudder

113 Dickinson St. (on the bay). ☎ **302/227-3888.** Dinner main courses $11.95–$25.95; lunch $4.95–$7.95. MC, V. Lunch daily 11:30am–5pm, dinner daily 4:30–11pm; Sun brunch 10am–2pm. AMERICAN.

Opened in 1979, this large, California-style restaurant is a favorite gathering place for young beachgoers. Situated right on the bay, it offers great water views from indoor and outdoor dining rooms, open decks, and terraces. Dinner entrées, which allow for unlimited trips to the bountiful salad bar, include chicken cordon bleu or Parmesan pan-fried backfin crab cakes, and prime rib, as well as enormous seafood and shellfish platters. Lunches range from salads and sandwiches to Cajun catfish and other fish specials. There's nightly entertainment, with frequent big-name concerts on weekends.

Starboard

2009 Hwy. 1. ☎ **302/227-4600.** Breakfast and lunch items $2.95–$10.95; main courses $7.95–$13.95. AE, DC, DISC, MC, V. Mid-Mar to end-Oct, daily 7am–1am. AMERICAN.

A popular Dewey Beach gathering spot for more than 30 years, this informal restaurant is situated on the bay side of the main highway at the corner of Saulsbury Street. It's famous for its large collection of hot sauces (more than 2,000) and for its Bloody Mary breakfasts with make-your-own omelets and pancakes with fruit toppings. Menu choices range from daily fresh-fish specials, cooked to order and served with a variety of sauces, to popular favorites such as shrimp salad, seafood lasagne, chicken cordon bleu, veal Parmesan, spaghetti and meatballs, and prime rib.

Waterfront

McKinley St. (on the bay). ☎ **302/227-9292.** Main courses $7.95–$16.95; lunch $2.95–$6.95. AE, MC, V. Daily noon–1am. Closed Oct–Apr. AMERICAN.

Bay-side sunsets and charcoal-grilled meats and seafood are the main draws at this restaurant, which boasts an open deck, a gazebo, and wide-windowed dining rooms overlooking the water. Known for its outdoor, open-pit barbecue cooking, it offers barbecue shrimp and burgers, plus soups, salads, and sandwiches for lunch; dinner entrées include barbecued ribs, chicken, steaks, and shish kebabs, as well as one-pound lobsters and a variety of other steamed, baked, and broiled seafood.

Moderate/Inexpensive

Crabbers' Cove

Dickenson St. ☎ **302/227-3888.** Main courses $8.95–$17.95. MC, V. May–Sept, daily 4–9pm. SEAFOOD.

Located on the bay in the Ruddertowne complex, this is a casual open-air family seafood restaurant featuring a variety of all-you-can-eat foods popular with children. Entrées include steak, fried chicken, barbecued ribs, fish fry, shrimp-in-a-basket, and steamed hard crabs, as well as filet of flounder, mako shark steak, gulf shrimp, steamed mussels, and crab cakes.

REHOBOTH & DEWEY BEACHES AFTER DARK

CONCERT HALLS/THEATERS

There's always music in the air at Rehoboth and Dewey Beaches, whether indoors or outdoors.

✪ Rehoboth Beach Memorial Bandstand

Rehoboth Ave. (at the Boardwalk), Rehoboth Beach. ☎ **302/227-2233.** Free. Memorial Day–Labor Day, Fri–Sun 8–9:30pm.

A unique Rehoboth tradition, this open-air bandstand presents more than 40 concerts and other musical events in the summer months. Check with the chamber of commerce office for an up-to-date schedule.

Sea Horse Cabaret

330 Rehoboth Ave. (at State Rd.), Rehoboth Beach. ☎ **302/227-7451.** Tickets $26.95–$27.95 per person plus gratuity.

Headquartered at the Sea Horse restaurant, this dinner theater features Broadway musical hits, preceded by a sumptuous buffet dinner. Seating is at 6pm, and show starts at 7:30pm, Mid-March through December.

CLUBS & BARS

Nationally known jazz and blues artists entertain year-round at **Sydney's,** 25 Christian St. (☎ 302/227-1339). Shows are nightly except Wednesday from mid-May through mid-September and on Friday and Saturday nights at other times; cover charge is $3 to $5 or free, depending on the group, and there is no cover charge for dinner guests.

The lilting sing-along sounds of Ireland are heard Thursday through Saturday in the summer at **Irish Eyes,** 15 Wilmington Ave. (☎ 302/227-2888). Classic rock and roll or DJ music is played on other nights. Cover charge varies.

3 Bethany Beach & Fenwick Island

12 miles S of Rehoboth Beach, 60 miles SE of Dover, 100 miles SE of Wilmington, 23 miles S of Lewes, 130 miles SE of Washington, D.C., 120 miles SE of Baltimore, 135 miles S of Philadelphia

Bethany Beach and Fenwick Island form a thin, fingerlike stretch of land between the Delaware Seashore State Park and the Maryland border. This southernmost tip of Delaware is referred to as the "land of the quiet resorts."

With the Atlantic Ocean on its eastern shore and various stretches of inland waters—from the Indian River Bay to the Little Assawoman Bay—to the west, these quiet resorts are relatively undeveloped, compared with the side-by-side condos, towering hotels, and bustling nightclubs of nearby Ocean City, Maryland.

Like Rehoboth, Bethany was named after a biblical place (Bethany was the home of Lazarus). Also like Rehoboth, Bethany Beach got its start when it was chosen as a site for 19th-century gatherings of a religious group, the Christian Church Conference.

Fenwick Island, of more recent origin, is located at the Maryland-Delaware border. It's divided into two distinct areas: the southern section is unincorporated and county zoned (multifamily dwellings, such as motels, are allowed); the northern section is an incorporated town with building codes that call primarily for single-family residences.

Both Bethany and Fenwick pride themselves on being quiet family style resorts. These communities are still residential, with strict control on the height and size of any new buildings. You won't find any large resort hotels, sophisticated tourist attractions, or entertainment complexes here. With almost everything geared to a tranquil atmosphere and a low-key pace (except at the height of July and August, when Ocean Highway has a constant stream of traffic), Bethany and Fenwick are unique finds, almost undiscovered by the average East Coast beach traveler.

GETTING THERE **By Plane** The closest gateways for regularly scheduled flights from all parts of the United States are Philadelphia International Airport and Baltimore International Airport. For commuter flights, the nearest gateways are Ocean City and Salisbury, Maryland.

By Train There's daily service from all parts of the United States via **Amtrak** into Wilmington (see "Arriving," in Chapter 8).

By Bus **Carolina Trailways** provides regular pickup and drop-off service during the summer season at Bethany Rental Services, 201 Central Blvd., Bethany Beach (☎ 302/539-6244).

By Car From points north or south, take Routes 113 and 13 to Route 1. From the west, take Route 50 to Ocean City and north on Ocean Highway to Fenwick Island.

By Ferry See "Lewes," earlier in this chapter.

ESSENTIALS **Area Code** The area code is 302.

Visitor Information The Bethany-Fenwick Area Chamber of Commerce, P.O. Box 1450, Bethany Beach, DE 19930 (☎ 302/539-2100 or 800/962-7873), is situated on Route 1 (known also as Ocean or Coastal Highway), adjacent to the Fenwick Island State Park at the Fenwick line at Lewes Street. The office is designed like a beach house, with wide windows overlooking the ocean and snow-white sands. The chamber publishes a helpful booklet called "The Quiet Resorts"; it also stocks brochures from motels, restaurants, and other visitor services.

The chamber is open during the following times: May through October, Monday to Friday from 9am to 5pm and Saturday, Sunday, and holidays from 10am to 2pm; November through April, Monday to Friday from 10am to 4pm and Saturday, Sunday, and holidays from 10am to 2pm.

GETTING AROUND Since Bethany Beach and Fenwick Island are within 5 miles of each other, the predominant mode of transport is car. Most visitors bring their own vehicles or rent cars from nearby Ocean City, in Maryland, or Dover and Wilmington. Like Rehoboth, many Bethany and Fenwick Streets are subject to meter or permit parking and the rules are strictly enforced. Fortunately, all the motels provide free parking for guests and most of the restaurants also have access to plentiful parking for customers.

WHAT TO SEE & DO

The 1-mile-long **Bethany Beach Boardwalk,** relatively free of commercial enterprises, is perfect for those who enjoy a quiet beachside walk and unobstructed views of the wide-open strand. The boardwalk is the focal point of the town, and most of the shops and fast-food eateries are located on Garfield Parkway, the street that runs perpendicular to the center of the boardwalk.

Fenwick, while lacking a boardwalk, has a wide-open beach with gentle dunes. There are no concessions or fast-food outlets along the shoreline, only private homes and rental properties. Most of the shops and business enterprises are concentrated one block inland along Route 1.

OUTDOOR ACTIVITIES

BICYCLING   The windswept flat land along Route 1 in Bethany Beach and Fenwick Island is ideal for bicycling. **Fenwick Golf and Cycle Center** (Ocean Bay Plaza, Route 1, Fenwick Island; ☎ 302/539-4922) rents single-speed cruiser bikes for $3 per hour, $5 for two hours, $10 per day, and $25 per week. The shop is open Memorial Day through Labor Day, daily 8am to 10pm; hours vary the rest of the year.

Bethany Cycle and Fitness Shop (Route 26 Mall, Route 26, Bethany Beach; ☎ 302/537-9982) rents beach-cruiser bikes with one to five speeds for $4 per hour or $10 per day. They are open Memorial Day through Labor Day, daily 8am to 8pm; Thursday through Monday 10am to 6pm the rest of the year.

WATER SPORTS   Ideal for swimming and sunning, **Bethany Beach** is a free and open to the public. **Bethany Rental Service,** 201 Central Ave. (☎ 302/539-6244 or 302/539-2224), operates a rental concession on the beach, offering eight-foot umbrellas, surf mats, boogie boards, highback or lounge chairs, and more.

A paradise for water-sports enthusiasts is **Fenwick Island State Park,** Route 1 (☎ 302/539-9060), just south of Bethany Beach. With the Atlantic on one side and Little Assawoman Bay on the other, this park has 3 miles of seacoast beaches and dunes as well as 344 acres of parkland and open bay front, ideal for fishing, crabbing, and boating. The facilities include a boardwalk with picnic tables, gift shop, and refreshments; shower and changing rooms; a first-aid room; and lifeguards. Surfing is permitted and access is allowed for four-wheel-drive vehicles. In addition, bird-watchers will find rare seabirds, such as tern, piping plover, and black skimmer, nesting in protected areas. Admission is $5 for out-of-state cars and $2.50 for Delaware cars.

Adjacent to the park on the bay side is **Bay Sports Watersports Rental and Lessons,** Route 1, Fenwick Island (☎ 302/539-7999), which rents sailboats from $35 an hour; and catamarans in three sizes, from $35 to $40 an hour. Sailing lessons are also available from $20 and up for an hour. Jet skis, kayaks, paddleboats, and wave runners are also available. Open late May to early September, daily from 9am to sunset.

Watersports Unlimited, 14 Second Street Marina (next to Harpoon Hanna's restaurant at the Delaware-Maryland state line), Fenwick Island (☎ 302/539-8666), rents a wide variety of pontoon boats, ranging from 20 to 31 feet long and priced from $65 to $75 per hour for smaller boats and $110 to $295 for a two-hour minimum on the larger boats. Parasail flights are also available at $40 to $60 per ride. In addition, this place offers jet skis, ski boats, fishing/crabbing boats, and other equipment. Open May through September daily from 7:30am to 8:30pm.

ATTRACTIONS

Chief among the sights here is the **Fenwick Island Lighthouse on the Transpeninsular Line,** Route 54, about a quarter of a mile west of Route 1. Built in 1859, this is one of the Delaware shore's oldest landmarks still in operation today, with beams that can be seen for 15 miles.

On the south side of the lighthouse you'll see the **First Stone of the Transpeninsular Line,** between Route 1 and Route 54, on the Delaware-Maryland border. This stone monument, erected on April 26, 1751, marks the eastern end of the Transpeninsular Line surveyed in 1750 and 1751 by John Watson and William Parsons of Pennsylvania and John Emory and Thomas Jones of Maryland. This line established the east-west boundary between Pennsylvania's "Three Lower Counties" (now Delaware) and the Colony of Maryland. The Transpeninsular Line served as the earliest foundation upon which the Mason-Dixon line of 1764 to 1767 was based.

ESPECIALLY FOR KIDS

The **Fenwick Island Boardwalk,** Routes 1 and 54, Fenwick Island (☎ 302/539-1644), is an inland amusement park across the street from the Fenwick Island Lighthouse. This summertime attraction features a water slide, miniature golf, and bumper-boat and go-cart rides. Hours are 9:30am to midnight, Memorial Day through Labor Day.

SHOPPING

Browsery
Route 26, Ocean View. ☎ **302/537-1505.**

Situated 1¹/₂ miles west of Bethany Beach, at the corner of West and Atlantic avenues, this shop is housed in a big red barn. It sells pottery, gifts, framed art, Amish-made Shaker-style pine furniture, and handcrafted Mennonite furniture. Open on Saturday from 10am to 4pm and Sunday from 1 to 4pm.

Japanesque
16 Pennsylvania Ave., Bethany Beach. ☎ **302/539-2311.**

Bringing the aura of the Far East to the Delaware beach, this shop carries a wide selection of Japanese jewelry, banners, kimonos, obi, hand-painted scarves, fans, gyotaku items (art of the Japanese fish rub), folk toys, miniature Zen rock gardens, gift wrap, note cards, hangings, tea kettles, chop sticks, and books. Open Monday through Saturday from 10am to 5pm and Sunday from noon to 5pm.

Sea Crest Gift and Gallery
Atlantic Ave. and Garfield Pkwy., Bethany Beach. ☎ **302/539-7621.**

Gifts and crafts that pertain to the sea are featured here, from dolphin, seagull, and dove art mobiles to framed sea art, as well as seashell-motif jewelry, wind chimes, pottery, music boxes, and colored glass. Open Monday through Saturday from 10am to 5pm and on Sunday from noon to 5pm or later.

Seaport Antique Village
Route 54 (at the bridge), Fenwick Island. ☎ **302/436-8962.**

This stores claims to have one of the largest privately owned antique collections in the United States. All the art and furnishings are for sale. Items range from paintings and decorative accessories made of crystal, sterling, brass, and bronze to china, chandeliers, jewelry, wicker, and furniture. Open daily from 10am to 6pm.

WHERE TO STAY

Like other Delaware coastal resorts, Bethany Beach and Fenwick Island depend on the summer season when the beaches are at their best. Rooms are booked months in advance for July and August, even though they're more expensive in peak season, often with weekend surcharges and two- or three-night minimums stays. Motels, for example, that otherwise would be considered in the moderate or budget category charge between $70 and $100 for a double. So, if you'd like to keep the costs reasonable, come during midweek or consider a visit in May, June, September, or October, when the weather can be almost as warm.

BETHANY BEACH
Moderate

Bethany Arms Motel and Apts.
Atlantic Ave. and Hollywood St., P.O. Box 1600, Bethany Beach, DE 19930. ☎ **302/539-9603.** 52 units. A/C TV TEL. $45–$95 double; $70–$130 apartment. MC, V. Free parking. Closed late Oct–early Mar.

Ideal for families who want to be close to the ocean, this modern complex offers basic motel units with a refrigerator and apartments with a fully equipped kitchen and an oceanfront view. The complex consists of two buildings right on the boardwalk and three situated just behind the first two, between the boardwalk and Atlantic Avenue; all are two or three stories high. A two-night minimum is in effect on summer weekends; holiday periods (such as Memorial Day and Labor Day weekends) often have three-night minimums and some surcharges.

Harbor View Motel
Route 1, R.D. 1, Box 102, Bethany Beach, DE 19930. ☎ **302/539-0500.** Fax 302/539-5170. 50 rms, 10 efficiencies. A/C TV TEL. $35–$100 double; $50–$115 efficiency. (Rates include continental breakfast.) AE, DISC, MC, V. Free parking. Closed Nov–mid-Mar.

Located 3 miles north of Bethany Beach at the southern edge of the Delaware Seashore State Park, this modern, two-story motel on the bay side offers views of the bay as well as the ocean. It has both rooms and efficiencies; some are equipped with an individual Jacuzzi, and all have a balcony. The guest facilities include an outdoor swimming pool, a sundeck on the bay, barbecue grills, a launderette, and a restaurant. There are weekend surcharges and three-day minimums in season.

Westward Pines
10 Kent Ave., Bethany Beach, DE 19930. ☎ **302/539-7426.** 10 rms. A/C TV $45–$70 double, $60–$85 for units with Jacuzzi and fireplace. No credit cards. Free parking. Open all year.

If you want comfort in a secluded setting, then you might consider this ranch-style motel. Situated in a residential area, four blocks from the beach and one block west of Route 1, it's surrounded by tall trees and leafy shrubs. The guest units, all on ground-floor level, have standard furnishings plus a small refrigerator and a coffeemaker; some have a fireplace and a Jacuzzi. A minimum stay may be required on weekends.

FENWICK ISLAND
Moderate

Fenwick Islander
Route 1 and South Carolina Ave., Fenwick Island, DE 19944. ☎ **302/539-2333** or 800/ 346-4520. 63 units. A/C TV TEL. $30–$105 double. AE, DISC, MC, V. Free parking. Closed Nov–Mar.

Situated on the bay side of the highway, between South Carolina and West Virginia avenues, just north of the Maryland/Delaware state line, this bright, modern three-story motel is ideal for families. All of the units are equipped with refrigerator and kitchenette facilities; second- and third-floor rooms have balconies. Children under 5 stay free and children aged 6 to 16 are charged just $5 each per night extra. Guest amenities include an outdoor swimming pool and a launderette. Weekend and holiday rates are subject to surcharges.

Sands Motel
Route 1 (Ocean Hwy.), Fenwick Island, DE 19944. ☎ **302/539-7745**; Dec–Mar 410/ 213-2152. 21 rms, 16 apts and efficiencies. A/C TV. $34–$70 double; $40–$99 apt and efficiency. AE, DC, DISC, MC, V. Free parking. Closed Nov–Mar.

Situated between Indian and James streets on the ocean side of the highway but not directly on the oceanfront, the Sands offers a choice of standard rooms, efficiencies, and apartments. It has a kidney-shaped outdoor pool, easy access to the beach, and welcomes well-behaved pets. Rates are subject to a three-day minimum stay in season, holidays, and weekends; surcharges also apply for certain weekend bookings.

Sea Charm
Oceanfront and Lighthouse Rd., Fenwick Island, DE 19944. ☎ **302/539-9613**. 19 units. A/C TV. $50–$80 double; $70–$140 apartment. DISC, MC, V. Free parking. Closed Nov– mid-May.

With wraparound porches on two levels, this homey, three-story inn, perched on the ocean amid the sand dunes just north of the Delaware-Maryland border, is the epitome of a vintage beach cottage. It may be a little time-worn and frayed around the edges, but it is the only place on Fenwick Island that has accommodations right on the beach. A favorite with families, which come back year after year, it offers a choice of motel rooms, oceanfront efficiencies, and one- to three-bedroom ocean-view apartments, some of which have a balcony. Facilities include an outdoor swimming pool and a ground-level patio and sundeck with picnic furniture and outdoor grills. A three-night minimum reservation is required throughout the season, and some surcharges apply on weekends.

WHERE TO DINE
The restaurants of the Bethany Beach and Fenwick Island area provide a pleasant blend of waterside and inland dining, all at fairly moderate prices. Because these two resorts are popular with families, there are also some fine lower-priced restaurants that offer quality, ambience, and creative cooking. Most restaurants serve liquor, unless otherwise noted. (*Note:* In Bethany, alcoholic beverages are available only in restaurants—there are no bars.)

Since most motels in Bethany and Fenwick do not serve breakfast, check some of the places below for breakfast, particularly **Holiday House, Libby's,** and **Warren Station.**

BETHANY BEACH
Moderate
Harbor Lights
Route 1. ☎ **302/539-3061.** Reservations recommended on weekends. Main courses $12.95–$20.95. AE, DC, DISC, MC, V. Apr–Oct, daily 5–10pm. SEAFOOD.

This restaurant is nestled on the bay side of the main highway, north of central Bethany, with views of the water. The menu emphasizes fresh crab (crab cakes, soft-shell crabs, crabmeat au gratin or imperial), and local fish platters, steaks, and surf-and-turf combinations. Two of the house signature dishes are veal Oscar and Harbor Lights Seafood Stew, made with shrimp, scallops, flounder, and garden vegetables.

Holiday House Seafood Restaurant
Garfield Pkwy. and the Boardwalk. ☎ **302/539-7298.** Reservations recommended for dinner. Main courses $8.95–$21.95; lunch $5–$10. AE, DISC, MC, V. Apr–Oct daily 8am–2pm and 5–9pm. SEAFOOD.

For oceanfront dining, try this restaurant on the Bethany Beach boardwalk. Light fare, sandwiches, and salads are available for lunch, but at dinner, the emphasis is on seafood—sautéed shrimp scampi, broiled scallops, local soft-shell crabs, and broiled crab-stuffed flounder. On many nights, a seafood buffet is featured. For meat eaters, the menu also includes prime rib, Delaware fried chicken, baked ham, and pork dishes.

Magnolia's Restaurant
Cedar Neck Rd., Ocean View. ☎ **302/539-5671.** Reservations recommended for dinner. Main courses $11.95–$18.95; lunch $2.95–$10.95. AE, MC, V. Daily 11am–11pm. SOUTHERN.

Situated 2 miles west of Bethany Beach off Route 26 and Central Avenue, this restaurant features Carolina-style cuisine and ambience. There are no great sea views or wide windows here, but there is an elegant decor of lace curtains and tablecloths, light woods, colored glass, and lots of leafy plants and flowers. The dinner menu is a medley of dishes influenced by the Old South—from baked Dixie chicken and scallops Savannah to Cajun-style stuffed flounder and seafood Norfolk. A light menu is also available, in an adjoining pub room, from 11am to midnight for lunch or snacks.

Inexpensive
Cottage Café
Route 1, Bethany Beach. ☎ **302/539-8710.** All items $2.95–$13.95. AE, MC, V. Year-round, Sun–Thurs 11am–9pm, Fri–Sat 11am–10pm. AMERICAN.

With a country cottage-style facade and interior, this homey restaurant and pub also displays the works of Maryland artist Joseph Craig English (his paintings and prints portray everyday scenes of the region). The varied menu offers everything from old-fashioned pot roast and country fried chicken to black beans and rice, meat loaf, steaks, burgers, sandwiches, and pastas throughout the day.

FENWICK ISLAND
Expensive/Moderate
✪ Harpoon Hanna's
Route 54 (on the Bay). ☎ **302/539-3095.** Reservations not accepted. Main courses $9.95–$21.95; lunch $4.95–$9.95. AE, MC, V. Year-round, daily 11am–11pm. SEAFOOD.

Dining in Delaware with views of Maryland is all part of the experience at this restaurant, located on Assawoman Bay near the state line. The half dozen large and lively dining rooms have a nautical decor. Lunch ranges from salads to sandwiches and omelets (try the Harpoon Seafood Omelet, overflowing with shrimp, crab, mild Cheddar, tomatoes, and sautéed mushrooms). In the evening fresh fish lead the menu: swordfish, sea trout, tuna, tilefish, shrimp, crab, lobster.

Nantuckets
Route 1 and Atlantic Ave. ☎ **302/539-2607.** Reservations required. Main courses $15.95–$23.95. AE, DISC, MC, V. Year-round, daily 4–10pm. SEAFOOD.

A New England cottage atmosphere prevails at this restaurant, with four cozy dining rooms, situated a block from the beach on the main highway. The chef-owner, David Twining, is known for innovative dishes, such as Madaket Beach Fish Stew (a potpourri of shrimp, scallops, crab, clams, mussels, and fresh fish in a tomato-saffron broth) and Veal Homard à la David (veal and lobster medaillons with brandy, hearts of palm, Dijon mustard, and cream). Other house favorites are quahog (clam) chowder (a rich scallop and clam chowder with traditional red potatoes and corn), lobster and scallops coquille, and jumbo shrimp sautéed with garlic, ginger, and chutney; for meat eaters, there are center-cut loin lamb chops with a fine horseradish-mint sauce and breast of chicken with crab and artichokes.

✪ Tom & Terry's
Route 54. ☎ **302/436-4161.** Reservations not accepted except off-season (Nov–Mar). Main courses $14.95–$25.95; lunch $5.95–$10.95. MC, V. Year-round, daily 11am–4pm and 5–10pm. SEAFOOD.

Situated 1¹/₂ miles west of Route 1, on Assawoman Bay, with a view of Ocean City skyline, this tropical-style restaurant offers seating in a wide-windowed dining room or on an outside deck. The menu focuses largely on seafood (there's a seafood market on the premises, too): crab-stuffed lobster tails, backfin crab cakes, soft-shell crabs, grilled tuna and swordfish steaks, and stuffed flounder. Steaks, prime rib, and chicken Marsala are also offered. There are early bird specials from 5 to 6pm each night. The sunsets are particularly worth the price of a meal.

Moderate
Galeano's
Fenwick Square Shopping Center, Route 1 and Farmington St. ☎ **302/537-1624.** Reservations accepted only for parties of five or more. Main courses $8.95–$21.95; lunch $3.95–$9.95. DISC, MC, V. Year-round, daily 11am–11pm. ITALIAN.

If you tire of sea views and crave straightforward Italian favorites, it's hard to beat this shop-front restaurant on the main highway. Specialties include veal cannelloni, chicken Tetrazzini, pasta primavera, steak pizzaiola, shrimp scampi, lobster fra diavolo. The menu also offers prime rib, steaks, and crab imperial, as well as fresh pasta served with a choice of six sauces or accompaniments. Lunch items, served in the lounge only, include pizzas, sandwiches, subs, and burgers.

Uncle Raymond's Ocean Grill

Route 1 and Atlantic Ave. ☎ **302/539-1388.** Reservations not accepted. Main courses $9–$16; lunch $2.50–$7.50. DISC, MC, V. Apr–Sept, daily 11am–1am. AMERICAN/SEAFOOD.

A casual atmosphere prevails at this restaurant, popular for its large, 200-seat outside deck, with picnic table seating, overlooking the main highway. The uncomplicated menu offers steamed hard crabs, backfin crab cakes, fried shrimp, charbroiled tuna or swordfish, and a house specialty of Seafood Raymond (shrimp, lobster, crab sautéed in spicy seafood gravy of wine, onion, peppers, and mushrooms). Surf-and-turf and lobster tails are also available at higher prices. The restaurant also serves pizza.

Inexpensive

⑤ Libby's

Ocean Hwy. ☎ **302/539-7379.** Reservations not accepted. Main courses $6.95–$18.95; lunch $2.95–$7.95; breakfast $2.65–$5.95. DISC, MC, V. Breakfast daily 7am–3pm; lunch daily 11:30am–3pm; dinner daily 3–9pm. Closed Dec–Feb. AMERICAN.

Known far and wide for its polka-dot facade, this restaurant is a particular favorite for breakfast. Choices include "pancakes with personality" (royal cherry, Georgia pecan, chocolate chip), old-fashioned buckwheat cakes, waffles, French toast, and omelets, as well as low-calorie fare. Lunch features a variety of overstuffed sandwiches, burgers, and salads. Dinner entrées, which include a huge salad bar, range from soft-shell crabs and shrimp to steaks and "chicken in the basket." The restaurant is situated between Dagsboro and Cannon Streets. *Note:* Libby's also operates a branch in the heart of Bethany Beach at 116 Garfield Pkwy. (☎ 302/539-4500), open May through September from 7am to 9pm.

⑤ Warren Station

Ocean Hwy. (Route 1). ☎ **302/539-7156.** Reservations not accepted. Main courses $6.95–$14.95; lunch $2–$6; breakfast $2–$5; MC, V. Mid-May to early Sept, Sun–Thurs 8am–9pm, Fri–Sat 8am–9:30pm. Closed Oct–Apr. AMERICAN.

For more than 30 years, wholesome cooking at reasonable prices has been the trademark of this homey and casual restaurant, located between Indian and Houston Streets. Designed to duplicate the look of the old Indian River Coast Guard Station, the decor features light woods, lots of windows, and bright blue canvas dividers. Turkey is the specialty of the house, roasted fresh daily and hand-carved to order, priced from $7.50 and up for a complete dinner. Other entrées include fried chicken, sugar-cured ham with raisin sauce, charbroiled T-bone steaks, crab cutlets, and flounder stuffed with crab imperial. Complete dinners—with appetizer or soup, salad, two vegetables, and beverage—range from $8 to $15. Sandwiches, burgers, soups, and salads are available for lunch. No alcohol is served.

INLAND EXCURSIONS

The end of the Delaware shoreline at Fenwick Island is by no means the end of the attractions in the region. There is much to explore inland.

Millsboro, 13 miles from the Atlantic coast and at the headwaters of the Indian River, is the home of **Carey's Camp Meeting Ground,** Route 24, one of the state's original camp meeting grounds, established by the Methodists in 1888. Listed on the National Register of Historic Places, it's still an active meeting site for families who return each summer. The open-frame tabernacle is surrounded by 47 open-front cottages, called "tents."

This area also has great links with the Nanticoke Indian tribe, whose ancestors were among the first residents of Delaware. Five miles east of Millsboro, on the banks of the Indian River, is the **Nanticoke Indian Museum** (Oak Orchard, at the intersection of Routes 24 and 5; ☎ 302/945-7022). Ensconced in a former Indian schoolhouse, it contains artifacts and various historical displays. It's open Tuesday through Friday from 9am to 4pm, Saturday from 10am to 4pm, and Sunday from noon to 4pm; admission charge is $1 for adults and 50¢ for children 3 to 11.

In addition, the culture of the Nanticokes is celebrated each September, when a powwow is held. Remaining members of the tribe, about 500 in number, convene for two days of ceremonial dancing, storytelling, crafts, and food. The public is welcome.

The largest city in Sussex County is **Seaford,** about 20 miles west of Millsboro. Established in 1726 on land settled by Thomas Hooper and his family, it was primarily a farming community until the arrival of the Delaware Railroad in 1856, an extension of service from Wilmington. Seaford soon became the main railhead for the entire eastern shore and the shipping point for seafood and produce bound for Philadelphia and New York. Seaford's role as the commercial hub was further enhanced in 1939 when the local Du Pont company produced the first strands of the synthetic fiber nylon. In the years since, Seaford has become the nylon capital of the world, as well as the county's largest business and commercial district.

Just over 10 miles southeast of Seaford is **Trapp Pond State Park,** R.D. 2, Box 331, Laurel (☎ 302/875-5153), a 966-acre inland expanse rich in freshwater wetlands. It's also the northernmost natural stand of bald-cypress trees in the United States. The pond is surrounded by hiking trails, from which visitors can observe native animal species, flowering plants, and birds, especially great blue herons, owls, hummingbirds, warblers, bald eagles, and pileated woodpeckers. The park's facilities include a guarded beach, picnic areas, a volleyball court, horseshoe pits, and camping sites. There's an admission charge of $2.50 for Delaware-registered cars and $5 for out-of-state cars from Memorial Day to Labor Day and on weekends in May, September, and October. The park is open year-round, daily from 8am to sunset.

Appendix:
For Foreign Visitors

Although American fads and fashions have spread across Europe and other parts of the world so that America may seem like familiar territory before your arrival, there are still many peculiarities and uniquely American situations that any foreign visitor will encounter.

1 Preparing for Your Trip

ENTRY REQUIREMENTS

DOCUMENT REQUIREMENTS Canadian citizens may enter the United States without passports or visas; they need only proof of residence.

British subjects and citizens of New Zealand, Japan, and most western European countries traveling on valid passports may not need a visa for holiday or business travel to the United States for less than 90 days, providing that they hold a round-trip or return ticket and that they enter the United States on an airline or cruise line participating in the visa-waiver program. (Note that citizens of these visa-exempt countries who first enter the United States may then visit Mexico, Canada, Bermuda, and/or the Caribbean islands and then reenter the United States by any mode of transportation, without needing a visa. Further information is available from any U.S. embassy or consulate.)

Citizens of countries other than those stipulated above, including citizens of Australia, must have two documents: (1) a valid passport with an expiration date at least six months later than the scheduled end of their visit to the United States; and (2) a tourist visa, available without charge from the nearest U.S. consulate.

To obtain a visa, the traveler must submit a completed application form (either in person or by mail) with a $1^1/2$-inch square photo and must demonstrate binding ties to a residence abroad. Usually you can obtain a visa at once or within 24 hours, but it may take longer during the summer rush from June to August. If you cannot go in person, contact the nearest U.S. embassy or consulate for directions on applying by mail. Your travel agent or airline office may also be able to provide you with visa applications and instructions. The U.S. embassy or consulate that issues your visa will determine whether you will be issued a multiple- or single-entry visa and any restrictions regarding the length of your stay.

MEDICAL REQUIREMENTS   No inoculations are needed to enter the United States unless you are coming from, or have stopped over in, areas known to be suffering from epidemics, particularly cholera or yellow fever.

If you have a disease requiring treatment with medications containing narcotics or drugs requiring a syringe, carry a valid signed prescription from your physician to allay any suspicions that you are smuggling drugs.

CUSTOMS REQUIREMENTS   Every adult visitor may bring in free of duty: one liter of wine or hard liquor; 200 cigarettes or 100 cigars (but no cigars from Cuba) or three pounds of smoking tobacco; $100 worth of gifts. These exemptions are offered to travelers who spend at least 72 hours in the United States and who have not claimed them within the preceding six months. It is altogether forbidden to bring into the country foodstuffs (particularly cheese, fruit, cooked meats, and canned goods) and plants (vegetables, seeds, tropical plants, and so on). Foreign tourists may bring in or take out up to $10,000 in U.S. or foreign currency with no formalities; larger sums must be declared to Customs on entering or leaving.

INSURANCE

There is no national health system in the United States. Because the cost of medical care is extremely high, we strongly advise every traveler to secure health coverage before setting out.

You may want to take out a comprehensive travel policy that covers (for a relatively low premium) sickness or injury costs (medical, surgical, and hospital); loss or theft of your baggage; trip-cancellation costs; guarantee of bail in case you are arrested; and costs of accident, repatriation, or death. Such packages (for example, "Europe Assistance" in Europe) are sold by automobile clubs at attractive rates, as well as by insurance companies and travel agencies.

MONEY

CURRENCY & EXCHANGE   The U.S. monetary system has a decimal base: one American **dollar** ($1) = 100 **cents** (100¢).

Dollar bills commonly come in $1 ("a buck"), $5, $10, $20, $50, and $100 denominations (the last two are not welcome when paying for small purchases and are not accepted in taxis or at subway ticket booths). There are also $2 bills (seldom encountered).

There are six denominations of coins: 1¢ (one cent or "a penny"), 5¢ (five cents or "a nickel"), 10¢ (ten cents or "a dime"), 25¢ (twenty-five cents or "a quarter"), 50¢ (fifty cents or "a half dollar"), and the rare $1 piece.

Note: The "foreign-exchange bureaus" so common in Europe are rare even at airports in the United States, and nonexistent outside major cities. Try to avoid having to change foreign money, or traveler's checks denominated other than in U.S. dollars, at a small-town bank, or even a branch in a big city; in fact, leave any currency other than U.S. dollars at home—it may prove more nuisance to you than it's worth.

TRAVELER'S CHECKS   Traveler's checks denominated in U.S. dollars are readily accepted at most hotels, motels, restaurants, and large stores. But the best place to change traveler's checks is at a bank. Do not bring traveler's checks denominated in other currencies.

CREDIT & CHARGE CARDS   The method of payment most widely used is credit and charge cards: Visa (BarclayCard in Britain), MasterCard (EuroCard in

Europe, Access in Britain, Chargex in Canada), American Express, Diners Club, Discover, and Carte Blanche. You can save yourself trouble by using "plastic money" rather than cash or traveler's checks in most hotels, motels, restaurants, and retail stores (a growing number of food and liquor stores now accept credit/ charge cards). You must have a credit or charge card to rent a car. It can also be used as proof of identity (often carrying more weight than a passport) or as a "cash card," enabling you to draw money from banks that accept it.

SAFETY

GENERAL   While tourist areas are generally safe, crime is on the increase every-where, and U.S. urban areas tend to be less safe than those in Europe or Japan. Visitors should always stay alert. This is particularly true of large U.S. cities. It is wise to ask the city's or area's tourist office if you're in doubt about which neigh-borhoods are safe. Avoid deserted areas, especially at night. Don't go into any city park at night unless there's an event that attracts crowds. Generally speaking, you can feel safe in areas where there are many people and many open establishments.

Avoid carrying valuables with you on the street, and don't display expensive cameras or electronic equipment. Hold on to your pocketbook, and place your billfold in an inside pocket. In theaters, restaurants, and other public places, keep your possessions in sight.

Remember also that hotels are open to the public, and in a large hotel, security may not be able to screen everyone entering. Always lock your room door—don't assume that once inside your hotel you are automatically safe and no longer need be aware of your surroundings.

DRIVING   Safety while driving is particularly important. Question your rental agency about personal safety, or ask for a brochure of traveler safety tips when you pick up your car. Obtain written directions, or a map with the route marked in red, from the agency showing how to get to your destination. And, if possible, arrive and depart during daylight hours.

Recently more and more crime has involved cars and drivers. If you drive off a highway into a doubtful neighborhood, leave the area as quickly as possible. If you have an accident, even on the highway, stay in your car with the doors locked until you assess the situation or until the police arrive. If you are bumped from behind on the street or are involved in a minor accident with no injuries and the situa-tion appears to be suspicious, motion to the other driver to follow you. *Never* get out of your car in such situations. You can also keep a pre-made sign in your car that reads: PLEASE FOLLOW THIS VEHICLE TO REPORT THE ACCIDENT. Show the sign to the other driver and go directly to the nearest police precinct, well-lighted service station, or all-night store.

If you see someone on the road who indicates a need for help, do *not* stop. Take note of the location, drive on to a well-lighted area, and telephone the police by dialing 911.

Park in well-lighted, well-traveled areas if possible. Always keep your car doors locked, whether attended or unattended. Look around you before you get out of your car, and never leave any packages or valuables in sight. If someone attempts to rob you or steal your car, do *not* try to resist the thief/carjacker—report the incident to the police department immediately.

Also, make sure that you have enough gasoline in your tank to reach your intended destination, so that you're not forced to look for a service station in an unfamiliar and possibly unsafe neighborhood—especially at night.

You may wish to contact the local tourist information bureau in your destination before you arrive, as they may be able to provide you with a safety brochure.

2   Getting To & Around the U.S.

GETTING TO THE U.S.

Travelers from overseas can take advantage of the **APEX (Advance Purchase Excursion) fares** offered by all the major international carriers. Aside from these, attractive values are offered by Icelandair on flights from Luxembourg to New York and by Virgin Atlantic Airways from London to New York/Newark.

The visitor arriving by air, no matter what the port of entry, should cultivate patience and resignation before setting foot on U.S. soil. Getting through Immigration control may take as long as two hours on some days, especially summer weekends. Add the time it takes to clear Customs and you'll see that you should make very generous allowance for delay in planning connections between international and domestic flights—an average of two to three hours at least.

In contrast, travelers arriving by car or by rail from Canada will find border-crossing formalities streamlined to the vanishing point. And air travelers from Canada, Bermuda, and some places in the Caribbean can sometimes go through Customs and Immigration at the point of departure, which is much quicker and less painful.

For further information, see "Getting There," in Chapters 1 and 7.

GETTING AROUND THE U.S.

BY AIR   Some large American airlines (for example, American Airlines, Delta, Northwest, TWA, and United) offer travelers on their transatlantic or transpacific flights special discount tickets under the name **Visit USA,** allowing travel between any U.S. destinations at minimum rates. They are not on sale in the United States, and must, therefore, be purchased before you leave your foreign point of departure. This system is the best, easiest, and fastest way to see the United States at low cost. You should obtain information well in advance from your travel agent or the office of the airline concerned, since the conditions attached to these discount tickets can be changed without advance notice.

BY TRAIN   Long-distance trains in the United States are operated by Amtrak, the national rail passenger corporation. International visitors can buy a **USA Railpass,** good for 15 or 30 days of unlimited travel on Amtrak. The pass is available through many foreign travel agents. Prices in 1995 for a 15-day pass were $229 off-peak, $340 peak; a 30-day pass cost $339 off-peak, $425 peak. (With a foreign passport, you can also buy passes at some Amtrak offices in the United States, including locations in Boston, Chicago, Los Angeles, Miami, New York, San Francisco, and Washington, D.C.) Reservations are generally required and should be made for each part of your trip as early as possible.

However, visitors should be aware of the limitations of long-distance rail travel in the United States. With a few notable exceptions (for instance, the Northeast Corridor line between Boston and Washington, D.C.), service is rarely up to European standards: Delays are common, routes are limited and often infrequently served, and fares are rarely significantly lower than discount airfares. Thus cross-country train travel should be approached with caution.

BY BUS   Greyhound, the sole nationwide bus line, offers an **Ameripass** for unlimited travel for 7 days (for $259), 15 days (for $459), and 30 days (for $559).

Bus travel in the United States can be both slow and uncomfortable, so this option is not for everyone.

BY CAR   Travel by car gives visitors the freedom to make, and alter, their itineraries to suit their own needs and interests. And it offers the possibility of visiting some of the off-the-beaten path locations, places that cannot be reached easily by public transportation. For information on renting cars in the United States, see the "Getting Around" sections in individual city and region chapters and "Automobile Organizations" and "Automobile Rentals" in "Fast Facts: For the Foreign Traveler," below.

FAST FACTS: For the Foreign Traveler

Automobile Organizations   Auto clubs will supply maps, suggested routes, guidebooks, accident and bail-bond insurance, and emergency road service. The major auto club in the United States, with 983 offices nationwide, is the **American Automobile Association (AAA).** Members of some foreign auto clubs have reciprocal arrangements with the AAA and enjoy its services at no charge. If you belong to an auto club in your home country, inquire about AAA reciprocity before you leave. You may be able to join the AAA even if you're not a member of a reciprocal club; to inquire, call the AAA (☎ 800/ 222-4357).

In addition, some automobile-rental agencies now provide many of these same services. Inquire about their availability when you rent your car.

Automobile Rentals   To rent a car you need a major credit or charge card. A valid driver's license is required, and you usually need to be at least 25. Some companies do rent to younger people but add a daily surcharge. Be sure to return your car with the same amount of gas you started out with; rental companies charge excessive prices for gasoline. (See the "Getting Around" section in individual city and region chapters.)

Business Hours   **Banks** are open weekdays from 9am to 3 or 4pm, although there's 24-hour access to the automatic tellers (ATMs) at most banks and other outlets. Generally, **offices** are open weekdays from 9am to 5pm. **Stores** are open six days a week, with many open on Sunday, too; department stores usually stay open until 9pm at least one day a week.

Climate   See "When to Go," in Chapters 1 and 7.

Currency   See "Money" in "Preparing for Your Trip," above.

Currency Exchange   You'll find currency-exchange services in major airports with international service. Elsewhere, they may be quite difficult to come by. A very reliable choice is **Thomas Cook Currency Services,** which has been in business since 1841 and offers a wide range of services. It sells commission-free foreign and U.S. traveler's checks, drafts, and wire transfers; it also does check collections (including Eurochecks). The rates are competitive and the service excellent.

Electricity   The United States uses 110–120 volts A.C., 60 cycles, compared to 220–240 volts A.C., 50 cycles, as in most of Europe. In addition to a 100-volt transformer, small appliances of non-American manufacture, such as hairdryers and shavers, will require a plug adapter, with two flat, parallel pins.

Embassies and Consulates   All embassies are located in the national capital, Washington, D.C.; some consulates are located in major U.S. cities, and most nations have a mission to the United Nations in New York City.

The embassy of **Australia** is at 1601 Massachusetts Ave. NW, Washington, D.C. 20036 (☎ 202/797-3000). There is a consulate in New York City at the International Bldg., 636 Fifth Ave., New York, NY 10111 (☎ 212/408-8400).

Other Australian consulates are in Honolulu, Houston, Los Angeles, and San Francisco.

The embassy of **Canada** is at 501 Pennsylvania Ave. NW, Washington, D.C. 20001 (☎ 202/682-1740). There's a Canadian consulate in New York at 1251 Ave. of the Americas, New York, NY 10020 (☎ 212/596-1600). Other Canadian consulates are in Atlanta, Buffalo (NY), Chicago, Cleveland, Dallas, Detroit, Los Angeles, Miami, Minneapolis, and Seattle.

The embassy of the **Republic of Ireland** is at 2234 Massachusetts Ave. NW, Washington, D.C. 20008 (☎ 202/462-3939). The nearest Irish consulates are: Chase Bldg., 535 Boylston St., Boston, MA 02116 (☎ 617/267-9330); 400 N. Michigan Ave., Chicago, IL 60611 (☎ 312/337-1868); and Ireland House, 345 Park Ave., 17th floor, New York, NY 10154 (☎ 212/319-2555). There's another Irish consulate in San Francisco.

The embassy of **New Zealand** is at 37 Observatory Circle NW, Washington, D.C. 20008 (☎ 202/328-4800). New Zealand consulates are in Los Angeles, Salt Lake City, San Francisco, and Seattle.

The embassy of the **United Kingdom** is at 3100 Massachusetts Ave. NW, Washington, D.C. 20008 (☎ 202/462-1340). There's a British consulate in New York at 845 Third Ave., NY 10022 (☎ 212/745-0200). Other British consulates are in Atlanta, Boston, Chicago, Cleveland, Dallas, Houston, Los Angeles, Miami, and Orlando.

Emergencies   Call **911** to report a fire, call the police, or get an ambulance. This is a toll-free call (no coins are required at a public telephone).

If you encounter traveler's problems, check the local telephone directory to find an office of the **Traveler's Aid Society,** a nationwide, nonprofit, social-service organization geared to helping travelers in difficult straits. Their services might include reuniting families separated while traveling, providing food and/or shelter to people stranded without cash, or even emotional counseling. If you're in trouble, seek them out.

Gasoline (Petrol)   One U.S. gallon equals 3.8 liters or .85 Imperial gallons. There are usually several grades (and price levels) of gasoline available at most gas stations, and their names change from company to company. The unleaded ones with the highest octane rating are the most expensive (most rental cars take the least expensive "regular" unleaded gas); leaded gas is the least expensive, but only older cars can use this anymore, so check if you're not sure. Note that the price is often lower if you pay in cash instead of by credit or charge card. Also, many gas stations now offer lower-priced self-service gas pumps—in fact, some gas stations, particularly at night, are all self-service.

Holidays   On the following legal national holidays, banks, government offices, post offices, and many stores, restaurants, and museums are closed: January 1 (New Year's Day); the third Monday in January (Martin Luther King Day); the third Monday in February (Presidents Day, Washington's Birthday); the last

Monday in May (Memorial Day); July 4 (Independence Day); the first Monday in September (Labor Day); the second Monday in October (Columbus Day); November 11 (Veterans' Day/Armistice Day); the last Thursday in November (Thanksgiving Day); and December 25 (Christmas). Also, the Tuesday following the first Monday in November is Election Day, and is a legal holiday in presidential-election years (1996).

Legal Aid The foreign tourist will probably never become involved with the American legal system. If you are pulled up for a minor infraction (for example, of the highway code, such as speeding), never attempt to pay the fine directly to a police officer; you may wind up arrested on the much more serious charge of attempted bribery. Pay fines by mail or directly into the hands of the clerk of the court. If accused of a more serious offense, it's wise to say and do nothing before consulting a lawyer. Under U.S. law, an arrested person is allowed one telephone call to a party of his or her choice. Call your embassy or consulate.

Mail If you want your mail to follow you on your vacation and you aren't sure of your address, your mail can be sent to you, in your name, **c/o General Delivery** at the main post office of the city or region where you expect to be. The addressee must pick it up in person and must produce proof of identity (driver's license, credit card, passport, etc.).

Generally to be found at intersections, mailboxes are blue with a red-and-white stripe and carry the inscription U.S. MAIL. If your mail is addressed to a U.S. destination, don't forget to add the five-figure postal code, or ZIP (zone improvement plan) code, after the two-letter abbreviation of the state to which the mail is addressed (MD for Maryland, DE for Delaware).

Domestic **postage rates** are 20¢ for a postcard and 32¢ for a letter. Check with any local post office for current international postage rates.

Newspapers/Magazines National newspapers include the *New York Times, USA Today,* and the *Wall Street Journal.* National news weeklies include *Newsweek, Time,* and *U.S. News & World Report.* All over Florida, you'll be able to purchase the *Miami Herald,* one of the most highly respected dailies in the country.

Radio and Television Audiovisual media, with four coast-to-coast networks—ABC, CBS, NBC, and Fox—joined by the Public Broadcasting System (PBS) and the Cable News Network (CNN), play a major part in American life. In big cities, televiewers have a choice of about a dozen channels (including the UHF channels), most of them transmitting 24 hours a day, without counting the pay-TV channels showing recent movies or sports events. All options are usually indicated on your hotel TV set. You'll also find a wide choice of local radio stations, each broadcasting particular kinds of talk shows and/or music—classical, country, jazz, pop, gospel—punctuated by news broadcasts and frequent commercials.

Safety See "Safety" in "Preparing for Your Trip," above.

Taxes In the United States there is no VAT (value-added tax) or other indirect tax at a national level. Every state, and each city in it, has the right to levy its own local tax on all purchases, including hotel and restaurant checks, airline tickets, and so on.

For sales tax rates in Maryland and Delaware, see "Fast Facts" in appropriate city chapters.

Telephone, Telegraph, Telex, and Fax   The telephone system in the United States is run by private corporations, so rates, especially for long-distance service and operator-assisted calls, can vary widely—even on calls made from public telephones. Local calls in the United States usually cost 25¢.

Generally, hotel surcharges on long-distance and local calls are astronomical. You're usually better off using a **public pay telephone,** which you'll find clearly marked in most public buildings and private establishments as well as on the street. Outside metropolitan areas, public telephones are more difficult to find. Stores and gas stations are your best bet.

Most **long-distance and international calls** can be dialed directly from any phone. For calls to Canada and other parts of the United States, dial 1 followed by the area code and the seven-digit number. For international calls, dial 011 followed by the country code, city code, and the telephone number of the person you wish to call.

Note that all calls to area code 800 are toll free. However, calls to numbers in area codes 700 and 900 (chat lines, bulletin boards, "dating" services, etc.) can be very expensive—usually a charge of 95¢ to $3 or more per minute, and they sometimes have minimum charges that can run as high as $15 or more.

For **reversed-charge or collect calls,** and for **person-to-person calls,** dial 0 (zero, *not* the letter O) followed by the area code and number you want; an operator will then come on the line, and you should specify that you are calling collect, or person-to-person, or both. If your operator-assisted call is international, ask for the overseas operator.

For local **directory assistance** ("information"), dial 411; for **long-distance information,** dial 1, then the appropriate area code and 555-1212.

Like the telephone system, **telegraph** and **telex** services are provided by private corporations like ITT, MCI, and above all, Western Union, the most important. You can bring your telegram in to the nearest Western Union office (there are hundreds across the country), or dictate it over the phone (a toll-free call, 800/325-6000). You can also telegraph money, or have it telegraphed to you, very quickly over the Western Union system. (Note, however, that this service can be very expensive. The service charge can run as high as 15% to 25% of the amount sent.)

Most hotels have **fax** machines available for guest use (be sure to ask about the charge to use it), and many hotel rooms are even wired for guests' fax machines. You'll probably also see signs for public faxes in the windows of local shops.

Telephone Directory   There are two kinds of telephone directories available to you. The general directory is the so-called **White Pages,** in which private and business subscribers are listed in alphabetical order. The inside front cover lists the emergency number for police, fire, and ambulance, and other vital numbers (like the coast guard, poison-control center, crime-victims hotline, and so on). The first few pages are devoted to community-service numbers, including a guide to long-distance and international calling, complete with country codes and area codes.

The second directory, printed on yellow paper (hence its name, **Yellow Pages**), lists all local services, businesses, and industries by type of activity, with an index at the back. The listings cover not only such obvious items as automobile repairs by make of car, or drugstores (pharmacies), often by geographical location, but also restaurants by type of cuisine and geographical location, bookstores by special subject and/or language, places of worship by religious denomination, and other information that the tourist might otherwise not readily find. The Yellow Pages also include city plans or detailed area maps, often showing postal ZIP codes and public transportation routes.

Time   The United States is divided into four **time zones** (six, if Alaska and Hawaii are included). From east to west, these are: eastern standard time (EST); central standard time (CST); mountain standard time (MST); Pacific standard time (PST); Alaska standard time (AST); and Hawaii standard time (HST). Always keep changing time zones in mind if you're traveling (or even telephoning) long distances in the United States. For example, noon in New York City (EST) is 11am in Chicago (CST), 10am in Denver (MST), 9am in Los Angeles (PST), 8am in Anchorage (AST), and 7am in Honolulu (HST). Maryland and Delaware observe eastern standard time.

Daylight saving time is in effect from the first Sunday in April through the last Sunday in October (actually, the change is made at 2am on Sunday) except in Arizona, Hawaii, part of Indiana, and Puerto Rico. Daylight saving time moves the clock one hour ahead of standard time.

Tipping   This is part of the American way of life, on the principle that you must expect to pay for any service you get (many service personnel receive little direct salary and must depend on tips for their income). Here are some rules of thumb:

In **hotels,** tip bellhops $1 per piece and tip the chamber staff $1 per day. Tip the doorman or concierge only if he or she has provided you with some specific service (for example, calling a cab for you or obtaining difficult-to-get theater tickets).

In **restaurants, bars, and nightclubs,** tip the service staff 15% of the check, tip bartenders 10% to 15%, tip checkroom attendants $1 per garment, and tip valet-parking attendants $1 per vehicle. Tip the doorman only if he has provided you with some specific service (such as calling a cab for you). Tipping is not expected in cafeterias and fast-food restaurants.

Tip **cab drivers** 15% of the fare.

As for **other service personnel,** tip redcaps at airports or railroad stations $1 per piece and tip hairdressers and barbers 15% to 20%.

Tipping ushers in cinemas, movies, and theaters and gas-station attendants is not expected.

Toilets   Foreign visitors often complain that public toilets are hard to find in most U.S. cities. True, there are none on the streets, but the visitor can usually find one in a bar, restaurant, hotel, museum, department store, or service station—and it will probably be clean (although the last-mentioned sometimes leaves much to be desired). Note, however, a growing practice in some restaurants and bars of displaying a notice that "toilets are for the use of patrons only." You can ignore this sign, or better yet, avoid arguments by paying for a cup of coffee or soft drink, which will qualify you as a patron. The cleanliness of toilets at railroad stations and bus depots may be more open to question, and some public places are equipped with pay toilets, which require you to insert one or more coins into a slot on the door before it will open.

Index

254 Index

The following Frommer's guides are available from your favorite bookstore, or you can use the order form on the preceding page to request them as part of your membership in Frommer's Travel Book Club.

FROMMER'S COMPLETE TRAVEL GUIDES

(Comprehensive guides to sightseeing, dining and accommodations, with selections in all price ranges—from deluxe to budget)

Acapulco/Ixtapa/Taxco, 2nd Ed.	C157	Jamaica/Barbados, 2nd Ed.	C149
Alaska '94-'95	C131	Japan '94-'95	C144
Arizona '95	C166	Maui, 1st Ed.	C153
Australia '94-'95	C147	Nepal, 3rd Ed. (avail. 11/95)	C184
Austria, 6th Ed.	C162	New England '95	C165
Bahamas '96 (avail. 8/95)	C172	New Mexico, 3rd Ed.	C167
Belgium/Holland/Luxembourg,		New York State, 4th Ed.	C133
4th Ed.	C170	Northwest, 5th Ed.	C140
Bermuda '96 (avail. 8/95)	C174	Portugal '94-'95	C141
California '95	C164	Puerto Rico '95-'96	C151
Canada '94-'95	C145	Puerto Vallarta/Manzanillo/	
Caribbean '96 (avail. 9/95)	C173	Guadalajara, 2nd Ed.	C135
Carolinas/Georgia, 2nd Ed.	C128	Scandinavia, 16th Ed.	C169
Colorado '96 (avail. 11/95)	C179	Scotland '94-'95	C146
Costa Rica, 1st Ed.	C161	South Pacific '94-'95	C138
Cruises '95-'96	C150	Spain, 16th Ed.	C163
Delaware/Maryland '94-'95	C136	Switzerland, 7th Ed.	
England '96 (avail. 10/95)	C180	(avail. 9/95)	C177
Florida '96 (avail. 9/95)	C181	Thailand, 2nd Ed.	C154
France '96 (avail. 11/95)	C182	U.S.A., 4th Ed.	C156
Germany '96 (avail. 9/95)	C176	Virgin Islands, 3rd Ed.	
Honolulu/Waikiki/Oahu, 4th Ed.		(avail. 8/95)	C175
(avail. 10/95)	C178	Virginia '94-'95	C142
Ireland, 1st Ed.	C168	Yucatán '95-'96	C155
Italy '96 (avail. 11/95)	C183		

FROMMER'S $-A-DAY GUIDES

(Dream Vacations at Down-to-Earth Prices)

Australia on $45 '95-'96	D122	Ireland on $45 '94-'95	D118
Berlin from $50, 3rd Ed.		Israel on $45, 15th Ed.	D130
(avail. 10/95)	D137	London from $55 '96	
Caribbean from $60, 1st Ed.		(avail. 11/95)	D136
(avail. 9/95)	D133	Madrid on $50 '94-'95	D119
Costa Rica/Guatemala/Belize		Mexico from $35 '96	
on $35, 3rd Ed.	D126	(avail. 10/95)	D135
Eastern Europe on $30, 5th Ed.	D129	New York on $70 '94-'95	D121
England from $50 '96		New Zealand from $45, 6th Ed.	D132
(avail. 11/95)	D138	Paris on $45 '94-'95	D117
Europe from $50 '96		South America on $40, 16th Ed.	D123
(avail. 10/95)	D139	Washington, D.C. on $50	
Greece from $45, 6th Ed.	D131	'94-'95	D120
Hawaii from $60 '96 (avail. 9/95)	D134		

FROMMER'S COMPLETE CITY GUIDES

(Comprehensive guides to sightseeing, dining, and accommodations in all price ranges)

Amsterdam, 8th Ed.	S176	Minneapolis/St. Paul, 4th Ed.	S159
Athens, 10th Ed.	S174	Montréal/Québec City '95	S166
Atlanta & the Summer Olympic		Nashville/Memphis, 1st Ed.	S141
Games '96 (avail. 11/95)	S181	New Orleans '96 (avail. 10/95)	S182
Atlantic City/Cape May, 5th Ed.	S130	New York City '96 (avail. 11/95)	S183
Bangkok, 2nd Ed.	S147	Paris '96 (avail. 9/95)	S180
Barcelona '93-'94	S115	Philadelphia, 8th Ed.	S167
Berlin, 3rd Ed.	S162	Prague, 1st Ed.	S143
Boston '95	S160	Rome, 10th Ed.	S168
Budapest, 1st Ed.	S139	St. Louis/Kansas City, 2nd Ed.	S127
Chicago '95	S169	San Antonio/Austin, 1st Ed.	S177
Denver/Boulder/Colorado Springs,		San Diego '95	S158
3rd Ed.	S154	San Francisco '96 (avail. 10/95)	S184
Disney World/Orlando '96 (avail. 9/95)	S178	Santa Fe/Taos/Albuquerque '95	S172
Dublin, 2nd Ed.	S157	Seattle/Portland '94-'95	S137
Hong Kong '94-'95	S140	Sydney, 4th Ed.	S171
Las Vegas '95	S163	Tampa/St. Petersburg, 3rd Ed.	S146
London '96 (avail. 9/95)	S179	Tokyo '94-'95	S144
Los Angeles '95	S164	Toronto, 3rd Ed.	S173
Madrid/Costa del Sol, 2nd Ed.	S165	Vancouver/Victoria '94-'95	S142
Mexico City, 1st Ed.	S175	Washington, D.C. '95	S153
Miami '95-'96	S149		

FROMMER'S FAMILY GUIDES

(Guides to family-friendly hotels, restaurants, activities, and attractions)

California with Kids	F105	San Francisco with Kids	F104
Los Angeles with Kids	F103	Washington, D.C. with Kids	F102
New York City with Kids	F101		

FROMMER'S WALKING TOURS

(Memorable strolls through colorful and historic neighborhoods, accompanied by detailed directions and maps)

Berlin	W100	Paris, 2nd Ed.	W112
Chicago	W107	San Francisco, 2nd Ed.	W115
England's Favorite Cities	W108	Spain's Favorite Cities (avail. 9/95)	W116
London, 2nd Ed.	W111	Tokyo	W109
Montréal/Québec City	W106	Venice	W110
New York, 2nd Ed.	W113	Washington, D.C., 2nd Ed.	W114

FROMMER'S AMERICA ON WHEELS

(Guides for travelers who are exploring the U.S.A. by car, featuring a brand-new rating system for accommodations and full-color road maps)

Arizona/New Mexico	A100	Florida	A102
California/Nevada	A101	Mid-Atlantic	A103

FROMMER'S SPECIAL-INTEREST TITLES

Arthur Frommer's Branson!	P107	Frommer's Where to Stay U.S.A.,	
Arthur Frommer's New World		11th Ed.	P102
of Travel (avail. 11/95)	P112	National Park Guide, 29th Ed.	P106
Frommer's Caribbean Hideaways		USA Today Golf Tournament Guide	P113
(avail. 9/95)	P110	USA Today Minor League	
Frommer's America's 100 Best-Loved		Baseball Book	P111
State Parks	P109		

FROMMER'S BEST BEACH VACATIONS
(The top places to sun, stroll, shop, stay, play, party, and swim—with each beach rated for beauty, swimming, sand, and amenities)

California (avail. 10/95)	G100	Hawaii (avail. 10/95)	G102
Florida (avail. 10/95)	G101		

FROMMER'S BED & BREAKFAST GUIDES
(Selective guides with four-color photos and full descriptions of the best inns in each region)

California	B100	Hawaii	B105
Caribbean	B101	Pacific Northwest	B106
East Coast	B102	Rockies	B107
Eastern United States	B103	Southwest	B108
Great American Cities	B104		

FROMMER'S IRREVERENT GUIDES
(Wickedly honest guides for sophisticated travelers and those who want to be)

Chicago (avail. 11/95)	I100	New Orleans (avail. 11/95)	I103
London (avail. 11/95)	I101	San Francisco (avail. 11/95)	I104
Manhattan (avail. 11/95)	I102	Virgin Islands (avail. 11/95)	I105

FROMMER'S DRIVING TOURS
(Four-color photos and detailed maps outlining spectacular scenic driving routes)

Australia	Y100	Italy	Y108
Austria	Y101	Mexico	Y109
Britain	Y102	Scandinavia	Y110
Canada	Y103	Scotland	Y111
Florida	Y104	Spain	Y112
France	Y105	Switzerland	Y113
Germany	Y106	U.S.A.	Y114
Ireland	Y107		

FROMMER'S BORN TO SHOP
(The ultimate travel guides for discriminating shoppers—from cut-rate to couture)

Hong Kong (avail. 11/95)	Z100	London (avail. 11/95)	Z101